The People and the King

The Comunero Revolution in Colombia, 1781

Books by John Leddy Phelan

*The Millennial Kingdom of the Franciscans in the New World: A Study of the
    Writings of Gerónimo de Mendieta, 1525–1604* (University of California
    Publications in History Series, Vol. 52, 1956; 2nd ed., 1970)
*The Hispanization of the Philippines: Spanish Aims and Filipino Responses,
    1565–1700* (1959)
*The Kingdom of Quito in the Seventeenth Century: Bureaucratic Politics in
    the Spanish Empire* (1967)
El reino milenario de los franciscanos en el Nuevo Mundo (Universidad
    Nacional Autónoma de Mexico, 1972)
The People and the King: The Comunero Revolution in Colombia, 1781
    (1978)

The People
and the King

The Comunero Revolution in Colombia, 1781

John Leddy Phelan

The University of Wisconsin Press

Published 1978
The University of Wisconsin Press
Box 1379, Madison, Wisconsin 53701

The University of Wisconsin Press, Ltd.
70 Great Russell Street, London

First printing

Printed in the United States of America

For LC CIP information see the colophon

ISBN 0-299-07290-8

To the Memory of

Pablo E. Cárdenas Acosta

Every Historian of the Comuneros Is His Disciple

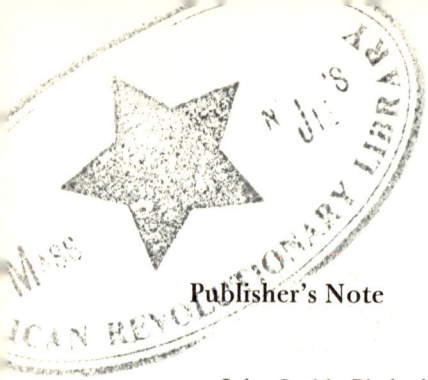

Publisher's Note

John Leddy Phelan's untimely death occurred as he was nearing the end of his work in preparing the manuscript of this book for publication. The Press thanks Peter H. Smith, the author's friend and colleague, for assuming responsibility for the final authorial chores that John Phelan did not live to finish. We are also grateful to Cathy Duke and Susan Fredston for their assistance.

This book is the third by John Phelan published by the Press in a close association that covered a period of more than twenty years. His sudden death, a blow to Hispanic studies and to this University, leaves all who have worked with him during this time with a sense of loss both professional and deeply personal.

Contents

III Antonio Caballero y Góngora

Illustrations

Maps

Preface

The research and the writing of this book were greatly facilitated by generous support from several foundations, and I am deeply grateful for all their assistance. Grants from the Midgard Foundation and the Social Science Research Foundation enabled me to spend a year in Spain and in Colombia. An American Philosophical Society grant took me to Bogotá again. A good deal of the writing was done during a year's leave of absence with funds provided by the American Council of Learned Societies and the Institute for Research in the Humanities of the University of Wisconsin-Madison. The Research Committee of the Graduate School and the Ibero-American Studies Committee, both of the University of Wisconsin, generously provided several travel grants.

I have received much assistance and unfailing courtesy in all the libraries and archives where I have studied. I would like to express my appreciation to the directors and the staffs of the following institutions: the Memorial Library of the University of Wisconsin, the Archivo Histórico Nacional (Bogotá), the Academia Colombiana de Historia, the Biblioteca Nacional (Bogotá), the private collection of José Manuel Restrepo (Bogotá), the Archivo de la Notaria in the Casa de Cultura (Socorro), the Archivo Parroquial (Socorro), the Archivo Histórico del Departmento de Antioquia, the Archivo Nacional de Historia (Quito), the Lilly Library at the University of Indiana, and the Archivo General de Indias (Seville). Among the directors and the staffs of those institutions a special word of thanks goes to Louis Kaplan, Joseph Treyz, Suzanne Hodgman, Carlos Restrepo Canal, Alberto Lee López, O.F.M., Alberto Miramón, Eduardo Santa, doña Pilar Moreno de Angel, doña Adiela Cajiao B., the late monseigneur José Restrepo Posada, doña Carmen Camacho de Villareal, the late Jorge Garcés, Elfrieda Lang, and doña Rosario Parra Cala.

This book owes much to my many Colombian friends. I am profoundly appreciative of the honor the Academia Colombiana de Historia bestowed on me in 1972 when they elected me a corresponding member. I cherish the friendship of its distinguished president, Dr. Abel Cruz Santos. I owe to Horacio Rodríguez Plata, a former president of the Academy and an illustrious son of Socorro, an extensive debt of gratitude for the liberality and good-fellowship with which he has shared with me his broad and deep knowledge of the history of his native land. Among the other academicians to whom I would like to express my appreciation are the following: the late Roberto Liévano, Guillermo Hernández de Alba, the dean of the Academy, Father Rafael Gómez Hoyos, Luis Martínez Delgado, Manuel Lucena Salmoral, Juan Manuel Pacheco, S. J., Luis Duque Gómez, Father Mario Germán Romero, General Julio Londoño, Rafael Bernal Medina, Colonel Camilo Riaño, José de Mier, and Armando Gómez Latorre.

I have spent many enjoyable hours in the home of doña Kathleen Romoli de Avery, who has more perceptive insights about Colombia than any other foreigner of my acquaintance. I also learned much from countless conversations I held in the hospitable home of Jorge Cárdenas García and his vivacious wife, doña María Elena. Don Jorge is a direct descendant through the female line of Juan Francisco Berbeo, the leader of the Comuneros, and he is the son of the late Pablo Cárdenas Acosta. Jaime Jaramillo Uribe, whose scholarship has won him an international reputation, proved a wise friend and a valuable counselor. Ramiro Gómez Rodríguez was generous to a fault in sharing with me his intimate knowledge of the archives of his native Socorro. While I was working in the archives of Bogotá over the course of several years, I had the privilege of several long and stimulating conversations with Indalecio Liévano Aguirre, currently foreign minister of Colombia and a former acting president of the Republic. My disagreement with some of his views in no way diminishes my respect for him both as a historian and as a statesman.

Among the other Colombians whose friendship and assistance I would like to acknowledge are the following: Germán Colmenares, Hermes Tovar Pinzón, Margarita González, Ines and Enrique Uribe White, Juan Friede, José Vicente Mogollón Vélez, and doña Beatrice Vila de Gómez Valderrama.

Among my American colleagues working in the field of Colombian history I have received much help and encouragement from José León Helguera, Jane Loy, Gary Graff, Allan Kuethe, Leon G. Campbell, Mark A. Burkholder, and D. S. Chandler. Frank Safford gave the manuscript a meticulous and constructive critique.

Among my colleagues in Madison I am particularly grateful to Peter H. Smith, Thomas E. Skidmore, William Courtenay, Morton Rothstein, Charles F. Edson, Maris Vinovskis, and Robert Halstead for sharing with me their expertise. A very special and personal expression of appreciation goes to my three research assistants, who aided me in countless ways. They are Peter De Shazo, Isabel Pepe Hurd, and David Lyles. I also have fond memories of the graduate seminar I conducted in the fall of 1972 on the topic of the Comuneros. Mary De Shazo ably translated four articles on the subject that appeared in the *Boletín de Historia y Antigüedades*. Mrs. Ruth Koontz patiently and efficiently typed the bulky manuscript.

In closing, I should like to thank all those countless and nameless Colombians from all walks of life who helped to make my many visits to their fascinating land both enjoyable and stimulating.

John Leddy Phelan
Madison, Wisconsin
November, 1975

Introduction

This study grew out of my previous book. In *The Kingdom of Quito in the Seventeenth Century,* I attempted to explore the inner workings of the colonial bureaucracy and to examine those conditions which enabled the administration to conciliate tensions and conflicts. This book looks at the other side of the coin. Under what conditions did the bureaucratic system of conciliation break down, so that various groups felt it necessary to resort to arms to achieve their political ends?

Such an occasion occurred in Colombia, then called the New Kingdom of Granada, in 1781. Some twenty thousand badly armed but rabidly irate sons and daughters of that poor but proud land marched to the village of Zipaquirá, a day's distance from Bogotá, to demand that the ministers of King Charles III of Spain repudiate a whole series of abrasively introduced fiscal and administrative changes. The capital was virtually defenseless. The portly, astute archbishop of Santa Fe de Bogotá, Antonio Caballero y Góngora, in the name of the authorities signed the capitulations of Zipaquirá in which the program of Charles III was abrogated.

This event, which has gone down in history as the Comunero Revolution, has been interpreted by some modern historians as the precursor of political independence, by others as a frustrated social revolution from below betrayed by those above. It was neither, as this book seeks to demonstrate, by focusing principally on how the men and women of 1781 perceived their protest. Rather than interpreting the Comuneros in terms of subsequent events, I have concentrated on the inner meaning of two key phrases: the word *Comunero,* by which the protesters identified themselves, and the slogan that the crowds shouted in all the squares of that mountain kingdom: " ¡Viva el rey y muera el mal gobierno!" "Long live the king and death to bad government."

The implicit political ideology of this movement cannot be found in the doctrines of the French and English philosophers who did so much to inspire the contemporary North American revolution of independence. Those ideas were unknown in New Granada in 1781. The intellectual nourishment of the generation of 1781 came from the doctrines of the classic Spanish theologians of the sixteenth and seventeenth centuries, the most outstanding of whom was the Jesuit Francisco Suárez. To the citizens of New Granada their kingdom constituted a *corpus mysticum politicum,* with its own traditions and procedures designed to achieve the common good of the whole community. That common good, according to the men of 1781, was being flagrantly

xvii

undermined by the fiscal changes introduced by Charles III's bureaucrats. The people of New Granada seldom invoked terms such as *nación* or *patria,* but they endlessly repeated the ancient Castilian phrases *el común* and *la comunidad*—the common good of all groups in the community.

The crisis of 1781 was essentially political and constitutional in nature. To be sure, it was triggered by new or increased taxes. The central issue, however, was who had the authority to levy new fiscal exactions. Animated by the goal of creating a highly centralized, unitary monarchy in order to meet the mounting expenses of imperial defense, the government of Charles III preached a new gospel, inspired by the French absolutism of Louis XIV and Louis XV, that subjects owed blind obedience to constituted authority. But deeply imbedded in the documents of the Comunero Revolution is the belief that unjust laws were invalid, and that inherent in the *corpus mysticum politicum* was the right to some form of popular approval of new taxation. The citizens of New Granada were the heirs of a tradition of bureaucratic decentralization that had slowly but steadily evolved in New Granada during the reigns of the Habsburgs and early Bourbons. The "unwritten constitution" provided that basic decisions were reached by informal consultation between the royal bureaucracy and the king's colonial subjects. Usually there emerged a workable compromise between what the central authorities ideally wanted and what local conditions and pressures would realistically tolerate. The crisis of 1781 was, in short, a constitutional clash between imperial centralization and colonial decentralization.

As often happens in revolutionary situations, goals escalated as the movement unfolded in time. The protest began as a demand to return to the "unwritten constitution." At Zipaquirá, however, a revolutionary goal inside a traditionalist framework emerged. The men of 1781 staked out a claim for creole self-government under the aegis of the crown. Both Charles III and his subjects in New Granada were compelled to abandon their respective revolutions. The definitive compromise was a modified restoration of the "unwritten constitution" tilting in the direction of greater royal centralization.

In organizing the march on the capital, the Comunero leaders and their followers were engaging in a campaign of massive civil disobedience in order to persuade the king to repudiate the policies of his ministers. The world without a monarchy was inconceivable in 1781. Hence the crowds furiously shouted, "Long live the king." But it was conceivable that new fiscal policies required some form of consultation with the people upon whose shoulders the burden fell. Hence they also shouted, "Death to bad government."

In 1781 there was only one principle of political legitimacy, and it enjoyed enthusiastic support from all groups in that society. The crown demanded and received obedience from its subjects, for the king, as the anointed of the Lord, was the fountainhead of justice. He would not will an injustice, if he were fully informed of all conditions. The citizens of New Granada in 1781 argued that the king had been deceived by rapacious and tyrannical ministers; his still loyal subjects were, somewhat flamboyantly, calling his attention to this fact.

Confined inside the boundaries of a traditionalist and providentialist form of political legitimacy, the generation of 1781 could not opt to overthrow the crown's sovereignty, nor could they advocate any basic reordering of society. They could only seek a redress of specific grievances—in this case the abrogation of the new fiscal program.

Those who have interpreted the Comunero Revolution as the first chapter of political emancipation or as a frustrated social revolution have concluded that the movement was a dismal failure. Viewed in the context of 1781, as I have defined it, the Comuneros achieved a solid success. Although the authorities soon repudiated the capitulations of Zipaquirá, Archbishop Viceroy Caballero y Góngora, after reestablishing the principle of royal authority, set about making significant concessions to the very sources of discontent that had precipitated the protest. He returned to the spirit of the "unwritten constitution," skillfully working out a compromise between the dissatisfactions in the New Kingdom of Granada and the fiscal exigencies of the central authorities in Madrid.

Perhaps the major failing in the extensive historiography of the topic is that most historians stopped their analysis at the repudiation of the capitulations, without examining carefully the administration of Caballero y Góngora.

The lesson that the Comuneros taught Charles III and his ministers was that they could not violate with impunity the deeply rooted political traditions of New Granada. Paradoxically, though inadvertently, Caballero y Góngora's sponsorship of the scientific thought of the Enlightenment and his belief in the state as renovator of the economy built the bridge connecting the colony with independence.

Independence would come a generation later, but the western world had profoundly changed between 1781 and the overthrow of the Bourbon dynasty in 1808. The introduction into New Granada of the scientific and political thought of the European Enlightenment, the impact of revolutions in North America and France provided the creole intellectuals of the generation of 1810 with the necessary tools with which to challenge the traditionalist and providentialist notion of legitimacy to which the men of 1781 were so deeply attached.

PART I
Charles III

1

From Kingdoms to Empire:
The Political Innovations of Charles III

The small group of incipient technocrats who gathered around Charles III (1759–88) envisaged a unitary state in which all the resources of Spain's diverse and far-flung dominions could be mobilized to defend the monarchy. They broke with the older, Habsburg notion that the settlements overseas were kingdoms, subordinate to and inalienable from the crown of Castile and León, and, in the eighteenth century, began to weld Spain's domains in the Indies into provinces of one theoretically centralized monarchy. The traditional Habsburg nomenclature of *rey de las Españas y de las Indias* gave way increasingly to *el rey de España y emperador de las Indias* or *América*. In the reign of Charles III, Spanish statesmen for the first time commonly used the word *colonias,* 'colonies,' a term borrowed from their enemies, the British, and their allies, the French, to describe the overseas possessions of the crown. This change in nomenclature represents a significant shift in emphasis.[1]

The original architect of the Caroline program was José dei Campillo y Cosío, whose *Nuevo sistema de gobierno económico para la América,* written as early as 1743, laid out the master plan of change; the treatise circulated in manuscript among high-ranking bureaucrats until 1762, when it was published with minor alterations in Bernardo Ward's *Proyecto económico.* For Campillo y Cosío *gobierno económico* was the application to the New World of the principles of Colbertian mercantilism. He advocated the abolition of inefficient monopolies such as the commercial monopoly that the Cadiz merchants enjoyed in the transatlantic carrying trade and the creation of fiscally lucrative monopolies, e.g., for tobacco. He envisaged America as an unexploited market for Spanish manufactures. In order to raise the consumption of that market he proposed to abolish restraints of trade and to

3

incorporate the Indians more fully into colonial society by distributing land to them. Silver production should be increased, and a more efficient system of tax collecting could be created by introducing into the New World the French system of intendants.

The humiliating defeats that England inflicted on Spain during the Seven Years' War galvanized the monarchy into implementing the grand design of Campillo y Cosío. Spain's weakness vis-à-vis England was analogous to the situation that the Austria of Maria Theresa faced with Prussia: modernize or perish. Yet the pace of reform was deliberately cautious and even slow in the context of the acute rivalry between Spain and Great Britain. Hence the technocratic and fiscal innovations of Charles III were nothing more nor nothing less than a cautious essay in what has come to be known recently as defensive modernization. The truly revolutionary aspect of the Caroline program was not its economic aspect, which merely amounted to a modified Colbertian neomercantilism, but the political and constitutional means adopted to implement these modest economic and fiscal changes.[2]

Charles III had one advantage over his royal predecessors. He had matured and developed over a period of some twenty-four years outside the Iberian peninsula, isolated from the entrenched interests and the traditional bureaucratic procedures of the Spanish court. During his reign as king of the Two Sicilies (1735–59) he had acquired a storehouse of experience in cautiously modernizing an antiquated monarchy.

The riots that erupted in several cities in Spain in March and April 1766 and compelled Charles III to flee briefly from his own capital were a warning to the king that he must proceed with prudence in introducing changes. Ostensibly precipitated by the new regulations prescribing the cut of capes and outlawing the wide-brimmed hats, the tumults were at once expressions of popular dissatisfaction with the king's Italian advisers, a classic bread riot, and a sharp reaction of traditional vested interests against change.[3] The lesson that Charles III drew from the riots of 1766 was that he must persuade and even cajole vested privileges into accepting his innovations. Some fifteen years later Antonio Caballero y Góngora, Charles III's viceroy in New Granada, drew the same lesson from the Comunero Revolution.

Although several of these changes were experimentally introduced in Cuba after 1763, the first large-scale attempt at applying defensive modernization occurred in the viceroyalty of Mexico during the *visita general* of José de Gálvez (1765–71). Triumphant from his Mexican experience, Gálvez returned to Spain, where he served as Charles III's minister of the Indies from 1776 until his death in 1787. During the late 1770's and early 1780's, Gálvez sought to apply the model of his Mexican experience to the viceroyalties of New Granada and Peru. If José del Campillo y Cosío was the principal architect of the Caroline program of defensive modernization, Gálvez was its

Charles III. (Portrait by Goya; Banco de España, Madrid.)

major executor. The regent visitor general Juan Francisco Gutiérrez de Piñeres and the visitor general Juan Antonio Areche were Gálvez's field lieutenants in New Granada and Peru respectively.

An understanding of the visita general of Gálvez in Mexico is, therefore, a necessary prelude to any solid comprehension of what subsequently occurred in New Granada. The goals and the tactics that Gálvez employed in Mexico were followed, with only minor alterations, by his appointee in New Granada a decade later. The creation of a profitable tobacco monopoly, direct royal administration of the fiscal system, the expulsion of the creoles from high office, and restriction of the powers of the viceroy were all tried first in Mexico. Militant popular resistance to these changes also occurred in Mexico, but the Mexican reaction lacked the intensity of the response in New Granada and Peru.[4]

The Caroline ministers did not set out to abolish traditional Habsburg institutions but merely to transform them to serve new ends. Needless to say, the holders of the old offices resisted these attempts, often successfully, vitiating the effectiveness of the proposed changes. Nowhere is this result more apparent than in the case of the viceregal institution.

The grand design was to restrict the authority of the viceroy to matters purely political and military, and strip him of all authority over the fiscal machinery. The royal exchequer would become a totally autonomous department headed by a *superintendente subdelegado de la real hacienda*. The superintendent would supervise a new provincial officer who was called a *gobernador intendente* or intendant. Since the intendant would exercise the political, judicial, and military functions of the old *corregidores* as well as having the financial jurisdiction of the royal treasury, a better trained and a more professionally qualified person could be recruited for the office. His major responsibility would be to promote economic development and to make the fiscal administration more efficient.[5]

Not only would the authority of the *audiencia* in the fiscal sphere be curtailed, but also the viceroy would no longer serve as its president. In 1776 the office of regent of the audiencia was created. Ranking just below the viceroy, the regent was to relieve him of the day-to-day administration of the audiencia.[6] The new governmental system seemed to resemble an eighteenth-century version of the troika, with supreme authority divided among the viceroy for political and military matters, the superintendent for the royal exchequer, and the regent for the administration of justice.[7]

The clash between the Caroline bureaucrats and the viceroys was due in part to an ancient hostility—the built-in conflict between the "ordinary" authority of the viceroys and the audiencias and the "extraordinary" jurisdiction of the visitor general. Although the viceroy came under the jurisdiction of a visita general only in his capacity as president of the royal audiencia, tension and conflict had characterized the relationships between the visitor and the viceroy under the Habsburgs.[8] During the reign of Charles III the old Habsburg system of the vista general was profoundly transformed and endowed with a much more dynamic role. Instead of being merely an instrument to expose and punish misconduct of officials overseas, the visita general was used by the crown as an instrument for imposing new policies. Gálvez in Mexico, Gutiérrez de Piñeres in New Granada, and Areche in Peru all had confrontations with the incumbent viceroys. In all three cases the visitor general temporarily triumphed over his particular viceroy, but the institution of the viceroyalty was not permanently weakened. The troika was administratively impractical. There was need of an official whose office shared some of the royal prestige to coordinate and to supervise the several administrative hierarchies. The vigor, the success, and the ability of viceroys such as Bucareli and Revillagigedo the Younger in Mexico and Caballero y Góngora in New Granada, all of whose terms in office were preceded by tumultuous visitas generales, enabled the viceroys to resume their traditional role as titular supervisors of the exchequer. The regents of the audiencia, on the other hand, remained until the end of the Spanish regime. They did perform a useful and necessary task in supervising the audiencia.

Although the hostility of Gálvez and his principal subordinates to the viceregal office can be partially explained by pre-existing tensions, there were other factors involved.[9] Gutiérrez de Piñeres, who clearly shared this hostility, pinpointed a principal source of dissatisfaction among the Caroline bureaucrats when he wrote to José de Gálvez:

> This way of proceeding is common to the viceroys: they think that they can do in their viceroyalty what the king would do if he were present. There is no lack of flatterers who approve of this erroneous maxim which is capable of [causing] fatal consequences.[10]

The Caroline administrators were embryonic technocrats; the viceroys were politicians, who traditionally followed the policy that the aspirations of the local creole elites should be taken into account and reconciled to some extent with a program of paternalistic protection for the nonelites. It was this tradition, of Habsburg origin, that Gálvez wanted to eliminate. The viceroys should no longer act as brokers between the central authorities in Spain and the regional elites and other classes. The creoles had too much power, Gálvez argued. He condemned their ascendancy in the audiencias and in the exchequer, for they were "too bound by ties of family and faction in the New World to provide disinterested and impartial government."[11]

Although the overwhelming majority of viceroys in the eighteenth century were Spanish-born, some 90 percent of those appointed between 1746 and

Manuel Antonio Flores, viceroy of New Granada. (Portrait by Joaquín Gutiérrez; Museo de Arte Colonial.)

1813 were career military officers, nearly one-half of whom had previous military experience in the New World.[12] Hence, many viceroys were apt to lend a sympathetic ear to creole points of view. The career of Manuel Antonio Flores (1723–99), who served as viceroy both in New Granada and Mexico, is not atypical. Born in Seville, Flores entered the naval service in 1736. He spent some ten years in Peru exploring the disputed boundaries with the Portuguese empire. He also did tours of duty in Havana and Buenos Aires before being appointed viceroy of New Granada in 1776. His wife was a creole from Buenos Aires, and several of his children were born in America.[13] It becomes clear why viceroys, with their previous American experience, were suspect in the circle of José de Gálvez, with its pronounced bias against creoles.

In the seventeeth century, a relatively small number of creoles had received appointments to the bench. Long-serving European magistrates, however, became significantly sympathetic to the points of view of the creole elites. During the reigns of the first two Bourbon kings, Philip V and Ferdinand VI, a basic change took place. When José de Gálvez began his celebrated visita general in Mexico, the creoles had long been a comfortable majority in both the audiencia and in the fiscal service.[14] After the 1730's creole majorities were frequent in the audiencias of Lima and Santiago de Chile.[15] It is less well known that the creoles were also immensely influential in the audiencia of Santa Fe de Bogotá during several decades prior to the beginning of the visita general of Juan Francisco Gutiérrez de Piñeres in 1778.[16]

To seek the reasons for this change, we must turn to the appointment policies of the Bourbons. The sale of judicial office had actually begun in the late seventeenth century under the Habsburgs, but the early Bourbons expanded its scope. Between 1701 and 1750, Philip V and Ferdinand VI appointed 108 creoles to 136 audiencia posts. Approximately two-thirds of these appointees had to purchase their offices, at prices varying between 4,000 and 20,000 pesos, whereas only 19 percent of the European Spaniards bought their posts—suggesting that the creoles even under the early Bourbons suffered from some discrimination. The purchase of office often but not always included the privilege of marrying a resident of the audiencia kingdom and the right to own property there. There were two categories of purchase (1) *de número,* a regular position to fill an existing vacancy, and (2) supernumerary, in which the magistrate so created did not take office until a vacancy occurred among the limited number of regular posts.

The council of the Indies vehemently protested the sale of judicial office, for historically it championed with considerable consistency the principle of a professional magistracy. In fact, there were only two periods when the crown sold these offices on a massive scale, from 1706 until 1711 during the War of the Spanish Succession, and then from 1740 until 1750 during the so-called War of Jenkins' Ear. Financial stringency created by war conditions was the evident cause.

Not only was there a close involvement between war periods and the sale of audiencia posts, but also the geographical distribution of the sales was a function of the international tension. English sea power represented the principal menace to the Spanish dominions. Hence the highest percentages of posts sold were in the less threatened inland or Pacific coast audiencias of Lima, Quito, Chile, Charcas, and Guadalajara, with the lowest percentages in the audiencias of Santo Domingo, Bogotá, Mexico, and Manila, all exposed to English naval aggression. In these areas the percentage of creole appointments ranged between 11 and 35 percent, for an average of 18 percent. Bogotá's percentage was 17. In those audiencias less vulnerable to English attacks the percentage of creole appointments varied from 68 percent for Charcas to 56 percent for Chile and 55 percent for Lima.

The governments of Philip V and Ferdinand VI sold audiencia posts with extreme reluctance. None was subject to sale after 1750, and in fact, after that time the government followed a discriminatory policy against creole appointments, in order to redress the balance in favor of European Spaniards. Yet the creoles appointed before 1750 were so numerous, and so many of them had bought their offices while young, that there were still creole majorities in the audiencias of Mexico, Lima, and Santiago as late as the 1770's.[17]

A vocal critic of creole influence in the audiencias, José de Gálvez certainly deserved his anti-American reputation. Yet he was not the author of the policy of excluding creoles from high office in the Indies, although he vigorously implemented the anticreole policy which he inherited. During his stewardship in the ministry of the Indies (1776–87) only 25 identified Americans out of a total of 126 magistrates received appointments to the audiencia.[18] The impressive statistical analysis of M. A. Burkholder and D. S. Chandler illustrates that Charles III's ministers inherited from the previous reign the program of reconquering America from the creoles by overthrowing creole predominance in the audiencias of the Indies. The Caroline objective was not too dissimilar from the aim of Charles V and Philip II, who set out to reconquer the New World from the original conquistadores by creating the audiencia bureaucracy. It found clearest expression in the recommendations of an extraordinary meeting of Charles III's most trusted advisers, precipitated by creole unrest in Mexico arising from the expulsion of the Jesuits in 1762 and the new policies introduced by the visitor general, José de Gálvez. The count of Aranda presided over this session, with fiscales Campomanes and Moniño, later the count of Floridablanca, presenting recommendations. Spain and America, the fiscales argued in their "position paper," should form one unitary state. In order to consolidate the loyalty of the creoles towards the imperial *patria,* a significant number of creoles should be brought to the peninsula and given high military, bureacratic, and ecclesiastical office:

> to adhere to the practice of always sending Spaniards to the Indies to hold the principal offices, bishoprics and prebends, appointing creoles to equivalent position in Spain. It is this which will bring the two together in friendship and unity, and make of them a single nation, for every creole who is brought to Spain will be a hostage to ensure that those lands remain subject to Your Majesty's mild rule.[19]

The recommendations of March 4, 1768, became governmental policy with the publication of the cedula of February 21, 1776, shortly after Gálvez took office. The king ordered the council of Castile to nominate Americans "for ecclesiastical benefices and legal posts in churches and tribunals in Spain." The cedula instructed the council of the Indies to nominate European Spaniards for equivalent posts in America "with the express proviso that one third of the canonries and prebends of the cathedrals there shall be reserved for American Spaniards."[20]

Gálvez's determination to reduce, if not to eliminate, the participation of the creoles in the overseas bureaucracy was not initially shared by the council of the Indies. Ironically, the council did not even include Gutiérrez de Piñeres among the candidates for the new post of regent of the audiencia of New Granada. That conservative-minded body proposed three members of the "old guard," all with proven procreole attitudes. Two, in fact, were creoles— Pedro Fagle, *alcalde de crimen* in Lima, and the Bogotá-born Nicolás Vélez de Guevara y Suescún, then serving in the audiencia of Quito. Heading the list was the aged Benito Casal y Montenegro, oidor in Bogotá and married to one of the daughters of the fiscal Manuel Bernardo Alvarez.[21] Gálvez swept aside the council's recommendation and appointed Gutiérrez de Piñeres, who had no previous American experience, but who had worked his way up in the fiscal and judicial administrations in Seville.[22]

The goal of a unitary state expressed in the cedula of February 21, 1776, was never reached. The deep-rooted and growing attachment of the creoles to their native soil—to the patria of the audiencia-kingdoms where they were born and lived—and their increasingly articulate self-consciousness as something different from European Spaniards made the creoles unresponsive to the ideal of empire-wide patriotism.[23] Two out of the many examples of incipient creole nationalism can be found in Mexico and in New Granada. On May 2, 1771, the cabildo of Mexico City complained to Charles III about the exclusion of the creoles from high civil, bureaucratic, and military office. The cabildo then went on to stake out a bold claim by demanding all public offices, not just some.[24] No less audacious a claim to creole power was the twenty-second clause of the capitulations of Zipaquirá, which demanded a virtual monopoly of office for the American-born.[25] It is not coincidental that both expressions of creole sentiment occurred shortly after Visitor General Gálvez in Mexico and Visitor General Gutiérrez de Piñeres in New Granada undertook to reduce drastically the number of creoles holding high office.

A quantitative analysis of creole representation and influence in the audiencia before the arrival of the visitor general in 1778 makes the situation very plain.[26] Table 1.1 shows the place of birth for officials of the audiencia over the period 1654–1819. If we accept the probability, earlier noted, that long-serving peninsular bureaucrats became partially coopted by local creole interests, the figures become even more revealing.[27] Excluding those whose birthplace is unknown, and combining the figures for creoles with those for Spanish-born magistrates who had served for periods of more than ten years, one arrives at the figures in Table 1.2. It will be remembered, moreover, that the number of offices sold to creoles in Bogotá was relatively low, because of New Granada's vulnerability to English naval power. It is clear that the voice of the creoles between 1700 and 1759 was loud indeed. It is also clear that

Table 1.1
Numbers of Creole and Spanish-born Officials, 1654–1819

	Creole	Spanish-born	Birthplace unknown
1654–99			
Oidores	2	14	2
Fiscales	4	4	–
	6	18	2
1700–58			
Oidores	5	13	4
Fiscales	4	4	–
	9	17	4
1759–88			
Oidores	1	9	–
Fiscales	1	3	–
	2	12	–
1789–1819			
Oidores	5	6	4
Fiscales	4	3	1
	9	9	5

Source: José M. Restrepo Saenz, *Biografías de los mandatarios y ministros de la real audiencia, 1671–1819* (Bogotá, 1952).

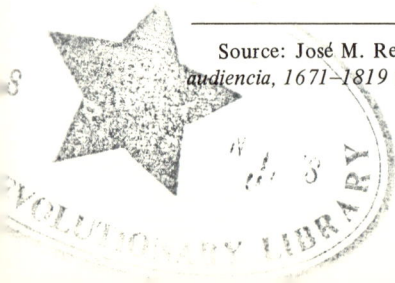

Table 1.2
Numbers of Creole and Procreole Spanish Officials, 1654–1819

	Creole and Procreole Spaniards	Spaniards
1654–99		
Oidores	5	11
Fiscales	6	2
	11	13
1700–58		
Oidores	12	6
Fiscales	6	2
	18	8
1759–88		
Oidores	3	6
Fiscales	1	4
	4	10
1789–1819		
Oidores	6	5
Fiscales	4	3
	10	8

Source: José M. Restrepo Saenz, *Biografías de los mandatarios y ministros de la real audiencia, 1671–1819* (Bogotá, 1952).

this represents a basic change from the earlier reign of Charles II. This assessment is borne out by the fact that only one of the four presidents of the audiencia during the reign of Charles II was a creole, and he was merely president ad interim.

But if the reigns of Philip V and Ferdinand VI were a golden age for creole magistrates, the succeeding reign of Charles III was a bleak time indeed. The one creole appointment to the post of *oidor* came very late in the reign—in 1787. Of the nine Spaniards, only two served more than ten years. The trend was reversed during succeeding reigns, however; generally throughout the empire the position of the creoles modestly improved, as the tables indicate.

On January 6, 1778, when don Juan Francisco Gutiérrez de Piñeres arrived in Bogotá, creole influence in the audiencia was still substantial, in spite of the fact that only one creole had been appointed between 1752 and 1775. In 1778 there were two creoles and four Europeans on the bench. Two of the Spanish judges had been in office for thirty-four years and twenty-eight years respectively. A Quito-born oidor had been serving for twenty-six years. The long duration of these magistrates suggests that in fact creole influence was much greater than the actual numbers would indicate, and it would be no exaggeration to claim that creole influence was something closer to two to one.

The full extent of the creole influence in the audiencia of Santa Fe de Bogotá is not adequately reflected in the quantitative analysis, impressive though these statistics may be. A complex network of marriages linked the fiscal bureaucracy and the audiencia with the leading creole families of Bogotá. Royal permission was necessary for marriage between Spanish officials and creoles, but it was usually granted, especially in the more lenient eighteenth century.[28]

To take one notable example, don Manuel Bernardo Alvarez, Spanish-born fiscal of the audiencia (1736–56), who lived in Bogotá until his death in 1774, was the founder of a veritable bureaucratic dynasty. On April 11, 1738, Ferdinand VI granted his request to marry a criolla, the well-born doña María Josefa del Casal. Of the ten children that survived to adulthood, seven married into wealthy creole families and into the fiscal bureaucracy of Bogotá.[29]

The Alvarez clan constituted a potential if not an actual *rosca*—a term used to describe an inner-centered pressure group—which could and sometimes did exercise an influence over the conduct of public affairs far out of proportion to its actual numbers, which were not insignificant. The visitor general, of course, never used the word *rosca,* but that is how he regarded them. Stressing possible conflicts of interests, Gutiérrez de Piñeres wrote to Gálvez, "I have attended meetings in which I have seen three brothers-in-law vote, one as oidor, the other as *contador mayor* and the third as *oficial mayor.*" He labeled this situation "a monstrosity."[30] The fact that these treasury officials sometimes, but not always, called in a magistrate who was not a relative by blood or marriage scarcely eased the visitor general's fears and suspicions.

After a careful examination, the visitor general confessed to José de Gálvez that he could discover no single example of outright fraud and collusion that could be ascribed directly to the Alvarez clan. He did argue, however, that the influence of this rosca was responsible for the appointment of Alvarez's son-in-law, Manuel García Olano, whom Gutiérrez de Piñeres dismissed as incompetent, to be director of the tobacco monopoly in Socorro.[31]

A royal cedula of January 20, 1775, ordering that no two blood relatives to the third degree nor in-laws to the second degree could serve in the same treasury office, provided the visitor general with a useful weapon, and also provoked a clash with Viceroy Flores that merits some attention. The viceroy argued that the cedula, though in theory reasonable, would impose undue hardships, and should be drastically revised or flexibly interpreted. The fact was that the most suitable candidates for office came from five families, all of

Manuel Bernardo Alvarez, fiscal of Santa Fe de Bogotá. (Courtesy of Cecilia Caro, Museo Nacional.)

whom were related by blood or marriage—the Prietos, the Ricaurtes, the Caicedos, the Oriundos, and the Alvarezes. The viceroy argued, "It seems harsh to me that persons who have neither wealth for their subsistence nor any other careers to give their children besides the few offices which their country offers, should be deprived of these posts and discriminated against by people of lesser talents who for this reason will not discharge their duties satisfactorily." The viceroy added to José de Gálvez that those who came from the peninsula without a royal appointment were "usually trash by birth, upbringing, and conduct."[32]

Gálvez, who then reposed complete confidence in Gutiérrez de Piñeres, sent a copy of the viceroy's letter to the visitor general for his comments. Gutiérrez de Piñeres attacked Flores's defense of the creole nobility: "It cannot be denied that the nobility should be given consideration, but the nobility of Bogotá would be notoriously insulted . . . if there should be an attempt to confine them solely to the Prietos, Ricaurtes, Caicedos, Oriundos, and Alvarezes, as the viceroy seems to be doing."[33] The visitor general argued that there were suitable candidates other than those coming from the five families and, citing the García Olano case, contended that not all the candidates for high office were qualified for the posts to which the viceroy appointed them.

The clash between Viceroy Flores and the regent visitor general is a graphic illustration of how the Caroline ministers intended to transform the bureaucracy. The viceroy, with decades of previous experience in America and a creole wife, was a partisan of the traditional Habsburg and early Bourbon policy of conciliating the creole elites. Gutiérrez de Piñeres, on the other hand, was aggressively implementing the new policy of reconquering the colonial bureaucracy from the creoles for the exclusive benefit of European Spaniards.

Gutiérrez de Piñeres proceeded with caution in dismantling the Alvarez rosca, following the example of Gálvez in Mexico.[34] Discretion was desirable, if not necessary, since these creole families were influential, and the regent had no hard evidence of graft.

Within two years, however, he could report triumphantly that the influence of the Alvarez family had been drastically curtailed. Only three members of the clan still retained fiscal office in Bogotá. Four others no longer held posts in the capital. One had died, one had retired, still another transferred, and yet another dismissed.

In 1778 the regent visitor general undertook to Europeanize the highest tribunal of the New Kingdom. He completed this task within two years. By the outbreak of the Comunero Revolution a solid phalanx of European Spaniards sat in the audiencia. Only one Spanish magistrate, it becomes apparent, enjoyed the confidence of the creoles—the senior judge, Juan Francisco Pey y Ruíz, married into a prominent creole family. The growing alienation between European and American Spaniards deeply influenced the character of the Comunero Revolution.

Article twenty-two of the capitulations of Zipaquirá takes on, then, an added significance. The creoles were demanding the restoration of a privilege to which they had long been accustomed. They were not a class systematically excluded from office but a bureaucratic elite that had been partially dispossessed only recently. The Caroline ministers were seeking to create a bureaucracy which would be exclusively responsive to orders emanating from Madrid. The leading families of Bogotá, long habituated to holding high office and accustomed to an informal influence in the councils of the government, saw themselves as the victims of a political upheaval. Their discontent was a major cause for the outbreak of armed resistance in 1781. It is no accident that Manuel García Olano, who had marriage ties not only to the Alvarez clan but also to the family of the marquis of San Jorge, was a major courier of information between certain elements of the creole elite in Bogotá and the leadership in Socorro. The alliance between Bogotá and Socorro was the hard core of the whole revolutionary movement.

Although the regent visitor general did much to restrict the power of the creoles, he could not totally eliminate their influence in less than three years. After Gutiérrez de Piñeres's fall from power on May 13, 1781, the government in Bogotá opted for a policy of reconciliation and concession. The besieged but still influential bureaucratic establishment that had informally governed New Granada during most of the eighteenth century played a key role in implementing the policy of reconciliation. Some of the leading protagonists in the hectic negotiations culminating in the capitulations of Zipaquirá were the senior oidor Pey y Ruíz, the regent of the tribunal de cuentas, Francisco de Vergara, and the marquis of San Jorge. The architect and consolidator of the policy, Archbishop Viceroy Caballero y Góngora, also realized the necessity of conciliating the creole bureaucratic elite.

Thus the essence of Charles III's political revolution was to abolish the "unwritten constitution" whose cornerstones were creole participation in the bureaucracy and government by compromise and negotiation. The economic and fiscal changes sponsored by the regent visitor general dramatized to dissatisfied creole patricians and mestizo plebeians alike the nature of the political revolution that the king's overzealous minister was seeking to impose on them. It is to these fiscal and economic innovations that we now turn.

2

From Kingdom to Colony:
The Fiscal and Economic Program
of Charles III

Bernardo Ward, in his *Proyecto económico,* succinctly expressed the fiscal goals of Charles III's ministers: "In order to understand how backward our dominions are, one has only to realize that France extracts from her colonies approximately forty million pesos annually, that is to say, four times more than Spain extracts from the New World."[1] What was disturbing to Ward was the fact that the overwhelming bulk of France's revenues came from the small but highly lucrative sugar colony of Saint-Domingue, whereas the extensive possessions of the Spanish crown stretched from California to the Strait of Magellan. José del Campillo y Cosío, the original architect of transforming the Empire, had urged his fellow statesmen to study and to copy the example of Spain's allies and foes—the French and the English. The central goal of the Caroline program of defensive modernization was to make the kingdoms overseas into veritable colonies producing the maximum revenue for the metropolis.[2]

The principal thrusts were technological and neomercantilist. Although the two shared the same goal of increasing economic productivity and hence royal revenues, benefits from technological changes would take longer to reap than neomercantilist innovations. Among the principal features of the technological program were the inclusion of the new science in the curriculum of the schools, the mining expeditions to Mexico, New Granada, and Peru in the 1780's, the botanical expedition to New Granada in the 1780's, the creation of branches of the *Sociedad Económica de Amigos del País* in various capitals of the Indies, and the speedy introduction of the new vaccination against smallpox.

But the pressing need in the 1770's and 1780's was an immediate and

18

dramatic increase in royal revenues to finance the rising costs of imperial defense. Potentially the most attractive sources were the royal monopolies, fundamentally mercantilist in origin and character, and including gunpowder, playing cards, salt mines, official stamped paper, mintage, and mercury. In New Granada the two which held the greatest potential for income were tobacco and liquor.

José de Gálvez's reorganization of the royal monopolies in New Spain became an astonishing fiscal success. The crown's net income rose to 14 million pesos annually. Six million pesos constituted the monopoly profits. Net profits from tobacco alone rose from 417,732 pesos in 1767 to 4,539,789 pesos in 1798. Royal legislation provided that all monopoly profits be converted into specie and shipped directly to Spain.[3]

While New Granada's economy and population were far inferior to Mexico's, the reorganized royal monopolies soon yielded a significant increase in royal revenues. By 1800 the treasury derived a net profit of some 373,966 pesos from the tobacco monopoly, and some 359,423 pesos from the liquor monopoly. New Granada's monopoly profits yielded 733,389 pesos annually, in contrast to Mexico's 6 million.[4] The tithes from the archepiscopal see of Bogotá, on the other hand, were some 222,983 pesos. While the royal treasury may have profited, severe hardship was imposed on the economy of New Granada, for that land suffered by the steady withdrawal to Spain of a significant portion of its metallic wealth, gold.

There was scarcely anything novel in the Hispanic context about royal monopolies. The tobacco monopoly was first established in Spain as early as 1630, and was leased to individuals for set periods of time until 1740, when direct royal administration replaced the contract system. As early as 1642 the energetic viceroy of Mexico, Bishop Juan de Palafox y Mendoza, urged his successor to create the monopoly there. The crown did make desultory efforts to extend the monopoly to America prior to 1764, but nothing came of these efforts.[5]

Mercantilists in the seventeenth century and neomercantilists in the time of Charles III justified their program on both practical and humanitarian grounds. Ward followed the classic mercantilist maxim that taxes should be low on necessities, moderate on articles of comfort, and steep on luxuries.[6] Tobacco and liquor were not necessities of life, but luxuries whose abuse could make their consumption vices. Hence royal control would not impose undue hardship on the poor. Such arguments, often repeated by Gutiérrez de Piñeres, scarcely impressed the small farmers who found in tobacco a lucrative cash crop, nor the consumers who indeed had come to regard both tobacco and liquor as necessities and not luxuries. But the combination of moral and commercial arguments made both products inviting targets to bureaucrats whose concern was to increase the coffers of the royal exchequer.

Tobacco Is King

The reign of king tobacco got off to a slow start in New Granada, where it was not extensively cultivated until the second half of the eighteenth century, when production dramatically increased.[7]

At the time that Gálvez was establishing an efficient royal tobacco monopoly in Mexico, Charles III ordered Viceroy Pedro Mesía de la Cerda (1761–72) to establish in New Granada a royal monopoly modeled after that of Spain. As was often the case with viceroys, Mesía de la Cerda flexibly interpreted the royal mandate. He paid a good deal of attention to the damage its implementation would cause local interests. Independent wholesalers and retailers would be put out of business. Stressing the expense that the government would incur under a system of direct administration, the viceroy pointed out that competent, efficient, and honest administrators were not easy to find, and resorted to the traditional method of tax farming. The viceroyalty was divided into districts and the privilege of administering the royal monopoly was leased for three to five years to the highest bidder.[8]

Tax farming had many disadvantages from the crown's point of view. Little control could be exercised over production, and overproduction periodically occurred. The true value of the tobacco production in each district was virtually impossible to measure, for tax farmers concealed its true worth. Prices varied from region to region. Paying low prices to the producers, the tax farmers tended to charge to consumers the highest price that the traffic would bear.

A second reorganization of the tobacco monopoly took place in 1774, during the administration of Viceroy Manuel de Guirior (1772–76). In response to a royal cedula on March 23, 1774, the viceroy began selectively to phase out tax farming, as particular contracts expired. In some districts, at least, he cautiously introduced direct administration. Under the new system the officers of the monopoly began to secure some control over the wholesale trade. Attempts were made to encourage quality production, but these changes were introduced piecemeal. Tax farming continued in many areas; other districts lacked any effective form of governmental control. Contraband flourished, and overproduction continued.[9]

The fiscal potential of a system of direct taxation was illustrated by what happened in the district of Honda, one of the most fertile regions in the New Kingdom for the cultivation of tobacco. In the first year of direct administration the district doubled its net profit to the treasury, from 6,000 pesos to 12,000 pesos.[10]

On October 24, 1776, Viceroy Flores introduced the third reorganization of the tobacco monopoly in less than a decade. The Flores plan was a major step in creating a more highly centralized royal monopoly in that it addressed itself to two major issues—overproduction and administrative structure. Both to avoid overproduction and to eliminate tobacco of inferior quality, such as was grown in the district of Bogotá, production was restricted to Girón and Zapatoca, San Gil, Charalá, and Simacota. The prohibition on growing tobacco in the parish of Socorro was not, then, an innovation of Gutiérrez de Piñeres, but of Viceroy Flores.[11] The principle of restricting areas of production had many advantages from the crown's point of view. Overproduction could be curbed, contraband cultivation could be more readily suppressed, and high-quality production could be more easily assured.

Another aspect of Viceroy Flores's reorganization was to move the headquarters of the Bogotá district from the capital city to Socorro. From here, it was thought, the industry could be better regulated: Socorro was the principal commercial center of the region and adjacent to the major tobacco production areas of the province of Tunja.

The real author of the Flores reorganization plan was his principal advisor, Francisco Robledo, the viceroy's *asesor general*. It was Robledo who persuaded the viceroy to appoint Manuel García Olano to the new position of administrator of the Socorro office.[12] Less than two years later, on June 8, 1778, Robledo married doña Rita Alvarez, the sister of García Olano's wife. Such a coincidence suggests that considerations of personal favoritism may have influenced the asesor general to recommend García Olano for the position in Socorro.

At the time of his appointment to the Socorro position, García Olano had a lawsuit of long duration pending because of his failure to render his final accounts to the treasury as administrator of the liquor monopoly in Mompós from 1760 until 1770.[13] It is clear that he owed his appointment more to his family connections than to his questionable professional qualifications. Indeed, José de Gálvez, in his capacity as *superintendente general de rentas,* not only refused to confirm García Olano, but curtly informed the viceroy on August 5, 1777, that he should be relieved forthwith of his post as tobacco administrator and that he should not be allowed to hold any other position in the royal treasury.[14]

Flores, who was on excellent terms with the Alvarez clan, did not dismiss García Olano until August, 1778, under pressure from Gutiérrez de Piñeres, who distrusted García Olano's family connections and knew him to be inept. These connections, however, resulted in García Olano's subsequent appointment as director of the postal service in Bogotá, at an annual salary of 1,500 pesos—a post from which the archibishop viceroy dismissed him in 1783.[15]

In order to avoid the kind of overproduction that García Olano had permitted, the regent visitor general restricted tobacco production even further than Flores had, limiting it to the small province of Girón and the parish of Zapatoca, where tobacco was of the highest quality. San Gil,

Charalá, Barichara, and Ocaña were now put on the forbidden list. This prohibition was abrasively enforced by Spanish-born policemen, the notorious *resguardos armados,* whom the populace accused of every sort of brutality including rape. Not only did the tough and rough policemen burn tobacco crops in forbidden areas, but those accused of illegally planting tobacco were subject to punishment in special courts set up to enforce the mandates of the royal monopolies.[16] The resentment of the small farmers was indeed a major cause of the outbreak of riots in March of 1781.

Charles III gave the regent visitor general a free hand in the cedulas of August 5 and August 15, 1777, when the monarch ordered the suspension of the Flores reorganization—an instruction Gutiérrez de Piñeres "obeyed but did not execute" until August 31, 1778, when he promulgated the fourth reform of the tobacco monopoly since 1766. Although this plan was a significant cause of the outbreak of the Comunero Revolution, it proved to be definitive, largely remaining in force until January 1, 1850, when the republican government of New Granada abolished the tobacco monopoly.[17]

The reorganization followed in large measure the model that Gálvez had earlier established in Mexico. Production was restricted to four carefully chosen areas producing tobacco of the highest quality: Ambalema in the upper valley of the Magdalena, Llano Grande on the eastern side of the Cauca valley, Girón and Zapatoca adjacent to the province of Tunja, and Pore and Numchia in the llanos de Casanare. Each area chosen was supposed to be able to supply enough high-quality tobacco for the consumers in each district. Trade in tobacco from one region to another was forbidden.

In view of the fact that other areas in the Empire were exporting tobacco to Europe, New Granada was not allowed to do so. The coastal provinces of Panama, Cartagena, and Santa Marta, where tobacco was not cultivated, received their tobacco not from the interior of the New Kingdom but by boat from Cuba.[18]

The world market for tobacco was limited: in what would soon become the United States tobacco growers at this time voluntarily burned tobacco in response to world market demands.[19] The Spanish state with its neomercantilist orientation adopted the policy that the state should directly intervene in order to achieve some stable equilibrium between supply and demand in the world market. New Granada, which was not allowed even to export tobacco to Spain, was a victim of this grand design.

The Spanish empire's chief competitor was English North America, which produced more tobacco than the rest of the world. Spanish American tobacco from Cuba and Venezuela (the "Orinoco tobacco," as it was generally called in Europe) was of superior quality, but it was much more expensive than the Anglo-American variety. It is an historical irony that France purchased the bulk of its tobacco not from her ally, Spain, but from her enemy, the English colonies along the Atlantic coast. Economic advantage overrode political considerations, and the French market annually absorbed approximately one-fourth of the total crop of English America. In 1778 increase in the price of the already more expensive Spanish American tobacco further restricted Spain's share of the French market.[20]

It is worth noting, by the way, that the Spaniards, whose entrepreneurial skills have not always been appreciated, were in this particular case more efficiently state capitalist than their French allies. Although the Caroline administrative, fiscal, and economic innovations were largely inspired by the mercantilist policies of Colbert, Louis XIV's minister of finance, in the specific area of the tobacco monopoly the "backward" Spaniards led and the "modern" French followed. The French tobacco monopoly was not created until 1674, and until it was swept away during the throes of the French Revolution, it was administered under the tax-farming system of the ancien régime.[21]

Gutiérrez de Piñeres rationalized the administration of New Granada by creating a *dirección general* in Bogotá with jurisdiction over all the royal monopolies. Tobacco and liquor, the two most lucrative, were separate subdivisions. Five administrative districts—Bogotá, Popayán, Honda, Panama, and Cartagena—were divided into a number of *estancos*, or retail outlets, which were usually coterminous with parishes. The producers sold their crop to the monopoly. It, in turn, manufactured the finished products which were sold to the public. The royal monopolies not only had their own police force but also their own tribunals to punish offenders. Full-time, salaried bureaucrats administered the system from top to bottom. A more efficient system of bookkeeping was established in order to discourage fraud. Gutiérrez de Piñeres sought to forestall any evasive scheme that regional administrators might devise in order to explain away a shortage of cash or to cover up any discrepancy between their account books and those of their superiors and inferiors.

The five administrative districts were to become the five intendancy units of New Granada, but the Comunero Revolution discouraged the crown from undertaking this step, and the intendancies set up elsewhere in the Indies were never established here.

Viva Aguardiente

The other lucrative royal monopoly in New Granada was that of *aguardiente de caña y anis*, rum and anisette. Aguardiente, meaning literally, in Spanish, 'fire water,' is a generic term for spirituous liquor. By the time of Viceroy Mesía de la Cerda the aguardiente monopoly was producing some

200,000 pesos, in contrast to the meager profits coming from the newly established tobacco monopoly.[22] To be sure, the aguardiente monopoly was of longer duration, for the crown authorized its establishment as early as 1736.

The manufacture and sale of aguardiente had a difficult struggle to secure legitimization. As early as 1693 Charles II forbade its production and sale on the grounds that it was injurious to health and public morality. On September 30, 1714, Philip V repeated the prohibition with severe penalties for noncompliance. But powerful vested interests made these royal mandates a dead letter. The consumption of rum and anisette among all sectors in the society was habitual. The sugar-producing haciendas, many of which were located in the coastal provinces of Cartagena and Santa Marta, needed a market for their product. Many of the haciendas belonged to the regular clergy.

Several times during the eighteenth century the crown ordered an investigation into the desirability of prohibiting the production of aguardiente. On each occasion the viceroys and the audiencia dutifully marshaled such expert opinion as there was. Both ecclesiastics and physicians testified that these beverages, taken in moderation, would endanger neither the moral standards of the community nor the physical well-being of its citizens. They further argued that governmental control of the price would diminish its potential harm. Drunkards existed everywhere, the authorities in Bogotá reminded the king, and it was not easy to legislate them out of existence. The total prohibition of the manufacture of aguardiente would be difficult to enforce in a land where rich and poor alike had been accustomed to consume it. The two most telling arguments that the authorities in Bogotá marshaled were that the prosperity of the sugar plantations would be jeopardized if they were deprived of this important outlet for their crop and, secondly, that the monopoly was a potentially lucrative source of royal revenue.

Although the crown's paternalist concern for the physical and moral welfare of its subjects overseas should not be discounted, the need for added revenues buttressed by the pressure of regional vested interests and custom proved an unbeatable alliance.

When first set up in 1736, the monopoly provided for free production of the liquor with each producer paying a specified tax to the royal treasury. Tax farmers, who secured a contract for a five-year period by bid, collected the tax and paid the treasury the stipulated amount. Aguardiente, like tobacco, proved initially to be a fiscal disappointment. In the early years the annual net profit for the treasury was only 8,528 pesos.[23] During the 1760's direct administration in many districts replaced tax farming. Hence Viceroy Mesía de la Cerda could report in 1772 a net annual profit of 200,000 pesos, which rose during the last decades of the eighteenth century to between 300,000 and 340,000 pesos.

Viceroy Flores paid as much attention to reforming the aguardiente monopoly as he did to reorganizing the tobacco monopoly. His asesor general, Robledo, drew up an equally comprehensive plan of reconstruction. The plan of November 26, 1776, envisaged direct state administration of the monopoly for the whole audiencia kingdom. New Granada was divided into districts, *administraciones generales,* which were provided with clerical staff and a corps of policemen. The monopoly bought the raw materials from the producers, manufactured the liquor, and sold it to the consumers. An estanco was to be established in every locality where there was sufficient demand. The *administrador general* usually appointed as the *estanquero* one of the richest citizens in the locality; he in turn was required to post bond as a guarantee of his compliance with the regulations of the monopoly.

The regent visitor general's instructions were to investigate the operations of the aguardiente monopoly and to make improvements if he thought desirable. Gutiérrez de Piñeres candidly admitted that the Flores-Robledo reorganization was a marked improvement, but argued that the centralization of all the monopolies in one administrative unit and detailed instructions for all levels of the bureaucracy were indispensable additions. On May 22, 1778, he issued his *Instrucción para el gobierno de la dirección general de la renta de aguardiente de caña,* which incorporated many of the features of the Flores-Robledo reorganization, but to which the visitor general added a dirección general to exercise supreme jurisdiction; tobacco and aguardiente became autonomous subdivisions. This definitive reorganization became embodied in the ordinance of May 27, 1780, which had the explicit approval of the king.[24]

Not only did the regent visitor general rationalize and centralize the administration of the aguardiente and tobacco monopolies, but in 1780, in response to orders from Spain, he increased the price that the estancos charged to the consumers. The increase amounted to two *reales* (twenty-five cents) for each pound of tobacco and every two liters of aguardiente.[25] The justification for the rise in price was to secure added revenues to finance the war against Great Britain.

During the course of the Comunero Revolution the two principal targets of popular wrath were the offices of the tobacco and aguardiente monopolies. The crowds burned the tobacco and emptied jugs of aguardiente into the streets of countless village squares throughout the province of Tunja. In fact, these activities represent the only massive destruction of property during all the commotions from March until June of 1781. The impact of these two products on producers and consumers should, however, be carefully distinguished.

In the capitulations of Zipaquirá, when the Comunero leaders had an opportunity to articulate their grievances, they did not demand the abolition of the aguardiente monopoly as such. They merely requested the abrogation of the recently imposed price increase. Although the bulk of aguardiente manufactured came from the sugar plantations in the coastal provinces of Panama, Cartagena, and Santa Marta, sugar production was also important in Socorro. These plantations were capitalist enterprises requiring large investments in both equipment and labor. The owners of the sugar plantations did not object to the principle of the monopoly, to which they had become accustomed in one form or another since 1736. Furthermore, the state monopoly guaranteed them a secure market for their product, and paid them in gold specie.

During the Comunero Revolution, the existence of a garrison of some 3,318 professional troops in Cartagena as well as smaller garrisons in Santa Marta and Panama no doubt accounted in part for loyalty of the coastal provinces to the government. That loyalty, however, was reinforced by the fact that economic grievances there were far less acute than those of the interior or mountain regions. While the consuming public on the coast had to pay more for aguardiente and tobacco, the sugar producers had no basic quarrel with the aguardiente monopoly, and the coast did not cultivate tobacco.

In the province of Tunja, on the other hand, the tobacco monopoly damaged both producers and consumers alike. Tobacco was cultivated in many regions of the province, often on small plots which provided countless small farmers with a modest cash crop. Hence the rage of the crowds intensified, for they were protesting both as consumers and producers.

One can only speculate what might have happened if the regent visitor general had merely restricted the areas of tobacco cultivation without increasing its price to the consumer. Popular wrath might have been less intense. But the restrictions and the price increase together proved an explosive combination that was further intensified by a whole series of other tax measures.

Before examining those aspects some brief attention should be paid to innovations that were introduced in the other royal monopolies. These were not insignificant in their impact, but compared to the tobacco and aguardiente monopolies and the sales taxes they belonged to the category of minor irritants. In the interests of expanding royal revenues, Gutiérrez de Piñeres increased the price to the consumers of playing cards, salt, gunpowder, and official stamped paper (necessary for all legal, commercial, and government documents). In the capitulations of Zipaquirá the playing card monopoly was abolished outright, and the recent increases in the prices of salt, gunpowder, and official stamped paper were rescinded.[26]

The regent visitor general's reorganization of the traditional sales tax system created almost as much antagonism among all groups as did his controversial reorganization of the tobacco and aguardiente monopolies.

Sales Taxes

The third most important single source of royal taxation in New Granada was the *alcabala*. By the end of the colonial period the sales tax yielded annually approximately 184,880 pesos out of a total revenue of 2,453,096 pesos.[27] Indeed, before the creation of the aguardiente and tobacco monopolies, whose total yield was around 700,000 pesos, the alcabala had been the single largest source of income for the royal treasury. One of the priorities of the regent visitor general was to reorganize this lucrative institution. In this important respect Gálvez and his lieutenants disregarded the advice of their mentor, Ward, who had urged the Spaniards to emulate the English colonies, whose prosperity he ascribed to the low rates of their excise and sales taxes.[28]

By the fourteenth century, the sales tax, of Arabic origin, was embedded in the fiscal system of Castile. In 1591 it was introduced into the southern viceroyalty of Peru, despite tenacious but unsuccessful resistance. By the eighteenth century the tax, now 4 percent, applied, with a few significant exceptions, to raw materials, consumer goods, chattels, and real and personal property on every change of ownership. Two groups in society enjoyed significant immunities: the Indians and the clergy.

The Indians did not have to pay the sales tax on crops they raised or on products produced in New Granada—an exemption that did not extend to goods of European or Asian origin. Secondly, the clergy and ecclesiastical institutions incurred no tax liability on products produced for their own benefit and on sales not entered into for the sake of gain. Ecclesiastical exemptions, however, were not spelled out fully enough to prevent endless controversy with the royal exchequer.[29]

Until the time of Charles III the alcabala was often farmed out to corporations such as *cabildos* or *consulados* or to individual tax farmers, usually for a three-year period. As Robert S. Smith has observed, "The price paid for the sales tax contract represented a compromise between the demands of the king for revenue, usually urgently needed, and the unwillingness or inability of the tax farmer to discover and to exploit the taxpayer's liability."[30]

Such a loose arrangement was unacceptable to Gutiérrez de Piñeres. One of his efforts at rationalization was to separate the alcabala sales tax from the sales tax for the *armada de Barlovento* (the Windward Island fleet), which had been introduced into New Granada in 1641 to help defray the costs of the Caribbean defense squadron.[31] In effect, the armada de Barlovento was an additional sales tax of 2 percent, and after 1720 the two taxes were jointly collected; by 1778 the armada de Barlovento had totally lost its identity as a separate tax. When Gutiérrez de Piñeres resurrected it from the dusty archives, this tax soon became a focus of bitter popular indignation.[32] It certainly was not a new tax, but the regent visitor general failed lamentably in his public relations campaign to convince the populace to the contrary. So deep was popular feeling that the tax was declared abolished in the first clause of the capitulations of Zipaquirá.[33]

Gutiérrez de Piñeres had no sympathy for the tax-farming system, which he regarded as an inefficient exploitation of the tax potential. He proposed to replace tax farmers in all large localities as their contracts expired, and, in smaller localities, rigorously to limit their contracts to three years, with intensified administrative supervision.

The regent visitor general's reorganization plan ordered a comprehensive census, which should be updated every January 1. Every person in the district should be identified by his economic activity. The alcabala administration was to be divided into subdivisions, such as products of Castile, products of New Granada, retail food outlets, retail merchandising outlets, cattle ranches, crop farms, and traveling merchants. While Gutiérrez de Piñeres reaffirmed the traditional exemptions of the alcabala, he sought to eliminate what he considered to be accumulated abuses, including practices involving slave-owners, the clergy, and the Indians.[34]

In order to guarantee that merchants paid the sales taxes, the regent visitor general set up a system of *guías* and *tornaguías*. A guía, issued by the local fiscal agent, was a certificate that a particular cargo of merchandise purchased in one locality and destined somewhere else had paid the appropriate sales taxes. When the merchandise arrived at its destination, the local representative of the royal treasury issued a tornaguía, that certified that the goods described in the guía had arrived with their taxes already paid or bonded for. This arrangement often meant that merchants had to incur the added expense of hiring the services of a bondsman, *fiador,* as well as to secure at their own expense the services of a notary.[35]

Although there had existed a rather primitive system of licensing goods in transit, the highly bureaucratic system of guías and tornaguías was the creation of Gutiérrez de Piñeres. Such an arrangement might promise to increase royal revenues, but the small merchants plying the treacherous paths of the Andes with their mule trains were livid with rage. These regulations were, indeed, greatly simplified in the aftermath of the Comunero uprising.[36]

The regent visitor general introduced yet another fiscal burden. In a cedula of August 17, 1780, Charles III requested from his vassals overseas a *donativo gracioso y préstamo* in order to meet the extraordinary expenses of the war against England—a Spanish form of forced loan that was periodically invoked by the crown during a war emergency. A forced loan, in effect, enabled the crown to mobilize substantial resources independent of the fixed ascriptive rights of the upper classes, but it was a poor substitute for an annual system of direct regular taxation.[37] If this tax were to be effectively collected, it would yield in New Granada more than a million pesos.

On March 20, 1781, the regent visitor general ordered that all white males, the so-called nobles, make a contribution of two pesos; nonwhites were required to pay one peso, and women, slaves, and the destitute were exempt.[38] False rumors that the forced loan was to be an annual tax gained general acceptance, so inflamed was popular opinion.[39] For the timing of the appeal was unfortunate.

The new regulations regarding the collection of the alcabala and the armada de Barlovento had been published in the city of Tunja on February 15, and in the town of Socorro on March 16.[40] In Socorro, publication precipitated a riot in which two thousand irate citizens participated. A revolution had begun.

The Visitor General and the Viceroy

Within a period of twenty-six months the energetic Juan Francisco Gutiérrez de Piñeres had reorganized the tax-collecting apparatus of the viceroyalty, in accordance with the efforts of Charles III's ministers to place the kingdoms overseas in a state of economic dependency that would benefit the metropolis. One could indeed argue quite cogently that the state of dependency— today an influential hypothesis in explaining Latin America's continued underdevelopment—did not effectively begin until the incipient technocrats of Charles III sought to convert the kingdoms of the Indies into a veritable economic empire.[41]

New Granada was then a relatively poor land with a modest if somewhat primitive economy.[42] Any increase in taxation, however moderate, would be felt. The tax and administrative changes hit every group in that society, suddenly and simultaneously. The tobacco and aguardiente increase affected a large number of consumers, the overwhelming majority of the population, who regarded these luxuries as necessities. The small farmers in the province of Tunja, who had only recently been accustomed to having tobacco as a cash crop, resented the prohibition against cultivation in most of the province.

While the rates of the sales taxes were not much increased, direct collection meant that more and more people were paying more of the taxes, of which only a fraction of the legal amount due had been collected in the past. The slaveowners and the clergy were not happy with the visitor general's zeal in eliminating some of their customary if extralegal tax exemptions. The Indians were bitterly restless over the expropriations of their community lands, the *resguardos*. Everyone's pocket was affected by the changes. All classes and ethnic groups had some cause for irritation. The creole elite families in Bogotá were alarmed at the loss of their traditional "rights" to high office. The local creole elites in the provincial towns such as Socorro and San Gil saw their political and social roles undercut, as the new fiscal administration imposed a host of new officials, usually European Spaniards who responded to the dictates of Bogotá rather than those of the localities where they were temporarily stationed. The lower classes were deeply alienated by the abrasive enforcement of the taxes and monopolies. The instinctive hatred of the plebeians toward the *chapetones,* as the European Spaniards were derisively called, became intensified.

New Granada, in fact, had been accustomed to a loose and decentralized administration in which the viceroy and the audiencia acted as brokers between local interests and the mandates of the central authorities in Madrid. Change did occur, but its pace was slow. The viceroys courted public opinion by enlisting the support of the parish clergy and the local elites, whose institutional strongholds were the cabildos, and sought to balance regional pressures with the demands of the central bureaucracy. No better example of this system can be found than the conduct of Viceroy Flores, who managed to accomplish a great deal to centralize the tobacco and aguardiente monopolies without arousing militant opposition.

Gutiérrez de Piñeres was certainly intransigent and uncompromising about implementing the fiscal program of Charles III, but he could be remarkably flexible and responsive to local interests on matters not directly affecting the royal treasury. He provided some paternalistic protection to the Indians in their desperate struggle to resist the land and labor hunger of the creoles and mestizos, as will be discussed in some detail in chapter 7. In the heated controversy involving changes in the curriculum of higher education the regent visitor general also demonstrated a willingness to listen to local vested interests. He was, indeed, quite capable of practicing coalition politics in almost every sphere excepting the fiscal. His instructions from José de Gálvez were to increase the royal revenues immediately, and he adamantly refused to consider any accommodation that might have reduced the initial intake of the royal treasury but might also have avoided the violent confrontation of 1781. He was not, like Viceroy Flores, a political conciliator, but a technocrat who wanted results immediately.

The only person of authority and prestige with a policy that might have avoided violence in 1781 was the viceroy. Flores urged that the militias be reformed and expanded so that the government would have sufficient military force in being to quell any riots. In 1777 he proposed an extensive military reorganization, but Gálvez rejected the plan. Madrid decreed that the fiscal program under the auspices of a visitor general should precede the military reorganization. When violence did break out in March of 1781, there were fewer than seventy-five professional soldiers in Bogotá, and the militia units in many interior provinces existed only on paper. The only effective military forces in the New Kingdom were stationed in the coastal fortresses of Cartagena and Santa Marta.[43]

Gutiérrez de Piñeres's opposition to the creation of disciplined militias in the interior provinces makes fascinating reading, in view of subsequent events. Good fiscal bureaucrat that he was, he deplored the cost to the royal treasury and the loss to agriculture and commerce of militiamen on active duty. He expressed intense loathing for the "vile mob," largely because they were the products of various kinds of race mixtures. These would constitute the majority of the common soldiers and, if armed, might lose their accustomed respect for their Spanish and creole social betters.

Viceroy Flores had pointed out that militias were needed to put down riots in which upper-class creoles sometimes participated. He had in mind the rum riot in Quito in 1765. Gutiérrez de Piñeres vehemently replied:

> I have been persuaded and still am that such allegations are willful and injurious to such a commendable group of vassals whose loyalty cannot be doubted without doing them a notorious injustice. I dare to affirm that nothing is to be feared from the nobility and the people of distinction nor from those honorable citizens residing in the villages who own real estate and farms or who engage in other industrious occupations, for they are white and of decent extraction.[44]

The regent visitor general would subsequently have occasion to repent those words. But the letter does explain why he so confidently refused to heed the advice of Viceroy Flores. Given his ignorance of American social conditions and his racist loathing for those of African extraction, he found it unthinkable that the well-to-do creoles would join the "vile mob" in an uprising. But the unthinkable did happen, within less than a year.

Flores proved to be a remarkably accurate prophet. In those areas where the military had been reorganized, such as Popayán and Quito, serious disturbances did not occur. One may speculate that if the authorities in Bogotá had had an effective military force, the Comunero uprising might not have taken place. In support of this speculation is the attitude of Flores's successor, Archbishop Caballero y Góngora.

While he pursued his policy of reconciliation, Caballero y Góngora, cleric though he was, proved more militaristic than all his military predecessors and successors in the viceregal office. He undertook a comprehensive reorganization of the military on the grounds that the government had to have in the background real coercive power.[45] He never forgot that at Zipaquirá he had no soldiers to protect him, but only the dignity of his archepiscopal office and his own political dexterity. Caballero y Góngora's tactics included both

REYNANDO LA MAGESTAD CATOLICA DE S.ᴼᴿ Dᴺ
CARLOS III.

EL YLUSTRISSIMO Y EXCELENTISSIMO Sʳ Dᴺ Antᵒ Caballero y Goncora Gran Cruz de la Rˡ y distinguida Ordᴺ de Carlos III
Dignissimo Arzobispo de Sᵗᵃ Fe de Bogotá Virrey Governᵒʳ y Capitᴺ Generˡ deste nuevo Reˢ de Granᵃ de cuyos empleos con la Presidenciᵃ de suˣ
Audiencia tomo posecion en 13 de Junio de 1782 por Fallesim. del Exmᵒ Sᵒʳ Dᴺ Juan de Torrezar Diaz Pimienta, y en Virtud de los Particu-
lares y distinguidos Meritos que contraxo en la Pacificacion del Socorro y demas Provincias se sirvio suMᵈ con fecha de 15 de Abril de 1783
CONCEDERLE LA PROPIEDAD DE DICHOS EMPLEOS POR EL TIEMPO DE SU VOLUNTAD.

Antonio Caballero y Góngora, archbishop of Santa Fe de Bogotá. (Portrait by Joaquín Gutiérrez; Museo de Arte Colonial.)

the proverbial carrot and the stick. He once confessed to José de Gálvez that if the king's vassals would not respond to orders couched in the language of "pastoral gentleness," he would not hesitate to use "repression and force." [46]

The second basic disagreement between Gutiérrez de Piñeres and Flores lay in tactics and political style. The two magistrates did not disagree over the need to increase royal revenues, but the viceroy argued for gradual and moderately diplomatic innovations. Such was the traditional approach of the viceroys toward the art of governing, fortified by Flores's long experience in the New World. Gutiérrez de Piñeres, on the other hand, wanted fiscal results immediately. He paid no attention to the political consequences of alienating every significant group in the land, for it was inconceivable to him that the patricians would join the plebeians in any kind of effective protest.

Gutiérrez de Piñeres shared none of the politician's concern for compromise and conciliation. His mentality as an efficient, if narrow-minded, tax collector was succinctly revealed when he wrote his mentor, Gálvez:

> The lower classes are not capable of understanding the justification for royal taxes. All they aspire to is their own self-interest which is absolute and unlimited libertinism. Since it is vain to anticipate that the multitude would gladly pay any tax whatsoever, the goal of government must be to force the plebeians to respect public authority so that their subordination and obedience to all magistrates will be preserved.[47]

Gutiérrez de Piñeres was a man in a hurry to get results. When José del Campillo y Cosío first proposed in 1743 a visita general for all the kingdoms of the Indies, its stated purpose was merely to gather information and to propose recommendations before introducing widespread innovations.[48] In his impatience to secure immediate results, Gálvez abandoned the original design, combining the information-gathering aspect of the visita general with the immediate introduction of changes. Had Gutiérrez de Piñeres confined his activity to gathering information and making recommendations—the actual implementation being left to viceroys of the political skill of Flores or Caballero y Góngora—the outbreak of violence might have been avoided.

From January, 1778, until August 11, 1779, when he left for Cartagena, the viceroy and the regent visitor general engaged in a polite but intense bureaucratic tug of war.[49] Leaving aside the inherited tensions of the two offices, the two magistrates were divided by a profound difference of tactics and political style. Gálvez, with his animus toward the viceregal office, resolved the conflict in favor of the visitor general, ordering Flores to submit to his jurisdiction in all matters relating to the royal treasury. Stripped of all real authority over the exchequer, which represented a major source of viceregal power, Flores saw himself virtually repudiated. The outbreak of war with Great Britain on June 16, 1779, provided him with a graceful pretext to depart for Cartagena to supervise the defense of that military bastion. On August 11, 1779, the viceroy delegated to the regent visitor general all his authority over the interior provinces except for the administration of the ecclesiastical patronage and military defense.[50]

Juan Francisco Gutiérrez de Piñeres was, in fact but not in name, viceroy as of August 11, 1779. But after twenty-one months of supreme power he had to face an outburst of popular fury that toppled him from his pre-eminence.

English and Spanish America

The crisis that agitated both Spanish and English America was triggered by the need of the metropolitan authorities to increase taxes sharply in order to pay for the mounting costs of imperial defense. When the enterprising Yankees disguised as Indians dumped tea into the harbor of Boston and when the infuriated citizens of Socorro dumped aguardiente and burned the tobacco from the state monopolies, they were not merely protesting against the increased taxation of these commodities. More profoundly, these actions symbolized the demand of the irate citizens of Boston and Socorro for the restoration of their respective constitutional systems, which they believed the new taxes violated.

The British and the Spanish empires prior to the great crisis of the 1770's and 1780's shared a tradition of political decentralization. In the case of the English, decentralization was largely legislative, whereas the Spanish tradition of decentralization was essentially bureaucratic in nature. As of 1778 the cornerstones of New Granada's "unwritten constitution" were cogovernment between European and American Spaniards, and government by consultation, negotiation, and compromise.

Although monarchical power was still well entrenched in the British world, that authority had been challenged twice during the seventeenth century, when one English king was beheaded, and another dethroned during the "Glorious Revolution" of 1688. Out of this crisis came the contract theory of political sovereignty, which provided that the king and Parliament share power, and which justified the right of revolution when the king violated the social contract. The central issue was the power to tax. The thirteen colonies claimed that Parliament's cherished right to approve all new taxes should extend to them as English citizens—a privilege which neither George III nor Parliament was prepared to grant. After the revolution of 1688 the colonial assemblies consolidated their claims to legislate over taxation.[51] During the same decades the Spanish American version of bureaucratic decentralization was consolidated.

Hence the celebrated slogan of 1776 in North America: "No taxation without representation." In Spanish America the slogan of protest was profoundly different in character and meaning: "Long live the king and death to bad government." In the Spanish American context the Anglo-American slogan had no meaning, for there was no tradition of legislative assemblies with the power to levy taxes. As early as the time of Charles V the *cortes* in the peninsula had been reduced to largely ceremonial functions. Nor would the crown sanction the emergence of formal representative assemblies in the Indies. What did develop in Spanish America, however, was an indigenous tradition of no taxation without bureaucratic negotiation. The crises that tore apart English and Spanish America were both basically constitutional and political in nature.

PART II
Juan Francisco Berbeo

3

The Crowd Riots

The conflagration that swept through the New Kingdom of Granada in 1781 began in Socorro, and that prosperous community provided the hard core of its leadership from beginning to end.

During most of the seventeenth century, Socorro was a grouping of a few huts and cabins—a *caserío*—and a way-station for changing mules and horses and securing fresh provisions on the *camino real* that as early as 1580 connected Vélez to the south and Pamplona to the north. It belonged to the territorial jurisdiction of the city of Vélez until 1689, when Nuestra Señora del Socorro del Chanchón became a parish. From 1694 until 1771 Socorro was attached to the town of Santa Cruz y San Gil, which was detached from Vélez by a royal cedula of October 27, 1694. In 1771 Socorro acquired town status from Charles III.[1]

During the course of the eighteenth century, Socorro developed into one of the most prosperous agricultural and trading centers of New Granada. By the 1750's the parish of Socorro was yielding its pastor an annual income of some 5,000 pesos, more than the annual rent that the bishop of Santa Marta derived from his whole diocese.[2] The only parish living to rival Socorro's was that of Neiva. By 1800 the whole jurisdiction of the towns of San Gil and Socorro, which stretched from Vélez in the south to Girón in the north, was the single largest producer of ecclesiastical tithes, some 39,993 pesos out of a total of 272,120 pesos for the archbishopric of Bogotá. The district of Tunja with a yield of some 25,360 pesos and the district of Bogotá with some 10,962 pesos ranked second and third.[3]

Socorro's rise to modest prosperity was due to several factors. One was its location, on a fertile shelf of land lying on the eastern slope of the Suárez

River in a warm valley about 4,000 feet above sea level. Sugar cane, bananas, corn, yucca, cotton, and cattle flourished. Not only did the large-scale production of cotton encourage the growth of a textile industry, but also Socorro's location made it a natural emporium of trade and commerce for a considerable hinterland. A high rate of population growth went hand-in-hand with Socorro's economic expansion.[4]

While there is abundant contemporary evidence about the importance of cotton cultivation, the information about textile production is scanty indeed. The section of the notarial archive in Socorro dealing with commercial transactions has not survived the ravages of time. Hence, next to nothing is known about the apparently primitive technology employed, nor about working conditions, nor to what extent there was some kind of credit system. What little evidence is available suggests that textile production was a primitive cottage industry confined to the homes of the poor, although there were some textile workshops. The work force was almost exclusively women. No evidence has yet come to light to substantiate the claim that the textile industry in Socorro constituted a nascent capitalism. This cottage industry was undermined by the flood of cheap English textiles imported into Colombia after independence.[5]

The ordinary pattern of settlement in this area was for a group of families to cluster into a hamlet, a *caserío*, which eventually became a vice-parish subordinate to the nearest parish. Then the parish in turn would acquire vice-parishes. Before the archbishop would authorize the creation of a new parish, the population had to be sufficiently numerous to support three *cofradías,* sodalities of laymen and laywomen. These voluntary associations had to provide the minimum stipend of a parish priest, between 150 and 200 pesos, and suitably furnish the church the requirements of ritual.[6] The legal definition of a parish was a community destined exclusively for the residence of Spaniards with a church, a jail, and civil magistrates. A parish's population could vary from two hundred to several thousand souls.

As their populations multiplied, the parishes in turn would acquire more political autonomy from their capital city by a process of cellular separation. San Gil, for example, was founded as a parish of the city of Vélez. In 1694 San Gil became a town with a cabildo and annually elected *alcaldes ordinarios* who were the executive and judicial officers of the community. The creation of new parishes as well as towns often aroused opposition from the older communities, which would lose revenues and privileges, but demography usually triumphed over local vested interests.[7]

Socorro's sense of its own identity grew, as it tenaciously fought to achieve autonomy from the jurisdiction of the town of San Gil, which lay some twenty-two kilometers to the northeast—in 1781 a day's journey from Socorro. No sooner had the parish of Socorro been created than her ambitious citizens petitioned the audiencia in Bogotá to grant them independence from San Gil. In 1711 the archbishop of Bogotá, Francisco de Cossio y Otero, who was then serving as acting president of the audiencia, granted Socorro's request. But San Gil initiated a lawsuit, as a result of which Philip V restored Socorro to the status of a subordinate parish.[8]

During the subsequent decades the authorities in Bogotá sought to placate Socorro by granting extensive powers to the alcalde resident there, and frequently appointing a Socorrano to the post of lieutenant corregidor. But as Socorro continued to grow in population and prosperity, the yearning of some of its citizens for municipal autonomy intensified.

On April 23, 1762, Socorro boldly took the offensive: a large number of its citizens petitioned the viceroy, not for the status of a town, but for the more prestigious rank of a city. What they eventually got was a township. In charge of this civic campaign was Socorro's then richest citizen, Juan Maldonado de la Zerda, who spent some 16,000 pesos from his own pocket to pay for the expenses involved in the long litigation, which culminated in the royal cedula of October 25, 1771, granting Socorro the coveted rank of town. Maldonado de la Zerda, however, was much less successful in persuading the city fathers of the new town to reimburse him for these expenses.[9] As might be expected, San Gil fought a tenacious but unsuccessful rearguard action in the audiencia, even dispatching a special representative to Spain to plead its case.[10]

Socorro not only had to wage a vigorous campaign to end its dependence on San Gil, but also it had to fight another battle in the courts to secure its boundaries. San Gil energetically tried to confine the limits of the new town to the parishes of Socorro and Oiba. Socorro argued that the ties of economics and geography justified placing of the populous parishes of Charalá, Simacota, and Chima under its jurisdiction, and once again won its case after a protracted legal battle.[11]

The rivalry of Socorro and San Gil is but one of many examples of the way that the process of cellular separation created new communities. In fighting San Gil to secure political autonomy, Socorro acquired a sense of self-identity, a feeling that its community was the leader of a prosperous hinterland. That vision of leadership was of paramount importance in 1781. In fact, Socorro's aspirations, as a *patria chica,* a regional homeland, to exercise some control over the destiny of the surrounding area planted the seeds from which federalism would grow in the nineteenth century.

The town council, the cabildo, of Socorro, exercised jurisdiction over eight outlying parishes with a total population in 1779 of 33,710 people.[12] By 1781 the urban nucleus of Socorro had a population of about 15,000, having grown from 4,000 or so in 1711 and 8,000 in 1753. Several adjacent parishes, such as Simacota, Oiba, and Charalá, had as many as 6,000 parishioners.

By legal definition Socorro was founded as a parish for whites, although in fact the area contained a large mestizo population with a smaller minority of blacks and mulattos. The ethnic categories in the late eighteenth-century census figures were: (1) whites, (2) Indians, (3) slaves, and (4) free population. The term "white" evidently included not only descendants of Spaniards but also some mestizos who, because of the lighter color of their skin or their prosperity, might pass as whites. The term "freemen," *libres,* included mestizos, blacks, and mulattos who were not slaves. By 1781 the process of miscegenation had so far advanced in the area of Socorro and San Gil that ethnic distinctions had become considerably blurred, although not totally eliminated.

The most reliable demographic information we have are censuses taken in 1779 and 1781. For the eight parishes of the town of Socorro, the figures are:

Whites	17,738	52.6%
Freemen	14,944	44.3
Indians	537	1.6
Slaves	491	1.5
Total	33,710	100.0

Between 1779 and 1781 the population increased by 2,139 persons, to a total of 35,849—an increase of 6.4 percent. The population of the town of San Gil was smaller than that of Socorro and the ethnic composition varied somewhat:

Whites	4,511	26.8%
Freemen	10,699	63.5
Indians	1,141	6.8
Slaves	489	2.9
Total	16,840	100.0

At the time of the conquest the Indian population of San Gil and Socorro was not so dense as in the southern part of the province of Tunja and the sabana of Bogotá, but it was not inconsequential. By the 1750's, however, it was very small indeed—the effect of epidemic disease and miscegenation. Although it was contrary to royal legislation, Indians and whites lived together in the same communities.

By the 1750's, the scant native population was mostly confined to the Indian village of Guane. Several Indian pueblos such as Chanchón, Oiba, and Charalá had disappeared or been abolished, and their community lands, the resguardos, sold by the royal treasury to enterprising white and mestizo farmers.[13] In 1754 the Indian pueblos of Guane, Curiti, Oiba, and Charalá had a total population of some 224 people.[14]

Spanish immigrants played a leading role in colonizing the fertile valleys on the eastern slope of the Suárez River. The population was predominantly white with a significant mestizo component and a very much smaller proportion of blacks and mulattos. In southern Tunja province, center of the preconquest Chibcha civilization, large Indian communities still survived, although their population had drastically declined since the conquest. Socorro had solved its "Indian problem" by miscegenation.

Blacks and mulattos represented only a small minority of the population in the area of Socorro and San Gil. In 1778 they constituted a mere 2.23 percent of the population of the province of Tunja.[15] The slave population of Socorro amounted to only 491 persons, and the overwhelming majority were women, creole and not African-born. Many were mulattos.

The fact that most slaves were women indicates that their role was domestic service. Male slaves, in any case, were not an important source of labor for agriculture. Salvador Plata, the richest man in Socorro, owned some eighteen slaves at the time of his death in 1802, and they were specifically identified as domestics.[16] Juan Francisco Berbeo left an estate consisting mostly of debts. His only substantial capital consisted of some five slaves. During the 1770's and 1780's he sold four slaves, purchased one, and freed two.[17]

These figures give us some clues to the economic role of slavery. It gave the well-to-do a form of capital investment. Ownership of a few slaves provided collateral with which to borrow money to purchase urban or rural real estate or to provide dowries for daughters. Berbeo's slave holdings enabled him to secure loans from convents in order to purchase a farm and a large house on the main square of Socorro. The dowry of doña Elena de Villar in 1774, for example, amounted to 1,242 pesos, 985 pesos of which represented the value of six slave women.[18]

There was a small but steady commerce in slaves—not more than twenty sales in any one year—and prices varied. A healthy slave woman in her early twenties would bring between 125 and 200 pesos.[19] There was also a trickle of manumissions—only two were recorded between 1781 and 1783.[20] Those who received their liberty were invariably favorite household servants.[21] Liberty, however, did not often represent a genuine change of social status, for manumissions were often conditional upon continued service for the ex-master or his family.[22]

Occasional manumissions by a benevolent master or mistress should not obscure the fact that in Socorro as elsewhere, relations between masters and slaves could be tense, if not violent. One slaveowner in Socorro reported to the viceroy in 1775 that slaves often became fugitives and that cases of slaves murdering their masters or other members of the families that owned them were not infrequent. Tension between master and slaves in all regions of the land significantly escalated during the second half of the eighteenth century.[23]

Socorro was a new settlement which in the course of a mere three generations had become one of the most prosperous regions in New Granada. Pedro Fermín de Vargas, a creole who was much influenced by the Physiocrat school in France, ascribed the prosperity of the whole region north of Vélez to Girón to the absence of latifundia.[24] A sampling of the land sales in the notarial archive confirms his observation. There were many sales of small plots that fetched prices as low as 20, 40, and 60 pesos.[25] Although upper-class creoles owned larger farms that could be sold for anything between 2,500 and 3,500 pesos, minifundia, not latifundia, was the prevalent form of land tenure.

Both the creole upper groups and the mestizo and mulatto plebeians were pioneers, tough, hardworking folk who created farms and towns from a wilderness. While regional or, for that matter, national characterology should be used with discretion, no one gave a more graphic, if earthy portrait of these early sons of Santander than Basilio Vicente de Oviedo, who during the 1740's and 1750's served as parish priest in San Gil and Charalá. That creole priest's observations were somewhat embittered by his tenacious but unsuccessful attempts to prevent his parish of San Gil from being reduced in size and in revenue by the creation of new parishes in Barichara and Cepita. He thus described the character of the people of the parish of Oiba: "In general they are uncouth, uncivilized, haughty, restless, and quarrelsome, just as the people from Charalá are, much given to fighting with machetes and sticks. They kill each other like savages, for they are bestial." No less acid was his description of the people from Charalá: "These rustic people are poor but restless, insolent, wild, coarse, and uncouth."[26] While we should make generous allowances for Father Oviedo's exaggerations, it is clear that these early sons of Santander were strong-willed, proud, and quarrelsome, fit colonizers for a new frontier.

Although the eighteenth century in general saw continuous colonization, modestly increasing prosperity, and a sharply rising population curve, there began in 1776, a year so decisive in the history of both English and Spanish America, an agonizing crisis whose impact was still being felt in 1781. A savage epidemic of smallpox followed by several bad harvests took a heavy toll in lives and undercut Socorro's prosperity. The local authorities claimed that the death toll approached 6,000 out of a total population of 33,710. Even making some allowances for exaggeration, the crisis was acute. The majority of the victims were from the lower classes, many of them infants.

The parochial archives are full of references to dead infants being left at the door of the parish church in order to secure a free burial. Although there is no hard evidence that there was mass starvation, poor harvests made food both scarce and more expensive. While the poor suffered most directly, the modest prosperity of the upper classes was badly shaken by the economic depression that swept through the community in the wake of the natural disasters.[27]

Hence it is no accident that the Comunero Revolution erupted in Socorro in March of 1781. A community of frontiersmen, whose toil had accustomed them to modest prosperity, had not fully recovered from an agonizing demographic and economic crisis when the energetic regent visitor general began issuing a barrage of fiscal changes which affected rich and poor alike.

In August, 1778, came the stringent reorganization by Gutiérrez de Piñeres of the tobacco monopoly reformed by Viceroy Flores only two years before. Hard on the prohibition on cultivation of tobacco in most parishes and hamlets in the jurisdiction of both San Gil and Socorro came increases in the price of tobacco and aguardiente, in May of 1780. On August 26, Gutiérrez de Piñeres promulgated the guías and tornaguías for merchants. On October 12, he announced his reorganization of the sales taxes. On November 4, in far-off Peru, Túpac Amaru II raised his standard in a rebellion that would influence the course of events in New Granada. On January 19, 1781, the corregidor of Tunja promulgated in his province the newly separated alcabala and armada de Barlovento taxes. On March 15, 1781, the alcalde ordinario of Socorro, José Ignacio Angulo y Olarte, published the new sales taxes.

The next day, March 16, the populace rioted. *Tumultos* occurred in the nearby parishes of Simacota on March 17, San Gil on March 24, Pinchote on March 25. A second and larger riot occurred in Socorro on March 30, quickly followed by similar outbreaks in Simacota on March 31, in Confines, Barichara, valle de San José, and Chima on April 1. Other popular uprisings broke out in Oiba on April 2, in San José de la Robada on April 3, in Simacota on April 6, in Guadalupe on April 8, in Charalá on April 16, and in Santa Ana on April 16. On April 16, Easter Monday, the third major riot occurred in Socorro. The next day the alcalde ordinario, Angulo y Olarte, fled. On April 18 the creole elite joined the movement by accepting the leadership posts. The revolution of the Comuneros began on March 16, but during its first month it was largely a protest of the lower classes.[28]

I shall focus attention on the dynamics of these popular outbursts of indignation before examining how the local elites responded. In Socorro there were three major riots in quick succession—March 16, March 30, and April 16. The number of participants on March 16 was about 2,000 people, on March 30 about 4,000; it climbed to 6,000 on April 16. Two riots occurred on the weekly market day, Friday, when Socorro had many visitors from neighboring parishes that belonged to both the political and economic orbit of the capital city. On Easter Monday, April 16, there were also many visitors in Socorro.

On March 16 the focus of the crowd's fury was the armada de Barlovento sales tax, which the populace erroneously believed was a new tax. During the second riot of March 30 the target of popular rage was the tobacco monopoly. The people were venting their anger both at the increase in price charged to consumers, and the prohibition on cultivating the crop which for many small farmers had recently become the only cash crop. On April 30 the crowd was demonstrating against the sales taxes and the tobacco monopoly as well as the aguardiente monopoly and the guías and tornaguías. Not only was tobacco burned but aguardiente from the royal monopoly was symbolically spilled into the square.[29] On April 16 more fuel was added to the conflagration in the form of a poem that was read to the rioters. Written in a vulgar and rustic language with which the plebeians could identify, this poem gave them an explosive, if primitive, ideology to articulate their grievances.

If these three riots were the expressions of popular anger, they were also expressions of the fury of the women. On March 16 it was a woman of the people, Manuela Beltrán, born in 1724, who tore down the armada de Barlovento ordinance.[30] The crowds lustily cheered her bold defiance of royal authority. Manuela Beltrán disappeared from history the day she entered it, but she became in the twentieth century a folk heroine of Colombian nationalism. All accounts of the riots agree that women were numerous, vocal, and angry participants. Some hostile accounts even suggest that men disguised themselves as women in order to escape recognition.

The only paramilitary force existing in Socorro was a handful of the hated monopoly police. The crowd's anger evidently frightened those few policemen, who appear to have taken no action. Yet the riots might have been brought under control, if the patricians had organized an informal militia. In general, the local elites remained barricaded in their homes, opting for a course of friendly neutrality toward the rioting crowds.

Responsibility for maintaining royal authority and quelling the disturbances rested with the two ranking magistrates of the town of Socorro, the senior alcalde ordinario, José Ignacio Angulo y Olarte, and the lieutenant of the corregidor of Tunja, Clemente Estévez. That they attempted to calm the crowds is amply documented, but the anger of the populace was too intense to be dissipated by words. The alcalde ordinario could find only half a dozen solid citizens who were willing to go into the main square to talk with the rioters.

Slightly but not very much more efficacious as an instrument of riot control were the clergy. Although several clergymen did go out into the streets dressed in their sacerdotal robes and clutching the exposed Host in their trembling hands, the crowds paid little attention to their pleas. The priests themselves were never physically harmed, for the populace had an almost superstitious reverence for the men of the cloth. To lay a hand on a priest with the exposed Eucharist in his hands was considered a sacrilege that few would dare to contemplate, let alone to execute. The strategy of the crowd was to encourage the priest to retire into the interior of the church, so that they might continue to riot in the square outside. Joaquín de Arrojo, the assistant pastor, was to the fore in organizing clerical support for the royal cause. For his contribution he subsequently received the proprietary appointment as pastor of Socorro.[31]

The audiencia in Bogotá, under the undisputed domination of the regent visitor general, reacted to the news of the first riot with instructions as contradictory as they were unenforceable. While the alcalde was urged to take no action that might provoke a fresh outbreak, he was also ordered to take a step that would, in effect, guarantee continued disorder. Angulo y Olarte was quietly to arrest the ringleaders and to dispatch them forthwith under armed guard to the capital. Bogotá further urged the beleaguered alcalde to conduct a public relations campaign to convince the populace that the armada de Barlovento tax was not a new tax but an old tax that had become confused with the alcabala. The people must be told firmly but kindly, Bogotá admonished, that all the taxes would be collected and that anyone caught destroying government edicts would be punished with "the exemplary severity that such crime merits."[32]

In distant Bogotá, Gutiérrez de Piñeres, true to his conviction that the elites would never join the common people, sought to minimize the importance of the disturbances in Socorro. Those events were portrayed to public opinion in the capital as something involving "four destitute, miserable, and vile foragers from the outskirts of Socorro who while attending the Friday fair shouted and made ridiculous demonstrations in a state of inebriation."[33]

On April 2 Bogotá made a concession that it hoped would mitigate popular unrest. The regent visitor general ordered that the collection of the armada de Barlovento tax on cotton thread be suspended.[34] Socorro, it will be remembered, was then an apparently thriving textile center in which cotton goods were manufactured in the homes of the lower classes. Cotton thread, in fact, was a kind of informal currency among the plebeians.

Whatever benefit the authorities in Bogotá hoped to derive from this was nullified on April 6, when the audiencia published the edict requesting a forced loan of two pesos for nobles and one peso for commoners. In the popular state of agitation the rumor circulated that this new appeal was to be an annual tax, rather than a once-only emergency tax.[35]

The regent visitor general subsequently denounced the cabildo for not promulgating his cotton thread concession. He cited their "culpable inaction" as evidence that the cabildo and the crowd were secret allies in fomenting the riots.[36] That the elites ultimately joined the others on April 17 is indeed a fact. But that precarious alliance was not forged during the early weeks. On April 3, the cabildo was still desperately trying to control the tide of popular wrath. They knew that the April 2 measure was too little and too late unless it was backed up by the arrival of military reinforcements from Tunja. But the corregidor of the province had evidently refused to appear in riot-torn Socorro until he, in turn, received military reinforcements from Bogotá.

After the March 30 riot, an increasingly discouraged alcalde begged Bogotá to send some two hundred troops to restore order.[37] But the cabildo was divided in its recommendation. On the day after Angulo appealed for soldiers, two aldermen wrote Bogotá asking only for munitions and not for troops.[38]

During the first week of April the policy of the audiencia drastically shifted from employing conciliation to a policy of force and coercion. On April 3, Gutiérrez de Piñeres ordered the corregidor of the province of Tunja, José María Campuzano y Lanz, to go to Socorro and place himself in charge of all those who remained loyal to the government.[39] The regent visitor general sharply rebuked the corregidor, who was the ranking royal magistrate in the province, for not going to Socorro immediately he had received news of the first riot.[40] The corregidor was then in Chiquinquirá, some eight days' travel south of Socorro. He steadfastly refused to take any other action save to dispatch orders to the various rebellious jurisdictions instructing them to obey the mandates of the audiencia. The corregidor partially justified his inaction on the ground that he was suffering from a severe attack of the gout.[41] He remained in the southern part of the province, in and around the capital city of Tunja, his habitual residence, where he was influential with the local elites. Notwithstanding his gout, Campuzano energetically organized a local militia which by late May consisted of some 6,000 troops, 4,000 of whom were cavalry.

Events in both Bogotá and Socorro were moving swiftly toward a confrontation. On April 9 the regent visitor general decided to abandon conciliation in favor of a demonstration of force and coercion. The audiencia instructed Oidor José de Osorio to lead a small military expedition to Socorro "in order to maintain respect for royal authority, to calm the spirits, to punish the guilty and to reestablish the royal revenues and public order."[42]

On April 16, Easter Monday, the third and most tumultuous riot erupted in Socorro; on the following day, the alcalde ordinario fled. All pretense of enforcing the mandates of Bogotá collapsed with his flight. On the next day, April 18, the elites of Socorro, led by Juan Francisco Berbeo, joined the movement, when in the main square the crowds enthusiastically proclaimed them *capitanes* of the "enterprise."

Both the success and the failure of the Comunero movement lay in the alliance of the elites and the nonelites. The story of that precarious coalition will be a central concern throughout this book. The Comunero victory in forcing the audiencia to accept the capitulations of Zipaquirá on June 7 may be ascribed in part, at least, to the existence of this alliance. The success that Archbishop Caballero y Góngora enjoyed in restoring royal authority was due, in some significant measure, to his political dexterity in dismantling the same coalition. Careful attention needs to be focused on patricians and plebeians in Socorro, where this alliance was initially forged.

4

Patricians and Plebeians in Socorro

Socorro was a new community that steadily grew in the course of the eighteenth century from a tiny hamlet into one of the most prosperous agricultural and manufacturing communities in the New Kingdom. An examination of the social structure of Socorro and of leadership patterns among the plebeians illuminates that alliance between patricians and plebeians around which the Comunero movement developed.

The leaders of the town in 1781 were, of course, creoles, in most cases the sons and grandsons of immigrants from Spain. A good deal of the material dealing with the nobles comes from the notarial archives in Socorro. That portion of the archive that survives is rich in references to wills, dowries, sales of land, and sales and manumissions of slaves but, like the records of commercial transactions, the acts of the town council have disappeared.

The richest citizen of Socorro in 1781 was Salvador Plata, but the town's most celebrated son is Juan Francisco Berbeo, who suddenly emerged in 1781 as the titular and real *caudillo* of that coalition. Berbeo was born in Socorro shortly before June 17, 1729, the date of his baptism.[1] He died there on June 28, 1795. Hence, he was a mature fifty-two during the climactic year of his long life.

The founder of the family's solid, but modest, prosperity was Juan Francisco's grandfather, don Domingo Antonio Berbeo, who was born in Oviedo, Spain.[2] He was rich enough to endow from his large farm located in Las Monas a chantry or chaplaincy, *capellania,* worth some 2,000 pesos. The two immediate beneficiaries were two sons, one a priest and the other the benefice's lay patron.[3] Juan Francisco Berbeo ultimately became the patron of the chantry that his grandfather created.[4] If Domingo Antonio Berbeo had

50

sufficient wealth to found a chantry for one of his sons, it may be assumed that his other children received similar legacies. How much is not known.

Juan Francisco's father, don Justino Berbeo, purchased the prestigious and solidly lucrative bureaucratic post of clerk, *escribano,* of the parish of Socorro. Juan Francisco in 1785 sold a farm inherited from his father for 800 pesos, but how much more he inherited it is not possible to determine.[5] Though born in Oviedo, Spain, don Justino spent most of his adult life in Socorro, where he married the well-born doña Juana María Moreno.

Juan Francisco Berbeo and his brothers belonged to Socorro's elite but none of them was wealthy. One brother, Juan Manuel Berbeo, bought a seat as an alderman of the town council, but although his wife came from the wealthy Maldonado de la Zerda family, the childless alderman left virtually no capital.[6] The extent of the estate of another brother of Juan Francisco, Albino Berbeo, is not known, but he was sufficiently prominent to hold the bureaucratic post of *alcalde de la santa hermandad,* a kind of rural police force.[7] Another brother was a priest.

Juan Francisco Berbeo was married not once, as has been commonly assumed, but twice. His first wife was doña María Blasina Montenegro, who bore him two sons and three daughters. Berbeo was her second husband; she had four children by her first husband, whose surname was Escobar. Each of these children from her first marriage received only twenty-seven pesos from her estate, which suggests that her capital was negligible, but her dowry did include a slave.[8] The expenses of raising a combined family of nine children must have placed a heavy burden on the meager resources of the future leader of the Comunero Revolution.

In 1771 Juan Francisco Berbeo contracted a second marriage, this time to doña Bárbara Rodríguez Terán, a niece of a priest. From this marriage came only one daughter, María Josefa, among whose illustrious descendants are Alberto Lleras Camargo, president of Colombia (1944–46 and 1958–62), and the late Dr. Pablo E. Cárdenas Acosta, the distinguished historian of the Comunero Revolution.[9] From his second marriage Berbeo acquired a solid amount of capital which enabled him to become an active and prominent member of the community. Doña Bárbara brought a dowry of some 3,608 pesos.[10] When Berbeo married her, the total value of his estate was a mere 1,102 pesos, consisting mostly of personal possessions, luxury items such as a few emeralds, some gold, some silver and pearls, silk shirts, and other finery for personal adornment.[11] No urban or rural property was listed in the meticulously detailed inventory. His most important capital asset was 425 pesos, consisting of two black slaves, one of whom he derived from the dowry of his first wife.

In 1781 the fortune of Juan Francisco Berbeo was modest indeed. His estate consisted of a house on the main square, a handful of slaves, two farms—one with a mortgage—and some luxury items, such as jewels, clothing, and furniture.[12] Berbeo's participation in the events of 1781 certainly weakened his financial solvency, but his capital worth was so modest that he can have spent little from his own funds. The Comunero caudillo's fortunes did not prosper between 1781 and his death in 1795. His only daughter by his second marriage, María Josefa, received a very much more modest dowry than her mother, some 649 pesos, mostly in jewels, when she married José Rito de Acosta on May 1, 1793.[13]

In his last will and testament, dated a month before his death, Berbeo asserted that nothing remained of his second wife's substantial dowry. His debts amounted to 3,250 pesos and his assets were something in excess of 4,108 pesos—a meager 858 pesos' net worth. His principal assets were his town house, purchased in 1782 for 2,308 pesos, and five slaves, whose total value was about 1,000 pesos. While it is difficult to estimate their precise monetary value, Berbeo's personal possessions, including a library of between fifteen and twenty books, probably did not exceed 600 pesos. Contrary to the standard view, Berbeo never was a rich man.

Whatever his political skills—and they were considerable—Juan Francisco was scarcely a successful businessman. His long-time rival, Salvador Plata, the Croesus of Socorro, claimed that Berbeo dissipated his wife's dowry in his passion for gambling at cards.[14] This charge may even have been true, for in the Socorro of those times virtually everyone, rich and poor alike, gambled at cards. After all, the three major social activities were attending mass, making love, and playing cards. Berbeo's lack of skill at cards is somewhat beside the point. It is clear that he simply lived above his means. His lifestyle was ostentatious, but he neither inherited sufficient capital, nor knew how to make it for himself.

If Berbeo's wealth did not qualify him for leadership, other considerations did. He had acquired military experience during several campaigns against hostile Indian tribes of the Carares and the Yareguies. Previous military experience was at a premium in 1781. His outlook and background were not provincial. He had traveled far and wide over the New Kingdom, not only in the provinces of Tunja and Sante Fe, but also in the eastern plains of the llanos. He once traveled to Maracaibo, even visiting the Dutch island of Curaçao and the coastal cities of Portobelo and Cartagena. Berbeo apparently did not reside in Socorro during the 1760's, for his name appears on none of the petitions soliciting township status. His brothers, on the other hand, were signatories.

Another asset that Berbeo possessed was that in his frequent visits to Bogotá he had acquired friendships and contacts with influential creole bureaucrats. One of his Bogotá friends was don Francisco de Vergara, regent of the *tribunal de cuentas.*[15] Vergara would play an important role in the negotiations culminating in the capitulations of Zipaquirá.

Berbeo's military experience, his travels, and his Bogotá connections all contributed to his acquiring the reputation of being "a very courageous and resolute man" who inspired confidence among both the patricians and plebeians alike. The only description we have of Berbeo written by a contemporary suggests that if he did not possess real charisma he did have several qualities that made him a natural leader of men:

> a handsome man, not tall, slender, long-visaged, clean-shaven, an elongated nose, lively eyes, chestnut brown hair, about 50 years old, who as he approached his fellow captains, would bow his head slightly and would greet them with a silvery voice. A skillful horseman, he rode a superb and fiery charger, a gift of the captains of Sogamoso.[16]

Salvador Plata y González possessed even more obvious qualifications to lead the coalition than did Juan Francisco Berbeo, though he apparently had no previous military experience.[17] He was Socorro's most opulent capitalist. In contrast to Berbeo, he had held several bureaucratic posts: he was *procurador general* of San Gil–Socorro and, in 1776, of Socorro; in 1776 he was also alcalde ordinario of Socorro and in 1779 judge conservator of the royal rents. Plata played an active role in Socorro's dispute over the boundaries of the two towns.[18] Furthermore, Salvador Plata had ties to the same influential creole circles in Bogotá with whom Berbeo was also in contact. But Plata opted to oppose the movement.

Salvador Plata (1740?–1802) was about forty in 1781, several years younger than Juan Francisco Berbeo.[19] The founder of the Plata clan, which gave the area many illustrious descendants, was Francisco Félix de la Plata Domínguez. Migrating from the Galician city of Lugo to New Granada in 1683, he ultimately settled in the San Gil–Socorro area where in 1688 he married a criolla, doña Josefa Moreno y Meneses. From this prolific union came eleven children. The eldest, born in 1691, was Hipólito José Plata, the father of Salvador; he died in San Gil in 1763.

Salvador Plata was born in the vice-parish of Pinchote, midway between Socorro and San Gil, where the family owned a large farm. His wife was the well-born doña Magdalena Alvarez y Lamo, the niece of Claudio Alvarez y Quiñones, archbishop of Santa Fe de Bogotá (1731–36). Doña Magdalena was evidently no relative of fiscal Manuel Bernardo Alvarez.

Salvador Plata's outstandingly successful career in business received an impetus from inheritances from his father, his mother, and his brother. The amount of his wife's dowry is not known, but as the niece of an archbishop, it may be assumed that she brought her husband a solid, if not munificent, dowry. By his death in 1802 Salvador Plata had expanded his initial inheritances of some 8,062 pesos into a gross estate of some 120,214 pesos. This amount does not include capital distributed to his children during his lifetime, in the form of dowries for his daughters and capital gifts to his sons.

Salvador Plata engaged in all forms of economic activity that were feasible in Socorro. He was a merchant who sold and bought slaves, textiles produced in both Spain and Socorro, cocoa, and cotton. His various houses, furniture, and slaves, of whom he owned eighteen or so, were valued at 29,606 pesos. His landed estates were worth some 40,000 pesos. His single most valuable farm was a hacienda in Chanchón whose value was assessed at 21,355 pesos.[20] The family farm in Pinchote was worth about 5,000 pesos, but he also owned smaller rural properties in Chochos and Bozque. His liquid wealth was even more impressive than his agricultural holdings: he left 25,684 pesos in gold currency and some 11,414 in silver currency. Surely don Salvador Plata y González of Socorro was one of the richest laymen in the whole New Kingdom.[21]

Some historians have accused Salvador Plata of being a traitor to the Comunero cause. This charge is misfocused: Plata opposed the movement from its inception to its end.[22] When he was serving as alcalde ordinario and judge conservator of the royal rents, he vigorously implemented the new regulations of the tobacco monopoly. He was one of the handful of prominent creoles who joined Alcalde Angulo y Olarte in vain attempts to restore order during the riots of March 16, March 30, and April 16.[23]

In view of his wealth and his prominence the populace demanded that Plata serve as one of the four captains general who took office on April 18. But Plata was so uncomfortable in his role as a titular leader of the protest movement that he refused to attend meetings, even pretending to be insane. He was soon replaced as a captain general by José Antonio Estévez.

Not trusting him, the Comunero captains did not allow Plata to go to Zipaquirá. Yet Plata worked closely in Socorro with Berbeo's associates in organizing a local military force to preserve law and order.

Salvador Plata took pains to remain on good terms with Berbeo, as the latter was marching toward Zipaquirá. On May 19, May 22, June 4, June 15, and July 3 Plata wrote letters whose tone was cordial and friendly to Berbeo, whom he always addressed as "my esteemed cousin"; Berbeo's wife, Bárbara, and Salvador Plata were, in fact, cousins. In one letter Plata wrote Berbeo: "I sincerely hope that the virgin of Socorro will lead you in such a way that peace will be restored and an agreement reached." In another, he expressed his preoccupation about maintaining law and order among the plebeians in Socorro. Plata, in fact, once loaned Berbeo 200 pesos as well as helping to secure for him lodgings in Bogotá.[24]

In order to counteract Plata's mountainous testimony, most of which was unfavorable to the Comunero chieftains, Juan Francisco Berbeo surrendered his correspondence with Plata to the authorities. Neither Plata nor Berbeo was being more deceitful than anyone else at this time. Plata opposed the Comunero Revolution, but he was determined not to sever his contacts with his friends and kinsmen who were leading the movement. And the same is true of the Comunero captains, who did not want to cut themselves off from the authorities and their partisans. Both the Comunero leaders and the authorities in the capital were committed to the principle of a negotiated settlement, and avenues of contact had to be kept open.

In spite of the tension and rivalry between Plata and Berbeo, the ties between the two survived the crisis of 1781. On May 1, 1793, when Berbeo's only daughter by Bárbara Terán married José Rito de Acosta, Salvador Plata served as the bride's attorney.[25]

If Juan Francisco Berbeo and Salvador Plata were Socorro's two most prominent citizens in 1781, the titular leaders of the community were the aldermen of the town council, the cabildo. Between March 16 and April 16 they attempted to contain the rising tide of popular discontent. While they pleaded with the plebeians to desist in their rioting in return for a promise to urge Bogotá to modify if not to suspend the new taxes, they desperately appealed for military assistance and advice from Bogotá. But neither reinforcements nor realistic counsel came from the capital. After the patrician captains were elected on April 18, the cabildo, without Alcalde Angulo who by then had fled, continued to work closely with the Comunero leadership. Two aldermen, Manuel Berbeo and Clemente José Estévez, were brothers of Comunero chieftains.[26]

It was Clemente José Estévez, in his role as lieutenant corregidor of Tunja, who publicly swore into office the captains general on April 19 and who administered their secret oath of loyalty to the king. Both the Estévez brothers had close ties with Manuel García Olano, the courier of information. Another Estévez brother was Filiberto José, parish priest in nearby Oiba, who was the most royalist of the three. While maintaining his ties with the Comunero chieftains, he was a diligent correspondent with Oidor Osorio and subsequently with Archbishop Caballero y Góngora, whom he provided with accurate intelligence about the Comunero camp. He was a well-placed intermediary between the Comunero leaders and the archbishop, and played a key role in the behind-the-scenes negotiations that ultimately culminated in the settlement of Zipaquirá. The differences in the attitudes of the three Estévez brothers highlight the choices facing the local elite of Socorro during the crisis of 1781: José Antonio an ardent Comunero, Clemente José with a foot in both camps, and Filiberto an ardent loyalist.

The other Socorranos besides Juan Francisco Berbeo and José Antonio

Estévez who held positions of leadership were Francisco Rosillo, Antonio José Monsalve, Ramón Ramírez, Pedro Alejandro de la Prada, and José Vicente Plata de Acevedo. None of these men held bureaucratic office before 1781, although Plata de Acevedo, like Berbeo and Estévez, had a brother who did—Juan Bernardo Plata de Acevedo served as alcalde of Socorro in 1777.

Municipal office was purchased from the crown, and between 1773 and 1796 the office of alderman fetched between 100 and 200 pesos. Income-producing offices such as that of town constable sold for as much as 600 *patacones*.[27] Hence municipal authorities were people of some prominence if not modest wealth.

Francisco Rosillo (1750–84) was born in Socorro of a peninsular-born father, Francisco José Rosillo, with whom he has sometimes been confused.[28] The father, who died before 1781, served as lieutenant corregidor of San Gil between 1760 and 1762. He was a merchant who traded in indigo, tobacco, textiles, and sugar. Apparently he was the victim of the economic depression that hit Socorro after 1776; at his death his estate consisted mostly of debts.[29] Hence, Francisco Rosillo inherited from his father not wealth, but a position of social respectability.

The notarial archives of Socorro contain only a few references to don Francisco's business activities. It is not implausible to suppose that when he married María Santos del Corral on April 27, 1778, she brought him a respectable dowry. He was sufficiently prosperous in 1780 to purchase a female slave for 160 pesos.[30] Yet the paucity of evidence in the notarial archives about his business activities suggests that he may have been socially prominent but not a rich man. Rosillo initially opposed the protest. He was one of the few *hombres buenos,* as they were called, who rallied to the standard of Alcalde Angulo y Olarte in his vain attempts to calm the populace during the riots of March and April.[31]

The notarial records provide only a few sparse facts about the activities of Antonio José Monsalve, another prominent chieftain from Socorro. He was born in 1745. He was sufficiently well-to-do to think it desirable, as early as 1779, to appoint a lawyer to defend his interests before the audiencia in Bogotá. He purchased a slave for 200 pesos in 1780, and in 1787 he sold a small farm. In 1782 he owed 400 pesos for a chantry that he created. And in 1790 he contracted a debt of 884 pesos.[32] These scattered facts suggest that although he may not have been rich, he was, nevertheless, modestly well-to-do. An irony of his career is that the same Comunero chieftain turns up in 1798 as the administrator of the alcabala in Socorro, the sales tax that was the target of popular fury in 1781.[33]

More is known about Monsalve's family connections than his business enterprises. One of his brothers lived in Bogotá, where he practiced law before the audiencia. A sister was married to Juan Dionisio Plata, a first cousin of Salvador Plata. Antonio Monsalve's mother was Margarita de Ardila, an aunt of Mateo Ardila.[34] The latter, who was the notarial clerk of the town council of Socorro in 1781, was a crucial link between the patricians and the plebeians of Socorro.

The most famous exploit of Ramón Ramírez (1754–88), another captain general, was that he led the expedition that conquered Girón, an event which will be chronicled in chapter 12. A native of Socorro, Ramírez held from 1779 on a concession basis the retail outlet of the aguardiente monopoly in Girón. In granting such contracts wealthy citizens were usually given preference. He evidently was a person of modest wealth, but his will, dated August 14, 1786, gave no detailed inventory of his goods. His son and namesake, who served as alcalde ordinario in 1791, was given blanket authority to arrange for his father's funeral and to dispose of his property.[35]

One of the wealthier leaders of the Comuneros, perhaps the richest if we exclude Salvador Plata, was Pedro Alejandro de la Prada. In his 1788 will the inventory of his estate includes two sugar estates, one cattle ranch, a large town house on the main square, and such luxury items as six forks, two mugs, and a pitcher all of silver. But he also left some debts and obligations. His second marriage to Juana Luisa Gómez was childless. Before his death he had created a chantry along with his in-laws, in which his share of the contribution amounted to 1,600 pesos. Indicative of his political prominence is the fact that he served as alcalde in 1785, an office which his son held five years later.[36]

There were in 1781 two intersecting circles of leadership among the patricians—the town council and the Comunero captains. No member of the cabildo held a formal position of leadership in the Comunero high command, but there are clear links between the two circles. Two Comunero leaders had brothers who belonged to the town council, and the brother of another was a former alcalde.

After the flight of Alcalde Angulo on April 17, these two leadership cadres worked together harmoniously, on occasion sending out parallel sets of letters to the authorities. The tone of the cabildo correspondence was apt to be a trifle more conciliatory than that of the Comunero chieftains. Yet both sets of letters shared a common thrust: i.e., an affirmation of loyalty to the crown coupled with a plea that the king's ministers must realize the urgency of discarding the fiscal program identified with Gutiérrez de Piñeres.[37]

The relationship between these two circles became even more apparent after the suppression of the Comuneros. The captains general underwent a rather intensive investigation in order to enable the authorities to determine where blame should be placed. The aldermen were often summoned as witnesses. They invariably testified that the captains were loyal to the crown, that they accepted office under duress in order to protect their lives and to moderate the anger of the uncontrollable crowd.[38] After the suppression of the Comunero movement the cabildo gave the captains a substantial amount of protection.

Of the ten patrician leaders among the Comunero high command, the notarial archives in Socorro provide solid information on seven. We know, for example, the ages of six. Berbeo was the oldest at fifty-two. Francisco Rosillo was the youngest at thirty-one, and Ramón Ramírez was thirty-four. The town clerk, Mateo Ardila y Oviedo, was forty-one. Plata was about forty and Monsalve thirty-six. None was a callow and inexperienced youth; all were mature individuals.

The age structure among the plebeian leaders whose dates are known follows the same pattern. Manuela Beltrán, who tore down the royal cedula, was fifty-seven, Isidro Molina was thirty-two, Manuel Ortíz, thirty-eight, and José Antonio Galán, thirty-two.[39] The average life span in those times probably did not extend much beyond forty. Thus, the lives of the older figures such as Berbeo, Plata, and Manuela Beltrán and their parents spanned the whole eighteenth century from the founding of Socorro as a parish in 1689 until the eve of the independence movement in 1808. The younger leaders were the third-generation descendants of the original settlers.

The size of their fortunes varied considerably. Salvador Plata was fabulously rich. Pedro Alejandro de la Prada was solidly wealthy. Monsalve and Ramírez were modestly well-to-do. And the Berbeo brothers and Rosillo were relatively poor. Wealth was clearly not an indispensable condition for enjoying social prestige and exercising political power.

Although some amount of property was necessary for being considered patrician, it did not have to be very much. The ownership of a slave or two, some rural property, even though small, a few luxury objects such as silk shirts, jewels, or table silverware were sufficient. No distinction, evidently, was made between land ownership and commerce, and members of the elite often engaged in commerce without any loss of social prestige.

A reasonable speculation is that the vast majority of nobles were worth between 1,000 and 10,000 pesos. San Gil's haughty claim that there existed in the parish of Socorro only eight persons whose net worth amounted to 10,000 or 12,000 pesos must, on the evidence of tithes, be dismissed as prejudiced and self-serving. And equally suspect is San Gil's assertion that only fifty persons in Socorro could don a cape on Sunday to attend mass, or owned land or cattle, enabling them to keep up decorous appearances.[40] But how many more there were is difficult to determine.

Plebeians seldom left wills; patricians almost always did. Although Juan Manuel Berbeo left virtually no property, he apparently felt that his social status required that he make a will. Patricians also provided their daughters with dowries, often in the form of a few slaves, jewels, and luxury household items. Nobles can also be identified as those who created chantries.

Marriage with social peers was another means of buttressing upper-class rank. Juan Francisco Berbeo's second marriage brought him the kind of solid dowry that allowed him to maintain the social appearances of the patrician status into which he was born. Salvador Plata's marriage to a niece of an archbishop of Bogotá brought him social prestige and presumably a respectable dowry. Juan Maldonado de la Zerda, born in Bogotá, married the well-born Francisca Javier Domínguez of Socorro, related to the Plata clan. That marriage strengthened his social position and his financial resources in the community where he settled and died the richest citizen of his generation (see chapter 3).

A net worth of 10,000 pesos, then, represented a solid but only a modest fortune. How many truly rich—worth substantially more than 10,000 pesos—there were, is also difficult to estimate. Certainly Juan Maldonado de la Zerda, who died around 1776, and Salvador Plata qualify for that status. Pedro Alejandro de la Prada probably belonged to this category also. But there are no other visible candidates for the honor.

The inevitable question of the real value of a peso at this time is difficult if not downright impossible to answer precisely. The Mexican silver peso was divided into eight reales; so also was the more commonly used gold peso in New Granada.[41] It would be impossible to translate the real purchasing power of that peso into present-day currency except to stress that the former was countless times more valuable than the latter.

What may elucidate matters somewhat is to compare the values of both capital and income in the context of those times. Alexander von Humboldt observed that in Lima no family possessed more than 130,000 pesos in capital and in Caracas the amount seldom exceeded 200,000 pesos. Only in Mexico were there some fortunes that were in excess of 1,000,000 pesos.[42] The Mexicans were the first millionaires in Hispanic America. Hence a modest fortune in Socorro might reasonably be classified as 10,000 pesos in capital, a large fortune, 20,000 pesos and up.

Looking at the matter from another perspective, let us observe the cost of acquiring capital assets. In Socorro a medium-sized farm cost between 800 and 1,200 pesos. A modest house on the prestigious main square fetched 800 pesos, and a more commodious dwelling located on a corner was worth about 2,300 pesos.[43] A young slave in good health fetched between 125 and 200 pesos.

The same comparative approach may be used in order to determine roughly what was a modest and what was a substantial income. The richest man in New Granada, the marquis of San Jorge, did not receive more than 18,000 pesos from his fabled entailed estate, the *mayorazgo de la dehesa de*

Bogotá.[44] That collection of rural properties comprised approximately one-fourth of the arable land of the sabana of Bogotá, some 60,000 to 70,000 hectares. It is exceedingly unlikely that any other large landowner derived more than 5,000 pesos annually from his latifundia.[45]

A comparative look at the salaries of bureaucrats and ecclesiastics is also revealing. Both the archbishop of Bogotá and the viceroy collected 40,000 pesos apiece. This income was astronomical by the standards of those times, but so were their expenses and their obligations. More to the point is that the salary of a judge of the audiencia was 2,941 pesos. The corregidor of Tunja received 2,812 pesos and the governor of Girón 1,375 pesos. In the fiscal bureaucracy the *contadores del tribunal de cuentas* received 2,068 pesos and middle-rank magistrates between 1,000 and 1,500 pesos.[46]

The 5,000 pesos that the pastor of Socorro earned is somewhat misleading. Socorro was then one of the richest ecclesiastical livings in the whole kingdom, for that pastor's annual rent exceeded that of the bishop of Santa Marta.[47] It will be recalled that the minimum stipend for a priest varied between 150 and 200 pesos (see chapter 3). Established and prosperous parishes in the Socorro area, such as San Gil, yielded their holder 2,000 pesos; the pastors of Simacota, Oiba, Girón, and Barichara collected 1,500 pesos annual rent.[48]

Hence an annual income of 1,000 pesos or less was scanty indeed. A salary between 1,000 and 2,000 pesos was solidly modest and anything over 2,000 pesos was substantial.

What is clear is that the nobles were only a very small minority among a very large plebeian population, of whom craftsmen constituted a kind of upper crust. Ordinary plebeians were the men and women whose dress style was the ruana; they wore sandals, or they went shoeless. The men might work for someone; many cultivated their own very small plots of land. The women often spun cotton in their homes in order to supplement the family's meager income.

Perhaps the single most important determinant of patrician status was ethnic origin. Pure Spanish ancestry was an indispensable certificate of admission to the upper echelon of society. But Spanish ancestry in itself was not sufficient. The majority of the inhabitants of Socorro in 1781 were second- and third-generation descendants of Spanish immigrants. Manuela Beltrán was no patrician, although her background was Spanish. Nor was José Antonio Galán, whose father was born in the peninsula. His mother, however, was a mestiza or a mulatta. The occupation of José Antonio's father ruled him out. He owned a tiny plot of land on which he cultivated tobacco, and his mother and sisters spun cotton cloth in their homes. Both of these activities were considered plebeian occupations, and occupation was also a determinant of social status. The town butchers, for example, may have possessed more capital and income than some nobles, but their trade condemned them to plebeian status.

Administrative posts such as alcalde, alderman, notary, were the exclusive domain of the patricians. Residence was another indication. The nobles lived on, or very near, the main square where the principal parish church and government offices were located. And the nobles' lifestyle was certainly an indication of their class. Wearing a cape at mass, in contrast to the ruana, owning a domestic slave or two, some luxury household objects, a few jewels and books, were other not insignificant marks of patrician status.

It is not easy to pinpoint the importance of education. Socorro, of course, possessed no institution of higher learning, not even a convent or a monastery. Perhaps the only truly well-educated persons in the community were the clergy, all of whom received their training in Bogotá. The proprietary pastor qualified for noble status also by an economic criterion, his income being the largest in the parish. Furthermore, there were no identifiable lawyers in Socorro. While it may be assumed that all patricians could write their own names, that was also a boast which many plebeians could make. Some of the bureaucrats such as notaries and alcaldes had to be reasonably literate in order to perform their duties. But there were not many books in Socorro, and only a handful of people received a formal education that went beyond the primary level. It may be assumed that some nobles were functional illiterates.

Patrician status was evidently determined by a complex and wide variety of factors, and any ranking of them is bound to be somewhat arbitrary. Spanish ancestry was evidently paramount; wealth was desirable but not indispensable. A little capital went a long way, provided that other conditions were met. Office-holding, education, lifestyle, and place of residence virtually guaranteed admission into the upper reaches of society.

What should not be forgotten is that Socorro in 1781 was a new community created by the hard toil of three generations. Social strata were still somewhat fluid. While there was an identifiable elite, its members were, in fact, the products of upward social mobility. And some families had both patrician and plebeian members.

In Socorro there was no custom of entailing estates. Primogeniture is often the hallmark of a truly patrician class. Even in older and more aristocratic Popayán this device was not employed in the seventeenth century.[49] Only in Bogotá were there a few entailed estates, such as that of the marquis of San Jorge. The relatively new society of Socorro sharply contrasts in these respects with the older societies of Mexico and Peru, where many entailed estates institutionalized and perpetuated the large fortunes of patrician families.

Given these conditions, some might question the appropriateness of calling the upper ranks in Socorro "nobles" or "patricians." Certainly they were not "noble" in the sense they held hereditary titles of nobility granted by the king. There were literally only a handful of such peerages in New Granada at this time, while in Mexico in 1775 there were some forty-seven titles of nobility.[50] While members of the upper class in Socorro may not have been hereditary peers, the point is that they perceived themselves as nobles, if untitled, and they were so regarded by their social inferiors. Nobility to some extent was a state of mind that pervaded the social values of all groups. They were nobles by a definition once formulated by the council of the Indies: "It is undeniable that in those kingdoms [in America], any Spaniard who comes to them, who acquires some wealth and who is not engaged in a dishonorable profession is regarded as a noble."[51] Alexander von Humboldt put it somewhat more crassly, when he observed: "Any white person, although he rides his horse barefoot, imagines himself to be of the nobility of the country." [52] A reflection of the accepted meaning of this term is that when Charles III imposed a forced loan on his loyal subjects in New Granada the figure was set at two pesos from the nobles and one peso from the plebeians.[53]

It is remarkable how the Spaniards were able to transfer to a new community such as Socorro, in the course of three generations, the basic aristocratic values of their society.

Children or sons-in-law of the Comunero captains Berbeo, Rosillo, Prada, and Ramírez held important administrative positions in the town of Socorro during the 1780's and 1790's. Two of the seven chieftains whose biographies have been recounted provided leaders a generation later during the war of independence—Antonio José Monsalve and Francisco Rosillo. This fact should not, of course, obscure the fact that the crises of 1781 and 1810 were sharply different. Nor should the virtues, or for that matter the vices, of the children be ascribed to their fathers. 1781 was not an incipient move toward independence. The incontrovertible point is, however, that the Rosillos and the Monsalves in both 1781 and 1810 belonged to the local elites and that members of both families played dramatic roles in the crisis that confronted each generation.

In addition to the cabildo and the Comunero captains, there was a third concentric pattern of leadership, centering on Mateo Ardila y Oviedo, the town clerk. Salvador Plata gave one plausible explanation for the power and prestige that Mateo Ardila exercised in Socorro, when he sarcastically posed and answered the following question:

> And what is the origin of the profound respect that everyone gives the clerk? It is that he is the only one with even a smattering of learning in that town. Because of his ability to write for others he can influence the outcome of the countless lawsuits that arise. There is even one alderman, a virtual illiterate, who depends on

him to write all his letters. He determines all the sentences of justice.[54]

Discounting Plata's animosity toward Mateo Ardila, to whom he was related by marriage, the fact is that the town clerk was a powerful and prestigious figure in a community, the overwhelming majority of whose population were illiterate. For that matter the literacy of many patricians was more nominal than real. The clerk controlled access to whole machinery of government for rich and poor alike. The father of Juan Francisco Berbeo, whose patrician status was beyond question, served as clerk of Socorro when that locality was only a parish. In such a community the two most powerful personalities were the priest and town clerk.

Not only was Mateo Ardila an entrenched member of the patrician elite by virtue of the office he held, but he was also the crucial link between the patricians and the plebeians. Many of his close relatives were the most active leaders of the plebeian riots. Some four blocks from the main square, where the main church and the homes of the patricians were located, was another parish church situated on the plaza of Chiquinquirá. This was the parish of the plebeians. It was here that the riots began, with rioters subsequently marching to the main square.

The rioters were not a faceless crowd; certain individuals exercised leadership and influence. Among them were Antonio Molina and his son Isidro, Roque Cristancho, José Ignacio Ardila y Oviedo and his son Ignacio Ardila y Olarte, Pablo Ardila, Miguel de Uribe, and Pedro Campos. All of them were closely related by blood and marriage to the town clerk. Juan Manuel Ortíz, another leader, was the official doorman (*portero*) of the town of Socorro, and the clerk's handyman. Ignacio Ardila y Oviedo was the clerk's brother. Pablo Ardila was a first cousin.

If the power and influence of Mateo Ardila rested on his office, the influence that his relatives exercised over the plebeians rested on their being the town's only butchers. Salvador Plata's upper-class prejudice should not obscure the essential veracity of his observation:

> If the vile trade of butcher in which they have been engaged all their lives makes them despicable in our eyes, this very activity is what has given them a kind of domination over the poverty-stricken plebeians who because of the frequent shortages of meat feel themselves forced to adulate and please the butchers.[55]

Alcalde Angulo y Olarte adds some further information about the sway that this plebeian dynasty of butchers exercised over the lower classes:

> Ignacio Ardila, his brothers, Roque Cristancho and Miguel de Uribe are the butchers of Socorro. Since that town does not have a slaughter house nor adjacent pasture grounds, they buy all the

cattle that comes here and retail it to the populace. When cattle is not brought to market, those butchers go out of Socorro and purchase some. Since there are periodic shortages of meat and they monopolize its retail sale, all the plebeians not only in Socorro but also in nearby Simacota whose retail trade they also control feel themselves so subordinated to the butchers that the people call them the magnates of the plazuela.[56]

The career of Mateo Ardila indicates that some social mobility existed in Socorro. Part of the family were patricians; and some of them, the butchers who were the "magnates of the plazuela," were important plebeians. In order to advance from one group to the other, some hurdles had to be overcome. One was ethnic. A person had to be of Spanish background or, at least, be able to pass as white; this requirement was not an insurmountable obstacle, given the predominantly European cast of Socorro's population. But to move from plebeian to noble, the candidate could not be employed as a skilled craftsman of any description. Given Socorro's modestly expanding economy during the eighteenth century, it was not impossible for the sons of plebeians to accumulate just enough income and capital to acquire the other symbols of noble rank.

Differences between nobles and plebeians have been defined in aristocratic terms such as ethnic origin, occupation, marriage, lifestyle, education, residence, and office-holding. Among the plebeians there were also clusters of power, but power derived almost exclusively from occupation. A small group of plebeians could exercise considerable informal authority over their peers, if they dominated a trade that directly affected the vital interests of the poor, such as the town's meat supply.

Figure 4.1, depicting the three circles of leadership in Socorro—the cabildo, the Comunero captains, and the magnates of the plazuela—illustrates the key role of the Ardila clan.[57]

It is not surprising that the plebeians had their own leaders or that tradesmen such as the town butchers were the magnates of the little square. Such a pattern was commonplace among the riots that took place in preindustrial England and France.[58] What is unusual is the way one family in Socorro belonging to both the upper and lower classes provided a bridge to link patricians and plebeians in a common cause.

Of the four original captains general—Juan Francisco Berbeo, Salvador Plata, Antonio Monsalve, and Diego Ardila—three were related to the town clerk. Diego Ardila was Mateo's brother. Antonio Monsalve's mother was an Ardila, the aunt of the clerk. The Plata and Ardila clans were related by marriage. Diego Ardila never took office, for he was absent from Socorro at that time, and was replaced by Francisco Rosillo.

Isidro Molina, a member of the Ardila clan and an active rioter in the

COMUNERO CAPTAINS*

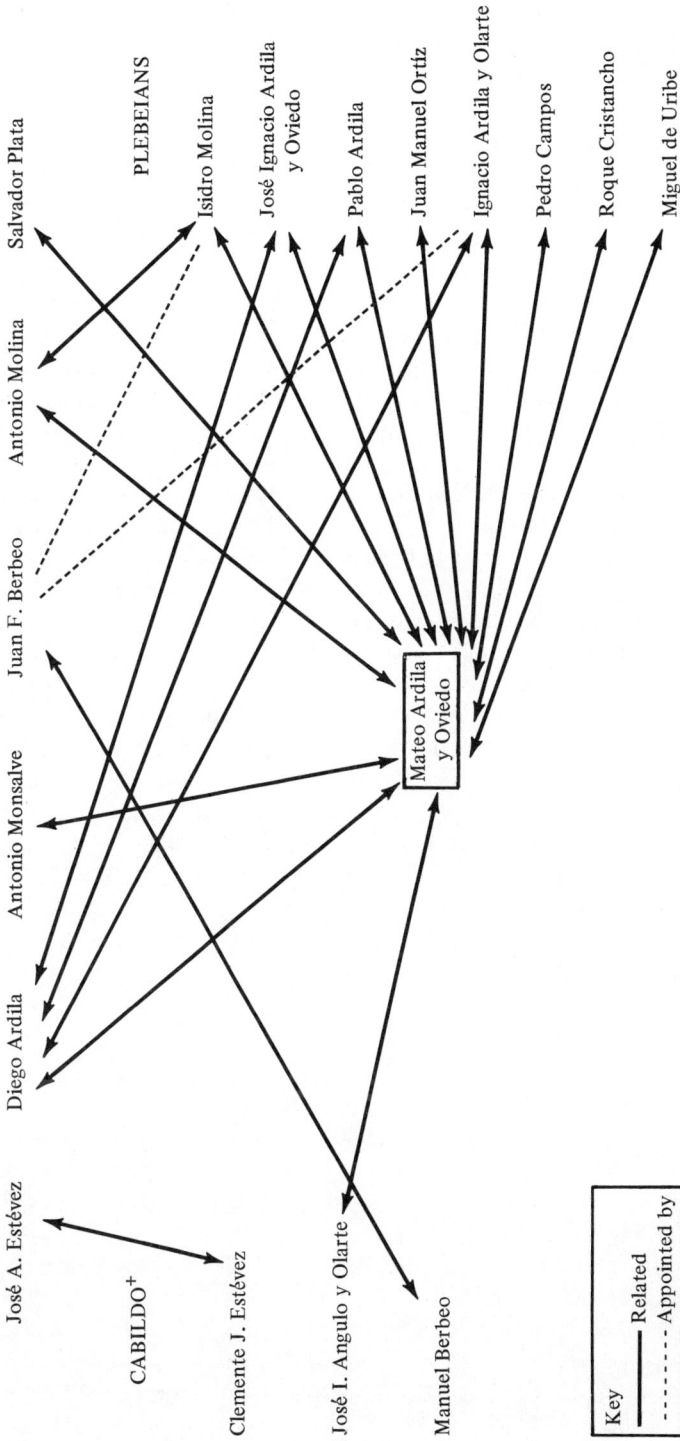

PLEBEIANS

Salvador Plata
Isidro Molina
José Ignacio Ardila y Oviedo
Antonio Molina
Pablo Ardila
Juan Manuel Ortíz
Juan F. Berbeo
Ignacio Ardila y Olarte
Antonio Monsalve
Pedro Campos
Roque Cristancho
Diego Ardila
Miguel de Uribe

Mateo Ardila y Oviedo

José A. Estévez

CABILDO+

Clemente J. Estévez

José I. Angulo y Olarte

Manuel Berbeo

Key
——— Related
------- Appointed by

*Ramón Ramírez, Francisco Rosillo, and Pedro Alejandro de la Prada have been excluded, since they lacked interconnections.
+Gregorio Roldán, Francisco Oribe y García, Francisco José Delgadillo, and Luis Céspedes have been excluded, since they lacked interconnections.

Figure 4.1. Role of the Ardila Clan in Socorro, 1781

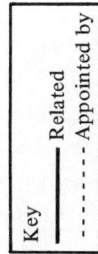

plazuela, received a roving commission as a *capitán volante*. His father Antonio held the position of *procurador del común,* which gave him the power of attorney as a kind of tribune to represent the interests of the plebeians in the Supreme Council of War. Ignacio Ardila y Olarte became the private secretary of Juan Francisco Berbeo.

The principal characteristic of a plural society is that two or more ethnic elements live side by side without mingling in one political unit and without forming a common social will.[59] By that definition Socorro itself, which had a disproportionate number of whites, was not a plural society, although most regions in New Granada were. The distinction between noble and plebeian in Socorro was less an ethnic and more an occupational distinction. Like the larger plural community of New Granada, however, Socorro lacked a common social will. In response to the political and fiscal innovations of Gutiérrez de Piñeres, Socorro became united for the first time in one broad political coalition comprising all groups in the community. Nobles and plebeians, creoles and mestizos began to interact as they forged a common political goal.

Mateo Ardila and his numerous clan provided the bridge to join the plaza of the nobles with the plazuela of the plebeians, just as the family and connections of the marquis of San Jorge formed the vital link between a united Socorro and an influential circle of creole patricians in the capital. Other communities such as the city of Tunja and the Indians would subsequently join the coalition. One meaning of the crisis of 1781 is that it represents the beginning of the end of the old plural society, with all ethnic groups for the first time united, if precariously, in a common political program.

5

A Utopia for the People

Three conditions were required to cement a precarious alliance between the elites and the plebeians in Socorro: a revolutionary example, a revolutionary ideology, and assurances of support from prominent creole circles in Bogotá. The uprising of Túpac Amaru II in Peru and an inflammatory poem originating in Bogotá more than adequately fulfilled these needs.

Not the contemporary revolution in British North America but the rebellion of Túpac Amaru provided a powerful revolutionary stimulus for New Granada. The outbreak of armed resistance in Peru occurred on November 4, 1780, just some five months before the first riot in Socorro. A rather sensationalized version of events in Peru was well known in Socorro during the months when popular dissatisfaction was germinating.

Manuel García Olano, then serving as administrator of the postal service in Bogotá, had three close friends in Socorro, from the days when he had been administrator of the tobacco monopoly there. To Salvador Plata, Francisco de Vargas—pastor of Socorro's principal parish—and Lieutenant Corregidor Clemente Estévez he periodically transmitted news of events not only in Bogotá but also in faraway Peru.[1] They in turn spread this information far and wide.

One of Manuel García Olano's sources of information about Túpac Amaru was Nicolas Vélez de Guevara y Suescún, Bogotá-born and Bogotá-educated, who was then serving as *fiscal del crimen* in the royal audiencia of Lima.[2] The reports that circulated among the elite and the populace of Socorro were to the effect that "the Inca [Túpac Amaru] must already be the master of the cities of Cuzco and Lima."[3] In fact, Túpac Amaru never occupied either city, but the belief that he was achieving spectacular success encouraged both the

67

plebeians to riot and the local elites to observe sullen neutrality during the critical month between March 16 and April 16, when revolutionary agitation was gathering momentum.

While the Socorranos were intoxicated by the alleged success of Túpac Amaru, the real situation was quite the opposite. After enjoying some initial victories in the months after November, 1780, the Inca leader was captured on April 6 and executed shortly afterwards. The authorities in Bogotá never discounted the impact of the revolutionary example of Túpac Amaru. Once royal control was reestablished, the audiencia decreed that his execution be proclaimed by town criers in every single parish of the New Kingdom.[4]

Padre Vargas was not in his parish on March 16, when his flock first rioted. On March 30, just two weeks later, he died in Tunja.[5] Was he en route to Bogotá? We do not know how he would have conducted himself between March 16 and April 16 with his tumultuous flock.

Manuel García Olano was not the only link between Bogotá and Socorro, although his epistolary activities were perhaps the single most important transmission belt. It will be recalled that Francisco de Vergara, regent of the tribunal de cuentas, was a friend of Juan Francisco Berbeo. Vergara's wife, doña Petronila, belonged to the prominent creole families of the Caicedos and the Vélez, many of whose members had long been well entrenched in the upper echelons of the bureaucracy. Doña Petronila's sister was married to Oidor Joaquín de Aróstegui y Escoto, who served from 1740 until 1775. Don Francisco was the father-in-law of another fiscal magistrate, don Antonio de Ayala.

Vergara had personal ties of friendship with Socorro going back to his childhood. He had lived there from 1735 until 1743, when his father, a widower who became a priest, was pastor of the church. Berbeo, the son of the parish notary, and Vergara, the son of the village pastor, may well have been playmates. As a fiscal magistrate Vergara returned several times to Socorro, where he nostalgically recalled having spent Christmas and Holy Week.[6] Vergara had a wide circle of friends there, including the influential town notary, Mateo Ardila.[7]

When it came time to negotiate the capitulations of Zipaquirá, Berbeo insisted that representatives from the prominent citizens of the capital participate in the discussions. Among those chosen were the marquis of San Jorge, Francisco de Vergara, and his brother-in-law, doctor Francisco Antonio Vélez. While there is no actual evidence that Francisco de Vergara undertook any action overtly favorable to the Comunero cause, the important fact is that Juan Francisco Berbeo enjoyed the friendship of that influential magistrate and he had confidence in his good will.

The most significant link between Bogotá and Socorro was not Manuel García Olano nor Francisco de Vergara, important though they were, but don

El Señor Dn. Jorge Miguel Lozano de Peralta, y Varaes, Maldonado de Mendoza, y Olaya, 1r. Marques de Sn. Jorge de Bogotá VIII. Poseedor del Mayorasgo de este nombre; ha servido los empleos de Sargento... or Alferes R. y otros varios de Republica en esta Corte de Sn. Fé, su Patria.

Jorge Miguel Lozano de Peralta, marquis of San Jorge de Bogotá. (Portrait by Joaquín Gutiérrez; Museo de Arte Colonial.)

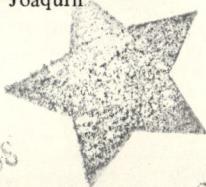

Jorge Miguel Lozano de Peralta, the first marquis of San Jorge de Bogotá. Both Francisco de Vergara and García Olano belonged to the family circle of the marquis—indeed, some eleven years after the Comunero Revolution, Vergara's son, don Juan de Vergara y Caicedo, married the youngest daughter of Lozano de Peralta. One of the sons of the late fiscal Alvarez was married to another daughter of the marquis of San Jorge, which made García Olano's wife and the marquis's daughter, doña Josefa Lozano, sisters-in-law. As a young man, the future marquis visited Socorro in 1751, and in 1762 he was one of the witnesses testifying in favor of Socorro's petition to acquire township status.[8]

Out of the circle of the marquis of San Jorge emerged the celebrated poem which the populace of Socorro called *nuestra cédula,* "our royal decree." That lampoon was first read to the tumultuous crowds in Socorro during the riot on April 16. Its importance cannot be exaggerated. It provided the plebeians with the one thing that they then needed—a revolutionary ideology expressed in a popular language that they could understand. Furthermore, the Bogotá origin of the lampoon was solid evidence to the patricians of Socorro that there were influential circles in the capital who were prepared to join the movement of protest. First, then, before analyzing in some detail the contents of that broadside, I shall look at the personality of the man from whose circle it emerged.

Don Jorge Miguel Lozano de Peralta, the first marquis of San Jorge de Bogotá (1731–93), was without any doubt the richest layman in the New Kingdom of Granada, as well as one of its most dissatisfied citizens. The founder of the Lozano de Peralta clan on the paternal side was the grandfather of the marquis, Jorge Miguel Lozano de Peralta, born in Spain, who served as an oidor of the audiencia in Bogotá from 1722 until 1729. The family fortune, however, came from the marriage of the oidor's son, José Antonio, to doña Josefa de Caicedo y Villacís. Their eldest son, Jorge, the future marquis, inherited from his mother the entailed estate, the mayorazgo de la dehesa de Bogotá, one of the largest latifundia of those times.

After being educated in the college of Rosario in Bogotá, Jorge Miguel held several honorific posts, such as alderman and standard bearer (*alférez real*) of the city of Bogotá. In the latter capacity, on August 6, 1760, he organized and paid for the most elaborate public fiesta that the capital had ever enjoyed in order to celebrate the ascension to the throne of Charles III. Several other prestigious positions came his way. On June 22, 1762, the viceroy named him *sargento mayor de las milicias.* The cabildo named him *mayordomo de propios* and *padre de menores.* The Holy Office of the Inquisition in Cartagena appointed him a *receptor.*

Lozano de Peralta, however, soon came into conflict with the cabildo over the monopoly that his famous estate, "El Novillero," enjoyed in supplying the meat market of the capital. The cabildo and its wealthiest alderman often quarreled over the price and the quantity of meat that was necessary to supply the needs of the capital city.

Indicative of the worsening relations between the creoles and their peninsular-born cousins was a clash in the city council between Lozano de Peralta and the Seville-born alderman, José Groot de Vargas. Groot de Vargas insulted the creole aristocrat, who took pride in his European descent, when he yelled at Lozano de Peralta: "You bear the stigma of this land, you are an enemy of the chapetones [European Spaniards] and you are a pagan."[9] Only the timely intervention of colleagues prevented the shedding of blood, and Lozano de Peralta subsequently resigned his seat in the cabildo. He then began a damage suit against Alderman Groot de Vargas that was still under litigation twenty years later, at the time of his death.

Jorge Miguel Lozano de Peralta was a proud, hypersensitive, and quarrelsome creole aristocrat who evidently reveled in the litigations that he vigorously conducted during his lifetime. By 1785 he had feuded with every judge of the audiencia, with the result that he requested the king to transfer his many pending lawsuits to a specially appointed judge not a member of that tribunal.

On the occasion of the birth of an heir to the prince and princess of Asturias, Charles III authorized the viceroy to grant titles of Castilian nobility to two citizens of high lineage whose personal wealth could amply support the maintenance of that honor. The acceptance of a title of nobility clearly implied the payment of a whole series of taxes, including the heavy tax of the *lanzas* and the *media anata*.[10] Lozano de Peralta eagerly accepted the title. He had his noble emblazon sculptured over the portal of his seignorial mansion, and gave an elaborate fiesta to celebrate his elevation to the peerage. Yet he stubbornly refused to pay the taxes, asserting that the title was a reward for his merits. In this he was grossly ill-informed, since titles of nobility at this time were just another means to collect revenue from the wealthy and the ambitious.

On May 5, 1777, the audiencia deprived him of his new peerage for his failure to pay the taxes involved. When he continued to style himself marquis and retained the noble coat of arms over his portal, the audiencia fined him 500 pesos. But his ambitions for honors did not abate. On October 7, 1778, his lawyer at the royal court in Madrid requested for his client the not very important position of corregidor of Zipaquirá, a minor post that had already been held by his son-in-law.[11]

The quarrelsome marquis perhaps did reflect in a highly exaggerated fashion the grievances that many creole patricians felt, when he wrote Charles III:

> What value do we in this part of the world gain from all the services and merits that we have rendered Your Majesty? What

> advantage do we derive from the blood our ancestors gloriously
> shed in the service of God, our Lord, and Your Majesty? . . . What
> benefits do we receive from the viceroys here and their retainers
> who insult, mock, humiliate, and oppress us? . . . Finally, Sire,
> the more distinguished the unhappy Americans are, the more
> they suffer. Once they are deprived of their wealth, then their
> honor and reputations are attacked, insulting them by depriving
> them of any honorific office of consequence.[12]

Immediately after the lampoon of 1781 appeared, the Spanish authorities made a sustained, but vain, attempt to identify its author. One fact is certain: the poem was composed in Bogotá. On April 7 at 2:30 A.M. a night watchman making his rounds found a copy attached to a pillar on the bridge of San Francisco on the calle real in Bogotá, and dutifully surrendered it to the regent visitor general. Other copies, however, were sent by private messenger from the capital to the Comunero captain general in the parish of Simacota, Pedro Fabio de Archila, a brother of one Friar Ciriaco de Archila, a Dominican lay brother who belonged to the outer fringes of the group surrounding the marquis of San Jorge. The fact that the poem so quickly arrived in the Socorro area suggests the possibility that either Manuel García Olano or the marquis of San Jorge arranged for the transmission of this explosive document to Simacota. Pedro de Archila had several copies of the poem made, and sent one to don Juan Bernardo Plata de Acevedo, who in turn distributed copies to Mateo Ardila and Isidro Molina, a plebeian leader.[13]

Suspicion of authorship fell primarily on the circle of the marquis of San Jorge, for that was the most visible center of pro-Socorrano sentiment in the capital, and, in particular, on the marquis himself and on the Dominican friar, Ciriaco de Archila. Both individuals were subsequently punished. Archbishop Viceroy Caballero y Góngora exiled Jorge Miguel Lozano de Peralta to Cartagena in 1786—he died there on August 11, 1793. Ciriaco de Archila was dispatched as a prisoner to the Dominican monastery in Madrid.[14]

Internal evidence suggests that the real author was not the litigious creole aristocrat but the Dominican lay brother. The rhetoric is coarse and vulgar, the language of the people of the Socorro region. It differs sharply from the style of the many known letters of the marquis of San Jorge, who, not being a native of Socorro, was unlikely to be familiar with its popular idiom. The emphasis on Socorro's role of leadership, with its blatant appeal to local pride, also suggests that the author may have been a son of that land. The poem contains several verses hostile to the creole-born fiscal, Francisco Moreno y Escandón, whose educational project had aroused the ire of the Dominicans. The tone and the spirit of the lampoon suggest an intelligent if unlearned man who was sufficiently clever to translate into a popular idiom the table talk and the theories that he picked up in his monastery.[15]

Friar Ciriaco was a native of Simacota, a subordinate parish located a few miles southwest of the town of Socorro. Born in 1724, he fulfilled a long-frustrated intention of becoming a Dominican friar when on December 19, 1776, after the death of his wife, he and his eight-year-old son entered the Dominican monastery in Chiquinquirá as novices. He remained, however, a lay brother. Transferring to the Dominican establishment in Bogotá, he held the humble post of porter.

On April 16, 1781, during the third riot, the lampoon was recited to the populace of Socorro, who joyously proclaimed it "nuestra cédula," *el superior despacho, la real cédula,* and *la santísima gaceta.*[16] The Spanish authorities considered the poem so inflammatory and subversive that all copies were destroyed. No copy of the full text, for example, survived in the archives of Bogotá. In 1880 Manuel Briceño published an incomplete text. It was not until 1960 that the full text was published by Pablo Cárdenas Acosta from a copy that he located in the Archivo General de Indias in Seville.[17]

The poem has some forty-two stanzas, each of eight lines, in a form known as *octavas reales*. It is very bad poetry, in extremely coarse language, but it was heady political wine for the populace. It is impossible to convey the spirit of this lampoon in English translation.

The lampoon has the sarcastic title, "Greetings, señor Regent." In these crudely composed verses Juan Francisco Gutiérrez de Piñeres was set up as the target of popular hatred. He was a tyrant imposing unjust taxes on a suffering people, a heartless magistrate with an insatiable appetite for robbing the poor and the downtrodden. This image became deeply embedded in the popular mind. The regent visitor general became a man seeking to impose tyranny, slavery, servitude, injustice, and oppression. Drawing on Biblical imagery, people compared what was happening in New Granada to the oppression that the Jews suffered in Egypt under the tyranny of Pharaoh. There is no more graphic illustration of the rhetoric and imagery of "our cedula" than the following phrases from a Comunero letter:

> Oh Sirs, we are determined in our resolve. Take heart, brave neighbors! Let the captive people be freed from the power of the Pharaoh! Long live our Catholic faith! Long live our Catholic King of Spain! Death to the Nero-like cruelties of those who would put us in bondage.[18]

A revolution must have a hate symbol. Note that it is the regent visitor general who is here singled out as a bloodsucking tyrant. Neither the king nor Viceroy Flores was so identified.

Another theme that recurs in the people's cedula is a simple but direct appeal to the regional patriotism of Socorro, an increasingly assertive local pride that had steadily grown as Socorro fought to achieve an independent political identity in the course of the eighteenth century. The poem rhetorically asks why Socorro and not Bogotá was the first community to raise the standard of rebellion. All the towns of the New Kingdom have equally suffered from the new taxes:

> Porqué no se levanta Sante Fe?
> Porqué no se levantan otros tales,
> En quienes opresión igual se ve,
> Y con mayor estrago de los males?
> Sólo el Socorro tiene que ser el que
> Ha de llegar primero a tus umbrales?
> Si pues tanta congoja dan a otros,
> Está sin duda aquí el dedo de Dios.

The "finger of God" points to Socorro. The citizens of Socorro are the "new chosen people," the instrument of Divine Providence's will to castigate the evildoers. Socorro's mission is to lead the suffering people of New Granada from the oppression of Pharaoh to the Promised Land.

The people's cedula waxes lyrical about Socorro's leadership in the "enterprise" that is now being undertaken. The word *empresa*, so often used in the novels of knight-errantry, and redolent of glorious feats for eighteenth-century Spaniards, is here invoked for the first time, and would be used countless times by the Comunero captains.[19]

The central purpose of "our royal decree" was to extend an invitation to the Socorranos to march on the capital, where they would receive an enthusiastic welcome.

The poem even provided a precise timetable and strategy. The Socorranos were urged to march on the capital in force within a period of two months. And indeed, by June 6 some 20,000 angry though poorly armed men—not the mere 5,000 troops that the poem requested—had assembled in Zipaquirá, one day's journey from Bogotá.

Several stanzas reassured the Socorranos that there were no serious obstacles to such a march. Corregidor Campuzano, for example, can be discounted. "Courageous only on parade," he is a gutless coward who "will wet his pants" upon merely seeing the legions of Socorro.

A more dangerous threat is constituted by the Capuchin friars. The poem warns the populace to pay no attention to their sermons, for "they will seek to persuade us in a submissive voice that it is just for the government to steal the shirts off our backs." This is the only occasion when the poem criticized any segment of the clergy. The Capuchin friars, who grew out of the Franciscan order, were then dominated by European Spaniards, to the virtual exclusion of the creoles. They also enjoyed a reputation as militant regalists who defended the authority of the crown over both church and state. These stanzas proved, indeed, to be an uncanny prediction. As a part of his grand design to pacify the new kingdom, Archbishop Caballero y Góngora established in Socorro a Capuchin monastery whose friars undertook a vigorous mission preaching the gospel of blind obedience to its erstwhile rebels.

The people should seek inspiration, the poem exhorts, not from the Capuchins, but in the events in Peru. (In none of these stanzas is there even a veiled reference as to what was then happening in English North America.)

If "our cedula" casts Gutiérrez de Piñeres in the role of principal oppressor of the people, next in order of villainy is the fiscal del crimen of the audiencia, Francisco Antonio Moreno y Escandón. Some ten stanzas, nearly one-fourth of the whole poem, attack him, especially for his efforts to remodel the curriculum of higher education, tenaciously resisted by the Dominican friars:

> Qué hizo con los estudios? confundirlos,
> Qué intentó con los frailes? acabarlos,
> Qué piensa con los clérigos? destruírlos,
> Qué con los monasterios? destrozarlos.
> Y qué con los vasallos? el fundirlos

Moreno had in fact proposed the abolition of the Dominican university of Santo Tomás in favor of a public university in whose curriculum scientific and rational methodology would replace traditional scholasticism.

Despite these echoes of Dominican concerns, there is no evidence to suggest that Friar Ciriaco might have been acting as an unofficial and anonymous spokesman of the Dominican order in authoring the pasquinade. A simple lay brother without sacerdotal status and of humble social background, he was far removed from the center of power and authority in that religious community. Although the Dominicans were engaged in an acrimonious battle to defend the monopoly of their university and were bitter opponents of the scientific methodology of the Enlightenment, the order as such was not even a silent partner in the coalition of 1781. On October 13, 1779, in a junta presided over by Gutiérrez de Piñeres, the Dominicans had won a substantial victory for their cause, and as will be discussed in chapter 19, they knew how to defend their interests inside the more orthodox channels of bureaucratic negotiation. The savage fury with which the poem assails Moreno is perhaps the most plausible bit of internal evidence to suggest that its author was Ciriaco de Archila. He was seeking to enlist the support of the Dominican order, but that prestigious corporation did not accept the invitation.

The poem portrays Fiscal Moreno as an ally of the regent visitor general, when in fact the two were opponents. During the period prior to 1778 when the creoles exercised considerable influence in the audiencia, Moreno, who was born in Mariquita, New Granada, and educated in Bogotá, had played a key role in selling off the Indian community lands, the resguardos—a policy sharply criticized by Gutiérrez de Piñeres, who also opposed Moreno's educational program. As a part of his plan to eliminate creole influence in the audiencia, Gutiérrez de Piñeres persuaded José de Gálvez to transfer Moreno to the audiencia of Lima, with the same rank. On May 7, 1781, Moreno left Bogotá for his new post, thus escaping on the very eve of the hurricane that was to descend.

"Our royal decree" not only assailed the fiscal for his alleged hostility to the friars but also made a direct appeal to the Indians, seeking to harness their discontent in the service of the rebellion, by denouncing the sufferings inflicted upon them in the consolidation of the resguardos. As we shall have occasion to observe subsequently, the creole leaders sought to incorporate this appeal into the grand design of forging a multi-ethnic coalition.

The political theory implicit, and to some extent explicit, in the people's cedula is capable of being interpreted in several ways. A new slogan emerges: "Long live Socorro and death to bad government." The cry, "Long live the king and death to bad government," which was the slogan of the riots of March 16 and March 30, was modified. In these verses there is no explicit affirmation of loyalty to the crown, and that in itself makes "our royal decree" one of the most radical political expressions of the Comunero Revolution. Yet in the vast majority of riots that swept through the province of Tunja in April and May the slogan of the demonstrators invariably was the traditional cry, "Long live the king and death to bad government."

The omission of "Long live the king" led some contemporary observers, such as the Capuchin friar Joaquín de Finestrad, to claim that the poem advocated political separation from Spain.[20] Rafael Gómez Hoyos in his masterful *La revolución granadina de 1810* concurs with Finestrad's assessment.[21] Their view stems from their interpretation of those verses which are most explicitly political in content.

> Pretender socorrer al Erario
> A costa de una injusta introducción,
> Que sin tener derecho hereditario,
> Logró el rigor, la envidia y ambición.
> Pero cómo, si no eres propietario,
> Así intentas del país la destrucción?
> Si de piedad no has visto ni aún el forro
> Cómo has de hallar en tu favor Socorro?
>
> A más de que si estos dominios tienen
> Sus propios dueños, señores naturales,
> Porqué razón a gobernarnos vienen
> De otras regiones malditos nacionales?
> De esto nuestras desdichas nos provienen,

Y así, para excusar fines fatales,
Unámonos, por Dios, si les parece,
Y veamos el Reino a quien le pertenece.

The poem falls far short of a condemnation of the Spanish conquest or a repudiation of the sovereignty of the Spanish crown, but it is understandable that Finestrad, chief executor of the "pacification" of Socorro after the Comunero Revolution, would interpret as subversive anything less than unquestioning obedience.

These stanzas imply not a repudiation of the Spanish crown as such but an affirmation of the notion that New Granada belongs to the people who were born and live there, "that this kingdom belongs to its citizens," i.e., the creoles, the mestizos, and the Indians. Gutiérrez de Piñeres is a chapetón, a "damned Spaniard." He has no hereditary right to rule. Nor does any other peninsular-born magistrate, "for all our misfortunes come from there [Spain]." To be sure, the verses vaguely allude to the sixteenth-century doctrines of Las Casas and Francisco de Vitoria that the Indians are the *señores naturales* of the New World. Yet it is scarcely conceivable that the poem, which originated in an aristocratic creole circle in Bogotá, would advocate the return of the Indies to the Indians. The new "señores naturales" are not the Indians but the creoles and the plebeians who look to them for political leadership.

These stanzas foreshadow in a crude and vulgarized form what article twenty-two of the capitulations of Zipaquirá spelled out in a more sophisticated fashion. Americans and not European Spaniards should be given preference for all bureaucratic positions in the New World. America should be ruled by Americans, under the aegis of Charles III. In practice, this would mean that the creoles as the only educated and propertied group would be the governors, under the general supervision of the crown. To Charles III and his ministers, such a claim constituted a revolutionary threat to the crown's sovereignty, but on the part of the creoles it was something less than a demand for outright political independence.

"Our royal decree" made a blatant appeal to the hatred that the populace felt toward the chapetones. They were outsiders who had exploited the people with unbearable taxes; the chapeton policemen violated their women, burned the tobacco crops, and brutally enforced the edicts of the hated royal monopolies. The creole elites in Bogotá were motivated by a similar feeling of resentment. What they wanted, however, was not relief from the oppression of the police but a virtual monopoly of all bureaucratic offices in the kingdom.

Too much can be read into the omission of "Long live the king." In the vast majority of cases, the crowds enthusiastically shouted their faith in the king as they lustily denounced the abuses of "bad government." For them "bad government" meant tyranny. Gutiérrez de Piñeres was the tyrant, and by extension so were all the Spanish-born magistrates who implemented his edicts.

The concept of tyrant and tyranny had precise meanings that had been developed by a galaxy of Spanish theologians from the thirteenth to the seventeenth centuries.[22] Neither the plebeians nor the patricians were prepared to deny the legitimacy of the royal authority. The king, if properly informed of all conditions, would never will an injustice.

The Spanish theologians had developed rather intricate and complex theories about the conditions under which it would be licit to resist a tyrant; of these, neither the author of the people's cedula nor the rioting crowd in Socorro were probably aware. What the poem clearly implied, however, is that the citizens of New Granada were justified in resisting the tyranny of the Spanish bureaucracy. In the capitulations of Zipaquirá the creole elites would advance a self-serving solution for this tyranny: creoles should be given preference for all bureaucratic posts.

Thus, the celebrated people's cedula gave the crowds a goal, a utopia to which they could aspire and which would stimulate their protest. They were fighting a cruel and avaricious tyrant whose only concern was to increase taxes upon a poverty-stricken and oppressed people. The utopia nostalgically conjured by "our royal decree" was the golden age of the early viceroys, when there were no royal monopolies of tobacco and aguardiente, when other taxes were low and not very efficiently collected.

Appealing to local patriotism and local pride, the poem urged the Socorranos to march on the capital in order to enforce the abolition of the hated royal monopolies and the new taxes. The hate symbols that the people's cedula exploited to such advantage were the chapetones in general, and Gutiérrez de Piñeres in particular. New Granada belonged to all those who were born there, those who tilled her soil and built her towns out of the wilderness.

Although half a dozen other poems appeared during the course of the Comunero Revolution, there was no verse which expressed more forcefully and boldly the aspirations of the people than the people's cedula.[23] Its contents were the intoxicating wine which stimulates revolutions. But if the utopia of the populace found its most heady, if crude, expression in "our royal decree," the utopia of the patricians had its most articulate and sophisticated expression in the capitulations of Zipaquirá.

6

A Utopia for the Nobles

The alliance between the elites and plebeians was sealed on Wednesday, April 18, two days after the third riot in Socorro, when "our royal decree" was first read to the rioting crowd. From the four corners of the main square of Socorro the cheering populace jubilantly proclaimed Juan Francisco Berbeo, Salvador Plata, Antonio José Monsalve, and Diego Ardila captains general of the "enterprise."[1]

The day before, Juan Francisco Berbeo had taken the first decisive military action of the revolution. In response to a rumor (it turned out to be false) that Corregidor Campuzano was approaching Socorro, Berbeo led an expedition to the nearby site of Polonia. There some two thousand people congregated, poorly armed with slings, bags of rocks, swords, pikes, staffs, spears, daggers, and a few firearms. Berbeo issued orders that made some kind of military clash with Bogotá almost inevitable. In order to protect Socorro from a possible invasion coming from the south, he stationed a military guard at Oiba on the Suárez River, and ordered the burning of the wooden bridge of San Bartolomé and the destruction of the bridge at Vargas, and the posting of armed guards at all localities adjacent to Socorro. His second act of bold leadership on April 17 was to order the interception of the royal mail pouch between Socorro and Bogotá.[2]

On the very day that the elites in Socorro made their alliance with the crowds, Oidor Osorio, on orders from the regent visitor general and the audiencia, left the capital at the head of a small military expedition whose purpose was to pacify tumultuous Socorro. Thus in Socorro and in Bogotá the antagonists had simultaneously resolved to settle their differences by a military confrontation.

The new leaders of the revolution proceeded with caution but firmness in assuming command. They insisted that the highest ranking representative of royal authority in Socorro, Lieutenant Corregidor Clemente José Estévez, provide an official and quasilegal sanction for their positions as captains general by swearing them into office in a public ceremony.[3] In approving these appointments, the lieutenant corregidor covered his flanks by reaffirming his blind loyalty to the king. Clemente José Estévez was in a difficult position. As the ranking royal magistrate in Socorro, he was required to maintain the authority of the crown. Yet the town was in a frenzied state of tumult, and it was clear to him that only the local elites could bring some order out of the chaos. With brothers on both sides and an intimate friendship with Manuel García Olano, principal link between Socorro and the pro-Comunero groups in Bogotá, he had no choice but to hedge his bets.

The new captains then met with the lieutenant corregidor, in private, and swore a secret oath:

> fearful lest they and their families meet death at the hands of the rioters and coerced by the latter and against their will, not wanting to incur upon themselves the unseemly blotch of treason to the king (may God preserve him) but rather to see if through the command given to them, they might through licit and gentle means contain, pacify, and subordinate the rebels, they accepted these appointments.[4]

Some historians have claimed that this celebrated secret oath is proof that the captains were from the beginning traitors to the very movement that they ostensibly led.[5] Even as articulate and erudite a defender of Juan Francisco Berbeo as Pablo E. Cárdenas Acosta described his conduct in this matter as Machiavellian. He argued that such a Janus-like posture was a characteristic means by which subjects protected themselves in an absolute monarchy where royal power could be arbitrary and capricious.[6] Cárdenas Acosta urged that the conduct of the Comunero leaders should be judged by the standards of their time. That argument must be rigorously pursued.

A careful examination of the conduct of the Socorrano leaders in the context of 1781 reveals that the controversial secret oath was neither hypocritical, traitorous, nor Machiavellian. On the contrary, the secret oath represents the Comunero leaders' honest estimate of their goals and their procedures. It is not wrong to assert that the captains were trying to cover their flanks in case their movement subsequently failed. Nor is it incorrect to argue that legalistically minded creoles were seeking to clothe in legal arguments an undertaking that was extralegal, if not downright illegal. But such explanations, while true in part, are superficial.

To what extent were the leaders of Socorro exaggerating, when they claimed that if they had not accepted positions of leadership their very lives would have been in danger at the hands of the irate crowds? Some exaggeration may be involved, but the pressure that the plebeians were exercising against the patricians was intense indeed. The crowds were outraged at the new taxes. They were the first to demonstrate. In a traditionalist society, they looked to the upper classes for leadership and direction, knowing instinctively that the abolition of the new taxes and a return to "the good old days" would never come about until the elites joined their cause. The nobles were just as unhappy about the fiscal program as were the plebeians, but it was not their style to demonstrate in the streets. Hence the vast majority of them remained sullenly passive between March 16 and April 16, as popular discontent escalated during three successive riots. But by April 16 popular dissatisfaction had reached such an intensity that it seemed to the patricians that their property and their lives were in danger unless they joined the movement. The resolve of the nobles was further buttressed by the solid assurances of support from dissatisfied creole circles in Bogotá, expressed in the concrete form of "our royal decree."

Even more plausible was the argument of the Socorrano leaders that they alone were capable of controlling popular fury, channeling the plebeians' wrath. In fact, the patrician leadership did exercise a remarkable control over the populace. Both pillage and anarchy were indeed avoided.

The leaders of Socorro were not being Machiavellian or hypocritical or traitorous to the cause they led, when they reaffirmed their fealty to the king. An oath of loyalty to the king's ministers, in particular to Gutiérrez de Piñeres, would indeed have been massive hypocrisy. But by carefully restricting their oath to the distant king, they were, in effect, reiterating the slogan of the rioting crowd: "Long live the king and death to bad government."

The apparently ambivalent position of the Comunero chieftains in reaffirming loyalty to the king while tenaciously resisting his minister's specific policies had several antecedents in the history of New Granada. There were three "tax revolts" before 1781. Each one was basically a constitutional crisis, for which the tax issue constituted the tip of the iceberg. They occurred in Tunja in 1592, when Philip II sought to extend the alcabala to New Granada, again in Tunja in 1641 with the establishment of the armada de Barlovento sales tax, and in 1740 in Puente Real de Vélez when Viceroy Sebastián de Eslava sought to raise a forced loan to defray the expenses of the war with Great Britain.[7]

The sales tax revolts of 1592 and 1641 made a substantial contribution to the evolution of the "unwritten constitution" of New Granada. While the crown's ultimate right to impose new taxes was preserved, the manner in which they were to be imposed was subject to significant restraints. First, the king's subjects had the right to petition the crown to reconsider. Second, the bureaucracy had to mount a sustained effort to persuade public opinion in favor of the new measures, thus implying some form of consent from those who were being taxed. Third, new taxes were subject to negotiation, with the crown informally committed to the principle of making concessions to regional interests. During the crisis of 1778–81 the regent visitor general violated every one of these powerful, if informal, traditional procedures.

The Spanish monarchy was absolute only in the original medieval sense. The king recognized no superior inside or outside his kingdoms. He was the ultimate source of all justice and all legislation. The late medieval phrase was, "The king is emperor in his realm." The laws that bore the royal signature, however, were not the arbitrary expression of the king's personal wishes. Legislation, and the extent to which it was enforced, reflected the complex and diverse aspirations of all or, at least, several groups in that corporate, multi-ethnic society. The monarchy was representative and decentralized to a degree seldom suspected. Although there were no formal representative assemblies or cortes in the Indies, each one of the major corporations, such as the cabildos, the various ecclesiastical groups, the universities, and the craft guilds, all of which enjoyed a large measure of self-government, could and did speak for their respective constituents. Their views reached the king and the council of the Indies, transmitted directly by their accredited representatives or indirectly through the viceroys and the audiencias, and their aspirations profoundly shaped the character of the ultimate decisions.

The most influential of these corporations were apt to be the city councils in the larger cities and towns overseas. Having purchased their positions from the crown as status symbols in a status-dominated society, the aldermen were the leading citizens both in social prestige and often but not always in wealth. In the second half of the seventeenth century and during the reigns of the first two Bourbons, the town councils were strongholds of the well-to-do creoles, although some wealthy European Spaniards were in their ranks. The cabildos were not reluctant from time to time to defend their own more selfish vested interests as well as to act as spokesmen for the interests of the larger community.

The cabildos, like the parliaments in northern Europe in the seventeenth century, represented property, both new and old wealth, but never people. Although they could never legislate about property and taxes but could only petition the viceroy and the audiencia, and ultimately the king, nevertheless those petitions always received a serious hearing and often influenced the ultimate formulation of royal policy. A formal representative assembly in one sense was superfluous. Through the cabildos the new and the old wealth in New Granada acquired an articulate voice in influencing the policies of the state. In the same period the new and old wealth in England and Holland played a similar role through their representative assemblies.

The views of the rising creole elites, institutionalized in the cabildos, influenced decision-making in the imperial bureaucracy through the application of the suspensive veto. In those situations where royal mandates sharply conflicted with local conditions or where enforcement might create an injustice, the viceroys and the audiencias possessed discretionary authority to suspend the execution of a law. In a picturesque ceremony in which the chief magistrate kissed the royal cedula, he invoked the celebrated "I obey but do not execute" formula. Upon applying the formula, the viceroy and the audiencia were required to submit to the council of the Indies concrete proposals by which the suspended legislation might be improved or modified so that it would not create an injustice or be in sharp conflict with local conditions. In making recommendations to the king, the viceroy and the audiencia usually took into account not only the views of the creole elites, but also the interests of the plebeians. What finally emerged was an accommodation between the initial directives from the central authorities in Spain, and the pressures generated by the regions involved. The difficult and complex responsibility of the viceroys and the audiencias was to act as brokers between what the central authorities wanted and what local conditions would permit. Everyone usually got something, perhaps not as much as each initially wanted. What emerged was a workable compromise that all could live with. The Spanish system of bureaucratic administration had a built-in flexibility in which local interests were able to influence significantly the outcome of events.[8]

The primary mechanism of bureaucratic decentralization was the "I obey but do not execute" formula. The phrase "I obey" denoted the respect enshrined in Roman law for the legitimacy of royal authority, which, if properly informed, would never will an injustice. Cementing the loyalty of all groups to the crown was the powerful myth of the king as the fountainhead of all justice. The phrase "I do not execute" represented the discretionary authority of subordinates, one of whose major responsibilities was to accommodate themselves to the pressures generated by both the central authorities and local conditions.

During the reigns of the first two Bourbon kings, Philip V and Ferdinand VI, the voice and influence of the creoles, as was observed in chapter 1, greatly increased. Under such circumstances the viceroys and the audiencias perforce pursued policies that enjoyed the positive acceptance of local interest groups. When in the 1760's orders came from Spain to organize the tobacco monopoly on the Mexican model, the viceroys interpreted these directives in the spirit of the "I obey but do not execute" formula. The tobacco monopoly was introduced gradually and piecemeal. During the 1770's, the viceroys and the audiencia, in effect, bowed to the pressure generated by demographic change and the land hunger of the creoles and the mestizos, when they sanctioned a wholesale reduction of the community lands of the Indians in the province of Tunja.

Until the arrival of the regent visitor general, Gutiérrez de Piñeres, the creoles were accustomed to a government of compromise, conciliation, and accommodation in which some creoles actively participated in the decision-making process. The basic goal of Charles III was to create a unitary and centralized state in which directives emanating from Madrid would be enforced without being diluted by any kind of compromise with local conditions and influences. In 1781 the Comunero leaders were frantically searching for a formula by which they could return to the kind of decentralized government which had evolved out of the tradition of municipal government in medieval Castile and the Habsburg system with its complex blending of centralization and decentralization. In seeking to abolish or, at least, to modify the fiscal program of Charles III, the Comunero leaders sought not to overthrow the crown, but to persuade the king to return to the traditional system of negotiating with his subjects. In organizing the march on the capital, they were, in effect, engaging in a campaign of massive civil disobedience in order to persuade the king to change the policies of his ministers.

The goals of the populace and the nobles must be carefully distinguished. Both groups were in a revolutionary state of mind in that they totally rejected the present, i.e., the innovations of Charles III, and both yearned for a return to a golden age of the past. In economic terms, the utopia of the plebeians was the abolition of the abrasively collected new and old taxes. Politically, it meant a return to the days of the early viceroys. If the people's utopia was tied to bread and butter issues, the central concern of the nobles was the distribution of political power.

The creoles took their point of departure in a utopian past—the Habsburg system of bureaucratic decentralization. Yet, when it came time for them to articulate their political and constitutional aspirations in the capitulations of Zipaquirá, they reacted to Charles III's political revolution with a revolution of their own. The concept of a "counterrevolution" is loaded in the context of the Comunero Revolution. Its use would imply that Charles III was "progressive" and the Comuneros were "reactionary." Such name-calling is both tendentious and ahistorical.

It is inappropriate to label the political and fiscal innovations of Charles III as "reforms." These were indeed changes, but they were differently perceived by different groups. To cite one outstanding example: the tobacco monopoly may have been a "reform" for the king's ministers in that royal revenues spectacularly increased. But the small farmers in the region of Socorro, who suddenly found themselves deprived of a cash crop, scarcely viewed the monopoly as a change for the better. For this reason, I have consistently preferred to use more neutral phraseology by referring to the "reforms" of Charles III as changes or innovations.

Equally, it was unthinkable in 1781 for the creoles, still deeply attached to the myth and mystique of the crown, to repudiate the monarchy as an institution. From our vantage point, the men of Zipaquirá may loom as precursors of nineteenth-century federalism, but the spirit and the tone of the capitulations of Zipaquirá conjure up the golden age of the Habsburgs, and their rhetoric employs key concepts of sixteenth- and seventeenth-century Spanish political theory. There is little evidence that the Comuneros had access to the political thought of the European Enlightenment that nourished the North American and French revolutions. Instead, they had another ideological tradition from which they drew inspiration.

Considerable controversy exists as to whether the ideology of the classic Spanish political theorists influenced the thinking of the generation of 1810. Some have claimed that the classic Spanish theologians were as influential as, if not more so than, the political philosophers of the Enlightenment—an assertion that has been hotly disputed.[9] What is incontrovertible is that a generation before in New Granada there was a profound coincidence between the implicit political theory of the Comunero Revolution and the rich body of classical Spanish political theory whose outstanding figure was Francisco Suárez (1548–1617). Among the notable sixteenth-century Spanish political theorists were Martín de Azpilcueta, Diego de Covarrubias, Domingo de Soto, Francisco de Vitoria, Domingo Bráñez, Alfonso de Castro, Luis de Molina, and Juan de Mariana. The outstanding figures of the seventeenth century were Diego de Saavedra y Fajardo, Pedro Fernández de Navarrete, Francisco de Quevedo y Villegas, and Jerónimo de Castillo de Bobadilla.

While there were several copies of works by these men in a few libraries in Bogotá, one cannot automatically assume that these books were read or that they directly influenced the thinking of the generation of 1781.[10] All the copies were printed in Europe, since Bogotá had no functioning printing press until the late 1770's. Tracing the paternity of ideas is a risky business at best. There is, for example, no hard evidence that the author of "our royal decree" or the framers of the capitulations of Zipaquirá had ever read these weighty tomes of political theory. It is nonetheless apparent that some of the basic doctrines of classical Spanish political theory coincided not only with the political posture of the Comunero leaders in 1781 but also with the "unwritten constitution" that had evolved in New Granada prior to 1778. The Spanish political theorists stressed the popular origin of sovereignty, limitations on political power, a social contract between the governors and the governed, resistance to tyranny, the invalidity of an unjust war, popular consent to new taxes, the primacy of the common good of the whole community, and the rule of natural law.

In eighteenth-century Bourbon Spain these doctrines had gone out of style, to be replaced with notions of French absolutism from the France of Louis XIV and Louis XV. No clearer expression of Bourbon centralism can be found than *El vasallo instruido*, by Friar Joaquín de Finestrad. In his denunciation of the Comunero Revolution, he seldom cited the classic Spanish political theorists of the sixteenth and seventeenth centuries.[11] He preached the gospel of blind obedience to constituted authorities, and assailed all rebellions, even those against a blatantly tyrannical government.

The most influential of the classic Spanish political theorists was the Jesuit, Francisco Suárez, whose major political treatises were *De legibus ac deo legislatore* and *Defensio fidei*. His works and those of many other Jesuit authors were banned from the curriculum of all Spanish universities in a royal cedula on May 23, 1767, shortly after the expulsion of the Jesuit order from all the Spanish dominions.[12] Suárez's cautious admission that tyrannicide might be justified under certain carefully prescribed conditions was a doctrine associated with the Jesuits that aroused the ire of the governing circles around Charles III.

Suárez was the heir of the tradition of Aristotle and Thomas Aquinas. His ontological formulation of the origin of the political community and civil power rested on the premise of the natural sociability of man. The end of all society is to achieve the common good, *bonum commune,* of all those who compose it, not as individuals but as members of the community. When a group of people decide to become a political society, they cease to be a mere collection of individuals, and become a *corpus mysticum politicum,* a political mystical body. God is the ultimate author, the efficient cause, of political authority, in that man's sociability made political society a dialectical necessity. Yet political power comes into being by a social contract either explicit or implicit between the people and the sovereign. Thus, Suárez stresses the popular origin and contractual nature of sovereignty.

It follows that there are certain limits on sovereignty: divine law, which restricts political authority to the temporal sphere, and natural law, which confines political society to the realization of the common good of the community. Thus, any law which infringes on the supernatural sphere or violates the common good of the community is invalid. A further restriction on civil authority is the specific character of the social contract by which the people created that society.

Although emphasizing the popular origin of sovereignty, Suárez argues that the granting of power to the prince is not a delegation, but a quasi-alienation. In answer to the contention of his celebrated adversary, King James I of England—who reasoned that if the people could delegate power to the prince, they could also revoke it, a prospect that James I found abhorrent—Suárez replied:

> In effect, after the people have transferred sovereignty to the
> king, they cannot, basing themselves on that sovereignty, with

justice recover their liberty on any occasion that they wish to. . . . At some later time the people will not be allowed to take away that authority nor to recover their freedom once more, even though the king might have originally derived his authority from the hands of the people either through a donation or a contract. After the people conferred power on the king, they deprived themselves of their sovereignty.[13]

Yet Suárez's defense of monarchical power did not exclude people's right to depose a legitimate king who had so grossly abused his power that he had become a tyrant:

And for the same reason, if the king converted his legitimate authority into tyranny, abusing his power with manifest harm to the people, they may use their power derived from natural law to defend themselves, since they never deprived themselves of that power. . . . But the entire commonwealth could rise against a tyrant. In such a case there would not really be sedition. The reason for this is that then the entire commonwealth would be superior to the king. Having given him power, they did so supposedly on the condition that he would govern politically and not tyrannically. If he did not do so, then the entire commonwealth could depose him.[14]

The Comunero Revolution produced no self-conscious political theorists. The men of 1781 were seeking the redress of specific political, constitutional, and fiscal grievances. In the public proclamations of the leadership, in "our royal decree," and in the text of the capitulations of Zipaquirá there hovers a spirit of diluted and popularized Suárecismo.[15] There is clearly implicit the notion that New Granada constituted a *corpus mysticum politicum* with its own traditions, whose end was to achieve the common good of the whole community. That common good, according to the men of 1781, was being grossly violated by the innovations of Charles III's ministers. The men of 1781 never appealed to the *nación* or the *patria*. The community, *el común*, a term that the leaders invariably used in their public proclamations, had the right to protest—hence the phrase that came to describe the movement, the Comuneros. Deeply embedded in the documents of the time is the notion of classical Spanish political theory, that the spirit of the *corpus mysticum politicum* of New Granada required some form of popular approval for new taxation and that unjust laws were invalid.

However different the aims of the Comuneros of New Granada were from those of the Comuneros of Castile who revolted against Charles V in 1521, both movements shared the same definition of the terms *común* and *comunidad* as the common good of all groups in the whole society.[16] The movement in New Granada, however, was no conscious emulation of its predecessor in Castile. In two different and totally disconnected crises an appeal was launched invoking the common good of the whole community. Long subsequent to the Comuneros of Castile that tradition was popularized by the classic Spanish theologians in the sixteenth and seventeenth centuries, and it still held sway in New Granada as late as 1781.

Monarchical sentiments had deep roots. The king was still the fountainhead of justice. But though the king was just, his ministers, in particular the regent visitor general, were tyrants against whom it was licit to offer armed resistance. Their policies were a flagrant violation of the common good of the community.[17]

Whether some of the Comunero leaders had read the texts of the classical political theorists of Spain is unprovable. That they were indirectly influenced by these doctrines is highly probable. The political theorists of Old Spain, on the level of high abstraction, and the generation of 1781 in New Granada, on the level of political activism, both came to grips with a central issue of political theory and practice: how to reconcile reverence for constituted political authority with the right of subjects to resist injustice.

7

A Utopia for the Indians: The Resguardos

It seems safe to conclude that no ethnic group in the society of New Granada was more profoundly dissatisfied than were the Indians. Moreover, in no area was the distress more acute than in the provinces of Santa Fe de Bogotá, Tunja, Vélez, and Sogamoso, which then included most of the present departments of Cundinamarca, Boyacá, Santander, and Santander del Norte.

Cundinamarca and Boyacá were the home of the preconquest Chibchas. Considerable controversy exists about the size of the preconquest population, but at the time of the conquest this area contained a dense Indian population, variously estimated at between 300,000 and 562,510 people.[1] By 1564 the population of the province of Tunja had declined to between 111,158 and 168,440 Indians.[2] The decline continued. Two well-documented visitas of some eighty-five Indian villages in the province of Tunja, one in 1635–36 and the other in 1755, indicate Indian populations of 42,334 and 22,543 respectively.[3] In 1778, the combined populations of the provinces of Santa Fe and Tunja amounted to 357,828 people, of whom only 68,881 were Indians.[4] These figures indicate that the rate of decline was much more severe in the sixteenth century than in the following two centuries, but a drop of some 47 percent between 1636 and 1755 suggests that the Indian community was living in a state of continuous societal demoralization.

Habsburg policy aimed to provide some paternalistic protection to the Indians, but a wide gap separated the crown's intentions from actual developments. The crown and its agents sought a compromise between protecting the natives and assuring the colonists of a plentiful and cheap supply of native labor. Between 1595 and 1642 the audiencia in Bogotá carried out a policy that was simultaneously adopted in many other kingdoms of the Indies. Substantial tracts of potentially fertile land in the provinces of Santa Fe, Tunja, Vélez, and Sogamoso were set aside as Indian communities. The Indians did not hold these resguardos, reserved lands, in fee simple, for the crown retained the ownership as part of its regalian rights, and in theory could increase or diminish the size of the resguardos. The Indians, however, did enjoy the usufruct. With the products of these lands, they would be able to pay their annual tribute taxes, to defray the costs of religious instruction and, it was hoped, create viable and prosperous communities. In order to protect the Indians, royal legislation forbade non-Indians from living in areas reserved for the Indians. Nor were the Indians allowed to lease their community lands to Spaniards, creoles, or mestizos.[5]

In order to meet the labor demands of the non-Indian groups, the Indians were required to offer their labor services for hire. The guiding principles were compulsion and rotation. About one-fourth of the tributary population at any one time was employed for nominal wages in mining, public works, or agriculture. The caciques, their eldest sons, and most of the officeholders were exempt, but it was their responsibility to provide the Indians. Similar systems of paid, quota, compulsory labor emerged in other parts of the Indies. In Peru it was the *mita,* in Mexico the *repartimiento,* and in the Philippines it was the *polo.* In New Granada this arrangement was called *mitayos agrícolas* or *mitayos concertados.* Forced labor, the mita, evidently came to an end around 1740 in the Chibcha areas, later in the south. But so-called free contract labor, the *concertados*—often nothing more than a disguised form of debt peonage—survived into the nineteenth century.[6] Although mitayos were legally obligated to work for a specified time span varying from two to ten months, many Indians continued to work permanently for their employers. This fact, of course, contributed to the gradual depopulation of the resguardos.

On October 15, 1754, King Ferdinand VI reaffirmed the crown's traditional policy of providing paternalistic protection via segregation, but with some significant modifications. Fiscal considerations were now more important. Land titles were to be reexamined to see if they were legally in order. All lands whose title of ownership could not be documented were to be sold by the royal treasury. Unoccupied lands belonging to the regalia of the crown might be sold by the exchequer in order to help defray the rising costs of imperial defense.[7]

In response to these royal directives the audiencia commissioned Oidor Andrés Verdugo y Oquendo to conduct a visita, an inspection, of the provinces of Tunja and Vélez. The inspection tour lasted nearly two years. On May 7, 1757, the oidor wrote a detailed report in which he stressed the sociodemographic and socioethnic revolution that had taken place since the visita of 1635–36. Not only had the Indian population greatly declined, but the other ethnic groups composed a population of some 59,323.[8] Clearly the policy of segregation had broken down, as whites, mestizos, and mulattos lived side by side with the Indians. The Indians themselves had become Spanish-speaking—the visitor had no need to use native interpreters.

In the northern portion of the province, specifically the area of San Gil and Socorro, which the judge did not visit, the demographic changes were even more dramatic. The preconquest population in the north was never as dense as it was in the south. By the 1760's the Indian population had virtually disappeared under the combined impact of epidemic disease and miscegenation.

Oidor Verdugo also reported that in violation of the law the Indians were renting to non-Indians large portions of their resguardo lands. He pointed out that these community lands were potentially fertile, but that the Indians apparently were unwilling or unable to exploit efficiently their holdings. They did not, for example, raise cattle.[9] Not only did cattle raising require less labor, but also the Indians had sufficient capital to acquire herds. There was apparently something in their lifestyle and value systems that discouraged them from engaging in potentially profitable pastoral activity. In the plains, the llanos lying east of the Andes, the Indians did raise cattle. The Indians in the Sierra were content with a modest rent, which was sufficient to pay their tribute taxes with something left over for their communal fiestas. The failure of the Indians to cultivate profitably their community lands was perhaps in part due to their declining population. Moreover, Indian labor was drained away from the resguardos by continuous *mestizaje,* and by the concertado system of recruiting Indians for work on non-Indian lands.

Expressing contempt for the inability, or the unwillingness of the Indians to develop the lands that they already possessed, Oidor Verdugo extolled the industry and the skill with which white and mestizo farmers had developed the resguardo lands that they had illegally rented. He recommended that the audiencia make de jure what had taken place de facto. The size of the resguardo lands should be drastically reduced to conform with the smaller Indian population. All the whites and mestizos renting resguardo lands should be given titles in fee simple in exchange for a modest payment to the royal treasury, as a measure of security and a reward for their productive labor. While the Indians should be provided with sufficient land to meet their basic needs, they should be deprived of those holdings that they could not efficiently cultivate.

Oidor Verdugo pointed out that the new settlers were not carving out large and inefficient estates. They were, for the most part, either immigrants from the peninsula, creoles, or mestizos—the latter becoming increasingly numerous during the course of the eighteenth century. The mestizos, who tenaciously refused to be considered Indians so as to avoid having to pay the tribute tax, passed themselves off as Indians in order to lease resguardo lands, and thus had the best of both worlds.

Oidor Verdugo actually moved few Indians off their community lands. What he did do, however, was to expose to the authorities in clear and precise language the nature of the changes that had taken place in the provinces of Santa Fe, Vélez, Sogamoso, and Tunja since 1636. A wholesale resettlement of the resguardo population was not attempted until the 1770's, when Fiscal Moreno y Escandón, in his capacity as protector of the Indians, under orders from Spain began to take a census of the Indians in the province of Tunja and to reduce and consolidate the number of Indian villages accordingly.

Under the vigorous supervision of Corregidor Campuzano y Lanz, scores of Indians were resettled.[10] Where formerly there had been sixty villages, now there were twenty-seven. The suppressed Indian villages became "Spanish parishes." The Indians reacted with bitter dismay. Deeply attached to the lands which their ancestors had cultivated for generations, they saw resettlement as, in effect, exile. A case in point is the pueblo of Sogamoso, where the Indian population did not exceed 700, and where the number of non-Indians had increased from 2,112 in 1755 to 3,246 by 1777. The Indians were resettled in the small village of Paita, but under conditions of hardship and privation, according to the testimony of the local parish priest.[11]

The anguished protests of the Indians of Sogamoso-Paita were repeated time and time again, and the fiscal himself met with criticism within the bureaucracy. In response to this controversy, Viceroy Flores requested the opinion of the all-powerful regent visitor general. On February 3, 1780, Gutiérrez de Piñeres handed down a lengthy formal judgment that constitutes one of the great state documents of that controversial bureaucrat.[12] The main thrust of his argument was to reject the goals and the procedures of the resguardo consolidation, and to opt for a modified form of Habsburg paternalism. Gutiérrez de Piñeres advocated the continuation of segregation, if the Indians were already isolated. In those localities where the races were mingled, this fact should be accepted. He did not reverse the sale of resguardo lands undertaken by Moreno and Campuzano, but he prohibited further sales. The Indians should be given assurance that they would continue to enjoy, under the protection of the crown, the usufruct of their remaining community lands. These policy recommendations were formalized in a cedula of Charles III on August 2, 1780.[13]

The regent visitor general's compromise won him only enemies. The active participation of the Indians in the upheaval of 1781 was due in large measure to their bitter opposition to the policy of Moreno and Campuzano, and this repudiation of their policy evidently came too late to appease the wrath of the Indians. Archbishop Viceroy Caballero y Góngora, with his acute awareness of the need to mold public opinion, was later to adopt the policy of Gutiérrez de Piñeres with considerable success. In any event Indian discontent, deep though it was, was far less causally significant in 1781 than the unrest among the creoles and the mestizos.

From the whole complicated issue of the resguardos, certain conclusions can be drawn. The decline of the Indian population, the labor demands of the whites, the increase in the white and mestizo populations and the process of mestizaje were decisive factors to which the imperial bureaucracy could only adjust, and which it could not truly control. But it is somewhat of an oversimplification to claim that local conditions altogether determined events. It is plausible that they often may have been more significant than the directives of the central authorities, but the royal bureaucracy always remained a basic factor in the equation of decision making. What often emerged was a mutually acceptable compromise between central directives and local conditions.

The Gutiérrez de Piñeres–Caballero y Góngora compromise is a classic example of how New Granada was actually governed in the eighteenth century. All sides received something; the elites, of course, much more than the rest. Creole-mestizo land hunger was significantly but not totally appeased in that their pre-1778 encroachments on Indian community lands were legalized. Yet the Indians received a guarantee of their remaining lands, which were not inconsiderable. And the royal law courts honored that guarantee, as long as the king of Spain reigned over New Granada.

The issue is somewhat misfocused by the assertion that Charles III and his ministers had in effect abandoned the policy of social justice for the Indians. Such a claim overlooks the return, after 1778, to a modified form of Habsburg paternalism whose real author was Gutiérrez de Piñeres.[14] This policy was continued by all succeeding viceroys.

The drive to eliminate the resguardos was led by the creole elites in alliance with the mestizos and those who sympathized with their aspirations in the audiencia prior to 1778.[15] Although the Comuneros made significant concessions to alleviate the deep distress among the Indians, they in fact sought to complete what the audiencia had begun. The seventh clause of the capitulations of Zipaquirá advocated that the remaining resguardos be divided up with each Indian being given title in fee simple to his share.[16] The Indians would be allowed to sell their lands—something which Habsburg legislation adamantly prohibited. Such a proposal meant that within a very short time white and mestizo farmers would acquire all the remaining resguardos by "purchase." The same proposal was repeated again in 1810 by the creole-dominated junta of Bogotá.[17]

Thanks to the decision of Gutiérrez de Piñeres and Caballero y Góngora to return to a modified paternalism, a significant number of resguardos survived into the republican period. The decisive break occurred on October 11, 1821, when the congress of Cúcuta picked up where the framers of the capitulations of Zipaquirá had left off. They decreed that all the remaining resguardos be distributed to the Indians in small parcels with titles in fee simple.[18] Within a generation these community lands disappeared in the old province of Tunja, although some survived in the south until the present century.

Now attention should be focused on the contrasts and similarities among four examples of Indian unrest—Peru, Tunja, Quito, and the llanos of New Granada.

8

A Utopia for the Indians:
Indians in Revolt

Túpac Amaru II of Peru

The deep-seated unrest in the provinces of Santa Fe, Vélez, Sogamoso, and Tunja in the New Kingdom of Granada finds both a parallel and a foil in what happened in Peru. There, in November of 1780, the sierra burst into rebellion under the leadership of José Gabriel Condorcanqui Noguera Túpac Amaru.[1] He claimed to be and was regarded as the direct descendant of doña Juana Pilcorvaco, daughter of the last Inca monarch, Túpac Amaru I, who was executed in the main square of Cuzco in 1572. He is better known in history as Túpac Amaru II.

The rebellion of Túpac Amaru was actually the second of two unconnected revolts in Peru in 1780. Beginning in January, the creoles and mestizos of the cities of Peru expressed their bitter dissatisfaction with the fiscal innovations introduced by Charles III's visitor general, José Antonio Areche; these were, of course, part of the same grand design that Gutiérrez de Piñeres was to implement in New Granada. Disorders erupted in Arequipa, Tarma, La Paz, Cochabamba, and Cuzco. Although some Indians participated, these disturbances were essentially antitax protests led by the creole noblesse de la robe, who rallied around the procreole viceroy, Manuel de Guirior. Establishment of *aduanas* (customs houses), increases in some sales taxes, imposition of a head tax on the mestizos—a tax identified with the Indians whom they scorned as their inferiors—provoked riots and vigorous protests, but no real bloodshed. The movement, in fact, was a war of words. A whole series of vulgar lampoons, many more than appeared in New Granada, was read aloud in the squares. A few even insulted the person of Charles III of Spain and had kindly words for Spain's enemy, George III of Great Britain. But the spirit of a majority of the lampoons was that of the traditional slogan, "Long live the king and death to bad government." The lampoons assailed with lusty wrath the new taxes and the tax collectors, who were denounced as public thieves, yet still expressed a deep-rooted, if primitive faith, that the king would redress the just grievances of his suffering subjects.

The revolt that broke out in November, 1780, had in actual fact very little connection with the protests of the creoles. But the coincidence in timing had disastrous consequences for its instigator, Túpac Amaru.

By birth a mestizo, Túpac Amaru lived in two worlds, the Hispano-Indian and the creole-Spanish. Well educated in the Spanish manner, married to a criolla, living a life of ostentation in the creole style, he had sought during the 1770's to act as a spokesman for the Indian community inside the norms of the colonial power structure in Lima. Hereditary cacique of Pampamarca, Tungasuca, and Surimana, he had sought relief for his people from some of the more vexatious burdens placed upon them—an end to the authority of the corrupt and arbitrary corregidores de Indios, relief from the forced labor of the mita system. He was rebuffed by the visitor general and ordered home to his estates. Here in November, 1780, he raised the standard of revolt.

A term that has been used in the context of Europeanized Africans in the twentieth century might apply also to Túpac Amaru. He was a marginal man caught between two cultures, a victim of "mutilated legacies." The tension between these two heritages exploded as a consequence of the disdainful treatment of the visitor general. He felt rejected by the Spanish creole world to which he felt he belonged, and he returned to the Indian world which was also his legacy. Pledging his loyalty to the king and to the church, Túpac Amaru sought to form a coalition of Indians, mestizos, creoles, and blacks against the hated chapetones. But he made two tragic miscalculations. The Indian plebeians, embittered by centuries of exploitation, were not responsive to the highly hispanized Túpac Amaru's integrationist program. Furthermore, by November, 1780, a good deal of the dissatisfaction of the creoles and mestizos had been appeased by timely concessions made by the Spanish authorities in Lima, and Túpac Amaru's appeals fell on deaf ears. In that multi-ethnic and plural society, it was improbable that large numbers of creoles and mestizos would join an Indian-led movement, in any event. Whiteness of skin was a major determinant of social prestige, and both the creoles and the mestizos felt an inherent sense of superiority to the Indians. Widespread destruction of property and the Indian plebeians' hatred of all non-Indians raised the specter of social revolution in which the privileges of the non-Indian groups might be swept away. The choice between an Indian-led social revolution and the maintenance of the Spanish colonial status quo was no choice for the creoles and the mestizos.

The Indian revolution did not end with the capture and the execution of Túpac Amaru on May 15, 1781—indeed it lasted in some areas for nearly three more years. But its failure was predestined. The only recipe that held some realistic promise of success was a grand coalition of all the ethnic groups against the European Spaniards.

New Granada, in this respect, represents a sharp foil to Peru. A multi-ethnic coalition did emerge for the first time in Spanish America. Demographic patterns largely explain this result. As was observed in the last chapter, the Indians in the provinces of Santa Fe, Vélez, Sogamoso, and Tunja were small minorities with the overwhelming bulk of the population consisting of whites and mixed groups. Indians never could aspire to lead a protest movement; the best that they could hope for was that their grievances would be included in a broader coalition led by the creole elites and their subordinate allies, the mestizos. In New Granada they were very junior partners, whose influence over the direction of events was not negligible but was limited.[2] Furthermore, the drastic decline of the Indian population in the provinces of Santa Fe and Tunja diminished the socio-economic bases of cacique influence. For this reason the effectiveness of Indian leadership in New Granada was much inferior to that in Peru.

By contrast, the Indian population in the sierra of Peru was still dense and compact; in many areas the Indians far outnumbered the non-Indians. Throughout Peru, the Indians, although declining in numbers, constituted a comfortable majority of the total population—in 1792, 608,894 Indians as against 467,228 non-Indians. Hence, the grievances of the Indians in Peru and New Granada sharply differed.

In Peru the Indians were bitter about the exactions of the corregidores de Indios and forced labor in the mines. In New Granada, the principal sources of unrest were twofold: the reduction of the community lands, the resguardos, and a fear of absorption into the non-Indian community—of a loss of identity as Indians.

Such was not the case in Peru, where the survival of the Indians as a group was not in question and Indians and non-Indians rarely lived together in the same localities as they did in New Granada. In New Granada, the Indians were Spanish-speaking; Quechua and Aymara vigorously survived as languages of the hearth in upper and lower Peru.

One Indian group was fighting for its survival in Peru. The class of hereditary Indian chiefs who claimed descent from preconquest royalty and nobility was still numerous and still functioned as a recognizable social group. But over the eighteenth century a whole network of pressures was undermining their economic and social position: the steady decline in Peru's economy as Mexico replaced her as the most lucrative source of silver in the Spanish empire; the continuing decline of the Indian population; the gradual stripping away from Lima of the immense administrative jurisdiction and bureaucratic monopoly of trade she had enjoyed. Added to all these factors was the innate distrust of the Caroline bureaucrats for hereditary privilege, which the caciques personified.

They were the modest beneficiaries of the colonial status quo. The preservation of the system was to their advantage. These hereditary chieftains, however, had to maneuver between the triple pressures exercised by the imperial bureaucracy, their desire for self-enrichment at the expense of their subordinates, and the discontents of the Indian plebeians. Only under conditions of acute stress did they abandon the Spanish cause for armed rebellion. One of those rare occasions, of course, was in 1780. But even then, in spite of the deterioration of the larger economy and the subsequent corrosion of their modest privileges, a large minority, some twenty caciques, embraced the Spanish cause. Their support significantly contributed to the defeat of Túpac Amaru.

In Peru there was a highly polarized situation, with the result that the revolution of Túpac Amaru became a race war of Indians against non-Indians. In New Granada, the salient factors combined to make a multi-ethnic coalition possible, and that coalition determined two basic aspects of the movement. In the first place, Indian demands were much less radical than in Peru. Secondly, the most extraordinary aspect of the Comunero Revolution was the notable absence of violence. It was *una revolución bien limpia.* Only a handful of people actually lost their lives in the shouting and screaming in the town squares. There were only two battles. At Puente Real de Vélez, for example, no lives were lost. Very little sacking of private property took place, leaving aside the burning of tobacco and the dumping of aguardiente, both of which belonged to the royal monopolies. In Peru, on the other hand, violence predominated. Several pitched battles occurred, with considerable loss of life; massive looting of private property was frequent. In Peru and Bolivia as many as 100,000 Indians may have lost their lives.

The Comunero Revolution would have taken place whether Peru was quiet or not. The grievances in New Granada were very deep-rooted. I noted in chapter 5 that the outbreak of revolution in Peru during November, 1780, had an indirect influence on the eruption of violence in Socorro the following March 15, 1781, but although the false rumor that Túpac Amaru had actually taken Cuzco and Lima evidently encouraged, it did not in itself cause, the plebeians to riot and the local elites to observe sullen neutrality during the critical month between March 16 and April 16.

It may seem paradoxical that the example of Túpac Amaru apparently exercised more influence over the creoles and the mestizos than it did on the Indians of the provinces of Santa Fe and Tunja. Ill-informed as they were, the creoles and mestizos of New Granada saw the events in Peru as an uprising against the king's ministers rather than a rebellion of the Indians. The paradox diminishes considerably in the face of the fact that the descendants of the Chibchas needed no Peruvian model of preconquest royalty around which to rally. They had their own indigenous monarchical symbol in the person of don Ambrosio Pisco, a direct descendant of the preconquest caciques of Bogotá.

Before turning to the sad and strange career of Ambrosio Pisco, something should be said about what did not take place in the audiencia-kingdom of Quito, for that nonevent provides a sharp contrast to both Peru and New Granada.

Quito, flanked on the south by Peru and on the north by New Granada, was strangely and remarkably tranquil during the tumultuous year of 1781. José García de León y Pizarro, president, regent, and visitor general of the audiencia of Quito, was understandably nervous. He complained about intrigues and discontents in the audiencia on the part of certain creole oidores, but no disturbances in the streets took place. He did assert that the capitulations of Zipaquirá had a more disquieting effect in Quito than did the sanguinary revolution of Túpac Amaru.[3] All of which suggests that whatever superficial unrest existed was confined to a small circle of upper-class creole bureaucrats.

The still dense Indian population was passive. One plausible explanation is that during the course of the eighteenth century there had been a chain of local Indian uprisings, possibly triggered by the decline of the *obrajes* (textile sweatshops).[4] Indian discontent may have been as acute in Quito as it was to the south and to the north, but the frustrations of the natives had gradually dissipated themselves in a long series of local revolts, whereas in Peru and in New Granada, discontent was concentrated in one massive burst of rage.

In 1765 Quito had a major riot of its own, when the royal monopoly of aguardiente was introduced. The rioters were plebeians. The authorities accused several prominent creole landowners of retiring to their estates and simply remaining neutral. Although the crowds captured the aguardiente headquarters, their attempt to storm and to capture the royal palace in the main square was thwarted by European Spaniards, some of them mere youths.[5] In response to the riot, the authorities could only opt initially, at least, for a prudent policy of conciliatory retreat. Within a year, however, the aguardiente monopoly was restored after the arrival of a contingent of troops from Lima.

Quito's antimonopoly riot, as early as 1765, was a warning to the authorities of the desirability of strengthening the military force in being. Bogotá, on the other hand, had no such warning. León y Pizarro, Gutiérrez de Piñeres's peer in Quito, was a firm partisan of the notion that military reorganization should precede the introduction of fiscal changes. So was

Viceroy Flores in Bogotá, but Gutiérrez de Piñeres flatly rejected this view. When the Comunero Revolution in New Granada broke out in the spring of 1781, the only garrison of professional troops in the provinces of Santa Fe and Tunja consisted of a corporal's guard of about 75 soldiers stationed in the capital. There were no functioning provincial militias. León y Pizarro, on the other hand, had a well-disciplined force of some 2,610 soldiers in the sierra and 1,540 troops stationed in Guayaquil. Allan J. Kuethe has suggested that while no direct relationship can be proved between military preparation and domestic tranquility, there is a striking correlation between the two. In the district of Popayán in southern New Granada, where a partial military reorganization had already taken place, there were no popular disturbances.[6]

Hence the explanation, if only partial, for Quito's tranquility lies in the interaction of three conditions: (1) the dissipation of Indian discontent over a long period of time in a series of local revolts, (2) the rum riot of 1765, and (3) the reorganization of the military.

Don Ambrosio Pisco, Prince of Bogotá and Lord of Chía

Nothing more dramatically exemplifies the sharp contrasts between the Indian uprisings in Peru and New Granada than the personalities and the careers of Túpac Amaru II and Ambrosio Pisco, the titular leader of the Indians of the provinces of Santa Fe, Tunja, Vélez, and Sogamoso. Both men claimed to be and were regarded as the descendants of preconquest royalty. Each also had Spanish forebears, making him a mestizo. Both had modest fortunes derived primarily from mule trains for transporting merchandise. Here the parallels end. Ambrosio Pisco was a very successful businessman who demonstrated no interest in politics until he was caught up in the dramatic events of the spring of 1781. Túpac Amaru, on the other hand, had spent fifteen years as the self-appointed spokesman of the Indian community before he chose the path of revolution in 1780.

The then fiscal of the audiencia, Francisco Antonio Moreno y Escandón, had in the late 1770's urged Pisco to assume an active role of leadership in the Indian community, but Pisco preferred to dedicate himself to business ventures.[7] Unquestionably the fiscal hoped that Pisco's intervention might tranquilize the already restless Indians, who were resentful of his policy of consolidating the resguardos.

Indian though Pisco was, his fortune was far greater than that of a majority of the socially superior creoles who led the movement. In Güepsa, where he ordinarily lived, he owned a well-stocked ranch of cattle and mules, and was also the administrator of the tobacco and aguardiente monopolies, a post that was usually reserved for a wealthy or socially prominent citizen. In

Moniquirá and on the calle real in Bogotá he owned profitable dry goods stores. In addition, he operated packs of mule trains to transport goods.[8] His whole career had been devoted to agriculture and commerce, in which he had accumulated a solid fortune. His last known letter, written shortly before his death while in exile in Cartagena, concerned a debt of ten pesos.[9]

His paternal grandfather, don Luis Pisco, and his elder brother, don Ignacio Pisco, had been hereditary caciques of Bogotá. Don Ambrosio's wife, his first cousin, was also a granddaughter of don Luis Pisco.[10] The Piscos traced their ancestry back to the preconquest royalty of the Chibchas and enjoyed considerable respect throughout the whole area over which the Chibchas had once ruled. During the colonial period they occupied dual positions. As caciques of Bogotá, they held a title whose legitimacy derived from their Chibcha royal ancestors. They also frequently served as governors of Chía.[11] Before the conquest the heir to the Chibcha throne bore the title of lord of Chía, a town located about fifteen miles north of Bogotá. In postconquest times, however, the governor of Chía was a bureaucrat appointed by, and responsible to, the local corregidor. The last cacique of Bogotá to maintain the pomp and prestige of the title was Ambrosio Pisco's grandfather, don Luis. Wealthy and elegant, he lived in a manner sufficiently grand to impress both his Indian followers and some Spanish observers.[12] But by 1781 the cacicazgo had diminished to a few very small villages near the capital.

In contrast to Peru, where the Indian nobility was still wealthy and numerous, the caciques as such had virtually disappeared by 1781 in the provinces of Santa Fe and Tunja.[13] Ambrosio Pisco, for example, still retained wealth, not because he was a cacique, but because he lived as if he were a creole or a mestizo.

Ambrosio Pisco had only two qualifications for leadership. One was the accident of his ancestry.[14] The other was his substantial fortune, which inspired confidence among both the creoles and the Indians. The more one contemplates his brief if pathetic career, the more he appears to have been caught in a sequence of events beyond his control. He was drafted for the role of titular leader of the Indians, not once but twice—by both the creoles and the Indians. The character of those two drafts will throw a good deal of light on the nature of both the Indian revolution on one hand and the multi-ethnic coalition on the other.

In the spring of 1781 Ambrosio Pisco was forty-four years old.[15] On the first Sunday after Easter, Comunero troops from Socorro arrived in his native village of Güepsa. A riot occurred on the usual pattern, in which the royal monopoly's tobacco was burned and the aguardiente was poured out of the casks into the streets. Ambrosio Pisco's response was typical of many of the well-to-do in his time. Bewildered, he went into hiding at the residence of the local parish priest. On his own initiative Pisco then went to Puente Real de Vélez to pledge his loyalty to the cause of the king by offering his services to Oidor Osorio and to Corregidor Campuzano. He promised to supply the oidor with mules, horses, and beef. Good businessman that he was, he looked forward to a solid profit. After returning to Güepsa to fulfill his contract, he received several disquieting threats from Comunero captains that if he did not join them, he would be murdered and his property confiscated. Concealing some of his movable goods in the residence of the parish priest, he again went into hiding. On May 7 his wife received a letter from the Comunero captains, Pedro Fabio de Archila, Melchor de Rueda, and Sergeant Pimentel, threatening both his property and his life if he did not join them in laying siege to the beleaguered forces of Oidor Osorio in Puente Real. Thoroughly intimidated, Ambrosio Pisco joined the Comunero cause, and returned to Puente Real. He claimed that he did not participate actively in the riots that led to the surrender of Osorio.[16] The victory of Puente Real converted a minor regional rebellion in the Socorro area into a much more formidable threat.

While in Puente Real, Ambrosio Pisco was proclaimed a captain of the "enterprise." Thus began the process by which the Comunero leadership drafted him as the titular leader of the Indian contingent of their coalition. What began at Puente Real was subsequently completed in Zipaquirá by Juan Francisco Berbeo.

The captain returned to his village of Güepsa, obviously unhappy and reluctant in his new political role. Summoning up all his courage, which was not limitless, he disregarded the threats of the Comunero leaders, and left Güepsa for Bogotá with a mule train loaded with cotton, cloth, and sugar. He evidently wanted to escape to the capital from the pressures that were building up around him.[17] If this were his desire, it was unfortunate that he did not flee to Bogotá without his mule train loaded with merchandise. But apparently he could not resist the temptation to turn a few pesos.

En route to the capital, at Boquerón de Simijaca, the Indians hailed him as their leader with delirious enthusiasm. They compelled Pisco to make what became a triumphant march through the Indian villages of Susa, Ubaté, and Nemocón until he reached Zipaquirá. Everywhere the Indians greeted him with drums, skyrockets, and bugles. In some localities the excited natives kissed the stirrup of his horse and hailed him as an angel sent by God to deliver them from oppression. They proclaimed him "prince of Bogotá" and "lord of Chía."[18] The long-suffering Indians perceived Ambrosio Pisco as a savior, although he saw himself merely as a merchant and a farmer.

Hesitantly he stepped into his new political role. He was persuaded to sign a letter with the dual title of prince of Bogotá and lord of Chía by the false argument that his grandfather had so styled himself.[19] Indian caciques enjoyed several honors, including the right to use the title of *don* and all the other privileges traditionally accorded to hidalgos of Castile. Caciques, however, were specifically prohibited from using the title of *señor,* let alone *príncipe,* for in Spanish jurisprudence both terms clearly denoted political sovereignty.[20]

In Ubaté the Spanish authorities accused Ambrosio Pisco of ordering the Indians not to pay the annual tribute tax. Pisco claimed in his defense that the original order came not from him, but from José Antonio Galán, who had passed through the village a few days earlier. All he had done was to confirm Galán's order until the audiencia decided otherwise.[21]

Pisco roundly denied the charge brought against him by the fiscal of the audiencia, Manuel Silvestre Martínez, that he had promised the Indians the restoration of their ancestral salt mines in Nemocón—expropriated a few years earlier—"even if it cost him his fortune and his life." Pleading for fair treatment of the natives, he admitted that he expressed to the Indians in Nemocón his hope that the audiencia would restore the salt mines to the Indians.[22] Accused by the fiscal of demanding tribute from the Indians, Pisco argued that it had been voluntarily offered on several occasions.[23]

Events were pushing the reluctant merchant into taking more aggressively his new political role. During the month of June, after the conclusion of the capitulations of Zipaquirá, he made a formal request to the audiencia to be recognized as the legal successor of his grandfather and his brother as cacique of Bogotá. In his petition to the audiencia, he implicitly staked out a claim for the leadership of the whole Chibcha area, asking that the jurisdiction of the cacicazgo be extended to include the provinces of Santa Fe, Tunja, Vélez, and Sogamoso.[24] Although Pisco ostensibly made the request in his own name, the real initiative came from both the Indians and the creole leadership of the Comunero movement.

The Indians wanted a chieftain, a kinglet if you will, with preconquest claims to legitimacy, who would be their spokesman and their leader. They drafted Ambrosio Pisco as their savior. The creoles needed an effective but pliable leader for the Indian contingent in their multi-ethnic coalition. They were well aware of the deep-seated dissatisfactions in the Indian community. They did not discount, and they probably exaggerated, the possibility that this unrest would lead to violence, destruction of private property, and even a more general social upheaval. Ambrosio Pisco was for them an ideal candidate as titular leader of the Indians. He was enthusiastically accepted by the Indians; he was a hispanized Indian who had no real political drive, and in fact proved to be a tractable instrument for channeling the wrath of the Indians.

During the hectic weeks preceding the signing of the capitulations of Zipaquirá on June 7, Pisco lent yeoman service in preventing Indian discontent from overflowing into violence. That the irate Indians did not engage in massive pillage and looting is largely due to his efforts.[25] A man of property, whose lifestyle was that of a white man and who possessed no real commitment to politics, don Ambrosio could play no other role than that of a pacifier.

Hence, the cooptation of Ambrosio Pisco by the creoles which began in Puente Real reached its completion in Zipaquirá. During the frenzied negotiations there, where the crowds yelled and screamed outside the parish priest's residence, Ambrosio Pisco dutifully acted as the titular spokesman for the Indians. The capitulations did contain some significant concessions to appease their discontent, but evidently creole leadership, and not Pisco, determined their scope and content.[26]

In summary, the revolution of the Indians of the provinces of Santa Fe, Tunja, Vélez, and Sogamoso was profoundly traditionalist. Although the legitimacy of Ambrosio Pisco rested on his descent from preconquest royalty, the Indians did not seek to repudiate hispanic culture. They did not reject the church nor its ministers to whom they were deeply, if superstitiously, attached, although they did protest against some exactions imposed on them by the clergy. They demanded the return of their resguardos and salt mines which had been granted to them by Spanish authorities centuries before. Above all else, they desperately yearned to retain their identity as an autonomous community inside that multi-ethnic society. Their protest was not against hispanic society in which they lived. Rather, they were demanding that the society live up to the principles that it professed.[27]

Rebellion in the Plains

In the hot lowland plains beginning at the foothills of the eastern cordillera of the Andes, *los llanos orientales,* a more radical Indian revolution took place in 1781. The province of Los Llanos de Santiago de las Atalayas lay east of the cordillera, northeast of the city of Tunja, and southeast of Socorro. The key variable in determining the traditionalist or the radical nature of these uprisings is the degree to which the natives were hispanized.

Until the second half of the eighteenth century, the llanos had been isolated from the valleys in the sierra, and there were very few Spanish colonists. These hot lowland plains, subject to frequent floods, began to be linked to the economy of the highlands when a road was opened through Cáqueza which enabled the lean cattle of the tropical plains to be exported to the highlands. Several profitable cattle ranches developed by the Jesuits before their expulsion in 1767 were sold at auction by the audiencia to affluent creoles from Bogotá. Among the purchasers was the rich and controversial marquis of San Jorge de Bogotá. He, in fact, helped to finance the

expedition, led by José Antonio Villalonga, which restored Spanish hege-
mony over the area after the Comunero revolt.[28] The governor of the
province in 1781 was don Luis de Caicedo y Flóres Ladrón de Guevara, who
belonged to a prominent clan of creole officeholders in Bogotá.

Rebellion swept through the plains in 1781. The rebels put to flight
Governor Caicedo. His personal property, carried on a mule train escorted by
two priests, was confiscated by a group of hostile Indians. Towns and
settlements such as Pore, Chire, Támara, Ten, Manare, Paya, Cravo, Pista, and
Labranzagrande rose. Fifteen hundred poorly armed Indians were mobilized.
Several white settlers were besieged in their homes. The hostility of the
Indians was directed against white settlers, much of whose property was
destroyed. Not only was the revolution in the plains antiwhite, it was also
ferociously anticlerical. Neither attitude expressed itself among the much
more hispanized Indians of the sierra.[29]

Before 1767 this thinly settled area had been a missionary territory of the
Jesuits. In 1779 the total population of the province amounted to a mere
22,159 persons, of which 14,627 were classified as Indians. There were 1,305
whites, 6,109 mestizos, and some 118 slaves.[30] After the expulsion of the
Society of Jesus, the Dominicans, the Franciscans, and the Augustinians took
their place.[31] The natives were only imperfectly Christianized by the Jesuits,
and their successors were patently ineffective. The neophytes showed acute
hostility to their spiritual mentors. The irate Indians attacked churches and
forced the clergy to flee. They spread the word that their new king, the Inca
Túpac Amaru, would provide them with priests who would not oppress them.
The Indian chieftains told their followers that they did not have to attend
mass or catechismal classes unless they so wished "because the priests cannot
oblige them to do anything."[32] In those localities where the men were away
from their homes engaged in cattle raising, the Indians named women captains. A shocked clergyman lamented:

> Finally this province seems like the confusion of hell. Everyone
> gives orders, everyone contradicts everyone else. One sees and
> hears nothing but crimes, proof of which is the childishness which
> has led them to appoint women captains whose principal activity
> is to mistreat white women.[33]

Although the Indians deposed several white aldermen and alcaldes ordinarios, and forced the governor of the province to flee, the ostensible caudillo
of the rebellion was a rich, white cattle rancher, Francisco Javier de Mendoza.
Mendoza received a commission from the supreme council of war in Socorro,
which obviously hoped to channel Indian discontent. But it is clear the
Indians on the plains were not as tractable as those of the sierra.

Although Captain Francisco Javier de Mendoza complained that he was not personally responsible for the misconduct of the Indians, he probably had more control over his followers than he wanted to admit publicly. Like everyone else in 1781, he was covering his flanks in case the "enterprise" failed. The circumstantial evidence to support this hypothesis comes from two extraordinary events.

The captains general of the small sierra village of Cocuy, in the northern portion of what is now the department of Boyacá, sent a fiery letter to the villages of Támara, Ten, and Manare in the llanos. They invoked the magic name of Túpac Amaru as the newly crowned king of all the Indies:

> We inform you that a new king has been crowned in the Indies. His name is the powerful don Josef Francisco Tupa Amaro [sic]. They say that he is going to do away with all the taxes. We have already rejected the taxes by breaking bottles of aguardiente and burning tobacco. We have seized the revenue of the administrator of the salt mines, and we have returned the money to their owners. Thus, we advise you that if the governor attempts to impose the taxes, do not let him do it. If he tries to punish you, rise up against him. If they do not lift the taxes, we are going to Santa Fe de Bogotá to make war on the Santafereños. If you have not done what we told you to by the time we return, we will make war against you. We inform you that many towns have already risen: the city of Vélez, the town of San Gil, Cocuy, Mogotes, Santa Rosa, and many other localities.[34]

Eight days before, on May 15, in far Cuzco "king" Túpac Amaru had met a cruel death at the hands of the Spanish authorities, but that event, of course, was then unknown in New Granada.

Four weeks later, in the sierra village of Silos, the Inca was again hailed as the monarch of the New World. These two proclamations merit careful analysis, for they reveal how the creole leaders in Socorro and Bogotá were apparently manipulating, to their partisan advantage, Indian discontent.

The Dethronement of Charles III of Spain: The Silos Manifesto

On June 14, 1781, in the tiny village of Silos in the mountains southwest of the city of Pamplona, one of the most extraordinary events in the history of the Spanish empire took place. Charles III, king of Spain and emperor of the Indies, was dethroned, and Túpac Amaru II of Peru was proclaimed Inca and king of all of Spanish South America. In ringing tones the proclamation so read:

> Don José, by the grace of God, Inca, King of Peru, Santa Fe, Quito, Chile, Buenos Aires and the continent, and of the southern

seas, Duke of the highest order, Lord of the Caesars and Amazons, with dominion in Great Paititi, commissioner and distributor of divine charity through our matchless treasury.

My council after extended discussions on many occasions both public and private, has resolved that the kings of Castile have usurped and maintained sovereignty over the dominions of my people for almost three hundred years, leaving me with vassals tormented by taxes, tributes, *sisas* [tax on food products], *lanzas* [tax on titled nobility], military service, custom houses, sales taxes, monopolies, contracts, tithes, fifths, viceroys, audiencias, corregidores, and other ministers. They are all equally tyrannical, selling justice at public auction, to whomever makes the highest bid in the same manner that the office of notary is sold. The ecclesiastical and secular bureaucrats of this kingdom also act in ' this way, killing those whom they could not or did not know how to rob. All of this is worthy of vigorous redress.

Because of the just complaints which often have risen to Heaven itself, I therefore command in the name of the Almighty God that none of the demands for taxes shall be met in any fashion, nor shall the intruding European magistrates be obeyed. Every respect shall be shown to the priests, paying them the tithe and handing over to them the first fruits of our labor, as this is owed to God, as well as the tribute tax and the fifth [mining tax] to their king and natural lord but in due moderation. In order to remedy the situation as quickly as possible and to observe the aforementioned commands, I order that the oath sworn to my royal crown be repeated and published in all cities and localities of my dominion, so that we may be informed of the willing and loyal vassals who should be rewarded as well as those who would deserve punishment, according to the terms of the oath.[35]

This document, with a few minor textual changes, had been found, five weeks before on April 6, in the baggage of Túpac Amaru II after his capture by the Spaniards. In the subsequent trial the prosecuting attorney cited it as evidence that Túpac Amaru was a traitor, whose deliberate purpose was to overthrow the sovereignty of the Spanish crown. One fact is incontrovertible. Túpac Amaru himself never published this manifesto. This fact has led some historians to conclude that the document was a fraud, perpetrated by an overzealous prosecuting attorney in order to nail down his case.[36]

While the authenticity of the manifesto probably can never be conclusively established on the available evidence, the Spaniards did not need to resort to forgery to convict Túpac Amaru. He had committed acts sufficient to justify his execution from a Spanish royalist point of view.

Some historians of the revolution of Túpac Amaru, such as Boleslao Lewin and Daniel Valcárcel, vehemently defend the authenticity of the Silos manifesto. Their enthusiasm, however, derives in large measure from their ardent conviction that Túpac Amaru was an advocate of political independence. [37] They may be right for the wrong reasons. While the authenticity of the document is plausible, it does not necessarily follow that Túpac Amaru favored political emancipation from Spain. While such an extreme step might appeal to the more radical elements among the Indian masses, it would certainly alienate the Indian caciques, not to mention the creoles and the mestizos whom he persistently but vainly courted. A more plausible analysis might be that the Silos manifesto was, in modern terms, a position paper drawn up by a member of Túpac Amaru's entourage—a radical option that he dared not take.

Casting aside the controversial question of authenticity, it is truly baffling that within five weeks this document traveled hundreds of miles from Cuzco to the remote and obscure little village of Silos. One can only speculate, but such speculation leads along just one road. There was collusion in the highest places. The document was not published at the time, for the trial was secret. Túpac Amaru was not sentenced until May 15. The only possible conclusion is that someone with access to the secret records of the ongoing litigation forwarded a copy to someone in Bogotá, who in turn sent it on to Silos.

In chapter 5, something was said about the lines of communication linking Socorro to Bogotá, and Bogotá to Lima. Fiscal Vélez de Guevara y Suescún was not directly involved in the trial of Túpac Amaru, but he had access to all state documents. Even if the fiscal were not the conduit in this particular case, someone equally highly placed in the audiencia of Lima had to serve in that capacity.

The proclamation of Túpac Amaru from Cocuy on May 24 and Silos on June 14 finds a plausible but not provable explanation in the war of nerves that Juan Francisco Berbeo was skillfully conducting to compel the authorities in Bogotá to negotiate a satisfactory settlement. The proclamation of Túpac Amaru in the isolated village of Silos provided Berbeo and his colleagues with a splendid opportunity to reaffirm their loyalty to the king, in sharp distinction to their militant criticism of his ministers. Within four days after the proclamation in Silos, the Comunero captains in Socorro publicly repudiated it as a grave insult to the royal person of Charles III, to whom they reaffirmed their undivided fealty.[38] By June 18, Socorro, of course, had received the news that the capitulations had been signed in Zipaquirá on the previous June 7.

Nor did the creoles need to invoke the name of Túpac Amaru to provide their Indians with a symbolic leader around whom they could rally. Ambrosio

Pisco was there as a pliant instrument of the creoles to channel Indian discontent.

The local leadership in both Cocuy and Silos was made up of men who owed their appointments in large measure to the supreme council of war in Socorro. Neither local captain would, on his own authority, assume the responsibility for authorizing such a bold step as dethroning Charles III. The inference is clear but it cannot be proven. To suggest a bold hypothesis, Berbeo may have planted the two manifestoes in remote and isolated villages in order to send a clear signal to Bogotá. He may have been warning the authorities that unless they made concessions to the moderate creole leadership, the protest would radicalize into a movement to repudiate the authority of the Spanish crown. As will later be observed, such a Machiavellian approach was within Berbeo's grasp: he made several other adroit moves in order to pressure Bogotá to come to terms.

Enough has been said about the origins of the manifesto. What remains to be discussed is its ideological content. One characteristic which leaps to the forefront is its Peruvian "viceregal imperialism."[39] Don José I claims sovereignty over the whole of Spanish South America—Peru, New Granada, Quito, Chile, and Buenos Aires. In historical fact, however, the Inca empire did not extend to New Granada in the north nor to Buenos Aires in the south. Thus, the Inca sovereign seeks to recreate not the boundaries of preconquest times, but rather the frontiers of the viceroyalty of Peru before the jurisdiction was substantially diminished by the creation of the viceroyalties of New Granada in 1739 and Buenos Aires in 1776. The territorial reorganization of Spanish South America, confining the viceroyalty of Peru to what became the republic of Peru, was certainly one factor contributing to the economic decline of Peru during the eighteenth century. The Silos manifesto sought to reverse the viceregal innovations of the Bourbons and to restore the preeminence that Peru enjoyed under the Habsburgs. It is difficult to understand why such a pretension would have any appeal in New Granada.

The fundamental ideological thrust of the manifesto is the traditional image of tyranny well developed by the neoscholastic theologians of sixteenth- and seventeenth-century Spain, the kernel of the argument that a generation later the proponents of independence would develop. For nearly three hundred years Spain had exercised a twofold tyranny, fiscal and bureaucratic, over America, an unjust regime that must be overthrown. The manifesto pointedly accused the Spanish regime of venality, and rejected the central myth of the king as the fountainhead of all justice. The king's ministers were so corrupt that there was no justice that could not be bought.

Furthermore, the manifesto expresses a stringent sentiment against the chapetones. Strongly implicit is the idea that all Americans, be they creoles, mestizos, or Indians, should unite against "the intruding European magistrates." The Silos manifesto foreshadows the winning formula of Simon Bolivar. All Americans share a common fatherland and a common future.

The program of the Silos manifesto, nevertheless, is not a total repudiation of the fiscal program of the Spanish colonial regime. The royal fifth, the traditional tax on mining production, would be retained as a major source of revenue for the new Inca regime. Nor would the Indians refuse to pay the tribute or annual head tax. Deeply attached to the Catholic church as the movement of Túpac Amaru was, the tithes—the principal source of revenue for the episcopacy and the secular clergy—would continue to be collected.

What the Silos manifesto explicitly rejected was the new fiscal program of Charles III. The attempts to collect more efficiently the taxes already on the books and to increase the traditional levies were pointedly rejected. The utopia implicit in the Silos proclamation was a return to the golden age of the Habsburgs with some taxes that were not burdensome.

The Utopia of the Blacks

There was still another utopia to emerge during the crisis of 1781. In contrast to the creoles, who aspired to self-government, or the plebeians, who dreamed of fewer taxes, or the Indians, who were struggling to preserve their ethnic identity, the utopia of the black slaves was the yearning to achieve their personal freedom.

By far the most interesting expression of black discontent in the New Kingdom of Granada in 1781 was a nonevent. Black slaves from the whole province as far south as Rionegro, perhaps some five thousand in all, were to congregate and march on Santa Fe de Antioquia, then the capital, in order to demand that the governor and the cabildo release a royal cedula granting freedom to all slaves. If freed, the slaves promised, they would pay an annual tribute tax "as if they were Indians."[40] They also expressed a willingness to work for their former masters as free men receiving the standard daily wage of two *tomines.* There was some talk among the blacks that if the authorities did not release the cedula, the slaves would flee to some inaccessible place and set up a *palenque,* a fugitive slave community. This option, however, included a commitment to pay an annual head tax to the crown.

The march never took place. It was betrayed; the fate of its ringleaders, all creole slaves and many of them mulattoes, is unknown, since the records have disappeared.

The myth of the royal cedula allegedly granting freedom to all slaves—a cedula which the local authorities willfully refused to publish—enjoyed widespread acceptance among the slaves in both New Granada and Venezuela during the late eighteenth and early nineteenth centuries.[41] How it originated, of course, can never be satisfactorily explained. Its significance can more easily be elucidated. The popularity of the cedula myth is dramatic evidence that many black slaves, certainly not all, accepted the cardinal myth of the Spanish imperial system enshrined in the traditionalist slogan, "Long live the king and death to bad government."

What is most striking is the modest character of the black demands. They were, to be sure, requesting their freedom, but they offered to continue to work for their masters and they were willing to pay an annual tribute tax. These slaves were not advocating social revolution: they merely aspired to move up one rung in the social ladder. The black slaves were requesting to be treated as Indians, who although free, were, legally speaking, not on a footing of equality with whites and mestizos. The reformist character of the black demands can largely be explained by the fact that the blacks were highly hispanized. They did not seek to destroy the status quo but merely to improve their own position within it. The less hispanized they were, the more radical would be their goals. The abortive black uprising in Antioquia is further proof of the moderate character of the crisis of 1781.

Now that we have examined the aspirations of the creoles, the plebeians, the Indians, and the blacks, it is time to consider the events that would lead to the capitulations of Zipaquirá.

9
Confrontation at Puente Real de Vélez

The four weeks after April 18 may be considered the most crucial of the Comunero Revolution. They began with decisions in both Socorro and Bogotá to escalate the conflict by a resort to force and coercion, and ended with the revolution institutionalized, the military forces of Bogotá in demoralized surrender, and the power of the regent visitor general in full eclipse.

A brief chronicle of events will help clarify the discussion that follows. On April 18 in Socorro, the captains general, under the leadership of Juan Francisco Berbeo, assumed formal command of the "enterprise." On that very day, Oidor Osorio left Bogotá at the head of a small military expedition whose purpose was to cow the rebels into submission. On May 2, the political structure of the revolution was institutionalized by the formation of the *supremo consejo de guerra.* Six days later, Oidor Osorio made an inglorious surrender to the Comuneros at Puente Real de Vélez.

Bogotá's inability to employ force successfully meant that a local protest movement became a revolution of substantial territorial extent, which ostensibly threatened, if only for a few weeks, the very foundations of imperial authority. On May 12, the authorities in Bogotá reversed their tactics and decided to negotiate. Juan Francisco Gutiérrez de Piñeres, the hated symbol of the fiscal changes, fled the capital. Into this power vacuum stepped the archbishop of Bogotá, Antonio Caballero y Góngora. On May 13 the newly created *junta de tribunales,* which ostensibly exercised royal authority in the absence of both the viceroy and the regent visitor general, granted the archbishop full authority to negotiate an agreement. On the following day, May 14, the junta de tribunales abolished in one session the principal fiscal

112

measures of Gutiérrez de Piñeres—the very program that had precipitated the outbreak of violence.

The consequences of the surrender of Oidor Osorio were as momentous in the camp of the Comuneros as they were in Bogotá. On May 17 Tunja joined the movement. So also did the restless Indians. The road to Bogotá seemed to be open. On May 14, the day that Caballero y Góngora departed from Bogotá in order to negotiate a settlement, Juan Francisco Berbeo left Socorro on his fateful march to Santa Fe de Bogotá.

On May 18, an event of great political and symbolic importance occurred in far-off Cuzco: Túpac Amaru II was executed. Symbolically, the ultimate restoration of the status quo in the New Kingdom was foreshadowed.[1] Several factors led the authorities in Bogotá to turn from conciliation to coercion. Alcalde Angulo y Olarte had clearly lost control of the situation in Socorro. The corregidor of the province of Tunja, José María Campuzano y Lanz, flatly disregarding orders to go in person to Socorro, remained in and around the city of Tunja, where he frantically but effectively organized a militia force. On April 9 the audiencia, under the still undisputed control of Gutiérrez de Piñeres, decided that a judge of the audiencia should lead a small military force from the capital to Socorro. His instructions were to enlist loyal subjects during his march so that he would arrive in Socorro with an impressive body of armed retainers to restore order. The audiencia granted him full powers "to maintain the reverence due the royal authority, to execute all the measures necessary to pacify those restless spirits, to punish the guilty, to reestablish the royal rents, and to restore public tranquility."[2]

A galaxy of blunders and miscalculations foredoomed the expedition, not the least of which was the choice of José Pardo de Osorio to head it. Among his outstanding liabilities was the fact that he was a very recent arrival on the bench in Bogotá, where he had been less than three months.[3] His ignorance of conditions in the New Kingdom was complete. Moreover, his health was far from robust. While serving in the audiencia of Santo Domingo, he had suffered an apparent heart attack. Shortly after his surrender to the Comuneros, Oidor Osorio took ill in Ubaté en route to Bogotá. He never reached the capital. He died of dropsy on August 11.[4]

The decision to appoint him was made by Gutiérrez de Piñeres, to whom it was an advantage that Osorio was a very recent arrival in Bogotá, with no ties to the creole elites. Furthermore, Osorio enjoyed the personal confidence of José de Gálvez, the minister of the Indies whom the regent regarded as his own patron.[5]

An even grosser miscalculation was the choice of Puente Real de Vélez as the immediate destination of the expedition. Its location had much to recommend it, since it blocked the path of invasion from Socorro to Bogotá. It seemed to be the best staging area for a march northward along the valley

Map 1. New Granada in 1810. (Based on *Atlas geográfico e histórico de la República de Colombia* [Paris, 1889], Plate V.)

of the Suárez River to Socorro. But it had a fatal strategic liability: it was located in a valley surrounded by hills, and its choice violated the universal military maxim that victory goes to those who control the heights. Puente Real was an inviting target for a siege, and that is precisely what the Comuneros proceeded to impose.[6]

When Viceroy Flores had departed for Cartagena, he had taken with him all the cavalry units stationed in the capital. It has been suggested that Osorio might have dominated the military situation with some cavalry units, but this hypothesis, though militarily plausible, is politically improbable. Discontent was so intense that Oidor Osorio simply could not recruit local volunteers. Without a large supporting force of locally recruited militia several dozen professional cavalrymen could not materially influence the course of events.[7]

Oidor Osorio, who lacked military experience, had as his second-in-command a veteran military officer, Captain Joaquín de la Barrera. In April of 1781, the military force in Bogotá consisted, literally, of a corporal's guard. When the crisis erupted, Bogotá could only muster fifty veteran footsoldiers, to which were added twenty-two much less professionally trained policemen employed by the tobacco and aguardiente monopolies.[8]

In addition to the appointment of Osorio and the choice of Puente Real de Vélez, the third decisive miscalculation was political in nature. Grossly minimizing the depth of popular discontent, Bogotá arrogantly and ignorantly assumed that the mere appearance of an expedition of seventy-two armed soldiers would act as a catalytic agent to enlist hundreds of recruits who would intimidate Socorro into submission.

If military force were to be the stick, there was also the proverbial carrot. Oidor Osorio's baggage was bulging with some 8,000 pesos in gold and silver coins, which he was supposed to distribute judiciously to enlist the support of influential persons.[9] In the event, this slush fund proved as ineffective as the military force.

Oidor Osorio arrived in Puente Real de Vélez after a five-day march from Bogotá, and immediately sent out an appeal to the cabildos of Pamplona, Tunja, Girón, and San Gil, the alcalde mayor of Bucaramanga, and the corregidor of Sogamoso.[10] Obviously he did not appeal to the cabildo of Socorro, which was then regarded as enemy territory. He instructed the cabildos to organize militias of dependable citizens, to arrest and to incarcerate the disloyal, and to be prepared to send him reinforcements when requested. The communication, which implied that he was going to restore respect for royal authority by force of arms, fell on deaf ears.

Leiva, which had promised a contingent of fifty men, procrastinated, alleging that their armed men were needed to defend the royal monopolies. One of Osorio's officers did go there in person, and brought back some forty-six soldiers. Only twenty met minimum military standards.[11] These were the only reinforcements that Osorio was able to secure. Without large-scale local recruitment a march northward to Socorro was impossible.

The military situation of Osorio rapidly deteriorated. Almost every day between April 7 and May 7, news overwhelmed him that yet another hamlet or parish had rioted and embraced the crimson flag that had now become the standard of the "enterprise."[12] The crowds burned the tobacco in the royal monopoly, and they poured the aguardiente into the squares, as they lustily shouted the slogan first heard in Socorro: "Long live the king and death to bad government."

While the military situation of Oidor Osorio swiftly worsened, Juan Francisco Berbeo was preparing to take the offensive. He controlled all the towns and parishes north of Puente Real along the eastern and western banks of the Suárez River to the city of Girón. All access routes were in his command. He had ordered the destruction of several bridges, and he had placed a garrison at the only available route northward at the bridge of Oiba.

On May 1, Berbeo dispatched from Socorro a military expedition against Oidor Osorio's troops in Puente Real de Vélez. The contingent, which left Socorro, consisted of some five hundred rather poorly armed but determined men, recruited from Socorro, Charalá, Simacota, Chima, and Oiba. An additional hundred troops joined the expedition at Moniquirá on May 6. The Comunero army picked up many more recruits along the route, where they were enthusiastically received by the populace. The sources are contradictory as to the precise numbers that actually encircled Osorio's skeleton contingent of increasingly demoralized soldiers.[13] Oidor Osorio may have exaggerated a trifle but not very much when he claimed that the enemy legions numbered four thousand.

The Comunero army was under the supreme command of Captain Ignacio Calviño. His principal lieutenants were Antonio José de Araque, Gregorio José Rubio, Melchor José de Rueda, Pedro Fabio de Archila, Miguel Monsalve, Antonio Becerra, Blas Antonio Torres, and Isidro Molina. Berbeo himself was not present at Puente Real, although he directed the whole operation from his headquarters in Socorro. Among those present at Puente Real were José Antonio Gálan and Ambrosio Pisco, both destined to play stellar roles in other situations.[14]

On May 3, Oidor Osorio received an alarming letter about the course of events in the enemy camp.[15] The author merited respect, for he was Filiberto José Estévez, the pastor of the parish of Oiba. "Here nothing is feared, nothing respected," he wrote, stressing the grim determination of the Socorranos. He warned that the lives of Corregidor Campuzano, Fiscal Moreno y Escandón, and especially Gutiérrez de Piñeres were in mortal danger if they ever fell into the hands of the men of Socorro, and offered Oidor Osorio some concrete advice:

> I fear that if your resolution, ardor, and discipline should make you come to Socorro, you will, needless to say, die. If your withdrawal is delayed unnecessarily, and then you decide to retreat, you will be surrounded by more than 4,000 men, and you will not know from whence they came. Who could but talk with the regent and Fiscal Moreno! Who could be lucky enough to let these words, at least, reach their ears.[16]

Father Estévez's alarming warning about the military build-up of the Socorranos was reinforced by other clergymen and those few spies of Osorio who had managed to penetrate into enemy territory.[17]

Within four days Father Estévez proved to be a remarkably accurate prophet. By May 7 the Socorranos dominated the heights surrounding Puente Real de Vélez. Osorio was, in fact, besieged. Negotiations between the two camps were initiated by some clergymen who offered their services as intermediaries. The captains and Oidor Osorio exchanged visits as well as correspondence. The Comunero captains addressed the judge of the royal audiencia with a tone of respect but also of candid firmness. Oidor Osorio had little alternative but to reply in a conciliatory tone. His metaphors of intimidation, invoked just a few days before, disappeared as his military situation dramatically worsened.[18] Initially he attempted to persuade the Comuneros to desist in their intent to march to Santa Fe de Bogotá. He urged them to lay down their arms. He assured them that he would go to Socorro in person, where with the full authority granted to him by the audiencia he would fully examine their complaints.

But the luckless oidor was in no position to impose any terms; all he could do was surrender. This is precisely what he did, when the victorious contingents of Socorro swept into the main square of Puente Real on May 8. In order to save what little face he had remaining, Osorio agreed that the disarmament of the two contending forces be mutual. The triumphant Comuneros obviously ignored this condition.[19]

After the Socorranos entered the headquarters of Osorio, some of the multitude spied three large boxes, which they assumed contained gunpowder. When they discovered to their delight that the boxes were bulging with coined money, the slush fund of Oidor Osorio, they proceeded to divide the contents of one of the boxes among themselves. Osorio and Barrera vigorously protested to the captains, who in turn ordered their more unruly followers to return every cent. The order was instantly obeyed. The captains assured Oidor Osorio "that their enterprise was not for the purpose of stealing but rather to insure the abolition of the new taxes and thus anything stolen must be returned."[20] This incident is just one of countless examples demonstrating that the Comunero Revolution was no mere exercise in pillage, and that the captains exercised a remarkably effective restraint and discipline over their followers.

While Oidor Osorio's cash was returned to him, his armaments were not. At Puente Real de Vélez the Comuneros received an impressive booty—148 muskets, a large number of bayonets, pikes, sabers, swords, other firearms, 20,000 bullets, and some four large boxes of gunpowder.[21] This bundle of arms was just the first dividend that the Comunero cause would reap from Puente Real de Vélez, one of the only two confrontations that occurred during the crisis of 1781 (the other was at Pie de la Cuesta near Girón). At Puente Real not a single life was lost.

A few days after the surrender one of the principal chieftains of Socorro,

Pedro Alejandro de la Prada, arrived in Puente Real, where he provided the dejected Oidor Osorio and his disarmed troops with safe-conduct passes to enable them to return to Bogotá.[22]

Perhaps the most curious incident of the whole episode was an offer that some Comunero captains made to Oidor Osorio in a conversation they had with him after the surrender. They proposed that Oidor Osorio be crowned king of New Granada, and that Captain Joaquín de la Barrera become the commander-in-chief of the armed forces, with the rank of captain general.[23]

This incident has provoked much speculation. Some historians have taken it so literally that they cite it as evidence that the Comuneros aspired to political independence from the Spanish crown.[24] There are two more plausible explanations. One is that the soldiers had a few too many glasses of aguardiente, and were exercising their facetious sense of humor.

If the incident is to be taken at all seriously, it may have been just another episode in the war of nerves that the Socorranos were waging against the authorities in Bogotá. Needless to say, the dejected Osorio, a prisoner, was not amused at this unexpected prospect of improving his status. The Comunero chieftains dropped the proposal as quickly as they had mentioned it. It is conceivable that the captains wanted to create a rift between Osorio and Barrera, on one hand, and the authorities in Bogotá, on the other.[25] The Comuneros, in fact, had no intention of deposing Charles III. But the offer to Osorio, made in one casual conversation, may also have been inspired by a desire to intimidate Bogotá into making concessions. Time and time again the forces of Juan Francisco Berbeo proved themselves adept tacticians of psychological warfare against their adversaries in the capital.

There were four momentous consequences of the battle of Puente Real de Vélez: Tunja joined the movement; the Indians became a part of the multiethnic coalition; the authorities in Bogotá, at long last, became acutely aware of the urgent necessity to negotiate a settlement; and the reluctant viceroy in Cartagena finally dispatched an expedition of some five hundred professional troops into the interior in order to contribute to the restoration of royal authority. The expedition commanded by Colonel José Bernet left Cartagena on June 1 and arrived in Bogotá on August 6.

The alliance with the city of Tunja was crucial to the Comuneros (see also chapter 13). The strategic importance of Tunja was as critical as was that of Puente Real de Vélez. Whereas Puente Real blocked the way to Bogotá and served as the gateway to the towns, hamlets, and parishes northward along the valley of the Suárez River of which Socorro was now the undisputed queen, Tunja, lying southeast of Puente Real, was on the main road to the sabana where Bogotá was located. Tunja was a three-day journey from the capital. Its adherence to the Comuneros was indispensable, if they sought to carry out their self-proclaimed intention of marching to Bogotá.

In contrast to Socorro, where the patricians joined the enterprise with some enthusiasm on April 18, the patricians of Tunja were obviously much more reluctant, if not openly hostile to assuming positions of leadership. Their adherence to the cause of Socorro was forced upon them by an external invasion; it was not a consequence of the dissatisfaction of their own elites or of pressures coming from the plebeians.

On May 2, an event of capital importance took place in Socorro, when the supremo consejo de guerra was established.[26] The captains general elected on April 18 exercised jurisdiction over only the town of Socorro. The office of captain general was military in character—for instance, in his capacity as captain general the viceroy was commander-in-chief of the armed forces. Serving under the captains general in each parish was a hierarchy of officers.[27] What needed to be created was a broader institutional and political body to exercise jurisdiction over the multitude of towns, hamlets, and parishes outside of the town of Socorro that had now joined the movement. It was on the initiative of Juan Francisco Berbeo, de facto caudillo of the captains of April 18, that the supreme council of war, which became the main governing body of the enterprise, was formed.[28]

The nomenclature by which various towns, hamlets, and parishes addressed the supreme council of war indicates its quasi-governmental status. The other terms often used were *ilustre consejo y congreso, superior consejo, real consejo, consejo de guerra, ilustre consejo de guerra, real consejo de guerra, consejo de justicia, guerra y hacienda del patriotismo.* The members of the council wore colorful and resplendent uniforms. They also enjoyed high-sounding titles: they were *generales, capitanes cristianísimos y caritativos, señores jefes superiores, jefes superiores, comandantes de la plaza mayor.* But there was no doubt that the undisputed caudillo was Juan Francisco Berbeo, who on May 2 was enthusiastically and solemnly proclaimed by the people in the main square of Socorro as *superintendente y comandante general* with the rank of *generalísimo.* So did Berbeo style himself in his public manifestoes.

Although this movement was a rather democratically organized confederation of towns, hamlets, and parishes, the town of Socorro, which provided the hard core of the leadership, was endowed with a particular glory. Socorro was hailed as the *ilustre villa, ilustre e inestimable Socorro, ínclita villa, reluciente Socorro, ilustre y noble villa,* and *invictísima y nobilísima villa.*

The choice of the word "council" is reminiscent of the Habsburg bureaucracy, whose fundamental unit of organization was conciliar and collegiate in nature—from the royal councils resident at court, such as the council of the Indies, to the audiencias and the royal treasury offices in the New World. The fact that the supreme council of war was sometimes referred to the supreme and royal council of war, the official nomenclature of the councils resident at the court of the Habsburgs, might suggest that the council of war in Socorro was repudiating the audiencia in Bogotá and, in effect, assuming the attributes of the *real acuerdo* which belonged exclusively to the audiencia.

Such is the opinion of Pablo Cárdenas Acosta, but I believe his interpretation is exaggerated. The creole leaders of 1781 had no choice but to invoke the rhetoric identified with the Habsburgs to whom they were nostalgically attached. A careful reading of the manifesto of the supreme council of May 4 suggests that that body was assuming only those attributes necessary to control, direct, and discipline all the adherents of the "enterprise," whose central goal was always to negotiate a settlement with the audiencia.

What the supreme council of war assumed were some but not all governmental attributes, in particular, the prerogative of enforcing military discipline. The council became in effect a provisional, subordinate authority whose purpose was to negotiate a settlement with the royal audiencia, whose jurisdiction the Socorranos never formally, or even informally, repudiated. The remarkable degree of control that the captains exercised over their subordinates was due in some measure, at least, to the discipline that the supreme council of war exercised over the captains, who constituted the officer corps.

Although the supreme council of war under the forceful leadership of Berbeo exercised a remarkably effective central control, the local structure of the movement was profoundly democratic. The council did send out capitanes volantes with a roving commission to organize resistance. Once a parish or a village joined the "enterprise" by the almost ritual act of burning the tobacco and pouring aguardiente into the streets, all the citizens, rich and poor alike, democratically elected captains. The election ceremony was a sui generis combination of ancient, Greek-style participatory democracy and a tumultuous riot. The supreme council in Socorro confirmed the elections and issued the official documentation, after the captains solemnly swore on the four gospels to uphold the mandates of Socorro.[29] In the larger settlements these officials were usually called captains general, in the smaller parishes merely captains.

In most but certainly not in all cases the captains belonged to the upper strata of society. What is more to the point is that these captains exercised influence and enjoyed prestige among their fellow townsmen. Whatever their social origins may have been, the profoundly democratic method of selecting them contributed to the cohesiveness of the whole movement and thus facilitated the task of the supreme council in providing the necessary centralized leadership.

The financial organization of the movement was a good deal more precarious than its political structure. The expedition to Bogotá, which ultimately became an army of 20,000 people, was financed in a variety of ways. The cabildo of Socorro provided a forced loan. The price of tobacco and aguardiente in the royal monopoly stores was reduced for the consumer, but the net profits were earmarked for the expenses of the expedition, as was the income that the royal treasury derived from the celebrated salt mines of Zipaquirá and Nemocón. Several private citizens, including Berbeo, volunteered individual subscriptions. Some may even have been cajoled into so doing.

Although no satisfactory figures are available, the "enterprise" was run on a "shoe-string" budget.[30] Yet it managed to feed an army of 20,000 men for several weeks, which was no mean accomplishment, and in the process to frighten the wits out of the august authorities in Bogotá.

Thus, the victory of Puente Real de Vélez, the formation of the supreme council of war, and the fall of Tunja facilitated the emergence of a grand coalition. Socorro, Tunja, patricians and plebeians, rich and poor, creoles, mestizos, and Indians were forming a formidable alliance. The road to Santa Fe de Bogotá was now open. And the invasion of the capital by the Comunero army was what the terrified authorities in Bogotá were determined to prevent, at all costs.

10

A Non-Battle in Bogotá
and the Invasion of Girón

The news that flooded into Bogotá was all bad. The "contagion of sedition" was rapidly spreading. The regent visitor general realized that he was rapidly losing control of the swiftly approaching crisis. His last initiative took place on May 12, when he reactivated the junta superior de tribunales. The junta was a standing committee of the royal audiencia and leading representatives of the fiscal administration that periodically met to deal with matters of common concern. This time, however, the junta de tribunales was expanded to include four representatives from both the city council and the royal exchequer, and two military officers. The junta was to meet every afternoon at 6 o'clock, in the residence of the regent visitor general, to transact all business relating to the crisis.

The major bureaucratic agencies were represented in the junta. Gutiérrez de Piñeres, in his capacity as regent of the audiencia, was the presiding officer. The entire audiencia, including Oidores Juan Francisco Pey y Ruíz, Joaquín Vasco y Vargas, Pedro Catani, and the new fiscal, Manuel Silvestre Martínez, were also members. With the departure of Fiscal Moreno for Lima on May 7, all of the audiencia were Spanish-born—mostly recent arrivals in Bogotá.[1] But in fact the newly powerful creole rosca had a comfortable working majority on the expanded junta de tribunales. The senior oidor, Juan Francisco Pey y Ruíz, had been serving on the tribunal since 1756, and two representatives of the fiscal administration had close ties with the creole élite: don Francisco de Vergara, regent of the tribunal de cuentas, and a friend of Berbeo and other prominent Socorranos, and don Manuel Revilla, married to one of the many daughters of don Bernardo Alvarez. Another member of the junta was the alcalde ordinario, the mayor, of Bogotá, don Eustaquio Galavis,

122

who was married to a daughter of the marquis of San Jorge. The cabildo traditionally had been dominated by the creoles, and that institution had four representatives out of a total of twelve members of the junta.

The composition of the junta general de tribunales, whose presiding officer after the flight of the regent visitor general was the senior oidor Pey y Ruíz, was a clear signal to the Comunero leadership in Socorro that the creole groups who for several decades had exercised considerable clout in governmental circles were again in power. They were prepared to resume the traditional pattern of negotiating a settlement. Thus, on the eventful night of May 12 the authorities in Bogotá, in effect, repudiated the political revolution of Charles III.

Gutiérrez de Piñeres's tenure as presiding officer of the junta general de tribunales lasted scarcely an hour. While the junta was holding its first session, an officer of Oidor Osorio's expedition, Francisco Ponce, was admitted into the chamber to give the stunned magistrates their first account of the debacle at Puente Real de Vélez four days before. Ponce had managed to escape from Puente Real disguised as a Franciscan friar. It was clear to the assembled magistrates that decisive actions had to be taken and that massive concessions had to be offered.

The first issue was the regent visitor general himself. Gutiérrez de Piñeres offered to retire to Cartagena, in view of the fact that Bogotá's military resources were negligible and that he was the target of popular wrath. He then withdrew from the chamber while the junta debated his offer. They ultimately reached a consensus that his departure might contribute toward appeasing the wrath of the approaching Socorranos and help to persuade them not to assault the capital. Two oidores initially expressed some misgivings about his departure, but they ultimately consented.[2]

The session of May 12 ended at midnight; Gutiérrez de Piñeres departed from Bogotá some three hours later.[3] His immediate destination was Honda on the Magdalena River, northwest of the capital; from there he subsequently fled to Cartagena. Although he returned to Bogotá on February 13, 1782, and remained in office until December 7, 1783, he lost effective political power as of May 12, 1781.

Thus the Comuneros had, in effect, deposed a powerful magistrate. The withdrawal of the regent visitor general from the capital was another signal that Bogotá was prepared to negotiate in earnest.

On that memorable first meeting the expanded junta de tribunales took other decisive measures. Its cardinal purpose was to negotiate an agreement, on whatever terms, with the Socorranos before the latter imposed a settlement by force after invading the capital. The leaders of Bogotá trembled at the prospect that their city would be the victim of pillage and anarchy. The nightmare that haunted the authorities was that with the Socorrano occupation of the capital the province of Popayán and the kingdom of Quito to the south, heretofore tranquil, would burst into flames. With upper and lower Peru already boiling with rebellion, the terrified magistrates were haunted by the prospective ruin of the proud and mighty Spanish empire and the end of their world. Perhaps these apocalyptical fears were somewhat exaggerated; but, on the other hand, they were not wild fantasies.[4] On May 12, there was unanimous agreement that the occupation of the capital by the Socorranos would escalate out of control an already perilous situation.

The most momentous action that the junta took on that eventful evening of May 12 was to accept the offer of Archbishop Caballero y Góngora to leave the capital immediately and to negotiate a settlement which would make the Socorrano occupation of the capital unnecessary.[5] The archbishop was accompanied by two other commissioners, both members of the junta general de tribunales, while Caballero y Góngora, of course, was not. One was Oidor Joaquín Vasco y Vargas, who was, in effect, the representative of the powerful audiencia bureaucracy. The other commissioner, chosen with equal skill, was actually the informal representative of the creole bureaucratic elite. A nephew of a former archbishop of Bogotá, the well-born Eustaquio Galavis y Hurtado was then serving as mayor of Bogotá. From 1771 until 1779 he had been the corregidor of Zipaquirá,[6] and had many local contacts which would facilitate the difficult task of the mission. This time the junta did not repeat the blunder of the Osorio expedition in sending out a magistrate totally unfamiliar with local conditions. Given the relationship of Galavis to the marquis of San Jorge, the signal that Bogotá was sending to Socorro was clear: a return to the traditional political system of cogovernment between European and American Spaniards and government by conciliation, consultation, and compromise.

The junta de tribunales gave the commissioners a broad and ample mandate. They were to negotiate whatever agreement was necessary to prevent the invasion of the capital. However well-chosen Vasco y Vargas and Galavis may have been, the mission was overwhelmingly dominated by the towering figure of the archbishop. The prestige of his august ecclesiastical office and the fact that he was totally unidentified with the fiscal program of Gutiérrez de Piñeres made him the obvious choice as a mediator. After the flight of the regent visitor general from Bogotá in the dawn of May 13, the political vacuum was not filled by the junta de tribunales but by the energetic and adroit archbishop. As of May 13, 1781, Caballero y Góngora was the de facto viceroy, although he did not become viceroy de jure until June 15, 1782.

The third decisive action that the junta took at the first meeting on May 12 was to reactivate the local militia in order to place the capital in some reasonable posture of defense.[7]

Two days later the junta general de tribunales took the dramatic step of

Eustaquio Galavis y Hurtado, alcalde ordinario of Bogotá. (Portrait by Joaquín Gutiérrez; Museo de Arte Colonial.)

repudiating the principal fiscal measures of Gutiérrez de Piñeres. The increase in the price of tobacco and aguardiente was abolished, the rate of the alcabala tax was lowered to its former 2 percent, the armada de Barlovento sales tax was abolished, and the guías and tornaguías were rescinded, as well as the collection of the forced loan.[8] The decree was valid for the whole of New Granada with the exception of Cartagena and Panama, where Viceroy Flores exercised direct authority and where no disturbances had taken place.

The grand strategy of the authorities in Bogotá—to negotiate a settlement before the Comuneros invaded the capital—rested on the premise that the capital itself would not fall to the enemy as a result of internal subversion. The authorities knew that there was a large measure of sympathy for the goals of the Socorranos among the plebeians in the capital. Even more alarming was the known or suspected fact that prominent creoles might be secret partisans of the invaders. The marquis of San Jorge de Bogotá, Manuel García Olano, and Dr. Monsalve, whose brother was an active member of the supreme council of war, among many other prominent creoles, were regarded as of doubtful loyalty. Hence the junta drew up several contingency plans in order to protect the capital against a potential fifth column.

Although frantic efforts were made to reactivate local militia units, the junta realistically recognized that the local militia, however much it might be expanded, would be unable to prevent the Socorrano army from entering the capital. If the Comuneros did approach Bogotá, the junta resolved that the entire clerical population, some 170 secular priests and 444 friars belonging to the various regular orders, should march out of the city, dressed in their ecclesiastical vestments, to implore the Socorranos not to violate the capital. The proposed scenario provided that they carry the exposed body and blood of Jesus Christ while singing Gregorian chants. If their pleas failed, then the capital would offer no further resistance and would surrender.[9] Hence the clergy were to be the first and the only line of defense to prevent the legions of Socorro from sacking the city. Without too much enthusiasm the clergy agreed to play this role. Fortunately for the men of the cloth they never had to redeem the pledge. The feverish military measures undertaken by Oidor Pedro Catani, whom the junta appointed commander-in-chief of the armed forces on May 15, had only a limited objective: to prevent an internal subversion in Bogotá so as to enable Archbishop Caballero y Góngora to reach a negotiated settlement outside the city.[10]

Oidor Catani quickly organized a military force of some 678 men. The cavalry unit was composed of 80 "distinguished citizens." Another infantry unit consisted of some 50 European Spaniards. There were also two other infantry companies totaling 168 militiamen. Another cavalry unit of 300 men was recruited from the neighboring localities. The cabildo of Bogotá also raised a company of 50 footsoldiers from the rural hinterland.[11]

Contingents of soldiers were stationed at all entrances to the city in order to prevent small-scale enemy infiltration. Squads of footsoldiers and cavalrymen periodically patroled the neighborhoods day and night. At military headquarters there was stationed a contingent of crack cavalrymen to meet any unexpected emergency. The palace, where the royal treasury was kept, was under constant military protection.[12]

As a further precaution the junta on May 17 imposed a 9 P.M. curfew which the military effectively enforced.[13] The junta further decreed that every *forastero,* or transient, had to report to either the senior oidor or the alcalde ordinario to explain why he was in the capital and to register his address.

The junta continued to be nervous about the large numbers of transients in the city. On May 18 they issued a draconian decree, in which they ordered all transients in the city who were originally natives of the towns of San Gil, Socorro, and Mogotes to leave Bogotá within twenty-four hours, on pain of death. The rectors of the two famous colleges of San Bartolomé and Rosario appealed to the junta, and the magistrates did grant a dispensation to all students coming from Comunero towns to continue their studies in the capital, on condition that their respective rectors guarantee their loyalty. Any person in whose home an unregistered transient was living was subject to confiscation of his property and six years' imprisonment in the fortress of Cartagena, if he failed to denounce the delinquents to the authorities.[14] While there is no evidence of any mass exodus of natives of San Gil and Socorro from the capital as a result of this severe measure, which evidently was not enforced, the edict does reflect the nervousness of the authorities.

The measures taken by Pedro Catani in the name of the junta were efficacious in maintaining royal control over the city.[15] That control was the sine qua non for carrying out the grand strategy of negotiating a settlement. By neutralizing the pro-Comunero factions inside the capital, the royal authorities took an important step in the complex process of restoring control over New Granada. The alliance between pro-Comunero creoles in Bogotá and the Socorrano captains, though not totally destroyed, was considerably weakened by the decisive act of placing the capital under a veritable state of siege. The royal authorities had, in effect, coopted several highly visible and influential creoles whom the Socorranos regarded as their allies.

If the royalists were successfully shoring up their control of their principal base in Bogotá, Juan Francisco Berbeo took some equally effective measures to insure that he would not be outflanked from the north, as he marched southward to Bogotá. San Juan de Girón, lying north of Socorro and just a few miles south of Bucaramanga, enjoyed a juridical and political status superior to that of Socorro. Girón was a city and not a town, as Socorro was, as well as the capital of a province headed by a governor. Although Girón enjoyed considerable prosperity from its fertile crops of tobacco, cotton, and cacao, it was not the peer of Socorro in population and wealth. The small province contained only 7,073 people, in contrast to the parish of Socorro with 15,000 inhabitants.[16]

Girón's location was highly strategic. To the west lay the Magdalena, and several of its tributaries, such as the Lebrija, the Cañabelares, and Sogamoso, were navigable to Girón. The lower Magdalena was firmly under royalist control. Hence the viceroy could sent reinforcements down the Magdalena from Cartagena or Mompós to the south and thence over the tributary rivers to Girón.

Juan Francisco Berbeo realized that a hostile Girón could become the gateway of an invasion from the north as he was marching southward to Bogotá. San Juan de Girón, however, refused all appeals coming from Socorro to join the "enterprise." Girón publicly proclaimed its loyalty to both the audiencia in Bogotá and the viceroy in Cartagena. The patricians and plebeians of Girón had much less cause to be angry about the innovations of the regent visitor general than did Socorro—it was, after all, one of the four areas in the New Kingdom where tobacco could be legally cultivated.

Rather than adhere to the cause of Socorro, the cabildo of Girón initially organized a defense force of some one hundred militiamen divided into three companies (whites, mestizos, and freed blacks).[17] As a reward for their loyalty, the government subsequently freed the blacks from the obligation to pay the annual tribute tax. The cabildo also appealed to Viceroy Flores, who on May 9 ordered some two hundred militiamen from Mompós to guard the bridges over the riverine approaches to Girón, but who, in view of his responsibilities in Cartagena, was reluctant to send an expedition of professional soldiers southward.

Without assistance from Cartagena and Mompós, Girón posed no real threat to Socorro: it could only muster, at the most, some three hundred poorly armed militiamen. Yet Berbeo could ill afford not to attack Girón. The supreme commander of the Comuneros showed just as much military acumen in organizing the expedition to conquer Girón in the north, as he did when he dispatched an army southward to capture Oidor Osorio at Puente Real de Vélez. On numerous occasions Berbeo showed skill and determination in choosing his strategy as well as his tactics. A generation later, General Francisco Miranda, the precursor of South American independence, praised the quality of Berbeo's military leadership.[18]

No less adroit was Berbeo's choice of a commander to lead the invasion of Girón. Doctor Ramón Ramírez (1754–88) was a native of Socorro. He was well know in Girón, however, for since 1779 he had held on a concession basis (*asentista*) the aguardiente retail outlet in that city. Hence he was well-to-do. On the urging of his parents in Socorro he returned to his natal city on May 1. The fact that he held a law degree undoubtedly facilitated his appointment as the private secretary of Juan Francisco Berbeo. With his close ties in both Socorro and Girón Ramírez was an ideal choice to lead the invasion northward. In order to endow him with greater prestige Berbeo arranged that the crowds elect Ramírez as a captain general with a seat on the supreme council of war.

While Socorro was preparing to invade, the patricians of Girón were making feverish military preparations at the same time that they publicly proclaimed their wish to live in peace and harmony with all their neighboring towns. For their three hundred recruits, the cabildo of Girón was able to assemble only 135 pieces of armament—more than half of their militiamen were unarmed. All sides in the crisis of 1781 actually lacked sufficient arms to wage a protracted military struggle. Hence the real decisions were reached in the political arena.

By May 20 Ramón Ramírez had arrived in the parish of San Francisco Javier del Pie de la Cuesta, two leagues from Girón. Pie de la Cuesta joined the Comuneros, as did Bucaramanga, which was just north of Girón. Girón took the offensive. Fifty militiamen, including a cavalry unit, attacked Pie de la Cuesta. Girón's cavalrymen won a victory that was to prove illusory. Two or three Socorrano soldiers were killed, and thirty others wounded or taken prisoner, including José Antonio Ramírez, the brother of the Socorrano commander. The expedition, however, failed in its main objective, which was to capture Ramón Ramírez himself.

The cavalrymen of Girón may have won the battle of Pie de la Cuesta, but they certainly lost the war. They soon freed Ramón Ramírez's brother. In the face of the overwhelming numbers of Comunero troops that were rapidly assembling at Pie de la Cuesta and Zapatoca, the patrician leaders of Girón lost the will to resist. They disappeared one by one, until by May 26 the city was virtually deserted. Only a handful of local magistrates, a few clergymen, some women, and some invalids remained.

On May 29 the victorious army of the Comuneros, consisting of some 4,000 troops, entered the virtually deserted city of Girón. Before Ramírez himself arrived at 4 P.M., an advance squad had pillaged a store, but the culprits were swiftly punished by Ramírez as thieves. This incident is another illustration of the high degree of discipline that the captains exercised over their followers. In the presence of Captain General Ramírez, Girón's clergymen, dressed in their ecclesiastical vestments with the exposed sacrament in their hands, went down on their knees and with tears in their eyes begged the victorious Socorranos to forgive Girón for its resistance.

Although Berbeo evidently exaggerated the threat to his northern flank posed by Girón's refusal to join his cause, he would have been negligent had he not dispatched the Ramírez expedition. While Berbeo was marching southward toward the capital, the revolutionary ferment was spreading north-ward and westward. On May 22 Pamplona rose in revolt and joined the "enterprise."[19] Also the "contagion of sedition" spread to the llanos, where the magic name of Túpac Amaru was invoked.

The royalists in Bogotá had a moderately firm grip on the capital, with Juan Francisco Berbeo controlling the whole area from the captaincy general of Venezuela south to the approaches of the sabana of Bogotá, the territory running east of the Magdalena River to the eastern cordillera and spilling over into the plains. Hence both the royalists in Bogotá and the advancing legions of the Comuneros had sources of strength from which to negotiate or to fight. The scene now must shift to the march on Bogotá.

11

"War, War, On to Santa Fe"

How is one to understand the willingness of Juan Francisco Berbeo's legions to negotiate a settlement at Zipaquirá, a day's journey north of Bogotá, without first occupying the capital? This is one of the most controversial issues in the history of the Comunero Revolution, and in a very real sense the following two chapters are nothing but an extended explanation.

The genesis of the expedition is somewhat obscure. It is not altogether clear when the Comunero leadership chose Bogotá as its objective. As early as May 3 Berbeo was appealing for recruits from neighboring towns and hamlets "in case it would be necessary to go to Santa Fe."[1] On May 8, after the fall of Puente Real de Vélez, the captive Oidor Osorio tried to talk his victorious conquerors out of their professed objective of marching to the capital.[2] The formal decision of Berbeo was not taken until May 11, when the supreme council of war ordered the triumphant army in Puente Real to march to Tunja as a preparatory move to occupy Santa Fe de Bogotá.[3]

Six days after the surrender of Puente Real de Vélez, Berbeo left Socorro for the capital of the kingdom. Although it was he who executed the grand strategy of marching on the capital, he apparently was not the first to formulate it. That plan did not originate in Socorro but in Bogotá. The *cédula del pueblo*, "our royal decree," which was first read to the multitudes in Socorro on the third riot of April 16—some two days prior to Berbeo's formal assumption of command—urged the people to invade Bogotá.[4]

The language of "our royal decree" contributed much to the belief of the plebeians that the immediate objective of the "enterprise" was to take the capital.[5] Only the occupation of Bogotá would guarantee that the regent visitor general would be ousted from power and that the hated taxes and monopolies would be abolished. Time and time again the populace shouted hoarsely, "On to Santa Fe."

One may question, however, whether the occupation of the capital was ever the real objective of the leadership cadres, in contrast to the plebeians who saw the occupation of Bogotá as the only guarantee of success. If redress of specific grievances was the real goal, the occupation of the capital was not a necessary precondition. As a proclaimed objective, however, it was a convenient ploy to bring the authorities to grant the desired concessions. Hence Berbeo kept open the option of taking the capital until as late as May 31. If Berbeo's objective were political independence, his failure to take Bogotá by storm would make him either a fool or a knave, neither one of which he was. By May 31 swiftly moving events made the seizure of Bogotá unnecessary, provided that the leaders' objectives were limited to redress of specific grievances.

Before he could leave Socorro for his march southward to the capital, Juan Francisco Berbeo had to secure his two northern flanks. One flank was military: the conquest of proroyalist Girón, which was discussed in some detail in chapter 10. The second was both political and military in nature: Viceroy Flores in Cartagena. Berbeo well knew that the viceroy was in command of a garrison of some 3,000 professional soldiers, whose primary responsibility was to defend the mighty fortress of Cartagena against a possible English attack.[6] Yet these soldiers, or at least some of them, might be diverted as an instrument of repressing the disorders in the mountain interior of the kingdom. It was also common knowledge in both Socorro and Bogotá that the viceroy and the visitor general had clashed over both the strategy and the tactics of introducing the Gálvez innovations and that the dissatisfied viceroy had used the declaration of war against Great Britain as a partial pretext to retire to Cartagena, thus implicitly dissociating himself from the policies of Gutiérrez de Piñeres.

Berbeo was determined to exploit to his advantage the rift between the two senior magistrates of the kingdom. On May 6 the cabildo of Socorro and the captains general sent separate but well-coordinated letters to the viceroy in which they sought to enlist his sympathy and his assistance. Anxious that their letters not fall into the hands of Gutiérrez de Piñeres, who was still in power, they sent them to Manuel García Olano, then head of the postal office in Bogotá, with instructions that they be forwarded directly to the viceroy in Cartagena. When the letters arrived in the capital, the regent visitor general had already fallen, and the junta de tribunales had come to power. Lest he subsequently be accused of treason, García Olano prudently showed his superiors these letters from Socorro, and the junta authorized him to send them to the viceroy.[7]

The more detailed letter was from the cabildo. Stressing the poverty that had overwhelmed Socorro since the epidemic of 1776, the town fathers in candid but respectful tones complained about the heavy burdens caused by the sales taxes, the forced loan, the guías and tornaguías, monopolies, and the brutality of their policemen. The cabildo urged the viceroy to intercede on their behalf before the king, to whom they pledged their undivided loyalty, in order to secure the necessary concessions to appease popular fury. Order and tranquility, the town council warned, could be restored only if the sales taxes were cut back to the 1750 rate, the armada de Barlovento tax and the guías and tornaguías abolished, and Socorro and San Gil again allowed to cultivate tobacco.

In a separate but shorter letter the captains general pledged their loyalty to the king and the viceroy, but not necessarily to all his ministers. They stressed, however, that granting the kind of concessions proposed by the cabildo would be crucial to the reestablishment of order. But the principal thrust of their letter was a defense of their own conduct. They argued that the infuriated crowds compelled them against their will and under the threat of death and the loss of their property to accept positions of leadership. Yet they also reminded the viceroy that they alone were capable of appeasing and controlling the anger of the populace.[8]

The viceroy apparently was in no hurry to reply to these statements. It was not until June 20 that he informed the Socorrano leaders that the authorities were prepared to grant the redress of legitimate grievances, provided the citizens of Socorro laid down their arms. The viceroy piously admonished the Socorranos to place their confidence in the benevolence of the monarch and his ministers, all of whom desired the happiness of their vassals. He warned the wealthy creoles that they had much to lose in a situation where rioting plebeians expressed no respect for private property and the rule of law.[9] Such a claim, in fact, was a gross distortion of the actual situation. Nevertheless, Viceroy Flores was following the grand strategy of Caballero y Góngora in seeking to drive a wedge between the patricians and the plebeians by creating the myth of a war between the rich and the poor.

Berbeo and his contingents arrived on May 23 at Ráquira, due west of the city of Tunja, from where he replied to a letter of the commissioners Vasco y Vargas and Galavis, written in Zipaquirá on May 14. The commissioners assured the advancing troops that they had full powers to negotiate a comprehensive settlement of all their grievances. Juan Francisco Berbeo's reply is perhaps the single most eloquent and dignified statement of his goals. Written in an elegant, if somewhat archaic, Spanish, it is, in fact, one of the great state papers of the Comunero Revolution.

> Public tranquility can only be restored in this kingdom by the completion of the enterprise which the community [el común]

of the towns of Socorro and San Gil and the other allied cities
and towns have thrust upon us, that is to say, relief from the
unbearable taxes under which we have suffered and which are
increasing daily, burdening and exasperating the people to such a
degree that they prefer to end their lives in an instant rather than
finish them miserably from day to day. In your letter of May 14
your lordships assured me that you are endowed with the full
authority of the audiencia [real acuerdo] whose authority comes
from both the king (may God preserve him) and the people upon
whom the king's authority ultimately rests. Since our purpose is
to seek the removal of these many taxes, which no one has
demonstrated to us that our benign monarch ever even authorized, and since we are his loyal subjects, we must request
your lordships to present yourselves in the territories of the
village of Nemocón where with all due courtesy and amenity we
may discuss and resolve all pertinent matters.[10]

In blunt and concise language Juan Francisco asserted the aims of "the
enterprise," and the determination of those involved: his followers "prefer to
end their lives in an instant rather than finish them miserably from day to
day"—a striking phrase indeed.[11] While he reaffirmed loyalty to "our benign
monarch," Berbeo made it very clear that the only basis of negotiation was
the removal of the hated taxes. Another feature of the letter is an unmistakable affirmation of the classic notion of Spanish political theory that the
sovereignty of the crown ultimately comes from the people and, by implication, that the crown must be responsible to the will of the people.

The proud tone of Berbeo's letter aroused resentment in Bogotá. The
president of the junta de tribunales complained to the viceroy in Cartagena:

The letter written by Berbeo gives a clear idea of the insolence
and predominance which all those inhabitants have acquired. In
addition to treating the commissioners without any courtesy at
all, the manner in which they are addressed seems to come more
from a spirit of sovereignty and absolute independence than from
someone who seeks peace with the intention of remaining a
subject.[12]

Berbeo's letter and Bogotá's reaction dramatically illustrate the feeling of
tension in the political drama of 1781, i.e., the clash between the "unwritten
constitution" of New Granada and Caroline absolutism. It is even probable
that neither Berbeo nor his private secretary ever read a single word of the
political treatises of Francisco Suárez and the other classic Spanish theologians of the sixteenth and seventeenth centuries. The really important point
is that they did not have to. The Suarecista notions of the popular origin of
sovereignty and other limitations on political authority were deeply em-

bedded into the fabric of the "unwritten constitution" that had gradually evolved in New Granada during the course of the seventeenth and eighteenth centuries, that is to say, government by compromise and conciliation in which the views of all ethnic groups in varying degrees would be taken into account. The Caroline bureaucrats instinctively abhorred this system. In their view subjects owed undivided obedience to all magistrates. Hence the deeply traditionalist tone of Berbeo's letter would strike them as an expression of "a spirit of absolute independence" not coming from "someone who seeks peace with the intention of remaining a subject." Berbeo was not looking forward to independence but looking backwards to restoring the traditional ways. Although both parties to the dispute may have spoken Spanish, neither one spoke the same political language. At this time it was a dialogue of the deaf.

On May 23 the advance guard of the Comunero legions arrived at Nemocón, some three leagues northeast of Zipaquirá. This was the victorious army of captains Ignacio Calviño, Antonio José Araque, and Blas Antonio de Torres. Two days later Berbeo arrived at Nemocón. In order to improve his negotiating posture either inside or outside Bogotá, the generalissimo took a series of decisive measures which conclusively demonstrate the high quality of his military and political leadership.

On May 25 he launched a bold and imaginative strategic plan, when he dispatched an expedition of about 150 soldiers southwest to Facatativá and then northwest to Honda. From Cartagena southward to Honda the Magdalena was navigable. It was, in fact, the most available route for Bogotá to receive reinforcements of men and matériel from the viceroy in Cartagena. Berbeo intended the expedition to occupy Facatativá, to intercept the mails between Bogotá and Cartagena, to capture there the artillery which Gutiérrez de Piñeres had dispatched from Honda for the defense of Bogotá, and then to invade the towns of the upper Magdalena valley, Guaduas, Mariquita, and Ambalema. The ultimate objective of the expedition was to capture strategic Honda and its most celebrated resident, the regent visitor general. The man whom Berbeo chose for this bold assignment was José Antonio Galán, one of the most famous chieftains of the Comunero Revolution.

Galán performed his mission brilliantly. Outmaneuvering a royalist detachment dispatched from the capital, he intercepted the royal mail pouch in Facatativá on May 30 (Berbeo eventually returned it unopened upon the heated insistence of the authorities in Bogotá). Between May 30 and June 7 Galán's small expedition swept through the towns and hamlets of the upper Magdalena valley to enlist these communities into the service of the "enterprise." Why Galán did not capture the regent visitor general in Honda, as Berbeo had instructed him to do, but instead sent a letter warning him to flee is a matter that perhaps always will be clouded with obscurity. An attempt to explain Galán's baffling conduct will be made in chapter 15.

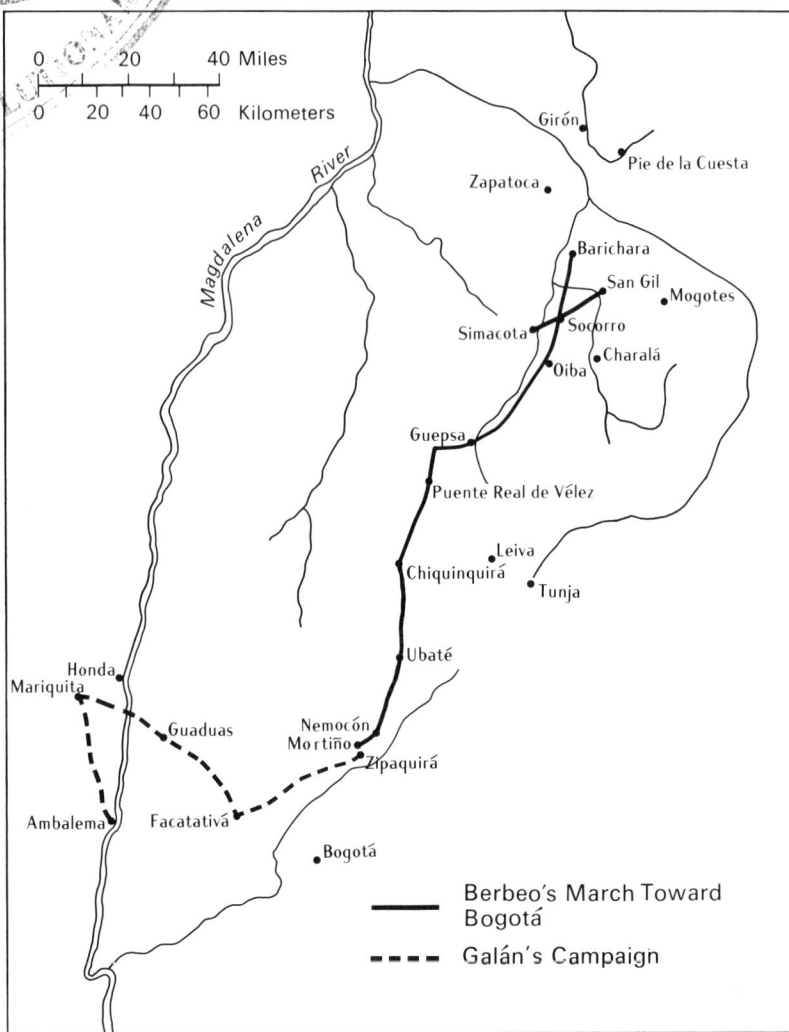

Map 2. Berbeo's march toward Bogotá and Galán's campaign. (See Map 1, p. 114.) (Based on Armando Gómez Latorre, *Enfoque social de la revolución comunera* [Bogotá, 1973].)

At this point it is important to stress that Galán's lightning campaign was a masterful military stroke which greatly strengthened Berbeo's hand at the negotiations in Zipaquirá, and created consternation both in Bogotá and in the entourage of Archbishop Caballero y Góngora in Zipaquirá. There is little doubt that Galán's exploits constituted one of the factors that compelled a reluctant Bogotá officialdom to approve the capitulations on June 7, the very day that Galán sent a warning to the regent visitor general to flee from Honda. Galán's campaign demonstrates not only his dexterity as a field commander but also the boldness and the vision of Berbeo's strategic thinking.

Another step that Berbeo took after his arrival in Nemocón was to incorporate Indian discontent into his multi-ethnic coalition, exploiting the wrath of the Indians as a means of putting pressure on the authorities in Bogotá.

The most celebrated event identified with Ambrosio Pisco, titular leader of the Indians, during the fast-moving events in Zipaquirá was the order that Juan Francisco Berbeo issued on May 31, a week before the signing of the capitulations. Reaffirming Pisco's dual role as the hereditary cacique of Bogotá and a captain of the "enterprise," the supreme commander commissioned

> don Ambrosio Pisco, the cacique of Bogotá, to go in person with his people to the outskirts of the city of Santa Fe to prevent by force anyone who attempts to enter Santa Fe in order to loot and desecrate. If it is desirable, he may erect two gallows, one at the entrance by the church of San Diego and another at San Victorino in order to punish the brigands.[13]

Berbeo's commission was ostensibly designed to prevent his own troops in Zipaquirá, a mere twenty-five miles away, from marching on the capital. A plausible inference is that Berbeo granted the commission to Pisco as a part of a broader tactic—to frighten both the archbishop in Zipaquirá and the junta de tribunales in Bogotá into making a settlement lest they face a possible onslaught on the capital. Bogotá reacted viscerally to Pisco's rather obsequious notification of his commission, seeing his approach as the beginning of the invasion of the capital.[14] His presence, with some 5,000 angry Indians, at the gates of the city was a nightmare that Bogotá wished to dispel. In the face of vigorous if not frantic protests from the capital, Berbeo did withdraw Pisco's commission before the latter reached the gates of Bogotá.[15] But he had scored his point.

The Pisco episode was not the only occasion in which Berbeo used Indian discontent in order to strike fear into the hearts of the royalist magistrates. The Cocuy manifesto of May 23, invoking the name of Túpac Amaru, and the publication of the manifesto in Silos on June 14 dethroning Charles III were apparently other incidents in the war of nerves that the supreme commander was waging against his opponents. It may not be an accident that these two proclamations of Túpac Amaru occurred in areas remote from Zipaquirá. Hence they posed little danger in further inciting the Indians in the sierra around the capital, who were already in an open state of rebellion. These descendants of the Chibchas had no need of the symbolism of a Túpac Amaru, for their own indigenous monarchical tradition was present in the person of Ambrosio Pisco, whom Berbeo had already adroitly coopted.

All these acts represented a clear signal to Bogotá: negotiate a settlement favorable to the Comuneros or run the danger that the "enterprise" would degenerate into an orgy of violence from below; either deal with the responsible leaders, or face a sanguinary Indian uprising whose aim might be to overthrow the sovereignty of the crown. The supreme commander's skillful manipulation of Indian discontent was one of the many factors that compelled Bogotá to come to the negotiating table.

The two great protagonists of the crisis of 1781—Archbishop Antonio Caballero y Góngora and Juan Francisco Berbeo—had their first face-to-face interview in Nemocón on May 26. Several clergymen, the most important of whom was the well-placed Filiberto José Estévez, acted as intermediaries between the two camps.[16] Their efforts were significant all during the hectic negotiations between May 26 and June 7.

The archbishop entered the first interview with the hope that his considerable powers of persuasion and the prestige of his high office would weaken the resolve of his adversaries to march on the capital. Berbeo flatly rejected Caballero y Góngora's first proposal that a treaty be negotiated immediately at Nemocón. He forcefully argued that the only guarantee that a negotiated settlement would be observed was the entrance of the Socorranos en masse into the capital.

Caballero y Góngora then made a counterproposal: that a small delegation of the Comunero captains, accompanied by the two other commissioners, should go to the capital to negotiate an agreement. In order to guarantee the personal safety of the Socorranos in Bogotá the archbishop offered to remain in the Comunero camp at Nemocón as a virtual hostage.

Neither the junta de tribunales in Bogotá nor Berbeo was happy with Caballero y Góngora's counterproposal. The junta never wavered in its conviction that the three commissioners had ample powers to negotiate an agreement outside of the capital. It did, however, reluctantly and nervously consent to the plan on May 28. But Berbeo bluntly refused his consent. He argued that if only a few of his captains entered the capital under these conditions, "they would be arrested and slaughtered."[17]

Berbeo, in fact, wished to postpone the beginning of meaningful negotiations. The supreme commander had several plans that he had already initiated or was about to launch; to accomplish them would greatly strengthen his bargaining position and would still leave the option of negotiating inside or outside the capital. Only two days before, he had dispatched Galán on his vitally important campaign in the upper Magdalena River valley; the full consequences would take some time to unfold. Ambrosio Pisco's commission had not yet been dispatched.

On May 27 a discouraged archbishop and his two colleagues retired from Berbeo's war camp in Nemocón to nearby Zipaquirá to await developments. Berbeo suspended but did not break off the talks on the grounds that all his military forces had not yet congregated. Once again he warned the delegation that the only satisfactory guarantee that his followers would not be deceived was the occupation of Bogotá.[18]

Before Berbeo could realistically negotiate with the archbishop from a position of maximum strength, he had to solidify his alliance with his newest ally, the city of Tunja. On May 30, at the private estate of Checua in the outskirts of Nemocón, Berbeo and the Tunjanos met. Tunja solemnly agreed that its military contingent would join Berbeo's legions for the march on the capital.[19]

On the day that he suspended his negotiations with the commissioners Berbeo moved his military headquarters from Nemocón to nearby Mortiño. The choice of the new war camp made sound sense both tactically and politically. Only half an hour by horseback from Zipaquirá, and hence only a day's journey from Bogotá, Mortiño could be effectively supplied with food from the neighboring towns and hamlets. Situated on a slope of the sierra, Mortiño had ample pastures and farmlands with many huts and enclosures that could provide some protection from the torrential rains that inundated the lower part of the valley during the rainy season, then in progress.

On the slopes of Mortiño a formidable if badly armed force gathered— some 20,000 people, housed in about seven hundred tents. Ten thousand came from the jurisdictions of the towns of Socorro and San Gil, and the city of Puente Real de Vélez. Another six thousand came from the jurisdictions of the city of Tunja, Leiva, Sogamoso, Santa Rosa, and Chiquinquirá. There were four thousand Indians under the nominal command of Ambrosio Pisco.[20] This host of soldiers was far larger than any army Simón Bolívar ever commanded during the wars of independence, although his troops were better equipped.[21] In view of the fact that the population of Bogotá was not many more than 18,100 in 1778, it is indeed understandable how this army, one day's journey away, struck consternation and panic in the minds and hearts of the defenders of royal authority.[22]

On May 30 Juan Francisco Berbeo made another clever move. A week earlier the supreme council of war in Socorro had written the generalissimo that, if the archbishop attempted to prevent the occupation of the capital by using his powers of excommunication and interdict, the council would exile him from his diocese and declare the see vacant. The fear that the archbishop might use these two most powerful weapons in his armory evidently came from the plebeians of Socorro, for it was their official representative in the council, the procurador Antonio Molina, who introduced the resolution which the council passed.[23] The fear was a very real one, for use of these weapons would probably have demoralized the Comunero legions.

Hence Berbeo showed the commissioners on May 30 this letter, putting the archbishop on notice that should he invoke his powers, the Comuneros were ready to exile him from his see. Since the initiative apparently came from the plebeians, the patrician captains could then subsequently disassociate themselves from such a bold threat, if it became desirable.[24]

In the course of the Spanish colonial period bishops frequently used these dreaded weapons, often for reasons that were more mundane than spiritual.[25] All the available evidence, however, indicates that in this case the wily archbishop had no intention of resorting to excommunication. He well knew that in his precarious position, with no soldiers to back him up, his only effective weapons were the prestige of his high office, his own cunning, endless patience, and pastoral words of conciliation. But Juan Francisco Berbeo had no certain intelligence as to what the archbishop intended.

On May 31 Zipaquirá formally joined the "enterprise" in appropriate ceremonies in which the supreme commander confirmed that parish's election of captains.[26] As early as May 16 the town had demonstrated sympathy for the Comuneros during a riot in which the home of a rich Spanish merchant was sacked. The archbishop, present on this occasion, was shocked by the crowd's disorderliness, but he was equally impressed by the fact that a few Socorranos who happened to be in the town were able to persuade the unruly crowd to repair the next day the damage that they had inflicted on the looted house.[27] The riot in Zipaquirá left an indelible impression on Caballero y Góngora. Not only did he observe firsthand the depth of popular anger, but he was impressed with the prestige of the Socorranos and the influence they exercised over the tumultuous crowd. The riot in Zipaquirá helped to persuade him that massive concessions were necessary to appease popular wrath, that only the Socorranos had the prestige to control that anger and finally, and most important at all, that the alliance between the patricians and the plebeians had to be severed. Henceforth he never wavered in his conviction that the Socorranos were the only group with whom he could conduct meaningful negotiations.

As of May 31 Juan Francisco Berbeo had reached the climax of his power. Demonstrating considerable military and political skill, he had recruited an army of 20,000 badly equipped but militant soldiers, and he had led them to within a day's march of the capital of the kingdom. Not only had he made an alliance with Tunja, but also he had skillfully coopted Indian discontent. Furthermore, Galán was executing a brilliant military stroke in overrunning the strategic upper Magdalena valley. On several occasions Berbeo had demonstrated uncanny ability in conducting on many fronts an extensive war of nerves in order to intimidate his opponents. Above all else, he had managed to keep open his option as to whether to negotiate inside or outside the capital.

Juan Francisco Berbeo played with considerable skill all the cards that he had in his hand. The point, however, is that he had only a few. Archbishop Antonio Caballero y Góngora, in contrast, had many more cards, and he knew how to play them with maximum dexterity.

12

Rendezvous in Zipaquirá

May 31 was one of the most eventful days in the history of the New Kingdom of Granada, for on that day the shape and course of the crisis of 1781 were largely determined.

In the morning Juan Francisco Berbeo formally installed in office the captains general of the parish of Zipaquirá and issued his controversial commission to don Ambrosio Pisco to go to the gates of the city of Santa Fe de Bogotá. Moreover, he appropriated, for a period of two months, the revenues of the royal salt mines of Zipaquirá and Nemocón to finance his expedition.[1] On that same day José Antonio Galán intercepted the royal mail pouch at the pass of Facatativá and, in effect, severed the communications between Bogotá and Cartagena.[2]

The most important event of the day, however, and one which largely shaped the final outcome of events, occurred in the afternoon. When Archbishop Caballero y Góngora received intelligence that the troops were on the point of breaking camp and starting their march to the capital, he and his fellow commissioners rushed posthaste to the neighboring headquarters at Mortiño. At three o'clock, the second conference began. The archbishop wrote:

> Seeing them resolved to march on Santa Fe and fearing that their idea to go on to Popayán and Quito would come true, thereby setting the entire continent on fire, I decided to meet once again with the captains. The toils I endured were incomparable, the insults I suffered from those people in this second conference were indescribable, many of them uttering the most infamous ideas. By dint of inalterable patience I was finally able to calm

142

them and get them to agree to capitulations. I also secured a promise from Juan Francisco Berbeo to remain in Zipaquirá and not to move his camp in spite of the opposition of many who were trying to make him go to Santa Fe in order to execute their depraved aims.[3]

During the course of that prolonged interview the archbishop learned about the existence of a deep cleavage in the Comunero camp that he could exploit to his own advantage. Powerful chieftains not only from Tunja and Sogamoso but also from Socorro's neighbor, San Gil, wanted to negotiate a treaty in Zipaquirá and not go to Bogotá. The grand coalition that Juan Francisco Berbeo had put together with infinite patience and considerable difficulty was threatening to come apart. In particular, the alliance with Tunja, which had only been sealed twenty-four hours before at the estate of Checua, was under severe strain. Tunja, the last to join the "enterprise," seemed now the first to defect.

Tunja's withdrawal had a strategic and military significance even out of proportion to the impressive size of her contingents. Tunja lay north of Zipaquirá; Berbeo's forces could be outflanked, if he marched south to the capital. Loyal to the commands of Bogotá until May 23, Tunja under the leadership of Corregidor Campuzano had raised an impressive military force during the months of March, April, and May for the ostensible purpose of defending royal authority. The battalions recruited from the jurisdictions of Tunja, Leiva, Sogamoso, Santa Rosa, and Chiquinquirá consisted of about 6,000 troops, whereas the components of the army that came from the territorial jurisdictions of Socorro and San Gil amounted to some 10,000 recruits. There were an additional 4,000 Indians whose alleged military ineffectiveness aroused only disdain on the part of the creoles and mestizos. Not only were Tunja's contingents large, but they were, in the opinion of the archbishop, "the most splendid of that army, the best disciplined, and the most obedient to their officers."[4] Some four thousand of them were cavalry-men with greater mobility than the San Gil–Socorro contingent, the majority of whom were footsoldiers.

On June 2, the Tunja regiments departed from the war camp at Mortiño in order to set up their war camp in Cajica, just south of Zipaquirá. Thus, they blocked the road to the capital. In Zipaquirá the Tunjanos publicly pledged to the commissioners their support of "all our forces to free the capital of Santa Fe de Bogotá from the affront and the outrage which those people [the Socorranos] with their monstrous fury are seeking to inflict."[5]

In his account, the archbishop gloated that he had tricked the Tunjanos into moving their headquarters to Cajica on the pretexts that it offered better pasturage for their horses and that in the congested war camp at Mortiño pestilence might break out.[6] The archbishop's account is self-serving, if not downright misleading. Captain Joaquín de la Barrera, who was the first to learn about the split between Socorro and Tunja, indicates that the Tunjanos made a deliberate decision that their forces should prevent the occupation of the capital.[7]

The archbishop by his own admission distributed presents of money to those whom he thought were potential or actual sympathizers for his proposal to negotiate at Zipaquirá.[8] But those who were so favored would have taken the actions they did in any event. Notwithstanding the archbishop's largesse and his considerable powers of persuasion, Tunja had good and sufficient reasons for breaking with Socorro.

The proud patricians of Tunja, whose economy had decayed during the eighteenth century as Socorro's prosperity had augmented, had been humiliated when the Socorranos invaded their city on May 23 and compelled them to join the "enterprise." But they did not lose control over their relatively well-disciplined army. Not without justification, the Tunjanos also had genuine fears that political power and control over the rural hinterland might pass to the aggressive Socorranos. One of the clauses of the capitulations provided that the extensive province of Tunja be partitioned, with Socorro–San Gil having their own corregidor. Not all the Tunja chieftains opposed occupying the capital, but a comfortable majority did.[9]

The extent to which San Gil sided with the Tunjanos is not clear. All the accounts indicate that the captains of San Gil expressed some sympathy for the position taken by Tunja, but their reservations about the matter cannot be clarified by the available documents. What has already been well demonstrated in chapter 3, however, is that rivalry between Socorro and San Gil had been a constant factor since the creation of the parish of Socorro in 1689.

Bogotá's repudiation of the whole program of Gutiérrez de Piñeres, the cooptation of the creole bureaucratic elite in the capital by the junta de tribunales, and the defection of Tunja were all significant events in pushing Berbeo into reaching a settlement in Zipaquirá and not in Bogotá. Yet there was still another equally important factor in this complex political equation: Cartagena.

Viceroy Flores commanded the only professional army in the New Kingdom of Granada, a force of 3,318 soldiers. At least Berbeo thought so. The viceroy claimed in his confidential dispatches that the number of effectively professional troops, of which only 400 were European Spaniards, came closer to 1,000 men.[10] Yet even this smaller number represented the most formidable military force in the whole New Kingdom. Berbeo's force was large, but on the whole lightly armed and poorly trained. He was very conscious of the existence of Cartagena's military might.

Bogotá kept the viceroy informed of the rapid spread of rebellion in the interior. On May 9, the audiencia urgently pleaded for reinforcements in the form of men and munitions.[11] Until the battle of Puente Real the viceroy would only send some arms and four veteran officers to help train the local militia in Bogotá. He emphatically refused to send a military mission to the interior until he had received reinforcements that he had urgently requested from Havana, contending that he needed all his troops concentrated in Cartagena lest the British attack any number of exposed coastal towns such as Panama, Portobelo, Veragua, Santa Marta, Ríohacha, or Darien.[12]

A soldier by profession, the viceroy apparently opposed using the military to quell civil disturbances. He expressed a certain lack of confidence in the reliability of his creole and black troops, especially if they found themselves involved in a civil war. Above all else, the viceroy wanted to avoid a blood bath. In his words, he did not want to precipitate another massacre of Saint Bartholomew or another Sicilian Vespers.

Like many professional soldiers before and after him, Flores had a loathing for using soldiers in a civil war. As often is the case, the real "hawks" here were the civilians. After the repudiation of his innovations Gutiérrez de Piñeres, from the safety of Honda and Cartagena, demanded military intervention with the ferocity of a frustrated civilian who has never known warfare at first hand.[13] The viceroy urged the junta de tribunales to negotiate with the rebels a settlement that would lead to their subsequent disarming. Then he would dispatch a small force of professional soldiers southward in order to consolidate the restoration of royal authority. The government could then revise or annul the agreement.

When news reached Cartagena about Oidor Osorio's debacle at Puente Real and the subsequent march of the Socorranos toward the capital, the viceroy was forced to reverse his timetable. Despite opposition from some of his staff officers who heatedly argued that Cartagena, at the most, could spare only 200 soldiers, Viceroy Flores on May 25 authorized an expedition to the interior of 500 troops under the command of Colonel José Bernet. Perhaps the staff officers were right in a narrow military sense, but the viceroy had to consider the larger political picture. The contingent included some 250 troops from the veteran *regimiento fijo*. Another 125 troops came from the white militia and 125 from the black militia. Colonel Bernet left Cartagena on June 1, but his expedition did not reach Bogotá until August 6.[14] The slow, inexorable advance of this small but potent military expedition was a powerful psychological instrument in helping the authorities to restore control after the conclusion of the capitulations. The Bernet expedition served the purpose for which Viceroy Flores intended it.

The expedition did not leave Cartagena until June 1, one day after Berbeo made his decisions to negotiate in Zipaquirá and some eight days before the junta de tribunales formally ratified the capitulations. It is impossible that either the archbishop or the generalissimo had received intelligence on May

31 of the viceroy's decision reached in Cartagena on the previous May 25. The fastest mail service between the coast and the capital took ten days. Although it might have been possible for news of the Cartagena decision to reach Bogotá by June 7, it is highly unlikely. Communications between the coast and the capital had been effectively severed after May 31 by José Antonio Galán. Nor would it have been to the archbishop's advantage to reveal such news. The Comunero camp was suspicious enough of Bogotá's intentions as it was. News that Cartagena was about to send an expedition into the interior would probably have resulted in the immediate occupation of the adjacent capital by the wrathful Socorranos.

As he faced the infuriated soldiers of the "enterprise," Caballero y Góngora could take some kind of solace in the hope that eventually Cartagena would come to the rescue of the interior, and that therefore any settlement that he reached at Zipaquirá could be reversed subsequently. The Comunero leadership never forgot the threat in distant Cartagena. Clearly, Viceroy Flores was one of the many factors leading to the decision to reach a settlement in Zipaquirá and not in Bogotá.

Tunja's decision to move its war camp to Cajica did not break irrevocably the alliance between Socorro and Tunja. The coalition, however, had to be rebuilt; this Berbeo proceeded to do. He insisted that the Tunjanos and the archbishop agree to certain conditions, if the negotiations were to be conducted in Zipaquirá. No one disputed the supreme commander's contention that it was necessary to appease the firm belief of the plebeians that only the occupation of the capital would guarantee the observance of any negotiated treaty. Berbeo insisted that the city of Bogotá formally join the "enterprise" by "electing" five captains general, who would participate in the negotiations in Zipaquirá. The captains general for Bogotá were, indeed, not elected but carefully handpicked by the generalissimo. His choice fell on five prestigious or wealthy creoles who were regarded, whether rightly or wrongly, as latent sympathizers of the "enterprise."

Berbeo's other condition was that the entire city council of Bogotá be present in Zipaquirá to participate in the discussions.[15] The cabildo was the political stronghold of the wealthy and socially prominent creoles. The cabildo expressed reluctance. In private they vehemently protested their loyalty to the king and to his duly constituted magistrates.[16] At the insistence of the junta de tribunales, however, the nervous aldermen and the captains general were dispatched posthaste to nearby Zipaquirá.[17]

The two most influential captains general for the city of Bogotá were Berbeo's friend, the fiscal bureaucrat Francisco de Vergara, and don Jorge Miguel Lozano de Peralta, marquis of San Jorge de Bogotá. Two other captains general from Bogotá were prominent and well-connected. They were don Francisco Santa María and Dr. Francisco Antonio Vélez, a creole fiscal magistrate, and brother-in-law of Vergara. Another of Berbeo's choices could not journey to Zipaquirá for reasons of health. He was the aged Ignacio de Arce, a retired fiscal officer who had served for many years as contador mayor. Francisco de Vergara exercised Arce's power of attorney.

Given the urgency and the delicacy of the fast-changing situation, the junta brushed aside any question of a possible conflict of interest in the case of Francisco de Vergara, who would be serving both as a member of the junta and a captain general of the "enterprise."

On June 4, in the war camp of Mortiño the four captains general from the city of Bogotá were installed in office in the presence of an enthusiastically cheering army.[18] Berbeo hoped to convince the plebeians, who still had their hearts set on taking the capital, that such a move was not necessary, since some of the most prominent and visible figures in the capital had formally accepted roles of leadership in the "enterprise."

Just as the royal magistrates in Bogotá had coopted the creole bureaucratic establishment when they created the junta de tribunales on May 12 in order to initiate a dialogue with the Comuneros, so did Berbeo execute the same process by insisting that those same creole magistrates share responsibility for drafting the final agreement. If negotiations were to be conducted in Zipaquirá, Berbeo was determined that responsibility would be widely shared and hence diluted. Like all sides in 1781, he was taking out a form of insurance policy in case the capitulations were subsequently annulled and the authorities might be looking for culprits. Not only did he need to involve in the process the creole political establishment in Bogotá, but also his reluctant allies, the Tunjanos, must be forced to participate in the formulation of the settlement.

Once again the supreme commander demonstrated his political capacity. Someone had to draw up a draft of the peace treaty which the junta de tribunales would ratify. Berbeo chose two Tunjano captains of impeccable patrician background, both partisans of marching on the capital.[19] Such a deft choice conciliated the "soft-liners" in Tunja and the "hard-liners" in Socorro. In order to define the limits of the negotiated settlement, Berbeo handed the two men from Tunja a preliminary working draft that he and don Pedro Nieto had already drawn up. During the course of two frantic days, June 3 to June 5, the supreme commander as well as many other captains from Tunja, Socorro, and Bogotá actively participated in the discussions that culminated in a final draft.

A more detailed analysis of the contents of the capitulations will be postponed until the following two chapters. Suffice it to say here that the Berbeo-Nieto draft foreshadowed some of the outstanding provisions of the definitive text of the capitulations.[20] Among their most important proposals were the abolition of the armada de Barlovento sales tax and the royal tobacco monopoly, a reduction in the price of salt, aguardiente, and the Indian tribute tax, the exile of the regent visitor general, preference for creoles in officeholding, military training for all Comunero troops on Sundays, and a separate corregimiento for Socorro—San Gil.

On June 5 at 10 P.M. the commissioners received from a messenger of Juan Francisco Berbeo the proposed text of the capitulations. The archbishop, appalled by the sweeping boldness of the demands, sent the text on to Bogotá without a recommendation either to accept it or to reject it. Wrote the archbishop subsequently of the junta's position: "They had no alternative, at least in the beginning, but to reject such shameless and insolent propositions."[21]

The next day the junta met in Bogotá. Its unanimous decision was to remand the text to the commissioners in Zipaquirá, who were curtly instructed to negotiate a revision of the many clauses which prejudiced the interests of the royal treasury.[22] The junta admonished the commissioners to conform to their commission, which was to negotiate and not to accept a dictate unilaterally imposed by the Socorranos.

Shortly after the junta on the evening of June 6 reached this decision, the supreme commander received an inflammatory letter from Bogotá. Although the text of the letter has disappeared, its contents can be pieced together. The anonymous correspondent evidently had access to the highest circles in the government, for he knew of the junta's decision. Two possibilities come to mind, although there is only the softest evidence to support either conjecture.

One possible author could have been Manuel García Olano. During the critical months of March, April, and May, García Olano did little to demonstrate publicly his loyalty to the authorities. Unlike his relative the marquis of San Jorge, he did not even accept a commission in the militia.

The other possible author could have been the Dominican lay brother, Ciriaco de Archila, the probable author of the inflammatory poem. The evidence is circumstantial, flimsy but still suggestive. The letter apparently contained many garbled Biblical and historical allusions reminiscent of the poem, and its message was identical with that of "our royal decree": only the occupation of the capital would guarantee that the authorities in Bogotá would not make promises that they had no intention of observing.

Archbishop Caballero y Góngora expressed his wrath when he wrote that the letter from Bogotá could only have been written in hell, for its author maliciously intended to undermine the credibility and the good intentions of the king, the junta de tribunales, and himself.[23]

In the war camp at Mortiño unrest and anguish prevailed both among the patricians and the plebeians. It rained heavily, with frequent cloudbursts, and a threatened shortage of foodstuffs further undermined morale. Among the common soldiers the feeling gained currency that the government was merely buying time with false promises until military reinforcements arrived from Cartagena. Berbeo's own leadership was being undercut by a persistent rumor that the archbishop had bribed him with a gift of 15,000 pesos not to lead the army to Bogotá. This gossip would not die even after the generalissimo publicly reprimanded one talebearer.[24] The captains expressed alarm and consternation when they learned of the contents of the anonymous letter.

In this rapidly evolving crisis Berbeo had to take energetic steps to reassert his jeopardized leadership. It was now his turn to put pressure on the archbishop. At noon the generalissimo and two hundred of his captains and soldiers, including don Ambrosio Pisco, arrived at the parish residence, where the archbishop was lodged. They politely but firmly pressed for an explanation of the alarming letter from the capital. The archbishop gave a lengthy exhortation reassuring the captains about "the good intentions" of the junta.[25] In a masterpiece of understatement he told his audience that the junta wanted only some minor revisions and clarifications in the text of the capitulations.

In the meantime a large and increasingly unruly crowd of plebeians gathered outside the parish residence, yelling and screaming "War, war, on to Santa Fe," as they beat drums and lit skyrockets. The captains ostentatiously refused to go to the balcony to attempt to calm the increasingly irate crowds, which suggests the high command may have orchestrated the demonstration. But the intrepid archbishop, who seldom minimized his powers of persuasion, did make an appearance on the balcony. The boisterous crowd hoarsely shouted, "Long live the king"; but they also threatened to burn the house down if the commissioners did not agree forthwith to the capitulations without any further modifications.

While the mêlée was erupting outside the parish residence, the archbishop and the captains inside were feverishly attempting to revise some of the clauses of the agreement. But genuine negotiations were impossible under these conditions. After several clauses had been modified or clarified, the din of the noise outside resulted in Caballero y Góngora capitulating. He agreed that the document would be returned to Bogotá forthwith. He further promised that he would warn the junta in unambiguous language that if it did not accept the capitulations without any further changes Bogotá would have to cope with an imminent invasion.[26] On May 31 the archbishop had won a major victory when Berbeo agreed to negotiate in Zipaquirá. Now he had to pay a steep price for Berbeo's concession then.

The archbishop was fully aware of the pressures upon Berbeo from the "hawks" inside his own camp. He also realized that only the supreme commander had the prestige and leadership to control and to discipline the Comunero legions. Hence Caballero y Góngora, realistically if sadly, recognized that Berbeo's terms had to be met.

Called into an emergency session at 11 P.M. on June 7, the junta explained to the king that it gave its very reluctant approval "with the clear understanding that it was null and void." Its argument was that consent was the only means of preventing the sack of Bogotá and the "total destruction of the crown's authority."[27]

This claim must be taken skeptically. Sacking was not in style in 1781. Nor was political independence the goal of the Comunero movement. By raising these alarming prospects, the junta was seeking to justify its conduct to Charles III and José de Gálvez.

The next day, before the archbishop celebrated mass and a solemn Te Deum, the two commissioners knelt before the prelate. They placed their hands on the missal and then "swore in the name of God our Lord and by his holy cross and by the four holy gospels and in the name of the king our lord to observe the capitulations confirmed by the said real audiencia y junta superior de tribunales."[28]

Because he did not occupy the capital, Juan Francisco Berbeo has been accused by some historians of venality and of disloyalty to the cause he ostensibly led. Such charges, if uncritically accepted, grossly distort the whole meaning of the crisis of 1781.

First of all, the charge of corruption should be considered. By his own admission, Archbishop Caballero y Góngora liberally distributed gifts of money to those whom he might incline toward his proposal to negotiate in Zipaquirá. Oidor Osorio had also gone to Puente Real de Vélez with a slush fund, but found no one to whom he could dispense his largesse. We do not know most of the names of the recipients of archepiscopal generosity, but we may assume that several of the Tunjano captains were probably beneficiaries. Yet they had good and sufficient reasons for opposing the occupation of the capital without any pecuniary encouragement from the archbishop. The power of money is often exaggerated. It is a gross and cynical oversimplification that individuals can be "bought" with bribes.

It is a fact that one of Caballero y Góngora's most trusted emissaries, Filiberto José Estévez, the pastor of Oiba, did give Juan Francisco Berbeo the sum of 1,000 pesos to help defray some of the costs of feeding the troops.[29] But this event occurred after Berbeo had agreed to negotiate at Zipaquirá. There is no evidence that the amount ever even remotely approached the 15,000 pesos rumored among the populace. The 1,000 pesos was not a bribe in the sense that the archbishop was seeking to reward Berbeo for agreeing to negotiate at Zipaquirá. If it were, it was a trivial sum.

The archbishop was deeply preoccupied on both humane and political grounds with the problem of feeding 20,000 troops in a small area that was unaccustomed to such a sudden and massive influx of outsiders suffering all the discomforts imposed by the season of torrential rains. He was genuinely fearful that hunger and disease would break out, with the probable result that the relatively well-disciplined army would turn into an unruly mob over whom their leaders would lose control. So alarmed was Caballero y Góngora by this prospect that he urged the junta de tribunales to raise a special tax among the rich in Bogotá, the proceeds of which would go to feed the Comunero army.[30] The archbishop argued that the wealthy in the capital ought to be willing to make a small contribution to spare their city from a possible sack. His extraordinary proposal was the only recommendation that the junta flatly rejected. The president of that body wrote the archbishop: "This proposal conforms to the charitable way your most illustrious excellency thinks, but in the actual circumstances the junta regards it as inadvisable to implement."[31]

The junta put its faith in the imminent conclusion of an agreement in Zipaquirá. But the strong-willed and wily archbishop, who was living within earshot of 20,000 shouting and infuriated people, undertook on his own to prevent the mass starvation and the anarchy and pillage that would have ensued. Hence the donation of 1,000 pesos was not a bribe but a contribution, to feed the troops.

Berbeo's decision to negotiate at Zipaquirá has received unfavorable criticism from two types of historians. Their unhappiness stems from the nature of their distinctive ideological commitments. One group believes that the Comunero Revolution was the first serious attempt to achieve political independence from the Spanish crown.[32] The other type of historian, with a leftist orientation, sees the crisis of 1781 as an incipient social revolution from below that was betrayed by upper-class creoles.[33] Neither one of these interpretations I share. If independence or social revolution were the underlying goals of the "enterprise," then one can indeed make out a solid case that Juan Francisco Berbeo of Socorro was both a fool and a traitor in not pressing on twenty-five miles further to occupy the capital of the New Kingdom.

The late Pablo Cárdenas Acosta, perhaps the most distinguished historian of the Comuneros, passionately believed that the main current of the movement flowed in the direction of political emancipation from Spain. A direct descendant of Juan Francisco Berbeo through the female line, Cárdenas Acosta offered an ingenious, but not convincing, explanation for the conduct of his illustrious ancestor.[34]

Cárdenas Acosta was the first historian to place considerable weight on Tunja's defection from the coalition. One cannot quarrel with this aspect of the analysis, but it should be emphasized that Bogotá's cooption of the creole political elite was equally decisive. Assuming that Viceroy Flores intended to dispatch a military expedition to the interior and was informed of the paucity of munitions in Bogotá, Berbeo decided to make a truce in Zipaquirá, according to Cárdenas Acosta, until he could secure arms from Great Britain. This line of reasoning was initially suggested by Manuel Briceño, whose classic account came out in 1880.[35]

Not only did Berbeo dispatch a trusted aide at the time of Zipaquirá to seek English assistance, but also, according to Briceño and Cárdenas Acosta, Berbeo and the marquis of San Jorge traveled in 1783 in some form of disguise to the Dutch island of Curaçao. There they appealed to Luis Vidalle to enlist the support of Great Britain for the resumption of hostilities in New Granada.

The Curaçao voyage is unadulterated fantasy. Luis Vidalle was a mendacious double agent offering his services to both Spain and Great Britain, and the documentation supporting his claims to be the agent of Berbeo and San Jorge is insufficient, internally contradictory, and quite untrustworthy.[36]

Los grandes conflictos sociales y económicos de nuestra historia, by Indalecio Liévano Aguirre, is one of the most influential works of history that has been published in Colombia in the twentieth century. Driven by a deeply felt patriotic urge to seek an historical explanation for Colombia's failure to escape from the domination of powerfully entrenched oligarchies, Liévano Aguirre concentrated much attention on the Comuneros. No objective historian can deny his wide-ranging erudition and his penetrating iconoclasm. He is in Colombia the most influential "revisionist" historian of our times, who has devastatingly and learnedly challenged a host of accepted myths of traditional Colombia historiography. But in so doing he has helped to foster some countermyths.

Minimizing somewhat unjustly the importance of Tunja's defection, Liévano argued that the basic split was not between Tunja and Socorro but between the creole elites and the others. Liévano commented:

> As we have already observed, the captain of the Comuneros [Berbeo] was a creole on all four sides of his family. His loyalty to the uprising remained inalterable as long as it did not overstep the limits of a revolt compatible with the interests of the creole oligarchy. His behavior changed, and not for reasons of personal dishonesty, when the revolutionary dynamic which propelled the crowds toward Santa Fe was transformed into acts contrary to those interests, such as land invasions, Indian uprisings, the proclamation of aboriginal monarchies and the rebellion of the slaves. . . . The revolution failed, not because the authorities subsequently disregarded the capitulations, but because its impetus and energies were cut off at Zipaquirá, when the creole oligarchy and its representatives refused to continue following the course the Comunero uprising had taken. [pp. 483–85]

Liévano has made the most eloquent case for the argument that the Comunero Revolution was a "revolution betrayed" by the creole "oligarchy" who feared the increasing radicalization of the movement.[37] Appealing though it may be to today's leftists, it is misleading to claim that the Comunero movement was a potentially radical social revolution in which the privileged position of the creoles was jeopardized by the lower classes.

The aspirations of the plebeians in no way threatened the patricians. The populace wanted the abolition of several royal monopolies, no territorial restrictions on the cultivation of tobacco, cheaper retail prices for tobacco and aguardiente, and reduced sales taxes—goals that the well-born creoles also shared. The basic difference between the two groups was not about objectives but tactics. The plebeians placed a simple faith in the belief that the occupation of the capital was the only secure guarantee that these specific grievances would be redressed. The patrician creoles, on the other hand, with their much greater political experience, had a long tradition of negotiating and compromising their differences inside the bureaucracy. Hence to the upper classes negotiating at Zipaquirá rather than in the capital was a reasonable approach and one that conformed to the spirit of bureacratic decentralization, a system of government they sought to restore.

Furthermore, the men of Zipaquirá took for granted a notion of political legitimacy resting on the principle of the authority of tradition sanctioned by Divine Providence. If the king could do no wrong and if he were the anointed of the Lord, there was little alternative but ultimately to negotiate with his ministers. A generation later, the men of 1810 had a more rational and secular principle of political legitimacy with which to challenge the traditional notion.

The Indian dissatisfaction did not arouse any deep fears on the part of the creoles of a social revolution from below. Ambrosio Pisco proved a pliant titular chieftain of the Indians, whom Berbeo effectively coopted both to control the Indians and to frighten the Spanish authorities in Bogotá.[38]

The rebellion of the slaves in Antioquia did not occur until several months after Zipaquirá. José Antonio Galán freed a few slaves, but after the first week in June when the fate of the Comuneros was being decided. And when myth and fact are carefully separated, José Antonio's exploits do not make him into a social revolutionary. As we shall observe in chapters 15 and 16, the archbishop and the audiencia several months after Zipaquirá created the myth of José Antonio Galán as a proponent of social revolution from below for the deliberate purpose of frightening the creoles into renewing their loyalty to the crown.

One of the most astonishing facts of the Comunero movement is how well disciplined and well behaved the plebeians actually were. There are, at the very most, not more than a half-dozen documented cases of the looting of private property. In most cases the captains promptly returned the stolen property to their owners. That is an extraordinary record indeed. The crowds usually burned the tobacco from the royal monopoly. Only seldom did they smoke it or steal for their private benefit. They also emptied into the streets the wooden kegs of aguardiente belonging also to the royal monopoly, but seldom drank it. Had they done so often, the Comunero revolution would have quickly degenerated into a drunken orgy, which it certainly did not become.

No less keen an eyewitness than the archbishop himself was impressed, if not somewhat horrified, at the disciplined control that the Socorrano captains exercised over their followers.[39] The passionately angry plebeians expressed their fury by yelling and shouting in the squares until their voices were hoarse. When they did riot, for example as on June 7, they were probably rioting on orders from Berbeo in order to put pressure on the archbishop. Living in an aristocratic society, the plebeians believed that their own grievances could be vindicated by the only leaders to whom they granted instinctive loyalty and respect, the local creole patricians.

It would be a grave error to read popular discontents of later ages into the world of 1781. The Comunero Revolution was not an abortive social revolution that the creoles betrayed, for neither the patricians nor plebeians wanted a social revolution. The Comunero movement was a socioconstitutional and sociopolitical crisis, in which the fiscal innovations introduced by the regent visitor general were but the tip of the iceberg.

Although the patricians and plebeians differed on tactics, they shared a profound unity of purpose. They both rejected change, the kind of change that Gutiérrez de Piñeres was seeking to impose on them. Everyone dreamed of going back to a golden age of the past, to a world before 1778. For the plebeians that idealized past was a world where taxes were light and rather inefficiently collected. For the patricians it was one in which they cogoverned with the European Spanish bureaucrats.

One final question merits careful analysis: did Berbeo anticipate that the capitulations would be subsequently annulled? Juridically speaking, capitulations were a treaty or a solemn agreement between the king and one or a group of his subjects in which the two contracting parties agreed to perform mutual services and obligations.

While recognizing that the capitulations at Zipaquirá had been won under the threat of force and intimidation, Berbeo and his captains evidently assumed that they would secure the indispensable royal ratification. Why? Both the European Spanish and creole political establishments were parties to the agreement, which also enjoyed militant popular support. Surely, the king would not reject a treaty signed under these circumstances, the Comunero captains must have reasoned.[40] Such an assumption was very plausible, given the time-honored tradition in which the creole elites were accustomed to have their views seriously taken into account by the various agencies of the government.

In fact, the creoles made a serious miscalculation. No sooner had the authorities disarmed the Comuneros and reestablished royal control than they formally annulled the treaty on the grounds that it had been imposed under duress. The juridical spirit of the capitulations belonged to the sixteenth century, when conquistadors often signed a formal contract with the crown in order to undertake a particular conquest. The privileges, rewards, and obligations of the conquistadors were precisely spelled out. Their heirs often argued in law suits that the crown was under a contractual obligation to fulfill its promises on the grounds that their forebears had conquered the New World. Implicit in the choice of the word "capitulations," so rich in six-teenth-century connotations and seldom used in the late eighteenth century, is the notion that the citizens of New Granada, as the heirs and descendants of the original settlers of the land, had some basic prescriptive rights that the crown should respect.[41]

Hence the political traditions animating the capitulations of Zipaquirá were anathema to the Caroline absolutists. The implicit political theory of the Comunero chieftains looked backward to sixteenth-century America, whereas the magistrates in Bogotá and Madrid were guided by the spirit of French-inspired enlightened despotism in which the sole duty of subjects was to obey constituted authorities.

Juan Francisco Berbeo's decision to negotiate at Zipaquirá was the result of a complex confluence of events. Certainly the reluctance of Tunja was significant. Even more decisive were Bogotá's willingness to make massive concessions and Bogotá's success in making an alliance with the long-entrenched procreole political establishment in the capital who were the silent allies of the Socorranos. And no one in Zipaquirá was unaware of Viceroy Flores's garrison in Cartagena.

The most persuasive demonstration that the Comunero movement was an acute political and constitutional crisis, not a move toward independence nor a betrayed social revolution, can be found in the text of the capitulations themselves—the topic of the following two chapters.

13

The Capitulations of Zipaquirá: Fiscal Aspects

Theory and Spirit

The treaty that the junta superior de tribunales ratified with the Comunero captains in Zipaquirá on June 8, 1781, is one of the most remarkable sociopolitical and socioeconomic documents in the entire history of the Spanish empire in the New World. It is an eloquent and poignant expression of the hopes and fears of a simple, but proud, people who were seeking to assert their own identity in a time of troubles.

The ideological origins of the capitulations are twofold. First, as was observed in the last chapter, the capitulations hark back to the period of the Spanish conquest. Second, woven into the text is the spirit and tone of the classic Spanish political theorists of the sixteenth and seventeenth centuries, the most notable of whom was the Jesuit theologian Francisco Suárez. Living in the age of the House of Habsburg, they advocated a strong monarchy, but they also vigorously defended the rights of public corporations and private individuals, founded on divine, natural, and customary law. In the course of this analysis the tensions and contradictions between these two distinct political traditions will emerge.

The men of 1781 faced the prime question that all political societies at one time or another must agonizingly confront: how to reconcile the coercive power of the state with the liberty of groups and individuals. In their search for answers the philosophical principles and the rhetoric they employed came not from the contemporary world but from the more remote medieval, Renaissance, and Baroque past of Castile and America.

There is, for example, no trace of the political ideology of the Enlighten-

156

ment which was influential in the contemporary North American movement for independence. There is no reference to the inalienable rights of man nor any explicit affirmation of popular sovereignty, as John Locke had defined it.[1] But the ancient Spanish phrase, el común, the community, was endlessly invoked. Deeply rooted in the document is the assumption of late medieval Castile, that the king could not impose new taxes without some unspecified form of consent from his subjects. An implicit premise is that the king and his subjects colegislate in all matters affecting the common welfare.

Nor is there any suggestion in the capitulations of representative government, as it had developed in the Anglo-American world during the seventeenth and eighteenth centuries. What is evident, however, is an affirmation of the Spanish American tradition of consent of the governed by means of bureaucratic negotiation. Although explicit political abstractions are notably absent, there is an implicit suggestion that government rests on the consent of the governed and supremacy of laws and customs over the will of the prince.

The New Kingdom of Granada is a *corpus mysticum politicum,* a political community with its own customs and laws that neither the king nor his ministers can violate with impunity. Under the House of Austria the ties uniting the overseas settlements to the peninsula were not, juridically speaking, those of colony to mother country as the Caroline bureaucrats viewed it. Each audiencia was in law an inalienable, if subordinate, kingdom united in a personal union with the crowns of Castile and León.[2] Indicating their sovereign status, the audiencias in their corporate capacity enjoyed the rank, title, and style of "highness"—and the capitulations used this old-fashioned nomenclature of the Habsburgs, which had gone out of style by the time of Charles III.

The text of the capitulations explicitly extols the early viceroys—Sebastián de Eslava, José Alfonso Pizarro, and José de Solís. Their regimes in retrospect became a golden age to which the Comuneros nostalgically wanted to return. Animating the text of the capitulations is the notion that New Granada had an "unwritten constitution," a kind of informal social contract based on custom and precedent, which the fiscal and administrative policies of the regent visitor general had grossly violated. The corrosion of the "unwritten constitution" gradually began in the 1760's, when Viceroy Pedro Mesía de la Cerda introduced the tobacco monopoly, and it reached its culmination during the administration of Gutiérrez de Piñeres. The ostensible goal of the capitulations was to return to the status quo ante 1760.

The final text consists of a preamble, thirty-four articles dealing with specific abuses and a final article concerning the procedure of ratification. It was hastily drawn up between June 3 and June 5 from an initial draft submitted by Juan Francisco Berbeo and Pedro Nieto. Its language does not lack its own form of archaic beauty and passionate dignity. In some places, however, the rhetoric is rustic and cumbersome. The language of the capitulations sharply contrasts with the coldly rational and finely chiseled bureaucratic prose of a Caballero y Góngora or a Gutiérrez de Piñeres.

There is no discernible logical sequence to the clauses. According to Rafael Gómez Hoyos, the organization and the spirit of the capitulations belong to the casuist tradition of the sixteenth- and seventeenth-century Spanish theologians.[3] Casuistry was that branch of moral philosophy in which the theoretical principles are developed and formulated on the basis of concrete themes and their application to practical circumstances. It has been criticized as oversubtle, intellectually dishonest, and even sophistical. The English reader should be warned not to apply the derogatory meaning that is the more common sense of the term in the English language. The capitulations were far from being oversubtle, intellectually dishonest, or sophistical. Rather, their theoretical principles are embedded in very specific and concrete issues. The capitulations, in effect, constitute a long list of particular grievances in which basic theoretical principles are implicit rather than explicit. In this sense they resemble the *cahiers* that French citizens presented to the deputies of the Third Estate in 1789, which emphasized specific grievances to the total exclusion of explicit principles of political philosophy.[4]

In the preamble, Juan Francisco Berbeo acts not as the representative of an unruly crowd but as the popularly elected spokesman of the political community of New Granada, the *corpus mysticum politicum*.[5] Taking for granted the time-honored principle of the popular origin of sovereignty, he, Juan Francisco Berbeo of Socorro, "the captain general and the commander of all the cities, towns, parishes, and villages which compose the larger part of this kingdom," seeks to make a treaty with the representatives of the crown in which public authority would be defined in order to achieve *bonum commune*, the common good, of the whole kingdom.

> I raise my voice in warning. Knowing that I speak with the unanimous voice of the people, I request the end of taxes and relief from the excesses from which this kingdom suffers. Because these taxes cannot be tolerated, either in their amount or in the odious way in which they are collected, the town of Socorro has found it necessary to rid herself of them by means which are already well known. The other cities, towns, parishes, and localities all continue to feel the same pain. In the meanwhile I have sought their advice, and we are unanimously in accord in our intentions. I appear before your highness [the audiencia] in all submissiveness both in my own name and also in the name of all those who have elected me to my command as well as in the name of all the others who have joined our enterprise. In view of

the fact that these capitulations have been drafted by the representatives of those men who elected me, I propose the following.[6]

The proud, even haughty, but always respectful tone of Berbeo's preamble, so reminiscent of the assertive conquistadors, profoundly shocked those Caroline bureaucrats who believed that subjects owed blind obedience to constituted authority.

A careful analysis of the capitulations reveals that Juan Francisco Berbeo headed a varied coalition. The aspirations of every important vested interest were amply represented in the document. The Indians, the poor mestizo and creole farmers, the small merchants, the petty elites in the rural towns, and the bureaucratic elites in Bogotá each received substantial concessions. And what each group received should be considered in turn.

The Indians

The Indians, who were contemptuously disdained by both the creoles and mestizos, were, at the most, junior partners in the coalition. Yet no one was more aware than the generalissimo of the need to alleviate their distress. Hence Berbeo insisted that don Ambrosio Pisco, the titular leader of the Indians, formally participate in the drafting of the settlement.[7]

The principal beneficiaries of the fourteenth clause were the Indians. Bitterly assailing the rise in prices that consumers had to pay under the new royal monopoly, the fourteenth clause advocated that the salt mines be restored to the Indian communities to whom they had belonged from time immemorial. Under the new royal monopoly the price of an *arroba* of salt had risen from two reales to three and one-half reales. Obviously the steep rise in the course of a few years hit the lower classes hardest. Another source of deep-rooted bitterness was that the new salt monopoly required consumers to pay for their purchases in currency, replacing the customary barter arrangement.

The fourteenth clause was directed to two different sources of discontent and two somewhat separate constituencies. All consumers, in particular the poor, would benefit by a rollback in the price of that necessity and the restoration of barter payment (gold and silver currency were becoming scarcer). The second constituency was the Indians in the region of Zipaquirá, who were ferociously resentful about the recent confiscation of their ancestral salt mines.[8]

The seventh clause, however, focused on the more virulent sources of Indian discontent: (1) the tribute tax, (2) the exactions of the clergy, and (3) the resguardos. The language expresses a paternalist sympathy for the plight of the Indians that is reminiscent of the Habsburgs:

> All the Indians are in a most deplorable state of poverty. It is as I write because I know what I see. I believe that looking at them with due charity such poverty will be evident to your highness [the audiencia]. You will also see that few hermits could display more frugality in their clothing and their food than the Indians because their limited knowledge and meager resources in no way reach the point of satisfying the increased tribute which is forcefully demanded of them. [CA, 2:20]

In no section other than the preamble did the supreme commander employ the first person. Its use in the seventh clause was to underline the urgency of the need to offer relief to the Indians, and the clause did go on to offer tangible and meaningful relief in some areas.

The clause urged that the tribute tax should be reduced to four pesos per married couple. It also contained a concession to free blacks, who were traditionally obligated to pay a tribute, although it was often unevenly collected. This tax, the *requintado,* was lowered to two pesos—suggesting that this group enjoyed a social status somewhat superior to the Indians. This, by the way, is the only specific reference in the capitulations to the freed blacks as a group, while the tiny group of black slaves received no specific mention at all. To be sure, men of color were also beneficiaries of the host of measures designed to lighten the burden of the poor. No one in 1781, either in English or Spanish America, was prepared to address himself in any significant way to the abolition of slavery.

In view of the drastic decline of the Indian population the income the crown derived from the Indian tribute tax was no longer a significant portion of the royal revenues. Some magistrates, such as Fiscal Moreno, had even admitted that it might be abolished without any serious damage to those revenues, but he had not pressed the suggestion.[9]

The seventh clause assailed the corregidores and the parish clergy as allies who cooperated in exploiting the Indians. The corregidores received the enthusiastic support of the clergy, since a portion of the tribute tax provided the stipend for those priests administering Indian parishes. The clause prohibited the clergy from collecting fees for the administration of the sacraments of extreme unction and matrimony, and for burial emoluments—a practice that had long angered the Indians, and that royal bureaucrats throughout the empire had long condemned, with varying enthusiasm, as an unnecessary burden on the natives.[10]

Significant though these proposals may have been in seeking to alleviate distress, the major complaint of the Indians was the absorption of their ancestral community lands, the resguardos, by the rapidly multiplying creoles and mestizos. The last sentence in the seventh clause addressed itself to the key issue of the community lands. The significance of these phrases has unfortunately escaped the attention of most historians.[11]

> These people [the Indians] should be restored to the lands that they have possessed since time immemorial. The resguardos that they now hold should be theirs not only in usufruct but also as full owners (*en cabal propiedad*) and be considered their property to dispose and to sell as they see fit as owners [in fee simple].
> [CA, 2:15]

Like the iceberg, the real meaning of these phrases lies underneath the surface. On one hand, the clause apparently repudiated the whole policy of consolidating the community lands that had taken place in previous decades. But it must be remembered that the driving force behind the "land reform" of the 1770's was the land and labor hunger of the rapidly multiplying creoles and mestizos. These ethnic groups were the hard core of the "enterprise." No responsible Comunero leader could afford to neglect their vested interests. What this language seems to say is that resguardo lands recently acquired by the creoles and the mestizo small farmers should be returned to the Indians and that no further consolidations should take place. On the surface such a proposal would be totally unacceptable to the creoles and to the mestizos.

The contradiction is more apparent than real. The last sentence is the key. The Indians would be given a title in fee simple to their community lands, and hence would be free to sell them. And that is precisely what the creoles and mestizos wanted. The Indians for decades past had partially alienated a large portion of their lands, in violation of the law, by renting them to the creoles and mestizos. In a regime of fee simple, the impecunious Indians, under the need to meet ordinary or extraordinary living expenses, could easily be pressured into selling their lands. Potentially cultivable land was plentiful. Labor was scarce. The creoles and mestizos needed to develop ways of pushing the Indians off their ancestral lands, thereby giving them no alternative but to enter the labor force as cheap hired hands. Had the seventh clause ever been enforced, the resguardos would have been liquidated within a generation and their Indian population would have been incorporated into the rural labor force at low wages.

In this important case the Comunero leaders were guilty of political duplicity. They were simultaneously proposing the restoration of the Indian resguardos and a formula by which the non-Indian farmers would be able legally to gobble up the remaining resguardo lands.[12] Juan Francisco Berbeo was the head of a diverse coalition. The vital interests of two components in this particular case were in conflict. While Berbeo recognized the gravity of

Indian complaints, the aspirations of the small creole and mestizo farmers rated a higher political priority than did the concerns of the Indians. The former, after all, constituted the hard core of his coalition, while the Indians were merely a peripheral component. The generalissimo had to make the kind of tough political decision that often confronts any successful practicer of coalition politics, and bend where the pressure was stronger. While making substantial concessions to the less influential Indian contingent in his alliance, he could not foreclose to his creole-mestizo allies what they had been doing for decades—encroaching upon the lands of the steadily diminishing Indian population.

Archbishop Caballero y Góngora, with a different set of political priorities from Berbeo, sought to redress the balance between the Indian and the creole-mestizo communities. The archbishop viceroy returned to the policy first formulated by Gutiérrez de Piñeres in his important memorandum of February 3, 1780. In leading a cautious return to a modified paternalism, the archbishop made no attempt to undo the consolidation implemented by 1778, but he forbade any further consolidations. Above all else, he insisted that the Indians could only enjoy usufruct and not title in fee simple. Hence, the Indians could not even rent their community lands; least of all could they sell them. During the last three decades of its existence the viceregal regime tenaciously clung to this policy.[13]

A Program for the Plebeians

If the capitulations offered some genuine relief to the Indians, the plebeians in the rural villages and parishes also received massive concessions in the area which hit them the most—taxes. The preamble had stated: "these taxes cannot be tolerated, either in their amount or in the odious way in which they are collected." The capitulations endlessly repeated that New Granada was an impoverished land that could not afford to pay the new taxes, and just as often they protested the abrasive manner in which the taxes were collected and administered, and which they saw as humiliating and degrading to the innate dignity of the loyal vassals of the king.

The capitulations did not foreshadow the equalitarian principle that all taxes should be collected equally on all classes, the kind of Enlightenment principle that Nariño and the other leaders of independence would demand a generation later. On the contrary, they looked back to the medieval notion of distributive justice, formulated by Thomas Aquinas and subsequently popularized in the Spanish world by Francisco Suárez.[14] Living in a society based on inherent inequalities and hereditary privilege, the citizens of New Granada were still attached to the old-fashioned medieval notion that taxes should be collected by a differential standard in accordance with wealth and social position.

Nor did the king's loyal vassals of 1781 deny that they should pay taxes. The fifteenth clause spelled out their attitude:

> We offer as loyal vassals that when a legitimate need of His Majesty either involving the defense of the faith or the defense of even the smallest part of his dominions is brought to our attention and he asks for a forced loan and gift, we shall contribute with great pleasure. Furthermore we shall pay more than just that tax. We shall spend as much as our meager resources allow, whether it be money, men at our own expense, arms, horses or supplies, as we have always done in the past. [CA, 2:24]

These sentences throw much light on the mood of the men of 1781. The citizens of the New Kingdom of Granada are to be the judges of whether the king has a legitimate need for new taxes to defend either the faith or the realm. The clear implication is that Charles III and his ministers have not persuaded his loyal vassals of the need for the taxes that the regent visitor general began imposing in 1778. Another unmistakable implication is that any new fiscal burden, however justified its cause, would have to secure in some unspecified form the consent of those being taxed.

These doctrines were profoundly alien to the mentality of the absolutist technocrats who governed the Spain of Charles III. Gutiérrez de Piñeres pithily expressed the wide chasm between his own technocrats and the king's subjects in New Granada when he wrote to Viceroy Flores:

> The plebeians are not capable of understanding the justification for royal taxes. All they aspire to is their own self-interest, which is absolute and unlimited libertinism. Since it is vain to anticipate that the multitude would gladly pay any taxes whatsoever, the goal of the government must be to force the plebeians to respect public authority so that their subordination and obedience to all magistrates will be preserved.[15]

The armada de Barlovento sales tax was abolished outright "and its very name may never be mentioned again [CA, 2:19]."[16] The rate of the traditional and older sales tax, the alcabala, was reduced from 4 to 2 percent. Furthermore, the kinds of merchandise subject to the tax were reduced to European products, cloth, linen, blankets, cacao, sugar preserves, tobacco, pack animals, real estate, houses, and cattle. Specifically exempted from the sales tax were all foodstuffs and cotton and cotton thread, "because only the poor plant and harvest it [CA, 2:21]." Moreover, since cotton thread was used by the poor of Socorro and San Gil as a sort of currency, the viceroy's inclusion of it in the sales tax was a political blunder of the first magnitude.

The single most visible target of popular wrath was the royal tobacco monopoly, principally for two reasons. First, most citizens rich or poor smoked the weed. Second, tobacco could be cultivated on small plots of land. During the years prior to 1781 it had become a lucrative cash crop for a legion of small farmers in the jurisdiction of the towns of Socorro and San Gil. The recent visitor general's increase in the price of tobacco and his restriction of tobacco production were among the principal sources of popular discontent. In its frantic efforts to turn back the rising tide of discontent, the junta de tribunales on May 14 had rescinded the increase.

The sixth clause of the capitulations made the sweeping demand that the tobacco monopoly itself be abolished. The clause further proclaimed that there be no territorial restrictions on cultivation. Tobacco was to be sold in the free market, subject only to a 2 percent sales tax.

The crowds also vociferously demonstrated against the regent visitor general's increase in the price of aguardiente. To express their wrath they dumped numerous casks of that liquor into the streets. Yet the capitulations did not advocate the abolition of that royal monopoly, but merely that the recent increase in price be rescinded. Such a concession the junta de tribunales had already granted on May 14. Aguardiente, which the populace plentifully imbibed, most directly concerned consumers. The poor could not cultivate sugar cane as they could tobacco, for sugar plantations required a large capital investment, and hence did not participate in the production of aguardiente. Their sole concern was that of consumers who wanted cheap liquor. Given the limited market for their product, the sugar plantation owners were evidently satisfied with the monopoly that guaranteed a partial outlet for their product. Moreover, sugar was much more extensively cultivated in the coastal provinces, which were unaffected by the disturbances that erupted in the mountain interior of the kingdom.

The capitulations swept away another ancient royal monopoly, that on playing cards. Since all classes found playing cards and gambling an endless source of amusement and relaxation, the royal monopoly provided a small but steady source of income for the crown.[17] Its abolition would obviously be even more welcome to the poor than to the well-to-do.

In the definitive text playing cards were to be sold in the free market by anyone who cared to manufacture them. In a previous draft, however, a puritanical note had crept in. Card playing as such was forbidden under any circumstances, a prohibition to be enforced with a rather draconian penalty: for the rich there was a fine of a hundred patacones; for the poor, a hundred days in jail. All playing cards produced in Spain arriving in American ports should either be dumped into the harbor or shipped back to the peninsula.[18] Among the Comuneros, as is often the case in social convulsions, there were some puritanical moralists, but their views did not prevail.

Another target for popular discontent was Charles III's appeal for a forced loan, "donavito gracioso y préstamo," in which the nobles would pay two pesos and the plebeians one peso apiece.[19] The two-tier structure of the tax is a graphic illustration of the hierarchical character of that society as well as a reflection of Suárez's notion of distributive justice. Obviously the burden of this tax would weigh more heavily on the poor than on the rich, even though the poor paid less.

The fifteenth clause annulled the collection of the loan, on the grounds that the king had not convinced his loyal vassals of the need for it. The clear implication was that the community had to consent to new taxes.

There were still other fiscal concessions to placate the wrath of the populace. The prices of basic necessities such as salt, gunpowder, and official stamped paper were rolled back to the price levels existing before the arrival of Gutiérrez de Piñeres. The new price of official stamped paper, which since 1638 had to be used for all government, legal, and commercial documents, also reflected the principle of distributive justice.[20] The clergy, the Indians, and the poor had to pay only half a real for a sheet, while the well-to-do were charged two reales.

There were other concessions whose particular beneficiaries were the plebeians. The thirty-fourth article provided for a general amnesty on all fines that were imposed by the regent visitor general for violations of his edicts. These were legion, and the vast majority were owed by plebeians.

Another source of popular discontent was arbitrary imprisonments. By putting up a bond, the socially prominent undergoing trial, even for serious crimes, might be put under house arrest or, for less serious indictments, under city arrest, whereas the plebeians might languish for months in jails where living conditions were primitive even by the standards of those days. The thirty-second article sought to remedy these abuses by providing that every prisoner, no matter what his social station, was to be promptly released from jail after his arraignment, upon payment of a small fee of two pesos. Those who had already been incarcerated for a long period without being tried were to be released gratis and immediately. The men of 1781 were sponsors of a modest but meaningful reform when they justified their proposal "that the prisons will not turn into warehouses for storing prisoners and thus causing riots there [CA, 2:28]." Any advocate of penal reform today would sympathize with these sentiments.

The plebeians looked to the patrician creole elites as their natural leaders. The evidence is abundant that the plebeians played an active and dynamic role during the course of the "enterprise" under patrician direction. Berbeo was acutely aware of the depth of popular discontent and the necessity of sponsoring substantial concessions to alleviate it. Only by following that course could he dissuade the populace from their cherished goal of occupying

Santa Fe de Bogotá. The concessions to the plebeians contained in the capitulations were far more sweeping than the edicts of May 14, frantically and hurriedly passed by the junta de tribunales.

At Zipaquirá, Berbeo did not betray his plebeian allies. On the contrary, the capitulations eliminated many major and minor sources of popular discontent, the majority of them fiscal in nature. Although the creole elites would also benefit from the return to things as they had been before Gutiérrez de Piñeres's reforms, it is clear that the fiscal burden had fallen more oppressively on the poor than on the rich.

The Social Function of Private Property

Victor Frankl and Rafael Gómez Hoyos have pointed out that the capitulations stressed the social function of private property.[21] This idea, of course, derived from the main line of late medieval social philosophy. In conformity with the casuist structure of the capitulations, attention was concentrated on very concrete issues. Yet the theoretical principle underlying the specific point is a clear, if implicit, affirmation that private property should be regulated in order to achieve the common good of the whole community—principles spelled out by Domingo de Soto, the Dominican theologian, in his classic treatise *De justitia et jure.*[22] Three clauses merit special attention. The twenty-sixth article provided that fields and pastures bordering on public roads not be enclosed, so that merchants and travelers might readily feed their animals—a clear limit on the rights of private property.

The same principle was emphatically implied in the twenty-seventh article:

> For the public benefit the nitrate found on the estate of don Agustín de Medina in the territory of Paipa will be sold at the price of two reales the half load, weighed and handled by his administrators. [CA, 2:27]

The social benefit principle was even more strongly stated in the next-to-final draft, which denounced the "greedy" who had been charging four reales "for the benefit of the few."[23] The twenty-eighth clause provided that no road nor bridge could be owned by private individuals. Only public corporations, such as cities and towns, could charge tolls over bridges. In a previous draft the affirmation of the supremacy of the general welfare over private interests was even more sharply focused.

However swiftly may have flowed the current of Thomist-Suárezist doctrine of the social function of private property in 1781, there was one notable exception. In the face of the acute land and labor hunger of the creoles and the mestizos the communal rights of the Indians were repudiated in favor of private property rights.

Commerce and Merchants

In the capitulations some seven articles deal with the promotion of trade and commerce. Perhaps the outstanding complaint of the small merchants was the recently imposed system of guías and tornaguías (see chapter 2, notes 35, 36). But most of all, the new bureaucratic machinery of Gutiérrez de Piñeres promised a much more efficient collection of sales taxes. Not only had rates just been increased but the taxes previously had been incompletely collected. That the small merchants bitterly resented the new bureaucratic procedures is amply attested in the second article which emphatically stated, "The guías, which have vexed the entire kingdom from the very moment that they were established, must cease forever [CA, 2:19]."

Not only was ownership of bridges and the right to exact tolls regulated, but improvements in the network of transportation were actively fostered. The twenty-ninth clause provided for building a new bridge of lime and stone at Chiquinquirá under the supervision of the cabildo of Tunja.

The concern for the redress of particular grievances as well as the intensity of regional rivalries is graphically reflected in the tenth clause. In 1750 Viceroy Pizarro had allowed the city of Bogotá to charge a special tax for animals and merchandise coming into the city, on the grounds that entry into the capital was extremely congested. That tax, designed to improve transportation routes into the city, had netted some 130,000 pesos since 1750. The tenth clause argued that the expenses involved in maintaining and improving entrance roads into the city had never exceeded 70,000 pesos during those three decades, and the city of Bogotá had made a net profit of some 60,000 pesos. The clause complained that it was not just that the merchants of Vélez, Socorro, and Tunja should pay for the improvements in the public access to the capital while their own transportation needs were being neglected or financed "out of left-overs [CA, 2:21]." The clause pointedly insisted that Bogotá should pay for its own transportation improvements.

Virtually all commercial contracts required the services of a notary, an escribano. Hence the nineteenth article provided for strict adherence to the set of fees, *arancel,* formulated by the government. "If the notaries are proven guilty of exceeding the official tariff three times, they can be removed from office without further cause [CA, 2:25]."

Still another article dealt with the public postal service which Viceroy Pizarro had founded in 1750. The eleventh clause charged that in a recent change in rates the director general, José Pando, "was advised by persons ignorant of the distances between localities" and hence the new tariff "assigned unjustly high rates [CA, 2:22]." The article requested a new tariff of postal rates based on a uniform principle of distance.

Still another concession to promote the interests of small merchants was the thirty-first clause, which stated: "Given the poverty of many men and women who with very little capital set up small retail stores, we request that they be obligated to pay no taxes other than the alcabala and the *propios* [CA, 2:28]."

The clauses dealing primarily with the promotion of commerce have no special ideological interest. There is no reflection whatsoever of the new economic doctrines of the European Enlightenment. There is nothing novel beyond the traditional aspirations of the commercial class since the sixteenth century. What these clauses do suggest is the depth of the merchants' discontent with some of the fiscal policies of the regent visitor general.

Perhaps the most arresting of the economic clauses is the one that dealt with the whole question of credit. The convents, monasteries, and the endless number of ecclesiastic charitable funds, *obras pías*, were the only sources of credit from which merchants could finance their transactions and farmers could secure mortgages either to pay off their consumer debts or to acquire new farmlands. A recent royal order required all ecclesiastical corporations to deposit their trust funds in the royal treasury, which in turn would pay them an annual 4 percent on their capital. In time of war, when prices were rising, as they did in 1781, the ecclesiastical corporations found themselves compelled to sell some of their capital assets in order to meet their expenses. Such a practice, however, violated their ecclesiastical statutes as well as the conditions under which the church received the endowments from private individuals. However much the royal treasury might have benefitted from the new regime, the thirteenth clause charged that under this arrangement capital for loans was rapidly drying up.

The article proposed that the royal order be rescinded. Let the clergy administer their own capital funds. Merchants and farmers would cheerfully pay the traditional 5 percent and not the new 4 percent in return for a more plentiful supply of credit. This request for a 1 percent increase in the interest rate is all the more remarkable in view of the fact that many other clauses in the capitulations are complaints against the alleged excessive exactions of the clergy. But the principal concern of the thirteenth article was to increase the amount of available funds. Long accustomed to paying 5 percent, the well-to-do in New Granada were quite prepared to continue to do so.[24]

The Birth of Anticlericalism

One of the most extraordinary features of the remarkable document that has gone down into history as the capitulations of Zipaquirá is the six articles dealing with the alleged abuses of the clergy. Heretofore they have not received from historians the attention that they merit.

It will be recalled that the seventh clause, concerning the Indians, had accused the clergy of exploitation. Not only were the Indians oppressed by the exactions and fees charged by the clergy, but so were the creoles and mestizos. The ecclesiastical notaries whose services were necessary for baptisms, weddings, and funerals were accused of overcharging their clients, sometimes grossly. The nineteenth clause used unusually blunt language: "From this day forward the law shall be obeyed and the ecclesiastical notaries shall be severely punished [for violations], since this kind of bureaucrat everywhere is a waster, a plague and a parasite [CA, 2:25]." The article went on to stress the lack of accountability of those scribes: "Because the ecclesiastical notaries have less to lose than the civil notaries, who are appointed by his majesty to hold their offices, the ecclesiastical notaries can ignore any kind of law which does not please them with greater facility than their civil counterparts."

Perhaps the most candid criticism of the clergy is the twenty-third clause, which stated:

> The heaviest burden weighing down upon all the cities, parishes, towns, villages and localities is the collection of the sacramental fees. This situation deserves the greatest attention, since not even the poorest person is free of this tax because the decrees of the church councils and ecclesiastical laws go unobserved. [CA, 2:26]

The article expressed the hope that the archbishop in the performance of his pastoral duties would bring about "a total remedy" of these abuses.

In another article the collectors of the ecclesiastical tithes were accused of charging illegal and excessive fees. Their emoluments, "which constitute an unbearable burden [CA, 2:27]," should be drastically scaled down. Still another clause complained of the problem of supporting the ecclesiastical visitors, periodically dispatched by the bishop to audit cofradía accounts, wills, and parish records. The twenty-fourth article concluded: "the priests shall be given provisions only in the places they actually visit . . . all the other expenses of the ecclesiastical visitors be the responsibility of the archbishop or the bishop who commissioned them [CA, 2:26–27]."

Another complaint was the high cost of securing the indulgences contained in the *santa bula de la cruzada.*

> Not even ten percent of the inhabitants of the kingdom benefit from the santa bula de la cruzada because of the poverty of the land and its high price. Its use would be doubled if its price were cut in half. [CA, 2:22]

The sum total of the six articles in the capitulations dealing specifically with the clergy clearly implies that there was a deep-rooted dissatisfaction with the heavy fees that all groups in society had to spend in order to maintain the ecclesiastical establishment. The crown with its new program of fiscal innovations was not the only exploiter of an impoverished and long-suffering people. The clergy's illegal and excessive exactions had imposed another intolerable burden.

The capitulations did not question the right of the church to charge certain fees for spiritual services, but they asserted in unmistakably clear language that the clergy were collecting excessively high emoluments for their services. Nor for that matter did the capitulations question the right of the king to receive certain taxes in order to administer the realm. But they argued that both the state and the church had grossly abused their legitimate authority to tax and that in the last analysis both institutions were accountable to the community they served.

While all the evidence indicates that the church and its ministers still enjoyed considerable reverence from all groups, nevertheless there was a strong undertow of resentment over the whole question of ecclesiastical fees.[25] What clearly emerges therefore is an embryonic anticlericalism that would become militant and virulent in the ranks of the Liberal party during the course of the nineteenth century.

The incipiently anticlerical tone of the capitulations might also have been in part, at least, a reaction against the role of the clergy during the crisis of 1781. While some parish clergy may have passively leaned toward the Comunero cause, none were active partisans. During the early weeks of the disturbances the parish clergy were the only instruments of riot control. They lent the full weight of their institutional prestige to pacify the anger of the crowd. However much many creole parish clergy may have personally sympathized with the complaints of their fellow creoles, the church as an institution was the very flesh and blood of the colonial establishment, in its corporate sense deeply committed to the preservation of the status quo. When the crowds resorted to rioting, the visceral and intellectual reaction of the men of the cloth was to side with constituted authority. Those few priests who were Spanish-born had no place to go but to the side of the authorities, given the clear hostility to the chapetones shown in the uprising. And, of course, the man to whom the creole parish clergy were directly responsible was Archbishop Caballero y Góngora.

There is not lacking a paradox in this situation. The Caroline technocrats were as anticlerical as the creole lawyers who drafted the capitulations. They, too, wanted to restrict the traditional privileges of the men of the cloth, for they regarded that institution's enormous wealth as economically unproductive and its vast influence over the people as a potential threat to the unitary authority of the crown. This was the principal but not the only cause for the expulsion of the Jesuit order from all the Spanish dominions in 1767. In

Mexico the Caroline bureaucrats undertook a wide-ranging offensive to curb the church's time-honored privileges. By 1810 the net result of that campaign was to weaken the lower clergy's loyalty to the crown, with men of the cloth providing many leaders in the war of independence.[26] While no such attempt was made in New Granada, the royal bureaucrats would reject not the content of these proposals but their form, which emanated not from them but from a popular assembly of "rebels."[27] Charles III's ministers were prepared to do much for the people but nothing by the people.

A content analysis of the capitulations reveals the following breakdown.[28]

Grievances	Concessions	Percentage
1. Taxes affecting the nonelites	12	21.4
2. Indians	10	17.9
3. Politics: local and "national"	8	14.3
4. Trade and merchants	7	12.5
5. Freed blacks	7	12.5
6. Anticlericalism	7	12.5
7. Social function of private property	4	7.1
8. Supremacy of private property	1	1.8
	56	100.0

This rather rough and ready analysis amply demonstrates that the capitulations of Zipaquirá addressed themselves to a broad spectrum of grievances, ranging widely over the whole social context of the New Granada of 1781. Almost everyone got some benefits: rich and poor, elites and plebeians, whites, Indians, and freed blacks. Only black slaves were excluded.

Given the late medieval and Renaissance inspiration of the capitulations, obviously there is no trace of the kind of egalitarianism that burst forth during the North American and French revolutions. Inherent inequalities and hereditary privileges were the way God made the world—or so men and women thought in 1781. Inside the context of a paternalist and aristocratic bias, the capitulations of Zipaquirá are an unusually responsive document in which the spokesmen of the creole elites adopted a generously humanitarian and a socially responsible attitude toward the hopes and fears of the plebeians. To be sure, the anger and the wrath of the plebeians encouraged their social betters to follow the path of responsibility.[29] Nevertheless, the framers of the capitulations were statesmen of the highest quality who spoke eloquently for the interests of virtually all the people of New Granada, rich or poor, white or dark-skinned.

14

The First Written Constitution
of New Granada

Important though the fiscal measures may have been, the core of the capitulations was constitutional and political in nature: (1) an aspiration for a larger degree of self-government on the local and regional level and (2) a claim staked out by the creole elites to self-government for the whole of the New Kingdom of Granada.

Regional rivalries played a major role in the events of 1781. The most important of these was the tension between Tunja and Socorro, and in this "tale of two cities" attention must be focused on the origins and development of their rivalry. Founded on August 6, 1539, a few years after the establishment of Santa Fe de Bogotá, Tunja was the rival of Bogotá in the sixteenth century. The initial source of its wealth was the dense Indian population in the adjacent areas. The encomienda took deep roots in Tunja, where there grew an aristocratic society based on relatively large landholdings and a servile Indian labor force.

Another source of Tunja's earlier prosperity was the large herds of sheep raised in the neighboring valleys. That wool helped to create a flourishing cottage textile industry. But during the eighteenth century the sheep herds declined and textile production sharply fell off.

As the political capital of a large territorial area which included Socorro, Tunja prospered during the seventeenth century. Her territorial extent was enormous. In the south it bordered on the province of Santa Fe. It extended northward to the coastal provinces of Cartagena and Santa Marta. The western frontiers touched the Magdalena River (the provinces of Mariquita and Antioquia) and its eastern extremity extended to the province of the Llanos. Inside this sprawling territory there were a few small, independent

172

governmental enclaves such as the governorship of Girón and corregimiento of Sogamoso-Duitama.

Splendid baroque churches and convents that remain to this day and a spacious main plaza adorned with stately seignorial homes provide ample testimony to Tunja's early opulence, which, however, was gradually declining during the course of the eighteenth century. The Indian population, Tunja's initial source of wealth, had sharply diminished by then. Indicative of decaying prosperity is the fact that the tithes collected from the province of Tunja amounted to 25,360 pesos in 1800, whereas in the then separate province of Socorro–San Gil the revenues had climbed to 39,993 pesos.[1] The social and political life of Tunja was dominated by an aristocratic class, some of whose members were able to or pretended to trace their ancestry back to the companions of Jiménez de Quesada.

Socorro stood in sharp contrast to Tunja. Socorro was a new area, an eighteenth-century settlement, many of whose citizens were second- and third-generation descendants of poor Spanish immigrants (see chapter 3). While there was a small group of new rich in Socorro, few of her citizens could lay claim to the aristocratic pretensions of the patricians of Tunja. Minifundia predominated. The Socorro–San Gil area never had a dense Indian population, and their numbers by the eighteenth century were insignificant. The region was predominantly white with a significant number of mestizos and a tiny minority of blacks and mulattoes.

The fertile valleys in the warm temperate climate of Socorro and San Gil provided for a diversified agricultural production as well as for a flourishing cattle industry. Cotton became a major crop, and Socorro replaced Tunja as a principal center of textile production.

By 1781 the population of the urban nucleus of Tunja was not more than 3,000 in contrast to Socorro's population of about 15,000 people. The pastor in Tunja, whose magnificent church was spacious enough to be a cathedral, received an annual income of 1,600 pesos, whereas in Socorro the pastor's annual income was 5,000 pesos—larger than the total rents of the bishop of Santa Marta.

As late as 1781 the seven religious houses of Tunja had not lost the wealth that they had accumulated in more prosperous times. Although Socorro's economy was expanding and Tunja's declining, the new wealth of Socorro often had to go to the "old wealth" of Tunja's convents to secure loans and mortgages to finance the expansion of their community. In 1781 Socorro had no convent. In the 1770's the citizens of that community were requesting that the Franciscans establish a convent there. Not only would such a foundation provide untold spiritual benefits and enhance the prestige of Socorro; but also a convent, as it accumulated capital, would constitute a growing source of credit. The debtor-creditor syndrome was yet another factor that intensified the rivalry of "old," aristocratic Tunja with the self-made men of "new" Socorro.

When Tunja had been the single most prosperous Spanish settlement in the New Kingdom, the encomenderos of Tunja in 1592 and 1641 formed a kind of *fronde* to resist the initial imposition of sales taxes in New Granada. But in 1781 Socorro, having replaced Tunja as the center of expanding wealth, now led the protest against Charles III's new fiscal exactions.

As her prosperity grew steadily, Socorro became increasingly restless under the political domination of outsiders. Long subordinated to San Gil, Socorro also continued to be subject to the political jurisdiction of the corregidor of Tunja. The corregidor ordinarily resided in the capital of the province, but after 1771 he was represented in Socorro by a lieutenant corregidor.

The leading citizens of Socorro yearned for a corregimiento of their own with its capital in their town. Thus, the Socorranos would have a greater degree of self-government. With a resident corregidor the local elites also could hope to have a louder voice in shaping the day-to-day political administration. Furthermore, with a corregidor of their own the local elites might be able to wield greater clout with the authorities in Bogotá.

In 1778 Fiscal Antonio Moreno y Escandón had proposed that the sprawling province of Tunja be divided up into smaller corregimientos based on some rational response to socioeconomic and sociodemographic facts. He proposed the suppression of the small governorship of Girón and the division of the northern portion of the province of Tunja into two corregimientos. One would have its capital in Pamplona and the other in Socorro–San Gil.

Gutiérrez de Piñeres, instinctively distrusting the creole-born fiscal, refused to consider that sensible proposal on its own merits. But the Socorranos did not ignore it. The seventeenth article of the capitulations stated in no uncertain terms:

> The community [el común] of Socorro requests that in these towns there be a corregidor and chief justice [justicia mayor] with an annual salary of 1,000 pesos. These magistrates will not have jurisdiction in the capital of Tunja and those chosen to fill the office must be creoles born in this kingdom. Neither of those two communities, San Gil or Socorro, should claim supremacy, even though the corregidor will reside in one of them. [CA, 2:24–25]

That the corregidor should be a creole clearly suggests that the Socorranos had in mind larger control over the local administration by their own elites. The provision that neither San Gil nor Socorro should enjoy supremacy was an effort to mute the intense rivalry between the two towns. It may be recalled that San Gil sided with Tunja against Socorro at Zipaquirá in opposing the occupation of the capital. In its fear of Socorro Tunja was able to exploit the tension between Socorro and San Gil.

The earlier draft made no mention of the corregidor's salary, whereas the final draft specifically mentioned the amount of 1,000 pesos.[2] That salary was respectable by the standards of the day. An oidor in the audiencia received 2,941 pesos annually. The corregidor of Tunja's salary amounted to 2,812 pesos per year.[3]

Socorro, in fact, did get its much coveted corregidor in 1781. He was none other than Juan Francisco Berbeo, who lingered in office for only a few months without exercising any real authority. The new corregimiento of Socorro was quickly abolished when the authorities in Bogotá gathered sufficient power to annul the capitulations.[4] Yet the claim of the Socorranos that they represented a regional center with a viable socioeconomic hinterland was vindicated a few years later in 1795, when a separate corregimiento was established in Socorro.[5] The new corregimiento became the nucleus of the state of Santander, which distinguished itself in so many ways during the history of the nineteenth century.

The capitulations of Zipaquirá did not foreshadow either political independence or social revolution from below, as many have claimed, but that celebrated document did sow the seeds of two great ideological trends that were destined to dominate in the nineteenth century—anticlericalism and federalism. The demand that the corregidor be a creole and the implication that Socorro formed a kind of patria chica for the surrounding hinterland staked out a claim that a substantial area of governmental authority should be regional. This is the essence of federalism.

It may be recalled that "our royal decree" made a powerful, if crude appeal to the regional patriotism and the local pride of Socorro. This fact does suggest that the sentiment of the patria chica had acquired a deep emotional content by 1781. The popular poem, that was endlessly recited and chanted in hundreds of village squares, emphatically stated that the "finger of God" pointed to Socorro. The citizens of Socorro were the new chosen people. They were the instrument of Divine Providence's will to punish the wicked magistrates in Bogotá, who were exploiting an impoverished people with their unjust and unnecessary taxes. Socorro's mission was to lead the suffering people of New Granada from the oppression of the Pharaoh to the Promised Land.[6] The message was a wine more intoxicating than aguardiente.

Colombian historians have generally regarded nineteenth-century federalism as a foreign importation from the United States. Socorro's tenacious battle with both San Gil and Tunja in order to achieve autonomy, of which the crisis of 1781 was but a significant chapter, amply demonstrates that federalism had deep roots in the native soil of eighteenth-century New

Granada. While the North American example may have exercised some influence in the nineteenth century, federalism cannot be dismissed as an exotic superimposition from abroad.

In a very real sense the men of 1781 began the dialogue that would dominate the history of Colombia during the nineteenth century—the nature of the political relationship between Bogotá and the provinces. The capitulations staked out a large area in which local authorities would exercise considerable jurisdiction over the fiscal and economic activities of the small rural towns and villages. Socorro led the campaign for regional autonomy because it was the most prosperous of the new communities that slowly but steadily developed during the course of the eighteenth century.

The Colombian origins of federalism have another source in addition to Socorro's tenaciously fought battle for autonomy: the tradition of municipal autonomy of medieval Spain, whose roots go back to the city-state, the *polis* and the *civitas* of antiquity. Socorro was a kind of city-state in the Greco-Roman sense, an urban nucleus which claimed political and economic leadership over an extensive web of subordinate rural settlements. Spanish medieval institutions of urban government, whose vitality was decaying in the peninsula, took on a new lease of life in America. They became instruments for promoting colonization and settlement as well as dynamic political vehicles for articulating to the central authorities in Bogotá and Madrid the aspirations of their communities.

A plausible case can be made for the hypothesis that the capitulations represented incipient democratic forces. No clause specifically championed the vested interests of the large landowners or the rich miners, in contrast to the multitude of measures defending the vital concerns of the plebeians, the small farmers, and the petty merchants. But there is little documentary evidence to support the argument of the distinguished scholar, the late Fernando Guillén Martínez, that the pro-Comunero party in Bogotá represented the latifundistas. According to him, there was a real conflict inside the Comunero camp between the small farmers and petty merchants led by Socorro and the large landowners in Bogotá, who rejected the new political centralization of the Caroline ministers for different reasons.[7]

To be sure, the circle of the marquis of San Jorge, the richest landowner in the kingdom, was the center of pro-Comunero sentiment in the capital. But the most influential allies of the marquis were a political group, not an economic class. They were the creole bureaucrats, long accustomed to holding high political office, whose network of activities was described in some detail in chapter 1. They were professional political brokers, who were intermediaries between the central authorities in Madrid and the aspirations of the creole elites and plebeians alike. While they may have paid some attention to the viewpoints of the large landowners, they were not the sole agents of that group. They were a noblesse de la robe, a political aristocracy, who saw themselves as brokers whose function was to conciliate tensions and conflicts and to formulate compromises which would be acceptable to the elites, the plebeians, and Madrid.

Three other clauses in the capitulations provide further evidence to indicate the depth of the aspiration for a greater degree of local self-government. The thirty-third clause provided that the aldermen select one of their number to replace the *fiel ejecutor*—the inspector of weights and measures for all goods and merchandise. Receiving fees for the services he performed to merchants, the inspector of weights and measures bought his office from the crown. This office, along with those of alférez mayor (standard bearer), *depositario general* (public trustee), and the *receptor de penas* (collector of fines), also carried an ex officio seat in the town council.[8]

What the thirty-third clause proposed to do was to transfer this office, which produced a modest income, from purchase from the crown to appointment by the town council. The aldermen could distribute this piece of patronage among themselves. It may be recalled that aldermen also purchased their office from the crown, but the office carried no salary. Furthermore, the inspector of weights and measures had a good deal to do with regulating commerce in the marketplace. The thirty-third article would have given the town councils, dominated by the local patricians, a more direct control over the economies of their communities.

The fifth clause sought to make the office of alcalde de la santa hermandad more attractive to the local patricians—at the expense of the crown—by abolishing the traditional requirement to pay the medias anatas tax. The alcalde de la santa hermandad, a kind of rural police officer and a court of first instance exercising original jurisdiction in the rural hinterland of an urban or village nucleus, collected fees for every service he performed. The clause justified the abolition of the tax on the grounds that these magistrates "must abandon their homes and receive in return very little income to maintain themselves." The clause added, "These and similar offices provide no benefits nor money for self-support, nor do they defray the cost of the losses encountered in abandoning their homes [CA, 2:19]," a hardly credible justification in view of the facts.[9]

It may be sheer coincidence that the person who held the office of alcalde de la santa hermandad in the town of Socorro in 1781 was Albino Berbeo, brother of Juan Francisco (see chapter 5).

An even bolder claim giving creole magnates a much freer hand in local self-government was the thirtieth article, which stated:

> In order to correct the bad results that have occurred from the demands which the judges of the residencia illegally make, we ask

that this practice of residencias be prohibited forthwith. If a citizen has a complaint, he should have recourse to the superior tribunals [presumably the audiencia]. [CA, 2:28]

Not only did the thirtieth clause advocate the abolition of the residencia on all levels of government from the viceroy and the audiencia to the corregidores and the aldermen, but the sixteenth clause formulated an even more audacious claim that the offices of regent and visitor general be abolished.

The cause of the spreading discontent in this New Kingdom as well as that of Lima has been the insolent conduct of the regents visitors general, who have tried to squeeze juice from our aridity and thus to destroy us with their despotic authority. Not even in this New Kingdom with such docile and submissive folk could the people allow them to achieve their purpose of increasing their extortions nor could they tolerate such despotic rule. Although some of the rising protest may have bordered on disloyalty, the intention was not that but merely a means to express dissatisfaction. Let don Juan Francisco Gutiérrez de Piñeres, visitor and regent of this royal audiencia, be exiled from this kingdom and be dispatched to the dominions of Spain. Let our Catholic Majesty, considering the results of his reckless conduct, take whatever further action seems appropriate. From now on, we must never be sent a regent and visitor, nor anyone else for that matter who would treat us with such cruelty and insolence. If it should ever happen again, we will rally a united and confederate kingdom to resist oppression by any bureaucrat thus trying to impose himself on us. [CA, 2:24]

These two proposals represent a truly revolutionary attack on the whole system of Habsburg and pre-Caroline Bourbon government. They strike at the heart of the traditional system of checks and balances in which the crown was able to hold all magistrates overseas to some amount of accountability for their conduct in office.

If the "I obey but do not execute" formula provided magistrates in the Indies with some measure of freedom to maneuver between the pressures created by the central authorities and local conditions, two other administrative devices, the residencia and the visita general, made these same officers sensitive to the wishes of their superiors in the peninsula.[10] Both devices were judicial investigations of the conduct of magistrates. The former took place immediately after an official left office; the latter during his incumbency.

For all their failure to achieve completely the stated goals of rooting out abuses—under the Habsburgs—or of imposing new policies—under Charles III—the residencia and the visita general nevertheless served several useful purposes. Both devices provided the crown with a documented survey of bureaucratic administration in its distant dependencies, conducted by a source supposedly independent of the regular administration. The residencia and the visita general gave the king's subjects a vehicle with which to protest abuses, real or fancied, committed by magistrates. In a very real sense the residencia and the visita general acted as a safety valve by which subjects could periodically release pent-up resentments against royally appointed bureaucrats. Furthermore, both devices provided the central government with an instrument with which to challenge periodically the instinctive urge of the local creole elites to coopt, if only partially, royal magistrates.

It is understandable that the Comuneros would demand the exile from New Granada of Gutiérrez de Piñeres. All the new administrative and fiscal policies that had aroused such bitter turmoil were identified with him personally. He was the visible target of popular wrath. This personal opposition was justified by a doctrine deeply embedded in classic Spanish political theory. Subjects have the right to resist tyranny. The clause denounced his *despótica autoridad* and his *despótico dominio.* The article concluded with both a demand and a threat. Send us no such magistrates again. If they do come, we shall resist their oppression.

But to advocate the abolition of the posts of regent and visitor general was quite another matter. In proposing to sweep away the twin devices of the residencia and the visita general, the men of Zipaquirá were the authors of a political revolution. Both instruments were integral parts of the "unwritten constitution" that the Comuneros had ostensibly set out to restore. If they were abolished, not only would the crown be hampered in its efforts to supervise the conduct of magistrates overseas, but also citizens of the Indies would be deprived of the most effective means that they possessed of protesting against the conduct and the policies of magistrates on every level of government from the viceroy down to the town alderman.

In the capitulations of Zipaquirá the spokesmen of the creoles sponsored a political revolution of their own in order to reply to that of Charles III, described in chapter 1. They started out asking for a return to the situation before 1778. In devising specific formulae to achieve this ostensible goal, they finished by seeking to overturn the traditional order. Not only did they advocate the abolition of the Habsburg system of checks and balances contained in the visita general and residencia, but also they made a bold claim that the whole government be turned over to the creoles to rule in the name of the king.

That audacious program was spelled out in the twenty-second clause of the capitulations.

> In governmental positions of primary, secondary, and tertiary rank nationals of this America should be preferred and privileged

over Europeans who daily exhibit the disdain they hold for the people from around here [America]. No amount of good will on the part of the Americans can rid them of this notion. In their ignorance they believe that they are the masters and that all Americans without distinction are inferior creatures. In order that this blind belief not be perpetuated, only in cases of necessity and according to their ability, good intentions, and favorable inclinations to Americans may Europeans hold some governmental positions. We are subject to the same king and lord, and we should all live together in a brotherly manner. Anyone who intends to lord himself over others or to take more than his equal share shall be banished from our company. [CA, 2:26]

The claim of the creoles to a virtual monopoly of bureaucratic office was not confined to New Granada. On May 2, 1771, the cabildo of Mexico in a letter to Charles III staked out the same bold claim that the capitulations of Zipaquirá did in 1781. The cabildo of Mexico sent copies of this letter to many other cabildos in the New World, including that of Bogotá.[11] It is not coincidental that both expressions of creole sentiment were articulated shortly after Visitor General Gálvez in Mexico and Visitor General Gutiérrez de Piñeres in New Granada undertook to reduce drastically the number of creoles holding high office.

In chapter 5 it was pointed out that "our royal decree" was saturated with the spirit that America belonged to the Americans. As Rafael Gómez Hoyos aptly observed, the twenty-second clause put in bureaucratic prose the crudely poetic sentiment expressed in the popular poem.

> Por qué razón a gobernarnos vienen
> De otras regiones malditos nacionales?[12]

The text never made explicit what was meant by primary, secondary, and tertiary. A reasonable inference is that primary referred to the audiencia, secondary to the fiscal administration, and tertiary to the provincial echelon of corregidores. There is no hint whether the article included the office of viceroy; probably not.

Hence in 1781 the creoles were asking for much more than the mere restoration of the system that existed before 1778. Prior to the arrival of Gutiérrez de Piñeres the creoles were, in fact, only a significant minority in the high bureaucracy, but their influence was greatly extended by an informal working alliance with long-tenured, Spanish-born magistrates, many of whose wives were creoles. In 1781 the creoles greatly expanded their demand by claiming an overwhelming majority of offices.

They did make one concession to the earlier spirit. They would not exclude a few European Spaniards "in case of necessity" and if they met the standards of "ability, good will, and favorable inclination to Americans." The framers of this clause clearly had in mind several Spanish oidores whose long tenure in Bogotá and whose creole wives made them responsive to American conditions. Among them were Benito Casal y Montenegro (1747–81), Juan Francisco Pey y Ruíz (1756–86), Joaquín de Aróstegui y Escoto (1740–75), and Bernardo Alvarez (1736–56).

In place of a pro-American coalition in which only a minority of creoles shared power with pro-American Spaniards, the twenty-second article proposed a coalition which would consist of an overwhelming majority of creoles and a small minority of pro-American Spaniards.

Although the creole elites invoked the rhetoric and the concepts of Habsburg times, the monarch as envisaged in the capitulations of Zipaquirá was not that of the House of Austria. Under that system an intricate web of checks and balances prevailed in which all groups received a minimum of what it wanted, but seldom did any receive the maximum. The monarchical ideal of Zipaquirá was the highly decentralized monarchy of fifteenth-century Castile. By virtually monopolizing the bureaucracy and eliminating the residencia and the visita general, the creoles would have a blank check to govern New Granada in the name of Charles III. Creole self-government would make a formal repudiation of the crown superfluous. Such an aim, if carried out, would constitute a de facto political revolution, i.e., the sudden transference of governmental power from one group to another.

In New Granada of 1781 the world without a monarchy was unthinkable. What was thinkable was a drastic shift of power away from European Spaniards toward the creoles under the protective umbrella of monarchical legitimacy.

There is, however, one visible thread linking the statesmen of 1781 to the independence movement a generation later. Camilo Torres did not aspire to a formal break with the Spanish crown. What he urged was creole domination of the bureaucracy under the continued reign of the House of Bourbon. [13] But it should be stressed that Torres represented a first stage in an evolution that was to culminate in independence.

There was a tension and a dichotomy in the political goals of the creoles. On one hand, they sought to return to the pre-1778 "unwritten constitution." This aim may be considered to be their minimum goal, or their real position. The dialectic of revolution, however, moved swiftly toward escalation of demands. When events forced them at Zipaquirá to spell out in writing their objectives, they formulated a kind of decentralized pre-Habsburg monarchy. This became their maximum goal or their bargaining position. One may question how seriously attached they were to achieving this bold program.

The capitulations represent an idealized world that had never existed historically in New Granada and one whose inspiration was rooted in the remote past.

The tactics of any negotiating situation require that the parties on the offensive ask for much more than they realistically expect to receive. Long accustomed to bureaucratic negotiation and settlement by compromise, the framers of the capitulations probably did not anticipate that their dreamworld would become a reality. But in order to achieve their minimum goal, they had to strike out audaciously with larger demands.

The political and moral assumptions of the capitulations are, as we have seen, embedded in the casuist traditions of the classic Spanish theologians. Yet those theologians lived in an age of a strong monarchy, and the framers of the capitulations advocated a weak monarchy. What the men of 1781 did was to invoke several of the basic principles of the classic theologians in order to justify a late medieval constitutional monarchy. Not only would the king's powers be limited, but also political power would be shared between the creole bureaucratic elite in Bogotá and the elites in the provinces.

The framers of the capitulations of Zipaquirá are the unsung and heretofore unknown authors of the first written constitution of New Granada. If a written constitution means a philosophical formulation of the goals of a community, as well as formulae for the distribution and the exercise of political power, the capitulations of Zipaquirá generously meet this definition. It is understandable that the document that they drew up lacked the durability and the political sophistication of the constitution of the new republic of the United States that was composed in Philadelphia a few years later.

Two extenuating factors exist in the case of New Granada. The capitulations were hastily if not frantically drawn up in the course of forty-eight hours, whereas the founding fathers of the United States deliberated for some four months. Secondly, New Granada had only one vein of ideological inspiration, admittedly rich, but still the only one: Spain's own theological tradition of the sixteenth and seventeenth centuries. In English America, on the other hand, there was a more varied mosaic of sources from which to fashion a written constitution. Not only were the founding fathers the heirs of a native American tradition of legislative decentralization, but also they received intellectual nourishment from a wide variety of political thought, all of which was totally unknown in New Granada in 1781: Enlightenment rationalism, seventeenth-century English jurisprudence, New England Puritanism, radical political and social theories formulated during the English Civil War and Commonwealth periods, and eighteenth-century opposition thought (Walpole, Benjamin Hoadly, Bolingbroke, etc.). Taking into account these two important differences between New Granada and the United States, the capitulations of Zipaquirá are a remarkable achievement worthy of comparison with any political document formulated in the eighteenth century in either the New or the Old World.

It was not until the generation of 1810 that New Granada had the necessary diversity of political traditions without which no political revolution can hope to germinate, let alone flower. By 1810 there existed the examples of both the North American and French revolutions as well as the political philosophy and the Enlightenment rationalism of Europe. These external influences blended with the classic political theories of old Spain and the "unwritten constitution" of New Granada to form the fuse that ignited the independence movement. Absent in 1781 was any criterion for challenging the traditional form of legitimacy, which everyone then accepted. A generation later the rationalism of the Enlightenment would provide such a measure.

The twenty-second article contains the clear implication that the kingdoms overseas were coequal with metropolitan Spain. The creoles were tenaciously attached to the Habsburg theory of the kingdoms of the Spains and the Indies united under one royal head—a notion that had fallen into disuse in Bourbon Spain. Under Charles III the settlements overseas had increasingly acquired the juridical status of colonies or provinces of the metropolis. The "federal" conception of the Habsburgs provided the proponents of independence after 1808 with a historico-juridical argument to justify the initial creole claim that provisional regimes should be set up in each of the kingdoms overseas in the absence of the legitimate king of Castile, Ferdinand VII, who was a prisoner of Napoleon from 1808 until 1813. But there were very real differences: in the early nineteenth century the claim was one of equality with the kingdom of Spain, whereas under the Habsburgs the Americas were considered as subordinate and inalienable kingdoms attached to the crown of Castile and León. The differences between these two theories should not, however, be equated with a shift from the neomedieval corporatism of the sixteenth and seventeenth centuries to the egalitarian attitudes of the American and French revolutions.[14]

The twenty-second article is dramatic and conclusive evidence that, a generation before the North American and French revolutions had any impact on the political thinking of New Granada's elites, the notion of the equality of the various kingdoms had taken deep root in the soil of New Granada.

A suggestion of a protonationalist undercurrent in the capitulations can be found in the twentieth clause.

In no way, by no decree nor cause should the laws and repeated cedulas concerning the right of immigration, residence, and naturalization of foreigners continue to be broken in any part of this kingdom. The coming of foreigners, both secular and ecclesiastical, could bring harm to our kingdom both now and in the future. Therefore, all those foreigners who are here now should leave within two months. Those who do not comply shall be treated as spies, as if in time of war. [CA, 2:26]

The term "foreigner" meant not European Spaniards but non-Spanish Europeans. The Habsburgs consistently prohibited such foreign migration to their American dominions, even though that dynasty reigned over many non-Iberian peoples in the Old World. The less foreigners knew about the Spanish New World the better, so the Habsburg regime believed. The only exception was the Society of Jesus, which obtained a royal dispensation to recruit some foreigners from Catholic countries of non-Spanish Europe for their American missions.[15]

The xenophobic sealing off of Spanish America to foreigners disappeared during the eighteenth century, as the new Bourbon dynasty sought not only ideas from non-Iberian, Catholic Europe but also foreign talent to reorganize the monarchy. Irishmen and Italians, in particular, filled some of the highest posts in the administration. One of these notable foreigners was the Irish-born Bernardo Ward, who was the co-author of the master plan of Charles III's innovations in the Indies. That monarch's initial reliance on Italian-born ministers, Squillace and Grimaldi, was one of the factors contributing to the hostility against foreigners that erupted into major riots in several cities in Spain during the spring of 1766.

While there are no precise figures about the number of foreigners in New Granada in 1781, they were evidently sufficiently visible to provoke a xenophobic reaction, if we can lend any weight to the very severe penalty involved. Once again the capitulations of Zipaquirá repudiated a Bourbon policy in favor of a return to a Habsburg tradition. Not only did the capitulations affirm in bold language the equality of American and European Spaniards, but they also displayed a pointed distrust of all foreigners. New Granada belonged only to those who were born there, so the statesmen of Zipaquirá believed. Hence the capitulations contain some of the seeds that would eventually grow in the nineteenth century into the tree of nationalism.

Everyone involved realized that the king's assent must also be secured before the capitulations could have the full force of law. In view of the deep suspicion among some circles in the Comunero camp that the authorities in Bogotá might renege on their solemn commitment to enforce the capitulations, there was included a kind of military guarantee. The eighteenth clause provided:

> All employed by and named in the current expedition including the commander-in-chief, the captains general, the territorial cap-

tains, their lieutenants, ensigns, sergeants, and corporals must retain their respective commissions. Each is obligated on every Sunday afternoon to drill his company in the exercise of arms, both of fire and steel, offensive and defensive; so that if any attempt is made to break the clauses of this concordat, which we are entering into in good faith, we will be prepared to serve our Catholic monarch. [CA, 2:25]

Although Berbeo and his captains agreed to disband their large army at Zipaquirá, then, they demanded and believed they had received a military guarantee that the capitulations would subsequently be respected by the authorities in Bogotá.

From the safety of the fortress of Cartagena the fugitive Gutiérrez de Piñeres exploded in wrath about the military clause:

> This is equivalent to agreeing [*capitular*] that the present rebellion shall be permanent, that within the state an armed association will be allowed to perpetuate the rebellion, that the members of that association shall recognize no other authority or power than the authority that they have usurped. In a word there would be no king, no law, nor any nation.[16]

Making allowances for the hyperbole to which he was addicted, the eighteenth clause conjured up for Gutiérrez de Piñeres and men like him a chamber of horrors. While that article was something less than the *levée en masse,* nation in arms, that the French revolutionary government decreed on August 23, 1793, a citizens' militia of some 20,000 men, even if they only trained on Sunday afternoons, was a prospect to appal Charles III's ministers.

It should be clear from the analysis developed in the last two chapters that the capitulations of Zipaquirá represented as radical a political revolution as the one sponsored by Charles III, which had precipitated the crisis of 1781. With the object of expanding the tax base to finance the increased costs of imperial defense, Charles III proposed a basic political restructuring, which would have replaced the traditional decentralization of Habsburg times with something approximating a unitary state. Violently reacting against this program, irate citizens from all ethnic groups in New Granada initially clamored for a return to the earlier political and constitutional status quo. But in the process of seeking specific formulae to achieve their ostensible objective, the capitulations ended up advocating a kind of decentralized monarchy in which political power would be virtually monopolized by the creoles. Such an ideal was the very antithesis of the theory and the practice of the Habsburg monarchy with its intricate pattern of checks and balances.

Neither Charles III nor his loyal vassals in New Granada achieved their utopia. Utopias have a habit of receding as they are approached.[17]

The responsibility for restoring royal authority in the wake of Zipaquirá fell on the broad and capable shoulders of Archbishop Caballero y Góngora. He was de facto viceroy from May 13, 1781, the day he set out for his rendezvous in Zipaquirá, although he did not formally take office as viceroy until June 15, 1782. A politician of consummate skill, the archbishop viceroy recognized the depth of discontent on the part of all ethnic and occupational groups in the land. Yet no matter how zigzag a course he traveled, he never wavered in his determination to salvage the fiscal substance of Charles III's program. Caballero y Góngora ultimately wove a fabric which blended several basic features of the traditional "unwritten constitution" with some, but not all, aspects of the "defensive modernization" of Charles III's incipient technocrats. How he performed this intricate task will be the topic of the rest of this book. But first, as a kind of coda to the events leading up to the capitulations at Zipaquirá, I shall examine the career of José Antonio Galán, one of the most interesting, controversial, and, in the truest sense, tragic figures to emerge from the Comunero movement.

PART III
Antonio Caballero y Góngora

15

José Antonio Galán: Myth and Fact

Around the figure of José Antonio Galán many myths have clustered, and to distinguish fact from legend is no easy task. In his own time the royal authorities vituperatively denounced the "infamous Galán" for a whole series of crimes, ranging from treason and banditry to incest. In the nineteenth century he was alternately vilified as a bandit or hailed as a hero of the people who dreamed of political independence from Spain.[1] In the twentieth century some men of the left have idolized him as an apostle of social revolution from below, a kind of remote precursor of Ché Guevara.

José Antonio Galán was born in 1749 in the parish of Mongui de Charalá, southeast of Socorro.[2] On October 26, 1766, he married Toribia Verdugo, who bore him several children.[3] We have no contemporary physical description of him.[4]

José Antonio's father, Antonio Galán, was a poor Spanish immigrant, originally a small trader in trinkets, who eventually settled in Charalá, where he married Ana María de Argüello, of either mestizo or mulatto background, who bore him a large brood of children. After settling in Charalá, Galán earned his living the way most of his contemporaries did. He owned a small patch of land on which he cultivated tobacco. In his modest home the women and children wove cotton goods.[5] In spite of his father's Spanish birth, poverty made Antonio Galán and his family plebeians.

The claim that José Antonio as a child studied in the prestigious college of San Bartolomé in Bogotá was eventually repudiated by the scholar who first asserted it.[6] While possessing only the rudiments of a formal education, he could sign his own name—some distinction in a society where the vast majority of the plebeian population were totally illiterate. His surviving

189

letters do not lack a certain beauty and vitality of style, but the syntax and vocabulary are rustic, primitive, and unlearned. Like most of his plebeian contemporaries, he was a small farmer.[7]

Another fact we know about his life prior to 1781 was that he lived for awhile in the nearby parish of Socorro, for there, in September of 1775, one of his sons was baptized. His stay in Socorro extended into 1777.[8]

The difficulties of ascertaining the truth about Galán's life are exemplified by a picturesque legend about his early youth which was invented out of whole cloth by Constancio Franco, who published a historical novel in 1891 called *Galán, el Comunero.* According to Franco, Galán, his social conscience aroused by the mistreatment of neighboring Guane Indians, organized a riot in protest, subsequently fled to the Indians, but was captured and sentenced to ten years' hard labor in the fortress of Cartagena, whence he escaped some time before the spring of 1781.

The account is riddled with inaccuracies of place and date, but perhaps the most devastating evidence of its falsity is the fact that no mention was made of it in Galán's death sentence, which listed in meticulous, if lurid, detail all his alleged crimes.[9]

Galán's death sentence does mention in a tantalizingly brief fashion that he was "punished several times by the law."[10] Evidently José Antonio had had several brushes with the authorities. It is not unreasonable to assume that he was hot-headed, aggressive, and quarrelsome—characteristics that some contemporary observers identified with the land that was to become the state of Santander.[11] This supposition is buttressed by the fact that, after the battle of Puente Real, Galán aroused the ire of none other than the victor of the battle, Captain Ignacio Galviño, his fellow townsman from Charalá, who stripped him of his captain's baton and imprisoned him for having committed "several outrages." What those "outrages" were has never been determined, but it could well be that Galán was involved in stealing the treasury chest of Oidor Osorio.[12]

Galán's death sentence reveals another solid piece of evidence about his pre-1781 career. José Antonio served in and deserted from the "fixed regiment" in Cartagena. Whether he volunteered or was sentenced as a judicial punishment is not known. Criminals sometimes were assigned to the "fixed regiment."[13]

Some of Galán's admirers have engaged in largely fanciful speculation about the influence of the Cartagena experience on their hero. Let us first deal with known quantities. Galán's length of service was brief, perhaps not more than a year. Second, he obviously did not enjoy being a common soldier in that hot tropical city. He did, of course, acquire some exposure to military discipline and tactics, experience that would stand him in good stead during the climactic year of his life.

Whether during his brief sojourn news about events in far-off English America fired his imagination is merely a tantalizing speculation. All the available information suggests that no leader of the Comunero movement was inspired to emulate the example of the thirteen colonies. Furthermore, Galán's posture did not deviate in the slightest from that of his fellow captains. While he furiously assailed the policies of the royal ministers, he always pledged allegiance to the crown of Charles III.

There are two principal chapters in José Antonio Galán's career during the crisis of 1781. One was his military campaign in the upper Magdalena River valley in June, just before and after the conclusion of the capitulations of Zipaquirá. The other major episode, of course, was his abortive march on Bogotá in the following September and October. Each event should be considered in turn.

On May 25, Juan Francisco Berbeo launched his bold and imaginative expedition against Facatativá and Honda under the command of Galán, who performed his mission brilliantly (see chapter 11).[14] Outmaneuvering a royalist detachment dispatched from the capital, in Facatativá on May 30 Galán cut off mail links between Bogotá and Cartagena.[15] Between May 30 and June 7 his small expedition swept through the towns and hamlets of the upper Magdalena valley to enlist these communities into the service of the "enterprise."

There are several episodes in the upper Magdalena campaign that merit careful scrutiny. One is Galán's correspondence with the courier Manuel García Olano. From Facatativá on May 30 José Antonio sent the following letter to García Olano in Bogotá:

> With a desire to communicate with you I have proceeded with this letter. I have no other person in whom I have confidence and with whom I may keep in touch in order to find out for certain what has been determined by those gentlemen [the authorities in Bogotá]. We are not violating reason nor the law of God. We are striving only to achieve a covenant for the common good. Since we are Roman Catholic Apostolic Christians, your Grace, I and everyone else cannot violate the law of God, nor can we be derelict in our obedience to our sovereign. We are all his subjects, and we obey all his orders. What we want is that which the regent has undone should be set right again. If not, we shall all perish, and there will be no one who will be able to help one another. If your Grace would be pleased to come and talk with us, we will hold you in great esteem. Only with your Grace can we vent our feelings, and our joy will be evident. All matters will be resolved in peace with God's grace, if our superiors so desire. If they do not, they will experience much ruination. May our Lord

give us peace, and may we live as His obedient children. We
expect an answer from your Grace through this messenger.[16]

The letter reveals that the plebeian José Antonio Galán, like the patrician
leaders of Socorro, reposed some confidence in Manuel García Olano, if not
as an active ally, at least as a friendly intermediary between themselves and
the royal authorities in Bogotá. In addition, the letter of Galán is not the
statement of a radical revolutionary. In more rustic language, Galán expressed
the same sentiments that the elite leaders enunciated to Viceroy Flores. Both
reaffirmed their loyalty to the crown, while they denounced the fiscal
measures introduced by the regent visitor general. And Galán, as of May 30,
supported the policy of Berbeo to negotiate "a covenant for the common
good" with the royal authorities. The date of the letter is significant. Events
were moving swiftly in nearby Zipaquirá, where Archbishop Caballero y
Góngora and Juan Francisco Berbeo were beginning the negotiations that
within a week would culminate in the signing of the capitulations.

Lest he subsequently be accused of treason, García Olano took the
precaution of showing Galán's letter to the junta de tribunales. With the
junta's permission he traveled to Facatativá, where he had an interview not
with Galán but with one of his associates, Nicolás José de Vesga y Gómez.
What transpired at this meeting is not known. When Vesga requested a second
interview, Oidor Catani refused to grant permission to García Olano.[17]

The reasons for the judge's refusal can only be surmised. García Olano was
suspected of being in sympathy with the Comuneros and hence untrustworthy. A royal mail pouch had just been confiscated by Galán's forces, and
suspicion fell on García Olano, who was then the director of the postal
service.[18] Negotiations were rapidly reaching their frantic climax in Zipaquirá. There was little need to negotiate with Vesga, who was a mere
lieutenant of Berbeo.

The second major episode in Galán's skillfully executed campaign, which
brought the upper Magdalena valley from Honda to Neiva into the Socorrano
camp, was his warning to the regent visitor general to flee Honda lest he be
captured by Galán's advancing troops. In this case, as in so many others, we
owe a debt of gratitude to the late Pablo Cárdenas Acosta, who published the
key documents.

José Antonio Galán and his triumphant little legion swept into Guaduas in
the evening of June 4. On June 7 the Spanish-born Manuel de Arejula penned
a hurried note with some alarming news to friends in Honda.[19] José Antonio
Galán had personally informed him that the principal objective of his expedition was to capture the regent visitor general. Galán explicitly requested
Manuel de Arejula to advise Gutiérrez de Piñeres to flee down the Magdalena.
Not only did Galán encourage Arejula to send this warning, but he sent a

personal appeal to the regent visitor general. Galán chose as his intermediary doña Ignacia Roa, the wife of don Joaquín de la Bodega Llano, administrator of the royal aguardiente monopoly in Honda. José Antonio had evidently met the couple in Facatativá, where he furnished them with a passport to enable them to pass through his lines to Honda.

In dignified, if rustic prose, Galán wrote the regent visitor general:

> Your Lordship:
> In the name of our Lord and Master and our Lady of Socorro I beg you to do me the favor to go into hiding, even if it were to a mountain underneath the earth, so as to avoid any ruination that might befall Honda and your honor should my troops find you. My troops should never know what you are doing, so that nothing may happen to me. The people are intensely rebellious because the explicit orders of our general [Berbeo] are for me to surrender your lordship's head to him. So that this may not happen, I am sending this dispatch with as much secrecy as possible, for I am baptized and redeemed with the blood of Christ. Your lordship may choose whatever is your pleasure, whether to await us in Honda or to go into hiding. May God keep you many years. I kiss your lordship's hand, your admirer.

Galán added a postscript:

> Your lordship will forgive the vocabulary and the grammatical errors because of my being so coarse in this business of writing words. I repeat a warning to your lordship: that you not head down the Magdalena river to Cartagena. If you proceed, there are many people there to oppose you. You shall hide, as I advise, and later as you proceed on your way, you may talk with me alone if you wish. This is all I can tell you. God be with you.[20]

Cárdenas Acosta has implied that Galán intentionally delayed his assault on Honda in order to allow Gutiérrez de Piñeres ample time to escape—a documentary revelation that has proved embarrassing to some of Galán's most zealous defenders.[21] Gómez Latorre, for example, flatly denied that Berbeo's instructions were to capture Gutiérrez de Piñeres, but such an interpretation squarely contradicts Galán's own words.[22]

A more plausible but not totally convincing explanation of Galán's baffling conduct has been offered by Luis Torres Almeyda. Galán was exercising the right of every field commander to interpret flexibly the orders of his commander-in-chief, with whom he could not immediately communicate. He foresaw that if his men entered Honda and captured the regent visitor general, they probably would tear that unfortunate magistrate limb from limb—a prospect abhorrent even to as tough and determined a warrior as José Antonio. Hence Galán's new strategy was to warn the regent visitor general not to flee down the Magdalena to the safety of Cartagena, for along that most obvious route of escape "there are many people there to oppose you." Gutiérrez de Piñeres and Galán would meet at a secret rendezvous where that magistrate would surrender. Galán would spare him the fate of being lynched by an angry crowd. Alive, he would be a trump card in any bargaining between the Socorranos and the authorities in Bogotá.[23]

Even if, for the sake of argument, we accept Torres Almeyda's explanation, Galán may have been humane, but he was also naive. He miscalculated on three counts. The haughty and strong-willed Gutiérrez de Piñeres would have chosen flight via the Magdalena River with all the risks involved rather than surrender voluntarily to a man he considered an unmitigated rebel and a vulgar plebeian at that. Second, Galán's war of nerves contained a little too much bluff. Although there were some Galánists, the area north of Honda was not firmly under their control. A well-armed Spanish vessel could have guaranteed Gutiérrez de Piñeres's safe exodus down the Magdalena even in the case of enemy hostility on the shore line. And in addition Galán did not take into account the rapidly changing situation, of which neither he nor his adversary had intelligence. On the very night of June 7, when Galán wrote Gutiérrez de Piñeres, the junta de tribunales in Bogotá ratified the capitulations of Zipaquirá. Unknown to Galán, Berbeo's orders to capture the hated Spanish magistrate had become inoperative.

There were only forty European Spaniards who could be depended upon to defend Honda against an anticipated invasion of the Socorranos. Within a few hours after receiving Galán's letter, the regent visitor general at 3 P.M. on June 8 fled down the Magdalena to the safety of the fortress of Cartagena. Before departing northward he ordered that a supply of munitions coming from Mompós to Honda, whose final destination was Bogotá, be returned to Mompós, lest they fall into the eager hands of the Socorranos. Gutiérrez de Piñeres, who loathed Galán as a plebeian and a rebel, never showed any appreciation to the man from Charalá for his timely warning to escape.[24] In war and in politics gratitude, however, is often a luxury that can be dispensed with.

Torres Almeyda's analysis is credible but not wholly convincing. Galán was within half a day's march of Honda, and he stopped. Instead of descending on Honda, he remained in Guaduas from June 4 until June 14, thereby allowing Gutiérrez de Piñeres ample time to escape. Did José Antonio have a failure of nerve? Was he afraid to touch the person of such a highly placed magistrate, even one who was the focus of intense popular wrath? Such an assessment is harsh and misleading.

If one regards Galán as a precursor of social revolution, his conduct in this episode was cowardly, if not traitorous. But if one places José Antonio in the context of 1781, his behavior becomes as comprehensible as that of the captains of Socorro, who took a secret oath of allegiance to Charles III shortly after assuming command of the revolution. Neither Galán nor Berbeo were traitors to the cause they so ably led. Neither one, however, advocated political independence or social revolution. Their aims were much more modest: to repudiate the fiscal and administrative changes identified with Gutiérrez de Piñeres. Their limited goals determined the essentially moderate tactics that all leaders in 1781 employed. Extremism of all sorts was to be avoided. Looting, by and large, was confined to the royal monopolies. Bloodshed was to be avoided if at all possible. Their aim was not to humiliate the royal magistrates but to negotiate with them.

Galán's reluctance to capture the regent visitor general is comparable to Berbeo's much criticized failure to take Bogotá. Yet that decision was forced upon the generalissimo by Tunja's defection, Bogotá's coopting of the creole elites in the capital, and the junta's willingness to conclude a comprehensive settlement. Galán's hand was not forced by external factors with which he had to cope, as was the case with Berbeo. Yet Galán, like Berbeo, studiously avoided extremist tactics that might jeopardize the realization of their essentially moderate goal of turning the clock back to 1778.

The third episode in Galán's Magdalena campaign that merits careful attention was his attitude toward black slavery. Unlike the patrician captains Galán, of plebeian background, had no hesitation in appealing to the lower classes in order to win popular support. On June 18, Galán appeared with fifty of his followers at the gold mine of Malpaso and the adjacent cattle ranch of La Niña. The owner of both properties, a resident of Honda, was the peninsular-born don Vicente Estanisloa Diago, who had the good fortune to be absent. Galán was not bashful about appealing to the feeling against the chapetones. He not only imprisoned the mayordomos of the two properties, but also confiscated a collection of jewels, which he subsequently returned to the owner. José Antonio won the support of the black slaves by proclaiming them free.[25]

There is no evidence whatsoever to suggest that Galán viewed the institution of slavery as morally wrong or economically exploitative. In spite of his modern admirers, who have falsely remodeled him into a precursor of Ché Guevara, Galán was no ideologue. This one particular incident—a matter of tactics—does not imply that he wanted to abolish slavery as an institution. Some have suggested that Galán's social conscience about the inhumanity of slavery was aroused by his brief stay in Cartagena, but no evidence can be cited.[26] The most conclusive proof that Galán's move was tactical and not ideological is that he only once resorted to this maneuver in spite of the fact that slavery was a major source of labor in the province of Mariquita.[27] Slave discontent was only a minor ingredient in the recipe that José Antonio Galán devised for winning over this fertile and strategic province. The most significant expression of slave discontent took place in the neighboring western province of Antioquia, where the blacks were even more numerous than in Mariquita.

The conclusion of the capitulations of Zipaquirá on June 7 did not immediately tranquilize the upper Magdalena valley, for the revolution had built up a momentum of its own. After the flight of the regent visitor general, Honda embraced the Comunero standard, although Galán himself never entered that river port.[28] On June 14, Galán crossed the Magdalena, marching from Guaduas to Mariquita. Subsequently he traveled to the fertile tobacco country of Ambalema, where he established his headquarters.[29] On June 18 Galán appeared at the gold mine of Malpaso. On June 19, in Neiva, there occurred a riot in which the governor, don Policarpo Fernández, lost his life.[30] To the west, in Antioquia, tumults took place, perhaps partially stimulated by the example of Galán but not directly under his instigation nor his command.

The junta de tribunales was deeply alarmed by the exploits, both real and fancied, of the chieftain from Charalá, whom they routinely described as the "infamous Galán." After Zipaquirá Berbeo went to Bogotá, where the authorities pressured him to order the cessation of hostilities in the fertile and strategic valley of the upper Magdalena. Colonel Bernet's expedition of five hundred soldiers was on its way from Mompós to Honda. Hence Berbeo appointed an influential commission to journey westward to order Galán to lay down his arms and to adhere to the capitulations.

The head of the commission was Pedro Antonio Nieto, one of Berbeo's trusted lieutenants and a captain general from Galán's own parish of Charalá, whom Galán supposedly respected. Nieto could not find Galán in order to deliver the letter, although the latter apparently knew its contents.[31] Galán quite correctly suspected that the real purpose of the Nieto mission was to take him into custody. He broke up his camp, went into hiding, and refused to adhere to the capitulations.[32]

A few days before Berbeo dispatched Nieto, another captain general, Marcelo de Ardila, arrived from Bogotá; on June 19 in Honda he proclaimed the capitulations to be in force. In Berbeo's name, he then proceeded to appoint three prominent citizens to the office of captain general. Ardila publicly warned the authorities not to allow Galán to enter their town. He called his previous conduct "reckless stupidity."[33] Under intense pressure from Bogotá, Juan Francisco Berbeo thus repudiated his most successful field commander.

The adherents of the government, who had abandoned Honda after the flight of Gutiérrez de Piñeres, had returned by June 16. One bloody riot occurred during the night of June 23; several lives were lost. The loyalist forces, however, carried the day. This tumult had some overtones of rich against poor, chapetones against American-born plebeians. The plebeian rioters sent frantic appeals to José Antonio Galán, but he pointedly refused to intervene.[34] Perhaps he was being prudent; certainly his failure to come to the rescue of his followers was something less than heroic. His reluctance was probably determined by two factors. He knew that Colonel José Bernet with his well-armed expedition was on its way from Mompós to Honda. And he always displayed a studied reluctance to participate in blood baths such as had occurred on the night of June 23.

The glittering series of victories that Galán had won in late May and early June were of no avail. An intensive public relations campaign conducted by the captains dispatched in the name of Berbeo did a good deal to calm public unrest by proclaiming the capitulations of Zipaquirá in force. Conciliation was backed up by military muscle when Colonel Bernet's expedition reached Honda on July 25, en route to Bogotá. Shortly afterwards Viceroy Flores dispatched from Cartagena a small, but well-armed contingent to garrison that strategic river port.[35]

Galán headed back to his native land of Charalá via Llano Grande, El Espinal, La Mesa de Juan Díaz, Facatativá, Zipaquirá, Ubaté, Chiquinquirá, and Santa Rosa de Cerinza, with about thirty well-armed followers. Among them were trusted lieutenants such as his brothers Hilario and Juan Nepomuceno, Isidro Molina, Manuel Ortíz, and Lorenzo Alcantuz, all of whom had shared his brief weeks of glory and who were destined to share his doom.[36]

As early as July 14, an impatient and vindictive audiencia gave a commission to Juan Antonio Fernández Recamán to capture Galán and his associates "for having committed various insults, robberies, and atrocities in diverse localities in the jurisdictions of Tocaima, Neiva, and Ibague."[37] On July 20 in El Espinal, Galán just managed to escape from a trap that Fernández Recamán had prepared.[38]

Galán's journey to Mogotes was not without its picturesque adventures. On August 3, in Zipaquirá, he boldly insulted the corregidor, who did not dare arrest him in the presence of Galán's well-armed escort. Subsequently the audiencia sharply rebuked the corregidor for his failure to act. In Chiquinquirá he even captured the lieutenant governor of Mariquita and Tocaima, whom he had apparently known in his previous campaign. That hapless official, Juan Félix Ramírez de Arellano, happened to be in Chiquinquirá on a pilgrimage to its celebrated shrine dedicated to the Virgin Mary. A Dominican friar gently chided the man from Charalá for capturing "a poor chapetón" who was performing the pious act of making a pilgrimage. Galán smilingly replied: "Reverend Father, you do not know what a rotten egg that Arellano is." Galán eventually released his prisoner to the priest, not before threatening to administer fifty lashes or, at least, twenty-five to the humiliated official. The man from Charalá was not without a prankish sense of humor and a healthy irreverence for pompous officials. It was the kind of material out of which folk heroes are made.

Galán had no qualms about insulting minor bureaucrats, but he was usually respectful toward high-ranking magistrates. While a mere corregidor or a lieutenant governor was an appropriate target for his prankish sense of humor, he hesitated to touch the person of Gutiérrez de Piñeres, the second-ranking magistrate of the New Kingdom.

That overused word *charismatic* should not be applied to Galán or, for that matter, anyone else in 1781. Galán represented no revealed truth, nor did he embody a moral purpose. No one in 1781 met Max Weber's definition of charisma as "devotion to the specific and exceptional sanctity, heroism or exemplary character of an individual person, and of the normative patterns or order revealed or ordained by him."[39] Though Galán was not charismatic, he was certainly a forceful and dynamic leader of men who could inspire personal loyalty.

José Antonio was no doctrinaire ideologue but a pragmatic tactician who dealt with each situation as he found it. He freed the slaves at the Malpaso mine not because he opposed slavery but because he wanted to enlist the support of those particular blacks. Of plebeian background, he did not hesitate to appeal to his fellow plebeians. He often appointed men of the people as his captains in those localities which joined his cause. This practice sharply contrasts with that of the supreme council of war in Socorro which usually but not always granted commissions to well-to-do and prominent creoles. It may be recalled that those creoles invariably enjoyed the respect and the support of the populace. They were elected by the whole population, and their nominations were confirmed by the council in Socorro.

Nor was Galán reticent about appealing to the antichapetón feelings of his plebeian followers. The property of rich Spanish merchants was on some occasions the target of Galán's supporters. But there was a mere handful of such incidents. The principal foci of popular wrath were the offices of the royal monopolies. Like his patrician colleagues in Santander, Galán usually returned any private property that his followers looted.

Nowhere is there a more striking example of his pragmatic approach to tactics than in the volte face he adopted toward the capitulations of Zipaquirá. Before Zipaquirá, Galán was a positive partisan of a negotiated agreement. In the upper Magdalena he pointedly refused to adhere to the capitulations, for that settlement was used quite effectively by his enemies to undercut his authority. Yet after he returned to his native land, he became their champion. By September there were enough indications to suggest that Bogotá was going to repudiate that settlement. Galán therefore sought to mobilize the ensuing popular unrest to organize a second march on the capital in order to enforce compliance. José Antonio chose his tactics in response to the particular situation that confronted him.

The only weakness of Galán's brilliantly executed campaign in the upper Magdalena valley was that he failed to forge an alliance between the creole patricians and the plebeians on the lines that had succeeded in Santander. Galán was no demagogue, playing the rich against the poor. When he returned to his native land, he sought to enlist the support of the nobles for the second march on Bogotá. He instinctively recognized that the recipe for success was a broadly based coalition of creole patricians and mestizo and mulatto plebeians. His leftist admirers today claim that his ideal was the "union of the oppressed against their oppressors." Such a phrase, of course, was never employed by Galán himself.[40] He took his support where he found it, and a good deal of it came from the plebeians.

His enemies, in particular the audiencia, who sentenced him to a cruel death, lashed out at him for appealing to the populace and appointing plebeians to positions of leadership.[41] But their word cannot be accepted at face value. The audiencia was grimly determined to create the image of Galán as a social revolutionary in order to frighten the creoles into renewing their loyalty to the status quo.

In the context of 1781 Galán was no radical but a man whose values and goals were rooted in the traditionalist society in which he lived. Never repudiating his allegiance to the crown, Galán had no conscious or even embryonic notion about the desirability of reordering society. He shared with all his fellow captains the simple goal of returning to the past by repudiating the fiscal innovations of Gutiérrez de Piñeres.

How and why the myth of José Antonio as a social revolutionary arose is the topic that now merits attention.

16

The Second Enterprise against Santa Fe

The tragic fate of José Antonio Galán was decided during the month of September in a swiftly moving, if at times confusing, sequence of events. Two earlier occurrences, however, drastically influenced the outcome during that fateful month. On June 25, Archbishop Caballero y Góngora departed from Bogotá for a pastoral visit to Socorro, to undertake what he fondly called the "task of reconciliation."[1] On August 6, Colonel José Bernet arrived in the capital with his well-armed expedition of five hundred professionally trained troops. Bogotá's negotiating position was immeasurably strengthened, for the authorities now possessed the threat of military force.

Accompanying the archbishop on his pastoral visit to Socorro and its neighboring towns and villages were four Capuchin missionaries. Caballero y Góngora did not leave the Socorro area until December 28. The archbishop and his colleagues conducted a veritable missionary campaign to reconquer the area from its "infidelity." A major instrument of this massive campaign, many of whose specific tactics will be discussed in more detail in the next chapter, was a series of sermons directed to both the plebeians and nobles. The archbishop's aim was to sever the alliance between the two groups by reassuring the nobles that the government would take into account their legitimate grievances and by preaching sermons of hellfire and damnation to the plebeians about the sin of rebellion against constituted authority.

Within a few weeks the archbishop's campaign had made solid headway among both patricians and plebeians. While Galán, in September, could still count on some influential adherents among both levels of society, Socorro's former militance was greatly eroded.

On September 1, Caballero y Góngora ordered the recently appointed

200

corregidor of the new province of Socorro, which had been established as a result of the capitulations, to leave Socorro for Pamplona, on the pretext that disturbances there required the presence of a prestigious official. The real reason, however, was that Caballero y Góngora suspected that Berbeo's continued residence in Socorro might have a disquieting influence on the pacification campaign.[2] Berbeo was absent from Socorro when Galán was captured.

The archbishop's chosen instrument to win back the allegiance of the local elites was Socorro's richest citizen, Salvador Plata. He had opposed the insurrection from its inception to its end. Never allowed to go to Zipaquirá to participate in the negotiations, Plata cheerfully and enthusiastically accepted the informal commission of the archbishop to rally the elites behind the government. Fearful that they might be punished, the captains general had little alternative but to cooperate with him.

During the month of September, however, a whole series of events threatened to undermine the obviously precarious loyalty of the patricians to the government and arouse new unrest among the plebeians. On the night of September 1 the Indians in Nemocón rioted. The tumult was repressed; several Indians lost their lives and others were dispatched to Bogotá for a speedy trial.[3] The audiencia proceeded to arrest, on grounds of treason, the harmless but nominal leader of the Indian community, don Ambrosio Pisco, the erstwhile cacique of Bogotá and Lord of Chía.[4] Pisco's arrest called into question the principle of amnesty enshrined in the capitulations. A few days later on September 7 the cabildo of Socorro received preemptory orders from the viceroy in Cartagena annulling the capitulations.[5] That news was shortly followed on September 12 by a mandate from the audiencia repudiating another key provision of the settlement reached at Zipaquirá. The captains general in Socorro and elsewhere were summarily ordered to relinquish their military commissions.[6] The militia, which was envisaged as a kind of military guarantee to enforce the capitulations, was abolished by fiat from Bogotá.

If the audiencia in Bogotá pursued a hard line, the resourceful archbishop in Socorro followed a soft line. On September 14, Caballero y Góngora authorized the cabildos of Socorro and San Gil not to publish the viceroy's edict annulling the capitulations.[7] This action reassured the patricians that the prelate was capable of acting effectively as their intercessor with the powers-that-be.

José Antonio Galán arrived on September 2 in Mogotes. That parish, belonging to the jurisdiction of the town of San Gil, lay about seven leagues southeast of the parish of San Gil, a distance of about two hours by horseback. Not yet under the direct influence of the archbishop's pastoral persuasions, which were then confined to Socorro and San Gil, the plebeians of Mogotes were restless and agitated. They implored Galán to lead a second expedition to Bogotá in order to guarantee compliance with the settlement reached at Zipaquirá. Galán at that time had two options. He could go into hiding in the remote eastern plains, the llanos, in the hopes that in time he would receive a pardon. Even without an act of grace from the authorities, he might, at least, hope to retain his personal freedom. Such was his self-proclaimed intention when he arrived in Mogotes. His second choice, of course, was to lead another "enterprise" to the capital. He evidently accepted with alacrity the invitation of the populace of the parish of Mogotes to do just that.[8] He remained in that parish for some forty days, hoping to rally the support of the parishes of Socorro and San Gil.

It is not without some irony that Galán's summons for a second march on the capital was to compel the royal authorities to comply with the capitulations of Zipaquirá, toward which his attitudes were always ambiguous and, it would seem, dictated in every case by the posture of his enemies. When the political establishment in Bogotá opposed the settlement of Zipaquirá, he favored it.

However enthusiastically the plebeians of the parish of Mogotes might rally to his support, Galán perceived that his only hope of success was in rebuilding the grand coalition of patricians and plebeians of the towns of Socorro and San Gil that had been the hard core of the first march to Bogotá. Galán consequently directed a forceful appeal to his former comrades-in-arms in Socorro to join him. Among those to whom he appealed were Isidro Molina, Ignacio Ardila, Miguel Francisco Monsalve, Blas Antonio Torres, and Juan Manuel Ortíz. Galán exhorted his would-be allies:

> What are we waiting for? For Bogotá to supply itself with all sorts of provisions, and for the arrival of troops from Bogotá. They are about to depart from there in order to come here and annihilate us without any exceptions not even sparing the innocent. So they have promised us. Let us take courage, and let us see even at the cost of our very lives we can restrain this pernicious cancer, which threatens to ruin our honor, our property, and even our lives with the infamous blotch and tether of shameful slavery!
>
> Long live God! Long live our holy faith! Long live our sovereign and death to his bad government![9]

Galán pleaded with his former colleagues for specific instructions. Socorro's reply gave him disquieting evidence of how effective the archbishop's pacification had been after a mere few weeks. The archbishop, Galán's correspondents wrote, had secured a "truce" of one month's duration with his word that he had already intervened personally with the audiencia in Bogotá requesting strict compliance with the capitulations. If they did not heed his warning, the archbishop would accompany the Socorranos to the capital where he would judge and punish the oidores.[10]

Not only were the nobles under the persuasive sway of Caballero y Góngora, but the will to resist of the plebeians of the plaza of Chiquinquirá, the "little square," had succumbed to the arguments of the Capuchin friars, that to resist the mandates of the king's ministers was tantamount to committing a sin against God. A manifesto containing a host of signatures, including those of seven members of the influential Ardila clan, was issued by the parishioners of Chiquinquirá. In it they proclaimed themselves "true vassals of King Charles III and subjects of his ministers."[11]

Another appeal from the newly elected captain of Mogotes, Miguel Rafael Sandoval, to the neighboring parishes emphasized bread-and-butter issues of interest to the poor. Sandoval stressed the same note that Berbeo and his associates had formerly emphasized—relief from the new taxes and the crown monopolies.[12]

Galán's secretaries dispatched many other appeals. Always the pragmatic tactician, he was prepared to appeal to the poor, although he never forgot the need to enlist the rich and prominent in his cause. But first, he must rekindle the fiery anger of the poor. Then the nobles would join the cause. Such was the way it had happened during the first march on Bogotá: the patricians had not assumed positions of leadership until after the crowd had rioted for several weeks. In appealing to the captains of Sogamoso the man from Charalá employed language designed to inflame the plebeians:

> The capital of Santa Fe, but not all its inhabitants but only those who have a great hunger to suck the blood of the poor, have arrived at the extreme of not being satisfied with anything less than our very lives, our honor and our property. . . . We must return a second time [to Bogotá] to see if we can destroy their lofty arrogance.[13]

Galán's cause was doomed, in fact; but before the end came, he received some encouragement from a few well-placed individuals in Socorro. Antonio Molina, a member of the supreme council of war whose son, Isidro, had been a trusted lieutenant of Galán in the Magdalena campaign, pledged his support. So did another lieutenant of Galán, Lorenzo Alcantuz, a small tobacco farmer from San Gil, who was then living in Socorro. Another lieutenant, Manuel Ortíz, the doorkeeper of the cabildo of Socorro, also joined the cause.[14] The Molinas, father and son, and Manuel Ortíz were related to Mateo Ardila, the influential town clerk of Socorro, but the influential Ardila clan, whose network included links to both the upper and lower echelons of Socorro, gave Galán neither massive nor sustained support.[15]

An offer of help came from an unexpected quarter. Juan Dionisio Plata and his two young sons, accompanied by Manuel Ortíz, turned up in Mogotes, where they presented Galán with a startling proposition. Plata urged that Galán march to Socorro and imprison Salvador Plata, Galán's most intransigent enemy. It so happened that Juan Dionisio Plata and Salvador Plata were first cousins, but that large and numerous clan were as noted for the bitterness of their family feuds as they were for their wealth. Galán flatly rejected the proposal.[16]

An equally reckless scheme was sponsored by Isidro Molina and Basilio Plata, Juan Dionisio's son. They proposed that the parishes of Pinchote, Culotas, Confines, Chima, and Simacota mobilize an army to invade San Gil in order to imprison Captain General Ignacio Tejada, whom Molina and Plata called an enemy of their cause. It may be recalled that at Zipaquirá San Gil had sided with Tunja in opposing Socorro's intention to invade the capital. Galán may have had some support in Socorro, but he had much less in more aristocratic San Gil. In his confession, written in the third person, Galán testified:

> the witness [Galán] told them [Molina and Plata] that he would not go to that town [San Gil], for they had not attacked him, nor did he have any enemies there. Those who are attacking him and who are their real enemies were in Santa Fe.

Molina and Plata taunted Galán as a weakling. Galán persisted in his resolve and wrote letters forbidding his followers to attack San Gil. Galán in his confession testified that he wrote the captains of those parishes reminding them, "This was not the time for vengeance, for they should regard each other as brothers."[17]

Galán sought to pour cold water on the internecine quarrels of his supporters. Vainly he aimed at uniting them against their common enemy in the capital. With friends like Isidro Molina and the Platas, José Antonio had no need of enemies; but unfortunately for him his enemies were legion, and they were ready to strike.

Two days before Galán arrived in Mogotes to establish his headquarters the audiencia in Bogotá issued peremptory orders to the cabildo of Socorro to capture Galán and to dispatch him forthwith to the capital. It was not until September 18, however, that the alcaldes in Socorro formally authorized an expedition.[18] The delay was probably intentionally orchestrated behind the scenes by Caballero y Góngora, to give him the needed time to consolidate his pacification campaign. On September 12 he secured his agreement for a one-month truce; on September 14, in another concession to pacify the troubled spirit of his flock in Socorro, he authorized the cabildos of Socorro and San Gil not to publish Viceroy Flores's annulment of the capitulations.

On October 6 the alcaldes accepted Salvador Plata's offer to lead the expedition.[19] The Croesus of Socorro was burning with enthusiasm to demonstrate his loyalty to the crown, and consumed with a ferocious disdain for the plebeians whom Galán obviously personified. On the morning of

October 9 Salvador Plata departed from the main square of Socorro with a contingent of some one hundred well-armed recruits. Accompanying Plata were several leaders of the first march against Bogotá, among them Captains Juan Bernardo Plata de Acevedo, Francisco Rosillo, and Pedro Alejandro de la Prada. While somewhat less vehement in their personal animosity toward Galán, they evidently wanted to demonstrate their loyalty to the crown in order to win exoneration for their immediate past.

Discouraged by his failure to rally support, Galán and a mere twenty followers abandoned Mogotes on October 10. Galán departed carrying not the red flag of the Comuneros but the standard of the king of Spain, to whom he had always pledged loyalty. On the night of October 13 Galán and his weary party had fallen asleep in a humble farmhouse in the parish of Onzaga. At ten o'clock that evening Salvador Plata's men captured Galán and eleven of his followers. Some escaped, some were wounded, but Galán himself surrendered without offering resistance.[20]

There is an interesting interplay between the roles of Archbishop Caballero y Góngora, who was then in Socorro, and the audiencia in Bogotá. It was the audiencia that ordered the arrest and trial of Ambrosio Pisco as well as that of José Antonio. Deeply humiliated by their enforced approval of the capitulations of Zipaquirá, they were anxious to justify themselves to the royal authorities in Madrid. Archbishop Caballero y Góngora's pastoral exhortations in Socorro and the presence of Colonel Bernet's five hundred soldiers in Bogotá encouraged the oidores to pursue a policy of exemplary repression. Galán was to be made a symbol of rebellion in order to strike fear into the hearts of would-be emulators. The archbishop shared the same conviction, but was determined to follow his own tactics. His soothing words of reconciliation did not contradict the audiencia's position but rather complemented it. The prelate, as often, was facing both ways. On the very day that Salvador Plata led his contingent from Socorro to capture Galán the archbishop wrote Bernet in Bogotá, expressing his approval of the action but making it clear that the whole matter fell under the exclusive jurisdiction of the civil authorities. He added:

> Of this resolution [the cabildo's commission to Plata to capture Galán] I have no opinion, being yourself aware of the delicate position of my holy ministry. If, in effect, they succeed as they think and plan, I believe that there will not lack those who will give thanks for having rid these villages of a man who aroused them and who has intended to form an army to march on the capital. . . . We shall see what this mission of Plata achieves against such a declared enemy of the peace. Your grace will subsequently find out if I am right in saying that Socorro will give unequivocal proof of its fidelity on that day.[21]

Two days after the capture of Galán, Alcalde Angulo y Olarte jailed several of Galán's most influential partisans. Among them were Juan Lorenzo Alcantuz, Manuel Ortíz, and Blas Antonio Torres. Galán and his associates were put in chains, under heavy guard, in Socorro's jail on October 16. After they were questioned under sworn oath, they made their confessions before Alcalde Angulo. Then José Antonio Galán and twenty-three of his companions were escorted under armed guard to the capital of the New Kingdom to stand trial before the audiencia. They reached their destination on November 6. All involved, it appears, were anxious to pass on the responsibility as quickly as possible: the nervous and impatient audiencia on October 20 sent orders to conduct the trial and to execute the death penalty in Socorro, but so anxious were the authorities in Socorro to get rid of Galán that by the time these orders arrived, Galán and his unhappy companions were four days away from Socorro en route to Bogotá.[22]

The trial began in early November, but it was not until January 30, 1782, that the audiencia handed down its verdict. While many of the key documents of the trial have disappeared, enough survive to suggest that the oidores observed all the outward forms of the cumbersome Spanish legal machinery. Galán certainly had benefit of counsel, presumably one of the state-paid public defenders, the *procuradores de pobres.* They were in 1781 Joaquín Zapata y Porras and Luis Marín Pastor, who brilliantly defended many other plebeians charged with crimes during the revolution. It is a pity that no brief has survived in Galán's case.[23] It was, undeniably, possible to construct an effective defense for Galán, largely based on the plausible argument that all of his actions in the Magdalena campaign were performed under the orders of the supreme commander, Juan Francisco Berbeo, who was, therefore, the real culprit. Such a defense had been invoked in other trials. Galán's warning to Gutiérrez de Piñeres to flee could have been used with devastating effectiveness by the defense. The public defender, however, would have more difficulty in defending Galán's self-acknowledged willingness to lead a second march on Bogotá.

However meticulously the legal forms may have been observed, Galán and his companions faced a kangaroo court. The audiencia regarded them as guilty of treason long before the trial had begun—as early as August 27, when they first ordered his capture. The audiencia's prejudice is graphically revealed in the draconian sentence that was handed down, and even more so in the actual text of the death sentence that was issued.

The audiencia added several gruesome touches to the standard punishment of hanging, drawing, and quartering traitors.

> We thus condemn José Antonio Galán to be taken out of jail, dragged and taken to the place of execution where he will be hung until dead, that his head be removed from his dead body,

that the rest of his body be quartered, that his torso be committed to flames for which purpose a fire shall be lit in front of the platform. His head shall be sent to Guaduas, the scene of his scandalous insults, his right arm shall be displayed in the main square of Socorro, his left arm shall be displayed in the square of San Gil, his right leg shall be displayed in Charalá his birthplace, and the left leg in the parish of Mogotes. All his descendants shall be declared infamous, all his property shall be confiscated by the royal treasury, his home shall be burnt, and the ground salted, so that in this fashion his infamous name may be forgotten. Thus shall end the life of that vile person of such detestable memory, and he shall leave behind him no remembrance other than the revulsion and horror of his ugly crime.[24]

Similar punishments were handed down for three of Galán's most trusted lieutenants—Lorenzo Alcantuz of San Gil, Manuel Ortíz, the doorkeeper of the cabildo of Socorro, and Isidro Molina.

Those four were considered to be ringleaders. Another group of seventeen Galanistas received somewhat less severe penalties, but they were harsh by any standard.

We condemn them to be marched through public and frequented streets after having received two hundred lashes. They shall also march under the scaffold with a hangman's noose around their necks where they shall attend the final execution of their captains and leaders. Their property shall be confiscated. Finally they shall be taken to the penitentiaries in Africa for the rest of their lives.

"Considering the involuntary and casual nature of their accompanying José Antonio Galán," four others were merely exiled perpetually from living within forty leagues of Bogotá, San Gil, and Socorro. They were captured with Galán, but evidently were not considered active partisans of his cause.

The sentences were carried out to the letter. The alcaldes in the communities involved dutifully reported to the audiencia about the arrival and display of the limbs of Galán and his three confederates.[25]

The death sentence was the third publication that was printed on the new printing press that Viceroy Flores had arranged to have set up in Bogotá.[26] Copies of the sentence were dispatched to every town and parish in the New Kingdom with instructions that the town crier read it word for word, when the populace gathered on three successive market days. That the audiencia regarded the severe punishment as a symbolic act to frighten the populace is clearly revealed by the text of the sentence.

This sentence shall serve as a veritable monument to the affront, the confusion and the shame of those who showed themselves to be unruly and disobedient. It will also serve as consolation,

> security, and trust to His Majesty's faithful and loyal vassals. . . . No one henceforth shall be able to excuse himself from the horrible crimes of conspiracy, revolt, or resistance to the king's ministers by feigning ignorance, rusticity, or timidity.

The text of the sentence paints Galán in lurid colors, making a systematic attempt to blacken his reputation. Not only is he a traitor to the king and an enemy of religion, he is a common ordinary thief who has no respect for the private property of individuals nor the public property of the crown, i.e., the royal monopolies.

Of the sixteen charges leveled against him, some eleven dealt with his "turbulent licentiousness" and "voracious and infamous plans" during his Magdalena campaign. Singled out for special opprobrium were his participation in the battle of Puente Real de Vélez, the interception of the royal mail pouch at Facatativá, the looting of various royal monopoly offices, his blatant disrespect for many local magistrates, and his alleged stealing of the jewels of Vicente Diago. Not mentioned, of course, was the fact that Galán returned the precious stones the next day.[27] The sentence puts particular emphasis on the celebrated incident at the estate of Malpaso "belonging to Vicente Diago, inciting the slaves to revolt and promising to give them their freedom as if he were their rightful owner."

Of the sixteen charges only two dealt with events after Zipaquirá. One charge dealt with the incident at Chiquinquirá, where Galán publicly humiliated a magistrate. And only one charge concerned the second march on Bogotá. That the audiencia feared his ability as a leader is suggested by one sentence:

> Finally he returned to Mogotes from where he spread terror and tumult among the populace who regarded him as invulnerable and who believed his fabulous stories and fantastic illusions.

Only three of the sixteen charges dealt with Galán's private life prior to 1781. One concerned his desertion from the army garrison in Cartagena. Another charge, that he was "scandalous and lax in his treatment of women of every social status" might shock some priests and pious old ladies, but not the general male adult public, many of whom practiced *don juanismo* in their daily lives, with varying degrees of success. Friend and foe agree that Galán was a successful ladies' man, and his letters reveal him as a gallant. The charge, however, that he committed incest—an act regarded with revulsion and horror—with his daughter was more serious. This rumor enjoyed some currency even before Galán's trial—Manuel García Olano, who knew Galán in 1777 or 1778 in Socorro, repeated it in a private letter addressed to his daughter.[28] The highly prejudiced García Olano's testimony cannot by itself vouch for the authenticity of the charge, and there is no other known documentary evidence on the matter. Whether true or not, the accusation must be viewed as an integral part of the audiencia's deliberate campaign to portray the man from Charalá as the personification of all types of evil.

A simple content analysis of the charges hurled against José Antonio Galán is, then, revealing if somewhat misleading. Of the sixteen specific charges some eleven dealt with his pre-Zipaquirá participation in the movement, some three dealt with his private life prior to 1781, and only two dealt with his post-Zipaquirá career. In one sense the only indubitable case for treason was the abortive march against the capital. Yet only one charge in the sentence dealt with that momentous event. Galán himself, and certainly his lawyer, could have made out a very credible defense that all his actions in the Magdalena campaign, some eleven out of a total of sixteen, were forgivable in that he was carrying out the orders of his superiors.

It is important to bear in mind that the audiencia was acting on several levels. The abortive march on Bogotá was, in its eyes, the most heinous crime of treason that Galán had committed. By imposing such a severe sentence, they were attempting to ensure that no one would dare follow his example. Hence every possible incident in his career was luridly magnified, and the widely publicized death penalty ordered in such gruesome, brutal, and meticulous detail.

In the sentence Galán is portrayed as the epitome of treason, theft, and licentiousness, and the king as the embodiment of benign justice. After reciting chapter and verse of the black litany of Galán's crimes, the text of the death sentence exploded in wrath:

> Finally he [Galán] is a monster of evil, an object of abomination, whose name and memory should be outlawed and erased among those happy vassals, who have had the good fortune of being born in the king's dominions, the most pious, the most benign, the most loving and the worthiest of being loved by all his subjects.

Lest the king's subjects labor under any misapprehensions, the text sternly admonished:

> that the punishment of this prisoner and his associates should serve as an exemplary warning, so that no one subsequently can claim ignorance of the horrible crime that a person commits when resisting or obstructing the laws and ordinances emanating from legitimate superiors, who in this remote area act as the direct representatives of the very person of our Catholic and beloved monarch.

The text provided to loyal subjects only one permissible remedy to secure redress of grievances:

in those cases where subjects have grievances toward inferior officials, they may only appeal to the superiors of those magistrates in a spirit of respect and submission without resorting to any other means. Any other procedure is scandalous, erroneous and a violation of the oath of loyalty, which binds all regardless of their privileges, their persons, their sex, their social position or ethnic status.

This message would become one of the ideological cornerstones of Caballero y Góngora's pacification program, discussed in chapter 17.

The death sentence was actually addressed to three distinct audiences, with a different message to each one. First of all, there was an admonishment to the local authorities in the towns and parishes to maintain a ceaseless vigilance to uncover and castigate any activity that might lead to sedition and rebellion. Bogotá officials tended to oversimplify the laxness of the local magistrates in failing to quell the first disturbances in March.

Secondly, the audiencia was addressing itself to the tough and boisterous plebeians who had enrolled with such enthusiasm under the red banner of the Comuneros. They were being warned that a repetition of Galán's example would be punished with all the severity that treason merited.

The most influential audience to whom the audiencia addressed itself, however, was the patricians, the socially prominent if not always rich creoles who formed the backbone of the leadership of the first march against the capital. The audiencia was saying, in effect, that the resort to arms and the use of coercion would ultimately lead to social revolution from below. José Antonio Galán was deliberately and falsely portrayed as a vulgar plebeian bandit who respected nothing, neither women, nor private property, nor the rights of the king. The patricians must look to the king's ministers for the peaceful redress of legitimate grievances. To ally themselves with the "uncouth mob" would only open up a Pandora's box out of which would leap anarchy.

In this celebrated death sentence, the audiencia of Bogotá created the myth of José Antonio as a social revolutionary. In historical fact, as we have seen, his social views differed little from those of his patrician contemporaries. He advocated no basic reordering of society.[29] Both nobles and plebeians were united in a common loyalty to the faraway crown as well as sharing a deep, if vague, feeling that the king and his magistrates should engage in some form of consultation about the extent and form of new taxation. Galán did not oppose taxes as such, but he, along with most of his contemporaries, argued that the fiscal burden should not exceed the ability of various groups to pay. He once admitted that the traditional 2 percent alcabala sales tax "was as much a part of natural law as death itself."[30] One is reminded of Benjamin Franklin's celebrated adage that the only certain things in life are death and taxes. Tough, courageous, and indomitable, José Antonio Galán was a man of his own times, a precursor neither of social nor political independence. To portray him as such is only to distort the meaningful role he did play in that eventful year of 1781.[31]

While Archbishop Caballero y Góngora approved the execution of Galán, he was astute enough to realize that repression had to be complemented by conciliation. How he implemented that policy is the topic of the final three chapters.

17

The Reconquest of Socorro
from Its "Infidelity"

Archbishop Caballero y Góngora clearly recognized the need to create a climate of opinion favorable to any innovations the government might propose. The failure of the regent visitor general Gutiérrez de Piñeres to mount any such campaign had clearly contributed to the outbreak of disturbances in 1781.

The prelate's chosen instruments were the Capuchin order, a branch of the Franciscans which was recruited from that order's peninsular province of Valencia. Before the 1770's their missionary activity in New Granada had largely been confined to the province of Santa Marta, and not until 1777 did they establish a monastery in Bogotá.[1] They had, therefore, no solid ties with the creole establishment, which dominated other branches of the regular clergy. As Spaniards, the Capuchins could be counted upon to defend zealously the authority of the crown. They were also noted for their staunch regalism, which asserted the power and authority of the crown over the church, and was the ecclesiastical concomitant of Bourbon political centralism.[2]

When the archbishop left on June 25 for a five-month pastoral visit to Socorro and its neighboring towns and parishes, he was accompanied by four Capuchin friars. The friar who dominated this mission was Joaquín de Finestrad, thirty-five years old, who had arrived in Bogotá on October 24, 1778.[3] In Socorro he became the archbishop's confidant and trusted lieutenant. He remained in the Socorro area for several years, for in 1783 Caballero y Góngora appointed him temporary pastor of populous Simacota.[4] As late as 1787, when the archbishop viceroy was directing from Cartagena the

212

conquest and the colonization of Darien, Finestrad recruited three expeditions of colonists from the Socorro area for that lackluster exploit.[5]

Joaquín de Finestrad was not only the field commander of the pacification campaign, but he was also its principal ideologue and apologist. Later, while in Cartagena serving as the chaplain to the Spanish fleet, he composed his *Vasallo instruido en el estado del nuevo reino de Granada y en sus respectivas obligaciones.* He finished the book on June 12, 1789, less than a month before the crowds in distant Paris, even angrier than those of Socorro in 1781, stormed the Bastille. That symbolic confrontation ushered in the French Revolution, which, of course, would shatter the world that Finestrad was seeking to defend with his pen. Although Finestrad's book was not published until 1905, and then only partially, many chapters, especially the unpublished ones, read like a collection of sermons and homilies.[6] It is fair to assume that the book is a version of the sermons that he often preached to his wayward flock just a few years before. As such it represents the most articulate formulation of Caballero y Góngora's policy of reconciliation, and its contents merit careful examination.

Finestrad recognized that the major ideological thrust of the Comuneros was a diluted and popularized form of the doctrines of the sixteenth- and seventeenth-century Spanish theologians whose most influential spokesman was the Jesuit Francisco Suárez. Finestrad turned his back on this whole classical theory. While he admitted the existence of an original social contract creating political society, his view of man in a state of nature was a Hobbesian nightmare of "everyman at war with everyman." Violence, homicide, rape, arson, sacrilege, and theft then prevailed. The primary goal of society was to achieve peace and stability, and not justice as the Spanish neoscholastics argued.[7] Justice was merely a subordinate attribute of peace.

The social contact created an absolute monarch who derived his authority directly from God and not from any action of the people. Finestrad added: "What else is a kingdom but one extended family in which the king is the father, for the authority of kings and fathers are both emanations of divine authority." As natural law provides that children obey their fathers, likewise subjects should obey their monarchs. As natural law provides that the arms and legs obey the brain, so also should all members of society obey the king who is the head of the body. As the anointed of the Lord: "The king is the living image of God, his minister, his vicar and his representative on earth ... to whom all subjects have sworn an ample and absolute obedience."[8]

Finestrad's vision of the limitless power of the king and innate powerlessness of his vassals is summed up in this passage:

> It is not the concern of the vassal to examine the justice and the prerogatives of the king but to venerate and obey blindly his

royal commands. His regal power lies not in opinions but in traditions as likewise does that of his royal ministers. It is a spirit of audacious and partisan presumption which claims otherwise. It is not the choice of a vassal to weigh or to examine the justice of the mandates of the king, even in a dubious case. It is to be presumed that all his orders are eminently just and equitable. The vassal may only humbly petition the sovereign, who if better informed, may repeal or modify his royal command.[9]

The Spanish neoscholastics shared the view that kingship was a divine institution, which was created by the people in a social contract with Providential sanction. Finestrad, however, was advocating not merely the divine right of kingship but the divine right of kings. In this respect he was following the views of James I of England, with whom Francisco Suárez had engaged in a celebrated polemic, and the French bishop Jacques Bénigne Bossuet (1627–1704), who had rationalized the particular version of royal absolutism personified by the Sun-King of Versailles.[10] Indeed, Louis XIV, "le grand monarque," was a model that his Bourbon descendants in Spain consciously emulated. Their cherished ideal was to create out of their diverse dominions in the Old World and in the New the centralized state that Louis XIV had previously fashioned in France.

Like Bossuet before him, Finestrad found his favorite sources in the Old Testament, the Roman empire, the Patristic fathers, and the early Church councils. In discussing the origin of political authority and the nature of regal power never once did he cite his Spanish predecessors. Only twice did he allude to Suárez, when he favored a particular opinion of his.[11]

Finestrad's most frequently quoted modern authors were the Abbé Raynal, William Robertson, Hobbes, and Machiavelli. The first two were usually cited to refute their hostile views of Spanish colonization overseas, whereas the latter two were mentioned, sometimes favorably, for their theories about the origin and the nature of the state.

Not only must all orders of the sovereign be obeyed to the letter, but so also should the commands of his ministers. The favorite slogan of the Comuneros aroused the ire of the Capuchin friar, who denounced it as "sacrilegious" and "reckless."

> To proclaim "long live the king and death to bad government" makes a phantom out of religion and the social policy created in the fashion and taste of those who would not recognize vassalage nor a government to rule over them nor a king to govern them. . . . To hail the king and then to deprive his ministers of the very breath with which to live is to grant the royal person only a vague shadow of his royal title. To separate the prince from command over his kingdom is to create a governmental monster

without a head. . . . The jurisdiction of the king's ministers emanates directly from the royal and public authority.

Finestrad drove home his point when he added:

> the ministers of the king are living images of his royal person; they are his vicars in temporal matters. . . . They merit the same order of veneration and obedience owed to the prototype by virtue of the respect and the relation that they bear to the royal person, whose character and power glitter and shine in them with greater clarity than the light of the sun and the stars.[12]

Finestrad roundly denounced the implicit assumption upon which the men of 1781 acted: that subjects had the right to resist tyranny. Under no circumstances were vassals justified in taking up arms against the king or his ministers. Subjects must endure patiently even those laws which seem unjust and oppressive and place their faith in the Almighty, for only he "can calm the winds and the waves."[13] Armed rebellion is a gross violation of the commandments of God—the king is the anointed of the Lord—and hence treason and sacrilege are synonymous. More than once Finestrad assailed the "horrendous sacrilege of rebellion."[14] Furthermore, the cure of rebellion is far worse than the disease of injustice, for "riots and disturbances are always more regrettable than tyranny itself."[15] For Finestrad, the price of social peace could never be too high.

Abandoning the level of political abstraction, Finestrad descended to the more practical level, developing at some length the argument that to take up arms against Charles III was particularly unjustified, since that benign and benevolent monarch sought only the happiness of his subjects.[16]

The Capuchin friar also appealed to the patriotism of his audience. "Our fatherland, our common mother, the American and Spanish people form one nation under one sovereign; we are the sons of one father, vassals of one king, limbs from the same body, branches from the same trunk, sheep from the same flock, and clients of the same patron."[17] These words expressed the views of all Caroline bureaucrats, that Spain and America formed a common *patria imperial*; the crisis of 1781 indicated the extent to which the creoles had come to identify, not with the empire-wide patria but with the regional patria of New Granada. Finestrad went on to appeal to the peculiarly Catholic quality of Spanish patriotism. In 1781 Spain was fighting its hereditary Protestant foe, Great Britain. Why should not the king's loyal subjects pay the taxes to undertake that war, he rhetorically, and often, asked his audience.[18]

In "our royal cedula," the inflammatory pasquinade which contained much of the implicit ideology of the Comunero Revolution, two stanzas cast some doubt on the legitimacy of Spanish rule over the Indies. Finestrad interpreted these lines as an outright denunciation of the Spanish conquest of America and a clear-cut repudiation of the sovereignty of the Spanish crown—an interpretation that is open to question (see chapter 5), but that so deeply offended his patriotism that he devoted an entire chapter of the *Vasallo instruido* to refuting the proposition that the Spanish kings were not the legitimate sovereigns of the Indies. He sarcastically referred to the anonymous author of the lampoon as the "new philosopher."[19] Finestrad paid only lip service to the traditional justifications of Spanish rule: the preaching of the gospel, the right of prior discovery, or the applicability of the just war doctrine. He did not even bother to defend at any length the conduct of the conquistadores, although he never criticized any of their individual or collective actions. His novel, and quite worldly argument was that time—some three centuries—had legitimized the conquest:

> If we must judge the legitimacy of thrones by their origin, we will have to overthrow the existing order, to turn upside down every kingdom and to dethrone every king so that every legitimate monarch may be restored. . . . What a monstrous proposition! . . . Possession from time immemorial is sufficient to guarantee the security of thrones. The common consent of peoples to venerate their kings as legitimate lords is sufficient and the recognition of their parliaments is enough for vassals to observe most rigorously obedience and allegiance to their sovereign.

Citing Machiavelli and Hobbes, Finestrad argued that most states originated by force and violence, but these political entities "have been legitimized by time."[20]

There is a deep if concealed contradiction in Finestrad's political theory. On one hand, he came close to idolizing the king as God's vicar on earth, whose mandates no subject might even question, let alone resist. Yet in his defense of the Spanish conquest he enthusiastically cited Machiavelli and Hobbes to the effect that political authority originated in violence and usurpation, and was legitimized by general acceptance of it over the span of time. Finestrad's king is a two-headed monster, both Bossuet's anointed of the Lord and Hobbes's Leviathan, whose power was originally acquired following the precepts of Machiavelli. Finestrad himself blithely ignored this contradiction, and it probably escaped the attention of his parishioners as well. Finestrad, after all, was first and foremost a preacher. Certainly not a political theorist of any noticeable originality, he sought to combine eclectically the Providentialist tradition of kingship with more worldly Enlightenment notions of naked political power.

Finestrad also took considerable pains to reject the argument of his New Granadine adversaries that the crisis of 1781 was caused by the "bad government" of the king's ministers. He devoted a whole chapter to the proposition that the "general corruption of morals which has inundated this whole kingdom" was the cause of their infidelity to the two majesties of God and king.[21] He paints a lurid picture of a land given to sodomy, incest, rape, robbery, and blasphemy. Like an Old Testament Jeremiah, Finestrad thunders that God has expressed his wrath against his sinful children by visiting upon them the earthquake of 1765, the epidemic of smallpox in 1766, and the famine in Socorro in 1776. He admonished his wayward parishioners: "Our sins are the cause of our misfortunes; we are the architects of our downfall and the authors of our miseries."[22]

Finestrad summed up his black impression of his flock:

> The children of this land vacillate between grace and sin, sometimes weeping with Peter for their sins and at other times reveling with Elagabulus in concupiscence. One month they are as penitent as a Mary Magdalen and the other month they are as scandalous as a Jezebel.[23]

He concluded by proclaiming their wickedness incurable, lest the people repent sincerely for their sins and the wickedness of their past rebellion. God in his infinite mercy might then forgive them.

Yet despite his religious absolutism, the Capuchin friar was very much a man of his times, "the century of light." He ardently believed that an enlightened elite could introduce economic and technological changes to increase wealth. He shared the view of most highly placed bureaucrats that the potential wealth of the New Kingdom was virtually untapped. He advocated congregating dispersed populations, eliminating vagabondage, hispanizing the Indians, and improving the mining industry.[24] In none of his concrete proposals was he original. But he was typical of the Caroline age in combining an ideal of blind obedience to constituted authority with an optimistic faith in the state as a dynamic instrument for socioeconomic change from above. His sermons provided one important part of the ideological foundation upon which Archbishop Viceroy Caballero y Góngora could reestablish undisputed royal authority, first in Socorro and subsequently in the whole New Kingdom.

Within a few weeks of the Capuchins' arrival, their sermons had blunted any major support among the plebeians for the cause of José Antonio Galán. In the evening of November 15 several hundred plebeians from the parish of Chiquinquirá, where the riots in March and April had begun, visited the archbishop, in a repentant and humble mood. Carrying an image of the Virgin Mary and bearing lighted candles they sang to their prelate a poem of some fifteen stanzas. In the poem his grateful flock thanked their good shepherd for restoring peace to "our afflicted town," and promised to obey the admonitions of the Capuchins. The poem neatly rhymed. The vocabulary was simple and grammatically correct. From the balcony of his residence the archbishop accepted with smiles and a blessing the peace offering of his once wayward, but now repentant flock.

The author of the poem has not been identified, but one may surmise that it came out of the Capuchin mission. The sedate, obedient, and humble tone of the verses sharply contrasts with the bawdy, earthy, and inflammatory pasquin that the people had lustily cheered.[25] The archbishop was fascinated, if not horrified, at the appeal of that provocative lampoon. He evidently was not displeased by a poem which proclaimed the gospel of blind obedience, as "our royal decree" had enthusiastically sung the praises of rebellion.

The authorities were still understandably nervous about the recurrence of popular outbreaks. Upon the advice of the local clergy the audiencia even issued an edict forbidding the celebration of bullfights and theatrical events, and closing taverns on the grounds that these activities where large numbers congregated might incite riots.[26] One parish priest acidly observed: "The bravery of these people comes from excessive drinking; without liquor they are mere lambs."[27]

On October 20 Viceroy Flores in Cartagena accepted the advice of the archbishop in Socorro and issued a general pardon. The text, of course, did not reveal that the amnesty excluded those who had been "movers and leaders in the past disturbances."[28] Leaders such as Berbeo, Rosillo, and Monsalve were understandably nervous about their fate. All three made elaborate defenses of their conduct. While they admitted to errors of specific judgment, the hard core of their defense was twofold.[29] They had been forced into accepting positions of command by an irate populace that would not have spared their lives nor their property. Secondly, only they exercised sufficient influence over the plebeians to prevent popular fury from overflowing into anarchy and pillage. While Caballero y Góngora made diligent efforts to learn how the movement originated, he was too adroit a politician to allow vengeance to dominate the need for reconciliation. The prelate was convinced that the English might have overcome their rebellion in North America had London pursued more conciliatory tactics. His principal concern was to win back the loyalty of the local elites. He eventually granted pardons to all the members of the supreme council of war and arranged that the pardons be confirmed by the king himself.[30]

As early as November 26 Juan Francisco Berbeo indicated to the viceroy that he was prepared to resign his newly won post of corregidor of Socorro, but not until the following March 22 did the audiencia abolish the post.[31] Berbeo and his fellow Socorranos were vindicated, however, in 1795, when the corregimiento was reestablished. Berbeo may have lost the bureaucratic prize that he won as a consequence of the capitulations, but he suffered no other form of overt punishment. He died in his bed in Socorro in 1795.

Amnesty was a necessary tactic to woo the loyalty of the local elites. Finestrad, for example, directed special efforts towards the five or six hundred patricians, without whose support, he estimated, no future protest movement could succeed. While he emphasized to them that to ally themselves with the "vile mob" would invite pillage and anarchy, he also reminded the upper crust of their obligation "to render blind obedience and spontaneous fidelity to the king without questioning the justice of his orders."[32]

José Antonio Galán's capture by a patrician contingent led by Salvador Plata was dramatic proof in the eyes of the prelate of Socorro's newly found loyalty. The fact that only plebeians were punished was but one aspect of the archbishop's policy of playing the plebeians against the patricians. The endless sermons of the Capuchin friars, in addition to Galán's draconian sentence and its gory implementation, intimidated all groups in the community. When the mutilated remains of Galán and his companions were ostentatiously displayed in the main squares of Socorro, San Gil, and Charalá in mid-February of 1782, not a murmur came from the cowed populace.[33]

As early as September 19 the cabildo in Socorro reorganized the local militia that had been sanctioned in the capitulations.[34] They argued that in spite of the evident success of the Capuchin sermons a local militia led by reliable and prominent citizens was still necessary to prevent or to suppress any fresh outbreak of popular unrest. Clearly the patricians of Socorro were uneasy about the possibility that Colonel Bernet's well-armed professional soldiers might be dispatched to their area to undertake military repression. Unknown to the town fathers of Socorro, however, the audiencia in Bogotá a few days earlier had issued an edict that the militias created in the capitulations be forthwith disbanded and that all officers immediately resign their commissions. The cabildo of Socorro promptly obeyed. Bogotá was flooded with resignations and declarations of loyalty.[35]

January 1 was the customary date when the town councils all over the kingdom elected their executive magistrates, whose term of office lasted a year. The elections in January, 1782, promised to be turbulent, with charges and countercharges about the loyalty or disloyalty of the candidates. In order to prevent an outbreak of factionalism the audiencia issued a blanket order canceling the elections and providing that incumbents also serve for the calendar year of 1782.[36] Their continuance in office was considered to be a desirable measure to consolidate pacification.

Although it is clear that the archbishop and his Capuchin allies conducted an adroit public relations campaign, their conciliatory efforts were significantly buttressed by a whole series of concessions issued by the viceroy on

October 20 in conformity with the advice of the archbishop. The viceroy had not only considerable prestige from his high office, but he was also popular in the Socorro area, since he was not personally identified with the fiscal program of Gutiérrez de Piñeres. On October 20 he not only issued the general pardon but also reaffirmed the concessions first offered by the junta general de tribunales on May 14 and reaffirmed at Zipaquirá. The increases in the price of tobacco and aguardiente were abolished, the rate of the alcabala sales tax was lowered to the traditional 2 percent, the armada de Barlovento sales tax was repealed, and the guías and tornaguías were rescinded. The viceroy also granted permission for the cultivation of tobacco in the jurisdictions of the towns of Socorro and San Gil under the same conditions that the city of Girón enjoyed.[37]

Caballero y Góngora's handling of the tobacco question in Socorro and San Gil offers a classic illustration of his tactics. He recognized that permission to cultivate the crop was a necessary concession during the fall of 1781, but he regarded it as a temporary measure. Installed as viceroy on June 15, 1782, the prelate was determined to salvage the essence of Gutiérrez de Piñeres's reorganization of the tobacco monopoly restricting cultivation to only four small areas of the New Kingdom. But he moved very carefully. On September 27, 1782, he addressed his flock in Socorro not as viceroy but as archbishop, in a pastoral and paternalist tone: "We are writing this letter to you not as a judge to confound you but as a father full of love and tenderness for our beloved children whom we wish to persuade."[38]

The prelate then went on to give his flock a homily in political theory much in the manner of Finestrad, arguing "that kings on this earth occupy the place of God; that the soul is subordinate to superior authorities and finally that he who resists the mandates of a king is resisting God himself." From these lofty political abstractions the prelate deduced that it was the duty of subjects to pay taxes to their monarch gladly and without any reluctance.

The archbishop viceroy took great pains to explain to his parishioners the standard theory that permission to cultivate tobacco belonged to the regalian prerogatives of the crown. Tobacco and liquor were not necessities of life, but luxuries, and royal restrictions would not impose undue hardships on the poor. He did not content himself with expounding principles of political theory, but also descended to more mundane arguments. He stressed, quite correctly in fact, that the tobacco crop in Socorro and San Gil was of inferior quality. Citing facts and figures, he pointed out that during the years when tobacco cultivation was prohibited the tithes increased from 12,340 pesos in 1779 to 15,528 pesos in 1781. Tobacco was not necessary for the prosperity of San Gil and Socorro, the archbishop contended. Cotton and sugar were the truly lucrative crops of the area.

The tone of the pastoral letter was sweet and practical reasonableness, for Caballero y Góngora always preferred to pose in his public utterances as a good shepherd caring for his flock. But in the same dispatch he confided to Gálvez, "If they do not obey with the gentle spirit which my pastoral letter conveys, I shall employ force and coercion in order to maintain the authority of the office [the viceroyalty] to which his majesty has honored me with his appointment." Caballero y Góngora never forgot that he wore two hats, nor was he reluctant to exchange one for the other. He observed to his faithful lieutenant in Socorro, Finestrad:

> If until now I have employed gentle and forbearing tactics appropriate to a mediator and a pastor in order to achieve my objectives, as viceroy and captain general of this kingdom I can employ force and coercion in order that I may be respected and that subjects will obey the just decisions of that benign and powerful king who governs us.[39]

Fortunately, there was no need for him to abandon his favorite posture. The indefatigable Finestrad had prepared the way for the acceptance of the new prohibition against cultivating tobacco. Using the archbishop's arguments in his sermons Finestrad managed to collect literally hundreds of signatures from all the parishes of Socorro meekly accepting the edict from Bogotá.[40]

The crowning achievement of pacification was the Capuchin campaign to persuade all the parishes of the town of Socorro to make a symbolic restitution to the crown for the damage that their citizens had inflicted on the royal tobacco and aguardiente monopolies during the disturbances. As of February 24, 1784, the cabildo of Socorro had diligently collected some 4,895 pesos that they surrendered to the royal treasury.[41]

The Capuchins had proven zealous missionaries in reconquering Socorro from its "infidelity" to God and king. The archbishop viceroy proposed to institutionalize the Capuchin presence in Socorro. To this end he exploited Socorro's yearning for a monastery in their community.

As early as 1776 the leading citizens of Socorro had petitioned the secular and ecclesiastical authorities in Bogotá for permission to found a Franciscan monastery in their town.[42] They contended that the dense and growing population, as well as the agricultural and industrial prosperity of their community guaranteed that Socorro could decorously support such a religious establishment. Clearly involved was Socorro's growing self-awareness and community pride. A Franciscan monastery would lend spiritual prestige to their community. It is also not unreasonable to infer that a convent, as it accumulated gifts from generous benefactors, would be a source of credit to finance agriculture and the textile industry. Socorro would, in effect, acquire a bank. No longer would it be necessary for Socorrano merchants and farmers to go to the monasteries of Tunja and Bogotá to secure mortgages and loans. Nothing, however, came of Socorro's pleas prior to 1781. The crisis of that year dramatized to the authorities the political and economic importance of that rural emporium. Socorro did get its much wanted monastery in 1786, but it was not a Franciscan establishment. The sons of St. Francis in New Granada had long been dominated by the creoles, from whose ranks virtually all the Comunero leaders had come. The archbishop viceroy arranged that the new monastery would be a Capuchin establishment, staffed by personnel from the peninsular Capuchin province of Valencia.[43] Their articulate loyalty to the crown had been amply demonstrated by the Finestrad mission.

On January 27, 1786, eighteen Capuchin friars (fourteen priests and four lay brothers) arrived in Socorro where they were enthusiastically received with the ringing of the church bells, fireworks, and flower-strewn streets. Leading citizens, some of whom had been active in 1781, pledged their support.[44] Among them were Salvador Plata, Francisco Rosillo, Ramón Ramírez, and Juan Manuel Berbeo, the brother of Juan Francisco. A location for a permanent edifice was secured on a high hill commanding a splendid view of the town below. To this day its simple but impressive façade dominates the skyline of Socorro. The cornerstone was laid on September 16, 1787, with appropriate ceremonies. The church and the monastery were completed by July 24, 1795. Always zealous defenders of the authority of the Spanish crown, the Capuchin friars were unceremoniously driven out of their monastery in 1815 when the first winds of the independence movement swept through Socorro.

Archbishop Caballero y Góngora acquired from his five-month pastoral visit to the Socorro area a wealth of experience that would prove invaluable in consolidating the pacification of the whole kingdom after he was installed as viceroy on June 15, 1782.

18

The Carrot and the Stick

The real focus of political power from the night of May 12, when the regent visitor general Juan Gutiérrez de Piñeres fled Bogotá, lay in the firm hands of Archbishop Antonio Caballero y Góngora. Titular authority, however, lay elsewhere. Viceroy Flores continued in office until March 31, 1782, but his real power was confined to the maritime provinces. The junta general de tribunales, composed of the audiencia and representatives from other bureaucratic agencies, exercised a kind of nominal authority in the interior of the New Kingdom until its formal dissolution on September 10, 1781, when sole authority passed to the audiencia.[1]

On February 13, 1782, a somewhat chastened but still testy Juan Gutiérrez de Piñeres ended his nine-month exile in Cartagena and returned to Bogotá, ostensibly to resume his duties as regent of the audiencia and visitor general of the kingdom.[2] But on January 21, 1782, all the holders of titular authority had received a pointed reminder from a grateful Charles III that the archbishop should be deferred to in all matters pertaining to the pacification of the kingdom. The king allowed the prelate carte blanche to grant amnesty.[3]

Charles III finally accepted the resignation of the weary Viceroy Flores. His successor, Juan de Torreázar Díaz Pimienta, a military officer who had been serving as governor of the province of Cartagena, was installed as interim viceroy on March 31, 1782, but died on June 11, only four days after his arrival in Bogotá.[4]

Gutiérrez de Piñeres immediately called the audiencia into session. That tribunal made an abortive power play. Deliberately refusing to open the sealed envelope containing the king's instructions as to who would succeed

223

in a case of viceregal vacancy, the audiencia opted for the standard statutory solution. Authority was divided between the regent of the audiencia in the military sphere and the audiencia exercising civil or political jurisdiction.[5] Two days later the archbishop arrived in Bogotá. He insisted that the sealed royal instructions be opened, and in the face of considerable resistance on the part of some judges cajoled a majority of the tribunal to his view. The sealed envelope contained the royal cedula of November 16, 1777, which provided that Caballero y Góngora should serve as interim viceroy in case either Viceroy Flores or Governor Pimienta died or were incapacitated.[6] Caballero y Góngora, who had been de facto viceroy since May 12, 1781, was duly installed as de jure viceroy on June 15, 1782.

Some members of the audiencia obviously resented the archbishop's rise to political influence after May, 1781. Several judges were also bitterly feuding with the regent visitor general. Their move to take over the government was ostensibly justified by the precedent that very seldom since the reign of Ferdinand VI had an archbishop served as interim viceroy. Under the seventeenth-century Habsburgs, 27 percent of the interim viceroys had been ecclesiastics; under the later Bourbons (1746–1813) there were only three episcopal viceroys, some 5 percent.[7] The Bourbons, who were increasingly anxious to trim ecclesiastical influence, had established the custom that the audiencia would temporarily replace a deceased viceroy until a permanent successor arrived at his post. The cedula of 1777 providing for Caballero y Góngora's appointment was a deviation from the rule. Why Charles III and Gálvez made that particular decision is not clear. It was fortunate for them, however, for the prelate possessed in abundance the necessary political skills to heal the wounds of 1781, whereas the audiencia was beset by personal vendettas and virulent factionalism.

Not only did the grateful Charles III confer on Caballero y Góngora the order of Charles III, but on April 7, 1783, he appointed him proprietary viceroy with the customary five-year term.[8] He was the only prelate between 1746 and 1813 who was thus honored. Even the Habsburgs had seldom appointed an archbishop as proprietary viceroy, for it was not considered desirable to combine in one person the highest ecclesiastical and civil office for more than a year or so. The signal honor conferred on Caballero y Góngora was due to the unique circumstance of his having restored order after a serious convulsion.

The new viceroy sought to maintain harmony with the audiencia. He remained on outwardly cordial terms with the magistrates, but he came to distrust several of them. Some judges were intriguing with individuals whose loyalty to the crown was suspect during the crisis of 1781. He was particularly incensed when one magistrate confided to Berbeo that the royal pardon could exclude leaders of the revolution. Caballero y Góngora patiently gathered evidence about the unreliability of certain magistrates. On January 31, 1783, he marshaled his arguments in a letter to José de Gálvez.[9] The minister of the Indies accepted forthwith the prelate's recommendations. Oidores Joaquín Vasco y Vargas and Pedro Catani and Fiscales Manuel Silvestre Martínez and José Merchante de Contreras were surprised to learn that they were being transferred to other audiencias.[10] With the departure of the regent visitor general for Spain on December 7, 1783, and the retirement due to age of the senior oidor, Juan Francisco Pey y Ruíz, Caballero y Góngora had pulled off a bloodless political coup. Thus he solidified his undisputed domination of the magistracy.

The most significant document of his viceregal administration was the general pardon he issued on August 7, 1782, less than two months after taking office. Along with "our royal cedula," the capitulations of Zipaquirá, and the death sentence of José Antonio Galán, the general pardon is one of the key documents of the Comunero Revolution. In a very real sense it is Caballero y Góngora's answer to the capitulations. As such it represents the definitive resolution of the crisis of 1781. Furthermore, in the text of the document the new viceroy outlined basic policies that his administration would pursue.

The manifesto offered a general and definitive amnesty to all those who had participated in the uprising, thereby confirming the provisional pardon granted by Viceroy Flores in August, 1781. Everyone then in prison was freed. Anyone in hiding merely had to register with the audiencia within a year in order to secure a pardon. Furthermore, the general amnesty included the right to hold any elective or honorary post in the commonwealth. The archbishop accepted at face value the standard defense of most captains that the irate crowds had forced them to take positions of leadership and that only they could prevent popular wrath from overflowing into anarchy and pillage. In his explanatory letter to Gálvez, Caballero y Góngora took great pains to justify the need to conciliate the local elites in the small towns and parishes from whose ranks the vast majority of the captains came. The ex-captains were more often than not the best qualified people to hold office. If they were disqualified, then the local governments might fall into the hands of "rustic sorts incapable of administering upright justice."[11]

Although the archbishop viceroy stressed the desirability of conciliating the petty rural elites, he was determined to uncover and punish the ringleaders in Bogotá. His suspicions centered on the circle of Jorge Miguel Lozano de Peralta. But the prelate had to proceed with caution lest he arouse the antagonism of the creole families—the Prietos, the Ricaurtes, the Caicedos, the Oriundos, and the Alvarezes—who had for decades played leading roles in the bureaucratic administration of the New Kingdom.

The archbishop ordered a secret investigation of the activities of Manuel

García Olano, related by marriage to the marquis. Positive and specific acts of treason, such as sending the text of "our royal cedula" or the Silos manifesto from Bogotá to Socorro, could not be proven. That García Olano provided his correspondents in Socorro with up-to-the-minute news of events in the capital and in Peru was clearly established. But these epistolary activities were significantly short of outright treason, as the archbishop recognized. In his family correspondence and in his conversations, García Olano often spoke harshly of Gutiérrez de Piñeres's policies.[12] So did most of New Granada, for that matter.

Hence Caballero y Góngora's decision to dismiss Manuel García Olano as the director of the postal service and to exile him to Cartagena on the pretext of administrative shortcomings was a political and not a judicial act. This tactic of exiling political troublemakers but concealing the real reasons for the decision was characteristic of the archbishop's political style. On another occasion he advised the president of the audiencia of Quito to adopt the same tactic in a similar situation.[13]

Francisco Antonio Vélez, a well-born bureaucrat, had served as one of the captains general from Bogotá at Zipaquirá, and hence was an object of suspicion. His son was tried by the audiencia for continuous acts of adultery "with women of the lowest extraction." His enraged father wrote an apparently libelous attack against the judges of his son, thus providing the archbishop viceroy with a convenient pretext to transfer father and son to bureaucratic posts far removed from the capital.[14]

Another captain general of Bogotá, Francisco de Vergara, Berbeo's friend, was also, inevitably, suspect. No derogatory evidence against him could be uncovered, but Caballero y Góngora took an unusual precaution. He dispatched secret orders to the postal office in Cartagena to intercept any mail Vergara might receive from Europe, lest he be in correspondence with his ex-Jesuit relatives exiled in Italy.[15]

Caballero y Góngora employed similar tactics when he lifted the embargo placed on Ambrosio Pisco's property but exiled him to Cartagena. The viceroy candidly confessed to José de Gálvez that he did not regard the titular leader of the Indians as a traitor. In fact, he credited the erstwhile cacique of Bogotá and lord of Chía with contributing to the pacification of the Indians. But political not judicial considerations were paramount in the viceroy's thinking. Ambrosio Pisco could not remain in the sierra. He might continue to be a potential focus of unrest among the Indians, as a descendant of the preconquest caciques of Bogotá.[16]

There are still other examples of Caballero y Góngora's predilection for exiling potential or actual troublemakers on a pretext. There was some circumstantial evidence to suggest that the author of the celebrated "royal cedula" was the Dominican lay brother, Ciriaco de Archila. In 1784 Archila was quietly dispatched as a prisoner to a Dominican monastery in Spain.[17]

The most prominent individual under suspicion was the richest creole in the New Kingdom, the first marquis of San Jorge de Bogotá. On June 15, 1784, Gálvez ordered the arrest of the marquis and of Friar Ciriaco. The archbishop viceroy flexibly interpreted these orders. He never directly accused the marquis of complicity in the events of 1781, but in 1786 don Jorge's boisterous and interminable feuds with certain judges provided a convenient pretext to exile him to Cartagena, where he died on August 11, 1793.[18]

In the case of Manuel García Olano, Caballero y Góngora could be both compassionate and politic. To provide the destitute and numerous family of García Olano with 500 pesos from his own purse and to recommend that his family receive a pension is a demonstration of the princely largesse of which that ruthless but compassionate politician was capable. The count of Floridablanca accepted the recommendation.[19]

Caballero y Góngora's conduct was as political as it was humane. García Olano was related by marriage to several influential creole families. The prelate must have recognized, realistically if perhaps wearily, that it was sheer folly to antagonize unnecessarily the whole creole bureaucratic establishment.[20] The government simply had to learn to live with them, instead of attempting to oust them from office, as Gutiérrez de Piñeres had vainly sought to do. The creole establishment was reassured that they would not be frozen out of the bureaucracy. In 1787 the first and only creole during the reign of Charles III was appointed a judge of the audiencia: he was Joaquín de Mosquera y Figueroa of Popayán, the uncle of the celebrated Mosquera brothers who played stellar roles in the history of the subsequent republic of New Granada.[21] With the creation of many more new positions necessitated by the fiscal innovations of Charles III, the creole bureaucratic establishment could best be conciliated by receiving a healthy share of the patronage.

In the text of the general pardon the archbishop viceroy invoked the fearsome image of José Antonio Galán:

> The scandalous crimes of the man named José Antonio Galán are as well known as the exemplary penalty with which he and his companions were punished. Let us consider, on one hand, that justice has been served. Those people have been taught a lesson. They allowed themselves to be seduced and deluded by a man of very obscure birth who by misfortune and fanaticism made the ridiculous claim of being an invincible leader. Let us consider, on the other hand, the heroic loyalty of those faithful vassals who overcoming difficulties and dangers rushed forward to apprehend

and to destroy that black blot on his country and thus to prevent the fire of rebellion from spreading to the most remote provinces.[22]

Now was the time to offer some symbolic act of reconciliation. The prelate instructed the alcaldes ordinarios of Socorro, San Gil, Charalá, and Guaduas to remove from the squares the rotten heads, legs, and arms of José Antonio and his three companions and to bury them according to the rites of the church in order "to obliterate from the memory of the people, if at all possible, that lamentable monument of infidelity."[23]

Caballero y Góngora squarely addressed himself to the importance of bread and butter tax issues that aroused the ire of all groups, in particular of the plebeians. His policy was to make enough concessions to placate the popular wrath without unduly damaging the interests of the royal treasury. Hence the prelate offered much less than the sweeping repudiation of Gutiérrez de Piñeres's program agreed on at Zipaquirá, but he did offer a meaningful and solid compromise. He candidly recognized the heavy weight of the tax burden: "As they [the people] are bled white to pay today's taxes, they have no blood to pay tomorrow's."[24]

While the Indians as such were not specifically mentioned in the text of the general pardon, the archbishop identified as the principal source of Indian discontent the land and labor hunger of the creoles and the mestizos, who were encroaching on the ancestral community lands of the Indians. Although he exiled Ambrosio Pisco, he reaffirmed the policy first formulated by Gutiérrez de Piñeres in his memorandum of February 3, 1780. He refused to undo the consolidation of the resguardo lands undertaken up to 1778, but he reassured the Indian community that no further reduction of the resguardos would take place. The return under these two men to a modified policy of Habsburg paternalism would prevail until the end of the Spanish regime. The creoles and the mestizos were not allowed to terminate the destruction of the Indian community lands until the republican era during the first half of the nineteenth century.

In regard to taxes and the royal monopolies the definitive pardon of Caballero y Góngora on August 7, 1782, was merely a modified version of the concessions formulated by Viceroy Flores on the previous October 20, 1781. It may be recalled that Flores had made these concessions in response to the advice of the archbishop, who was then in Socorro. Now installed in the viceregal chair, Caballero y Góngora let stand the decrease in the price of tobacco and aguardiente, the reduction of the alcabala sales tax to the traditional 2 percent in the interior provinces and 4 percent in the maritime provinces, and the abolition of the armada de Barlovento sales tax.

In October, 1781, Viceroy Flores had rescinded the guía and tornaguía sales tax forms. Caballero y Góngora in his general pardon, however, partially restored them, in a greatly simplified form, in the hope of simultaneously placating the merchants outraged by the tedious formalities of Gutiérrez de Piñeres and protecting the royal treasury against possible fraud.

The August pardon did not specifically mention tobacco cultivation in Socorro and San Gil. Less than two months later, on September 27, 1782, Caballero y Góngora addressed his pastoral letter to the towns of Socorro and San Gil in which he rescinded Flores's concession. The persuasive efforts of the Capuchin mission in Socorro prepared the population of that area to accept the archbishop's prohibition without any murmurs of protest. Thus, Caballero y Góngora salvaged Gutiérrez de Piñeres's royal tobacco monopoly, which remained in force until January 1, 1850, when a republican regime abolished it.

The prelate frankly recognized that the popular anger against the royal monopolies and the taxes was due in some significant measure to the abrasive manner in which they had been collected by subordinate treasury officials in the small hamlets and rural parishes. He made a solemn promise to the king's subjects to eliminate "that intolerable harshness, rudeness and coarseness, characteristic of only barbarous times, which has caused so many protests."[25] Caballero y Góngora did not need to rely, as Gutiérrez de Piñeres did, on brutal coercion to protect the interests of the royal treasury, for he could rely on the persuasions of his Capuchin friars to mold public opinion.

As a direct consequence of the Comunero protest the crown did not dare establish in New Granada the five intendancy units designed to supervise the fiscal administration. Their creation in the other viceroyalties of the New World were one of the principal administrative changes of Charles III. How effective the intendancies were in promoting prosperity and increasing the royal revenues is a moot question.[26] Even without these administrative units the innovations of Charles III in New Granada must be viewed as a solid success, as public revenues during the subsequent decades dramatically increased.

The sum total of Caballero y Góngora's fiscal concessions represents a significant victory for the men and women of 1781 who had taken up arms against the fiscal innovations of the regent visitor general. Obviously they did not secure their maximum demand for the total abolition of the new program, but neither did the archbishop viceroy follow the advice of Gutiérrez de Piñeres to restore in toto his fiscal program.

What requires explanation is the sharp rise in public revenues, from 950,000 pesos in 1772 to 2,453,096 pesos by the end of the colonial regime.[27] A little over one-third of the increase can be attributed to new sources of royal revenue. The tobacco monopoly, yielding some 470,000 pesos, was not profitably established until after 1781. Another source of revenue after 1772 was the 65,000 pesos that the crown collected from the direct administration of the salt mines, formerly the community property of the Indians.

After 1781 the crown continued to rely on traditional avenues of taxation. The income from the aguardiente monopoly, which as early as the administration of Viceroy Mesía de la Cerda (1761–72) was earning 200,000 pesos annually, had climbed to 295,048 pesos. Other significant and traditional sources of treasury income were the alcabala (184,880 pesos), external custom taxes (191,000 pesos), and the royal mint (150,000 pesos). The ecclesiastical tithes came to 100,000 pesos. These longstanding items represent some 920,928 pesos out of the total of 2,453,096 pesos.

Hence, if we discount the 535,000 pesos derived from the post-1772 monopolies, the nearly 1,000,000 pesos extra that the crown collected subsequent to the Caroline fiscal innovations cannot be explained by any increase in the rates of traditional royal taxes. The replacement of the inefficient tax farming method with a system of direct administration by salaried bureaucrats was perhaps the single most important factor in explaining the dramatic success of the Caroline fiscal program. After 1781 the government was collecting more efficiently the old taxes that were still being assessed at the traditional rates. All the indications are that the three decades following the Comunero Revolution were dominated by moderate economic expansion and a significant increase in the population. The application of the policy of free trade within the empire after 1778 and the introduction of some new forms of technology probably contributed to solidifying the modest prosperity that New Granada continued to enjoy during the last decades of the Spanish empire.

The tobacco monopoly, more efficient methods of tax collection, and a modest expansion of the economy, then, made it possible for Caballero y Góngora to make some significant tax concessions without jeopardizing the cardinal Caroline objective of expanding the income of the royal treasury. The single most important contribution of the archbishop viceroy was the salvaging of the tobacco monopoly, which alone accounted for nearly a third in the increase of public revenues. But to accomplish that end Caballero y Góngora had to exercise considerable political skill.

Gutiérrez de Piñeres was an energetic but literal-minded technocrat with little sensitivity to the subtle nuances of tactics. Possessing all the cunning of a Renaissance ecclesiastical prince, Caballero y Góngora, on the other hand, was a compassionate and patient political realist. He never wavered in his goals of salvaging the Caroline fiscal innovations and at the same time alleviating the principal sources of discontent among both the elites and the others. His recipe for success was to introduce Caroline fiscal and economic innovations with the paternalist tactics reminiscent of the Habsburgs. His political style was Habsburg, but the solid content of his policies was

Caroline. A politician's politician, he understood that in order to reach a determined goal the shortest distance between two points is not necessarily a straight line. Compromise, persuasion, dissimulation, temporary retreats must be employed in order to cajole entrenched vested interests into accepting change. He once confided to José de Gálvez, "It is necessary to travel slowly in order not to exasperate the minds of people."[28]

Gutiérrez de Piñeres was confused and annoyed by Caballero y Góngora's tactical zigzagging. In restrained language he complained to Gálvez about the prelate's "policy of indulgence and dissimulation."[29] But Gálvez paid no attention. Caballero y Góngora handled Gutiérrez de Piñeres with his usual finesse. While he recognized his abilities as a fiscal bureaucrat, he politely disregarded his advice on political tactics. The viceroy, however, continued to consult the regent on all matters of policy. Both men were gradually drawn together by their common distrust of Oidores Vasco y Vargas and Catani and Fiscales Silvestre Martínez and Merchante de Contreras. Not only did Gutiérrez de Piñeres resent their having accused him of cowardice in fleeing Bogotá, but both the archbishop and the regent visitor general shared a common revulsion at their revealing confidential information to persons outside the government. Hence he supported the viceroy's recommendation that those judges be transferred to other posts.[30]

In 1782 Gutiérrez de Piñeres was no longer the zealous warrior he had been prior to May 12, 1781. In poor health and weary of the political battles in Bogotá, he looked forward to his promised promotion to a seat on the council of the Indies in Spain. On December 7, 1783, the regent visitor general left Bogotá on the long journey home.[31] Ill-health notwithstanding, the first regent of the audiencia of Bogotá served in the council of the Indies some nineteen years until his death in 1802.[32]

In the general pardon Caballero y Góngora issued an amnesty and some tax concessions, but he also offered the creole elites more than a partial return to the traditional procedures of consultative joint government by American and European Spaniards. While he stressed the potential dangers of allying themselves with the "uncouth mob" personified by José Antonio Galán, he presented the patricians with something new, positive, and alluring. The crown, he argued, merited unquestioned obedience from its subjects, in particular from the prosperous and influential, not only because God ordained it so but because only the state possessed the capacity to introduce science and technology. In this manner wealth would increase, jointly benefitting both the crown and the creoles. The archbishop appealed to the elites to form a new alliance with the crown in order to promote economic development and increasing prosperity.[33]

There was little original in Caballero y Góngora's economic thinking. Most of his ideas were first expounded by José del Campillo y Cosío and Bernardo

Ward. The archbishop's much quoted praise of the martial valor of the conquistadores and their alleged ineptitude as agricultural settlers, his opposition to latifundia, his criticism of the exploitation of Indian labor, his desire to congregate dispersed rural populations, and his disdain for sloth and vagabondage all first appeared in the Campillo-Ward recommendations that constituted the master plan to modernize the Spanish empire during the reign of Charles III.[34] Caballero y Góngora's outstanding contribution was the vigor with which he sought to implement these goals.

The visita general of Oidor Mon y Velarde contributed to the subsequent prosperity of Antioquia.[35] As early as 1783, the tenth book published by the new printing press in Bogotá was a treatise dealing with inoculation against smallpox.[36] An Economic Society, all of whose branches were dedicated to spreading the new technology, was founded in Mompós in 1784. Another branch was established in Bogotá in 1801. The former, however, did not receive the personal patronage of the archbishop viceroy.[37]

Without a doubt the most glittering scientific achievement of the archbishop viceroy was his active and sustained patronage of the celebrated botanical expedition that ultimately aroused the admiration of scientists around the world.[38] Caballero y Góngora organized it in 1783. He had the good fortune of entrusting its leadership to the Spanish savant José Celestino Mutis. In over twenty-five years of active investigation, the expedition accumulated a library of six thousand volumes, an herbarium of more than 20,000 plants, a nursery, a collection of samples and domestic products, a series of paintings of Colombian fauna, and more than three thousand carefully colored botanical plates, which made Humboldt's mouth water when he saw them. It studied geodetics, geography, and zoology, and founded the Observatory. Less successful in its practical results was the archbishop's sponsorship of the mineralogical expedition headed by José Elhuyar, but that venture does attest to the vigor of his efforts to introduce into New Granada the useful knowledge of the Enlightenment.[39]

In order to increase the productive wealth of the land and to win back the loyalty of the creoles, especially the youth, the archbishop stressed the need to introduce both applied and pure science. The curriculum in higher education had to be drastically changed. Scholasticism had to be replaced by philosophical eclecticism; in the study of the sciences the authority of the ancients and religious revelation must give way to systematic observation, exact measurement, and experimentation. Like all the "enlightened" ministers of his time, Caballero y Góngora was a disciple of Benito Gerónimo Feijóo. He advocated that only in the realm of theology should natural reason be guided by supernatural revelation and authority. The archbishop viceroy stated his goal concisely, when he observed to his successor:

The whole purpose of this plan is to substitute for the merely speculative sciences, on which until now students have wasted their time, with the useful and exact sciences. In a kingdom full of valuable products to exploit, mountains to subdue, highways to open, mines and swamps to drain, rivers to tame and precious metals to purify there is more need of people who are trained to observe nature and to use calculus, the compass, and the ruler than people who are trained to understand logical being, prime matter, and substantial form [traditional categories of scholasticism].[40]

All during the 1770's a veritable war of words had been raging between the defenders of the old scholasticism and the proponents of the sciences. Talk of reorganizing higher education began in 1768 after the expulsion of the Jesuit order and the extinction of their Javeriana University. Bogotá was left with only one university, Santo Tomás, entitled to grant the degrees of *bachiller, maestro, licenciado,* and *doctor.* That institution was under the administration of the Dominican order, whose members zealously defended as the sole truth the scholastic heritage of their founder, Saint Thomas Aquinas. In spite of the determined efforts of Viceroy Guirior, Mutis, and Fiscal Moreno y Escandón, the forces of pedagogical traditionalism won a solid victory on October 13, 1779. The newly formed *junta de estudios* opted for a modified form of scholasticism.[41]

Caballero y Góngora was as determined to salvage the basic content of the Moreno educational program as he was to reestablish the tobacco monopoly of Gutiérrez de Piñeres. In both endeavors he followed his usual zigzag tactics, never deviating from his own maxim that it is necessary to travel slowly. His policy was to undercut the Dominicans indirectly and to postpone a direct confrontation with them for at least several years. His grand design was to woo support for the cause of the sciences among the creole youth, so that the pressure of public opinion would undermine the defenses of scholasticism.

The archbishop's patronage of the botanical expedition spectacularly succeeded in advertising the benefits of modern science. Mutis's team of researchers was a de facto faculty of the natural sciences in which many creoles were trained. José Celestino Mutis was Caballero y Góngora's chief lieutenant in the world of higher education, just as Joaquín de Finestrad was his field commander in Socorro. In fact, Mutis looms as the first minister of education of New Granada, although that honor might also be given to Fiscal Moreno y Escandón.

To put pressure on the colleges of Rosario and San Bartolomé, the archbishop dispatched visitors to those institutions. They reported irregularities in the administration of the funds as well as notable deficiencies in the curriculum. The prelate made no flamboyant accusations.[42] He took pains to avoid the tactical blunder of Moreno, who had assailed scholasticism with obviously indiscreet gusto. But the archbishop did insist that the physical and natural sciences be taught in both colleges by properly qualified professors. He arranged that the chair that Mutis had held at the Rosario since 1762 be filled by a substitute when Mutis was totally absorbed in the botanical expedition. The choice of the candidate was sound on both pedagogical and political grounds. Fernando Vergara y Caicedo was a disciple of Mutis and the son of Francisco de Vergara.[43] Thus, a scion of the creole bureaucratic elite was preaching the new gospel of the natural sciences inside the classrooms of the Rosario. Young Vergara belonged to both God and science, for he eventually died in a monastery in Spain as a Trappist monk.[44] Caballero y Góngora persuaded one of the professors at the college of San Bartolomé to teach the latest theories in mathematics, although he did not hold a formal chair in that field. The students enthusiastically supported their professor's decision.[45]

Another move the archbishop took was to enforce the separation between the faculty of the college of San Bartolomé and the diocesan seminary. The prelate insisted that the two institutions be housed in separate buildings. He was particularly adamant that lay students in law and in the sciences not receive the same education as future priests.[46]

Perhaps the most effective measure Caballero y Góngora took to increase enrollment in the natural sciences was his insistence that students in the two colleges be given the option of choosing between speculative philosophy (scholasticism) and practical philosophy (the physical and natural sciences). Given the climate of opinion favorable to the sciences that the prelate had done much to foster, the number of students in scholastic philosophy declined as science enrollment sharply increased.[47]

It was not until 1787 that Caballero y Góngora felt that he had molded public opinion sufficiently to afford a direct confrontation with the Dominicans. He dusted off Moreno y Escandón's proposal to abolish the Dominican university of Santo Tomás. In its place he proposed a state and public university, to be named the university of San Carlos in honor, of course, of Charles III. Avoiding Moreno y Escandón's polemics against the schoolmen, Caballero y Góngora envisaged a university in which the "useful and exact sciences" such as mathematics, physics, chemistry, and natural history would reign supreme.[48] The prelate's university of San Carlos remained stillborn. The Dominicans still had enough political muscle at court to preserve their monopoly of tertiary education until the end of the colonial regime. But they were defending an empty shell. The new generation of creole students clearly saw the sciences as the wave of the future.

The proponents of educational innovation had to contend not only with the defenders of the status quo but also with an even more insidious and perennial foe, the lack of public and private funds. Given the enthusiastic support of several viceroys, the innovators undoubtedly could have accomplished even more had more revenue been available. As is usually the case, funding lagged far behind their ambitious plans. In Caballero y Góngora's time only 13,132 pesos annually were available to support chairs in the natural sciences.[49]

The Dominicans may have won the battle to save their university of Santo Tomás, but Caballero y Góngora won the war to solidify and to expand the place of the exact sciences in the curriculum of higher education in New Granada. The archbishop viceroy was only exaggerating a trifle when he confided to Mutis:

> Although one cannot say that the natural sciences have not been cultivated with happy results in this kingdom (since your grace first introduced them here), nevertheless I can flatter myself by claiming to be the restorer of the natural sciences. I am the one who has recalled them from a long and shameful exile to which ignorance and an indiscreet zeal for the learning of antiquity had condemned them.[50]

Mutis was indeed the pioneer and Caballero y Góngora was the consolidator of a veritable intellectual revolution. Moreover, although it is true that curriculum change was a standard objective of all Caroline ministers, resistance to change was much more entrenched in New Granada than in other parts of the empire. Mexico, for example, was a pioneer. As early as the 1760's the Jesuits had transformed the curricula in their schools, and by the 1780's the new science was a flourishing intellectual movement. This opposition makes all the more decisive the role of Caballero y Góngora.

Much though the archbishop viceroy believed in a political solution in which he combined paternalism and conciliation with firmness, he never forgot that without military force at Zipaquirá his only defense against popular wrath was his own acumen and the prestige of his high ecclesiastical office. As viceroy he was determined that never again would a representative of the king be in such an exposed position. His remedy was to strengthen the military establishment.

In his final statement addressed to his successor he warmly praised Viceroy Flores for his advocacy of strengthening the local militias before introducing fiscal changes. The crisis of 1781 had made a mockery of Gutiérrez de Piñeres's prediction that the patricians and the plebeians would never form an alliance against the government.[51] Caballero y Góngora was the only viceroy of New Granada who was not a military officer by profession. Yet the only sacerdotal viceroy turned out to be more militaristic than any of his military predecessors or successors.

The warrior-archbishop confided to his successor:

> In the past, when the policing of the interior provinces, the administration of justice and the authority of the king's ministers lay in the fidelity of the people, the military forces were concentrated in the maritime provinces. But, once the inestimable original innocence was lost, the government and the loyal vassals—which came to include all of them—desired the establishment of military bodies in order to perpetuate order and tranquility.[52]

Under Caballero y Góngora's administration, the total number of soldiers did not rise appreciably, but they became more evenly distributed between the maritime provinces and the interior. In 1789 there were 3,959 regulars, 1,200 of them stationed in Bogotá; in 1781 there had been only 75 regulars in the capital. In 1779 there were 14,592 disciplined militiamen, all of them confined to the maritime provinces and none in the interior. In 1789 there were 15,032 disciplined militiamen, of whom 800 were stationed in Bogotá, with other contingents in Honda, Tunja, and Socorro.[53] During his tenure the archbishop viceroy gave the military a new role as a domestic police force in the interior. The reorganized militia was Caballero y Góngora's answer to article eighteen of the capitulations. In place of a militia under the exclusive control of the creole elites, as was envisaged at Zipaquirá, the militia would be the instrument of the government, although many commissions would go to creoles.

Caballero y Góngora wished to combine pacific persuasions with an organized military force as a reminder to the hesitant that only the state possessed legitimate coercive power. In this sense he was typical of most Caroline bureaucrats all over the empire who, in contrast to the Habsburgs, saw the military and not the clergy as the mainstays of royal authority. He was atypical in continuing to place considerable reliance on the clergy, but he was, after all, an archbishop as well as a viceroy.

Caballero y Góngora's reliance on the military as a domestic police force did not long survive his administration. In 1789 the army was the single largest item in the budget. Under his immediate successors, however, the scope of the military was drastically cut back, its personnel reduced, and its influence diminished. By 1794 the number of disciplined militiamen had declined from 15,032 to 6,960, none of them stationed in the interior provinces. Only 564 regulars composed the garrison in Bogotá. The expense of maintenance seems to have been the paramount factor in the government's decision to reduce numbers.[54]

When Caballero y Góngora departed for Spain in 1789, he was heavily in debt, despite an annual income of 80,000 pesos. Obviously, he lived in a princely manner. Generous to a fault, he donated his extensive library and sizable collection of paintings to the archbishopric of Bogotá.[55] When a devastating earthquake struck Bogotá in 1785, Caballero y Góngora's generosity was not found wanting. He donated his salary as archbishop to help defray the costs of reconstruction. While he lived in Cartagena, he built a comfortable if not luxurious residence in Turbaco, costing some 20,000 pesos. He gave this house to the crown so that his viceregal successors would have an appropriate residence in a climate somewhat more healthy and agreeable than steaming Cartagena.[56]

The archbishop evidently gave generous and frequent alms to worthy ecclesiastical institutions. But his generosity was not exclusively a series of disinterested acts of Christian charity. His largesse often had a more mundane political purpose. In explaining the lamentable state of his finances, he confided to the count of Floridablanca with discreet candor, employing the third person,

> that the archbishop of Santa Fe is burdened with debts because he had permitted his obligations as pastor and viceroy to consume all his rents, spending some of his income on acts of charity and allotting other rents for political purposes in order to buy and preserve (if one is permitted to use these words) with liberality the fidelity and loyalty of the king's vassals.[57]

Antonio Caballero y Góngora's recipe for restoring royal authority after the convulsion of 1781 was an intricate mosaic of old and new. In order to salvage the substance of Charles III's rather moderate neomercantilist program, he sacrificed the more radical political goals of the monarch. The complex web of political procedures and customs that had gradually evolved in New Granada over more than two centuries could not be ignored, he came to realize. The crisis of 1781 had taught him that in sponsoring innovations the government could move only as fast as it could mold public opinion. Such a process made compromise and concessions inevitable. The Caroline ideal of a highly centralized monarchy with Madrid imposing changes by bureaucratic fiat from above had to give way to the traditional system of consultation and compromise that may be called New Granada's "unwritten constitution." The Caroline program had to be packaged in a Habsburg wrapping. Paternalist tactics came naturally to an archbishop.

The long-entrenched bureaucratic establishment could not be threatened with the prospect of being frozen out of office, as Gutiérrez de Piñeres had unwisely attempted to do. Nor could the government abrasively enforce the new taxes and the regulations against the equally self-assertive creole and mestizo small farmers who in the towns of Socorro and San Gil had carved out of a wilderness modestly prosperous agricultural communities during the course of a mere three generations.

Ideologically, Caballero y Góngora sought to replace the Comunero slogan, deeply rooted in the traditionalist ways of Spain's past—"Long live the king and death to bad government"—with the Bourbon doctrine of blind obedience to all forms of constituted authority. Though he took pains to form public opinion, he was not reluctant to offer concessions. He sought to frighten the creole elites into renewing their allegiance to the crown by creating the myth of José Antonio Galán, social revolutionary. But not only did he present the creoles with a threat, he also offered them an alluring prospect: the crown as a creator of rising prosperity through the systematic introduction of modern science and the new technology.

Reconciliation was the archbishop viceroy's paramount goal. Vindictiveness would only be counterproductive. Hence he granted amnesty widely; the notable exceptions were Galán and his nearest followers—a grim object lesson—and the exiling from Bogotá of a handful of potential troublemakers. While he gave the government a new and powerful weapon in the form of a revitalized military, Caballero y Góngora preferred to use the tactic of persuasion and conciliation, as long as it produced the desired results.

The political skills of Caballero y Góngora cannot be underrated. Yet the relative ease with which that artful politician put the system back together again is perhaps the most convincing demonstration that the causes of the Comunero Revolution lay not in the moderate neomercantilist content of Charles III's fiscal changes but in the revolutionary political means by which his overzealous agents originally introduced those innovations into New Granada.

19

Caballero y Góngora and the Independence of Colombia

The crisis of 1781 was not an abortive social revolution, nor was it a first step toward political emancipation from the Spanish crown. But 1781 did foreshadow two movements of outstanding importance in the history of the nineteenth century: federalism and anticlericalism.

The persisting consequences of the crisis of 1781 should be sharply distinguished from its historical antecedents. Strictly in the context of 1781, the Comunero Revolution conformed to dialectic that often operated during the colonial regime. The central authorities proposed new policies—the thesis; the elites and the others in New Granada vigorously protested against both the content of the new policies and the tactics by which they were administered—the antithesis. Caballero y Góngora provided the synthesis: a remarkably workable and stable compromise between the two forces.

In this process neither side won its maximum demands; neither one, however, remained empty-handed. Charles III did not succeed in institutionalizing his centralized and unitary monarchy, but the central power was strengthened to some significant extent. Yet even this proved to be a pyrrhic victory. Spain's involvement in the wars of the French Revolution after 1789 soon led to a gradual paralysis of Madrid's control over its overseas possessions. What the crown did win by means of its fiscal and technological innovations was a rising prosperity in its American dominions and a consequent sharp increase in royal revenues. The creoles of New Granada did not achieve the political utopia enshrined in the capitulations of Zipaquirá: creole self-rule under the aegis of the crown. But they wrested a major victory in compelling the authorities to act within the spirit of the "unwritten constitution" whose guiding principles were consultation, cogovernment, and compromise. The creole bureaucratic establishment was not uprooted from office, as Gálvez and Gutiérrez de Piñeres had envisaged. Juan Francisco Berbeo may have lost his post as corregidor, but the incipient federalism that he personified was vindicated in 1795 with the creation of the corregimiento of Socorro, the genesis of the nineteenth-century state of Santander. And the men and women of 1781, especially the poor, won a whole series of tax concessions and a much less abrasive procedure for their collection. The Indians, also, received some meaningful protection.

In order to reach a compromise both the crown and the Comuneros made their heaviest concessions in the political sphere. Both, in fact, tacitly renounced their respective political revolutions. The definitive settlement provided for a return to the constitutional status quo ante 1778, with some significant modifications in favor of greater centralization.

The dialectical character of the crisis of 1781 and its resolution was not a novelty. This was the way that New Granada, and for that matter the other kingdoms of the Indies, had been governed for over two centuries. The crown proposed, the colonists opposed, and the bureaucracy compromised. By the judicious use of the "I obey but do not execute" formula, this process of accommodating conflicting interests was carried out peaceably inside a bureaucratic framework.[1] What was different in 1781 was that a new factor entered into this traditional political equation: coercion and the threat of violence. The government deliberately refused to employ the suspensive veto. Twenty thousand irate, if poorly armed citizens had to assemble within a day's march of Bogotá before the authorities realized the need to negotiate a compromise settlement. One may speculate that if undivided power had remained in the experienced political hands of Viceroy Flores rather than being surrendered to an autocratic and rigid technocrat such as Gutiérrez de Piñeres, there would have been no confrontation in Zipaquirá in June, 1781. Such was the tacit evaluation of Caballero y Góngora.[2] But, of course, that confrontation did take place. Even with the new element of violence, however, the resolution of the crisis conformed to the traditional pattern of proposal, opposition, and compromise.

Juan Francisco Berbeo has not fared well in historiography. Many historians who would like to regard the Comuneros as the precursors of political independence have criticized him with varying degrees of intensity for his failure to occupy the capital and his willingness to accept the capitulations of Zipaquirá. I have argued earlier that he was neither incompetent nor disloyal; that his real objective was the modest one of demanding that the authorities return to the spirit of the "unwritten constitution" of New Granada. Seen in this context Berbeo solidly succeeded. Skillfully leading a multi-ethnic coalition not without its share of internal tensions, Berbeo and his legions taught

Spanish officialdom from Charles III downward that the aspirations and the traditions of New Granada could not be ignored with impunity. This is not the kind of stuff of which folk heroes are made, but it does represent a meaningful, if unspectacular, political achievement.

José Antonio Galán has been enshrined in historiography as the precursor of a frustrated social revolution from below, when in historical fact he no more stood for social revolution in 1781 than did Juan Francisco Berbeo.

Paradoxically enough, the man who allegedly defeated the Comuneros, Antonio Caballero y Góngora, has received a more kindly treatment from historians than Berbeo has. To be sure, some have assailed his Janus-like duplicity, but most have applauded the conciliatory fashion in which he restored royal authority. Above all else, many Colombians understandably view with gratitude his active patronage of Enlightenment learning.

Few historians would disagree that 1781 represents a major watershed in the history of Colombia, although there exists some honest disagreement about the meaning of that watershed. Some economic historians have stressed the continuity of Gutiérrez de Piñeres's reorganized tobacco monopoly that spanned the decades from 1778 until its abolition in 1850.[3] During that period tobacco, which provided a major source of governmental revenue, continued to be produced for the domestic market. Only in the 1840's did tobacco become a major export crop, thus creating a new watershed. In his examination of patterns of land tenure and labor mobilization, William McGreevey sees the period from 1760 until 1845 as a historical unit. Under the later Bourbons and the early republic the pace of change was real, but slow in comparison to the acceleration that took place with the coming to power of the Radical Liberals, the "Gólgotas," during the decades between 1845 and 1885.[4]

In what sense does Caballero y Góngora represent continuity in the history of New Granada? The question remains to be explored.

The prelate received the reward that he had specifically requested. On June 19, 1789, he arrived in La Coruña, Spain, from where he traveled to Córdova in his native Andalucía, to take up the duties of bishop of that historic see. Perhaps the most dazzling personal triumph of his tenure occurred on March 12 and 13, 1796, when he received King Charles IV and his queen in Córdova during their royal progress through Andalucía. A recommendation from the cathedral chapter that the king should request from the pope a cardinal's red hat for the archbishop-bishop of Córdova proved abortive. A few days after the departure of the royal couple, death suddenly claimed Antonio Caballero y Góngora on March 24, 1796, at the age of seventy-two.[5]

Hence, during his last years from the apparent tranquility of Córdova,

Caballero y Góngora witnessed the first tidal waves of the French Revolution. That convulsion, however, did not entirely destroy the world that he defended with such skill in New Granada.

The French Revolution ultimately swept away the principle of traditional and providentialist legitimacy upon which the Spanish crown's authority in the New World had rested for centuries. On one hand, the archbishop viceroy frightened the creoles with the phantasm of social revolution, to destroy the coalition between the elites and the plebeians. On the other hand, he sought to forge a new alliance between the creoles and the crown, based not only on theories of kingship but on economic self-interest. He was the expositor of an Enlightenment doctrine that fostered a new conception of political legitimacy which has exercised considerable appeal even in our times, not only in Colombia but also throughout Latin America. Peter H. Smith has aptly called this conception of political legitimacy *achievement-expertise.* That term, when translated into eighteenth-century terminology, means *enlightened despotism.* Smith adds:

> This notion of achievement-expertise rests on the claim that authority should reside in the hands of people who have the knowledge, the expertise or the general ability to bring about specific achievements—usually, but not always, economic achievements. In this case authority derives essentially from the desirability of the achievement itself; the commitment is to the goal, not the means.
>
> Political obedience is thus demanded, and presumably accorded, for nonpolitical reasons. The political structure per se loses importance. Leaders are free to adopt any method, no matter how repressive, as long as they can demonstrate progress after the sought-after goal.[6]

In the late nineteenth century this form of political legitimacy won widespread acceptance in many countries of Latin America as the Positivist slogan of "order and progress." Two of its most successful personifications were Porfirio Díaz in Mexico and Rafael Núñez in Colombia. The similarities and continuities between Caballero y Góngora and Núñez are striking. Both statesmen shared the same goal of using the state as the creative instrument to promote economic prosperity by the introduction of technology. Obviously the content of Núñez's specific policies differed from that of Caballero y Góngora, for a century separated the two. Núñez's technology was steam navigation, telegraphs, railroads, and improved postal service; Caballero y Góngora's consisted of the botanical expedition, the consolidation of the new science in the curriculum of higher education, new methods of mining extraction, and the introduction of smallpox vaccination. In contrast to Caballero y Góngora, whose empire-centered goal was to increase government revenues by means of more efficiently administered royal monopolies, Rafael Núñez in the 1880's and the 1890's envisaged a nationalist-inspired autarky. The state should introduce a high tariff to protect nascent industry, in particular textiles. Núñez could not sponsor in such a stark form Caballero y Góngora's ideal of blind obedience, but he stood for a somewhat milder form of political authoritarianism. Each one, to be sure, had to devote inordinate energy to political means, for the prelate's task was to liquidate an uprising and the conservative chieftain's was to transcend the political legacy of the Radical Liberal era. Yet both shared the conviction that the goal of economic prosperity—differently viewed—overrode the political means employed.[7] They both demanded political obedience for essentially nonpolitical reasons. They both were advocates of statism in the name of economic development.

Achievement-expertise did not disappear with the Positivist generation of the late nineteenth century. It has reemerged in our times in new incarnations as scores of regimes have pursued the goal of developmental modernization. Achievement-expertise has been the claim of several contemporary military regimes as varied as the tyranny of Trujillo in the Dominican Republic and the present dictatorship in Brazil. During the 1960's, under the inspiration of the Alliance for Progress, many far less authoritarian regimes invoked that principle of political legitimacy. They were all the remote heirs of the enlightened despotism of Charles III.

As Smith has emphasized, achievement-expertise was not the only form of political legitimacy to emerge in Latin America after the overthrow of the traditional legitimacy of colonial times. Legality, charisma, and personality dominance provided other equally important appeals to justify governmental authority.[8]

One enduring legacy, then, that Antonio Caballero y Góngora left the land he governed with a maximum of benevolence and a minimum of repression was the notion of a dynamically interventionist state as the promoter of economic prosperity. Of all the Caroline ministers who pursued this aim, he was undoubtedly the most articulate and successful. The prelate left New Granada another important legacy. He, more than any one person in 1781, laid the foundation for political emancipation a generation later. What made repudiation of the Spanish crown in 1781 unthinkable was that everyone, creole patrician or plebeian mestizo, accepted a principle of political legitimacy that was providentialist, authoritarian, and traditionalist. For three centuries the crown had demanded and enthusiastically received obedience from its subjects scattered on four continents because all believed that God had so ordained the world.[9] Even in the sphere of the natural world explanations were sought that were rooted in the authority of the philosophers of antiquity and guided by religious revelation as expounded by the scholastic theologians. The men of 1781 had no yardstick other than the traditionalist and providential authoritarianism of their ancestors. Their anguished and massive protest, enshrined in the slogan, "Long live the king and death to bad government," was simply the demand that Charles III and his ministers should govern in the time-honored way.

It was Caballero y Góngora who gave the creoles the intellectual tools with which to undermine the very foundations of the ancien régime. He ensured the victory of a pedagogical revolution in consolidating the supremacy of natural reason unguided by supernatural revelation as the explanation of the natural world. His almost evangelical sponsorship of the new science and technology was inspired by his twin objectives of extricating New Granada from its perennial poverty and forging a new alliance between the creoles and the crown.

But the long-range consequences of his pedagogical revolution were different from those he anticipated. The generation that grew to maturity between 1781 and 1810 avidly grasped the new science, but after 1808 they applied its rational methodology not only to the physical and natural realm, but, more important, to the political world as well. The political philosophy of the Enlightenment, emphasizing the right to revolution, popular sovereignty, the social contract, and representative government, provided a veritable arsenal of arguments. The creole intellectuals thus had after 1808 a hostile criterion for judging the ancien régime—something noticeably lacking in 1781.

The viceregal administration of Caballero y Góngora was a watershed in the decisive sphere of political legitimacy. On one hand, he sought to strengthen the providentialist tradition of legitimacy by replacing the "I obey but do not execute" spirit of the Habsburgs with the doctrine of blind obedience inspired by the model of Louis XIV. Yet he was no intransigent ideologue. As a practical politician, he was quite prepared to make significant concessions to the spirit of New Granada's "unwritten constitution" that had gradually evolved during the two centuries of the reign of the House of Austria. But his ideal of "enlightened despotism," shared by all the Caroline ministers, was a new form of political legitimacy that could easily be separated from traditionalist legitimacy. And that is precisely what the generation of 1810 did. The ideal of the state as the promoter of prosperity could just as well be implemented by a creole-led republic as by a traditionalist monarchy.

Caballero y Góngora's stress on science and technology did much to broaden the intellectual horizons of the generation of 1810. The independence movement was essentially aristocratic and intellectual. It was not the uprising of the toiling and oppressed masses but the work of intellectually oriented, upper-class creoles, whose minds and attitudes had been stimulated by the scientific thought of the Enlightenment. Some may argue that the introduction of the new science did not necessarily reflect a more critical cast of mind. The creole aficionados of science may have accepted the new science as they did the old scholastic science—received doctrines inculcated in an authoritarian manner.[10] While this may be true in part, the new science stood for a rational and secular way of viewing the world, and the world they saw was that of the French Revolution and Napoleon. It is indeed an irony that an archbishop who sought to create a new partnership between creole patricians and the crown would provide the next generation with the intellectual tools with which to break New Granada's ancient links with the motherland. Caballero y Góngora's own nephew, Manuel Torres, for that matter, served as the first diplomatic representative of the infant republic of Gran Colombia to the government of the United States.[11]

But in 1810 a new set of circumstances had come into play, and no one in the 1780's could have anticipated them. By 1810 the impact of the North American Revolution had penetrated. The French Revolution and Napoleon had provided other explosive examples, and the crisis of monarchical legitimacy in Spain offered to the generation of 1810 the seductive invitation to strike out for political independence.

Much though the memory and the deeds of Juan Francisco Berbeo and José Antonio Galán should be respected by Colombian patriots, the Comuneros, in the last analysis, were the spokesmen of a world that would quickly fade into the past. It was Caballero y Góngora who inadvertently opened the door that would lead to the future.

REFERENCE MATTER

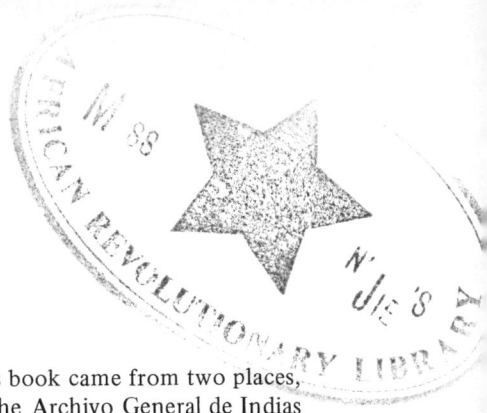

Note on the Sources

The great bulk of the documentation for this book came from two places, the Archivo Histórico Nacional in Bogotá and the Archivo General de Indias in Seville. It is no exaggeration to affirm that the history of the Comuneros cannot be written without long periods of investigation in those two famed depositories. The greatest single treasure of the Archivo Histórico Nacional is eighteen bound volumes of manuscripts entitled "Los Comuneros." It is particularly rich in the documentation of events in New Granada, especially the correspondence exchanged among the Comunero chieftains themselves and with the authorities in Bogotá. The other extensive holdings of the national archives only fill in important details about the crisis of 1781. This solid core of documentation was bound thanks to the foresight of Germán Arciniegas when he served as minister of education in the government of President Eduardo Santos.

The second richest depository in Colombia, although more restricted in scope than the Comunero collection in Bogotá, is the Archivo de la Notaria housed in the Casa de la Cultura in Socorro. That institution was founded with the enthusiastic sponsorship of Horacio Rodríguez Plata. This collection, consisting of some twenty-eight thick volumes covering the period from 1691 until 1802, contains many of the primary sources for the history of that community, notably dowries, wills, land sales, and sales of slaves. What it does not contain are the records of commercial transactions. The archive of the town of Socorro has not survived.

The Academia Colombiana de Historia, the private collection of José Manuel Restrepo, the Lilly Library at Indiana University, and the British Museum also contain valuable documents, but most of them are duplicates that can be found in the Archivo Histórico Nacional in Bogotá or the Archivo General de Indias in Seville. In view of the dangers of piracy or the possibility of ships being captured in wartime, standard practice was to make duplicates of all correspondence exchanged between Bogotá and Madrid, and one copy usually remained in either place.

The documentation in Seville usually supplements the holdings in Bogotá. Seville's treasure consists of the voluminous reports of the viceroys, the audiencia, and the regent visitor general dispatched to the central authorities in Spain. Many of these accounts also contain as appendices copies of correspondence exchanged in New Granada, many of which also exist in Bogotá. Among the most useful sources are the following: Audiencia de Santa Fe 658–61, 696–700, 590–93, 573, 662, 663-A, 577-B, 594, 663–64.

249

Notes

Abbreviations Used in the Notes

AGI/ASF The Audiencia de Sante Fe section of the Archivo General de
Indias (AGI), Seville
CA Pablo E. Cárdenas Acosta, *El movimiento comunal de 1781 en el
nuevo reino de Granada.* 2 vols. Bogotá: Editorial Kelly, 1960
CR Private Collection of José Manuel Restrepo, Bogotá
AHN Archivo Histórico Nacional, Bogotá
ANS Archivo de la Notaria, Socorro
BHA *Boletín de historia y antigüedades*

Chapter 1
From Kingdoms to Empire:
The Political Innovations of Charles III

1 See my *Kingdom of Quito in the Seventeenth Century: Bureaucratic
Politics in the Spanish Empire* (Madison, 1967), pp. 119–21.
2 For stimulating recent interpretations, see David A. Brading, *Miners and
Merchants in Bourbon Mexico, 1763–1810* (Cambridge, 1971) and Stan-
ley and Barbara Stein, *The Colonial Heritage of Latin America: Essays on
Economic Dependence* (Oxford, 1970), pp. 86–119. Brading can be
faulted for not sharply distinguishing between the political and the
economic-fiscal aspects of the Caroline program. He referred to the sum
total of Charles's changes as a "revolution in government," when, in fact,
that monarch adopted a rather revolutionary means in order to introduce
modest fiscal changes. The Steins quite correctly stress the moderate
character of the fiscal program, but their brief account minimizes the
political aspect.
3 For an economic interpretation of the riots of 1766 see Pierre Vilar, "El
motín de Esquilache y la crisis del antiguo régimen," *Revista de occidente*
36 (1972):199–247.
4 Herbert I. Priestley, *José de Gálvez, Visitor General of New Spain,
1765–71* (Berkeley, 1916); Brading, *Miners and Merchants,* pp. 26–81;
María del Carmen Velásquez, *El estado de guerra en Nueva España,
1760–1800* (Mexico, 1958), pp. 80–85.
5 Brading, *Miners and Merchants,* pp. 33, 45–47, 63–69, 69–79, 87–92,
241–46; John Lynch, *Spanish Colonial Administration, 1782–1810: The
Intendant System in the Viceroyalty of Río de la Plata* (London, 1958);
Luis Navarro García, *Intendencias de Indias* (Seville, 1959).

251

6 Clarence H. Haring, *The Spanish Empire in America* (Oxford University Press, 1947), pp. 132–33. Consulta, August 10, 1779, and dispatch from Gutiérrez de Piñeres to Gálvez, February 28, 1779, both in AGI/ASF 912; Gálvez to audiencia, May 15, 1777, AHN, Historia Civil, 4:345.

7 Brading, *Miners and Merchants,* p. 45.

8 See my *Kingdom of Quito,* pp. 243 ff.

9 Brading, *Miners and Merchants,* pp. 44, 45.

10 Gutiérrez de Piñeres to Gálvez, May 15, 1778, AGI/ASF 659.

11 As quoted in Brading, *Miners and Merchants,* p. 35. Both George Ade and Mark Burkholder are undertaking studies on the career of Gálvez as minister of the Indies.

12 Michael Flamingo, "Viceregal Recruitment Patterns in the Spanish-American Colonies," seminar paper for Professor Peter H. Smith, fall of 1971, University of Wisconsin–Madison.

13 Biography of Manuel Antonio Flores by María Luis Rodríguez Baena, in José Antonio Calderón Quijano, *Los virreyes de Nueva España en el reinado de Carlos IV,* 2 vols. (Seville, 1972), 1:3–5. Flores's successor, Pimienta, had a creole wife from Cartagena; see Pablo E. Cárdenas Acosta, *El movimiento comunal de 1781 en el nuevo reino de Granada,* 2 vols. (Bogotá, 1960), 2:196–97. This work, frequently cited throughout, is hereafter abbreviated as CA.

14 Brading, *Miners and Merchants,* p. 35.

15 Jaime Eyzaguirre, *Ideario y ruta de la emancipación chilena* (2nd. ed., Santiago de Chile, 1969), pp. 54–57. For the important role played by the creoles in the Brazilian bureaucracy see Stuart B. Schwartz, "Magistracy and Society in Colonial Brazil," *Hispanic American Historical Review* 50 (1970):715–30. In 1777 in Lima, 7 of the 8 oidores and 3 of the 4 judges in the sala de crimen were creoles, belonging to the leading families in Lima, and in many cases wealthy. For creole participation in various audiencias, see Leon G. Campbell, "A Colonial Establishment: Creole Domination of the Audiencia of Lima during the Late Eighteenth Century," ibid. 52 (1972):1–25; Mark Burkholder, "From Creole to Peninsular: The Transformation of the Audiencia of Lima," and Jacques A. Barbier, "Elite and Cadres in Bourbon Chile," ibid. 52 (1972): 395–415, 416–35.

16 See my "El auge y la caída de los criollos en la audiencia de Nueva Granada," *BHA* 59 (1972):597–618.

17 The information that precedes is drawn from the seminal studies of M. A. Burkholder and D. S. Chandler, reported in part in "Creole Appointments and the Sale of Audiencia Positions in the Spanish Empire under the Early Bourbons, 1701–50," *Journal of Latin American Studies* 4 (1972): 187–206. Their findings on creole participation in the audiencias are summarized in *From Impotence to Authority: The Spanish Crown and the American Audiencias, 1687–1808* (Columbia, Mo., 1977).

18 "Anti-Americanism and the Audiencias: The Years of José de Gálvez, 1776–1787," unpublished paper by M. A. Burkholder. Professors Burkholder and Chandler have generously shared with me their data on the audiencia of Bogotá, and I am deeply grateful.

19 Eyzaguirre, *Emancipación chilena*, p. 53. For the English translation see R. A. Humphreys and John Lynch, *The Origins of the Latin American Revolutions, 1808–1826* (New York, 1965), p. 257.

20 Eyzaguirre, *Emancipación chilena*, p. 53. The career of Joaquín de Mosquera y Figueroa (1748–1830), born in Popayán and the uncle of the celebrated president of the republic, conformed to the new Caroline policy of granting office in Spain to qualified creoles. After serving as oidor in Bogotá (1787–95), he held high posts in both Mexico City and Caracas before being promoted to the council of the Indies in 1810. He was briefly regent of Spain in 1812. José María Restrepo Saenz, *Biografías de los mandatarios y ministros de la real audiencia, 1671–1819* (Bogotá, 1952), pp. 388–93.

21 Consulta, September 23, 1776, AGI/ASF 547.

22 For a brief biography see Restrepo Saenz, *Biografías*, pp. 509–14. For his pre-New Granada career see his "Relación de Méritos" published in José Manuel Pérez Ayala, *Antonio Caballero y Góngora* (Bogotá, 1951), pp. 394–98.

23 Humphrey and Lynch, *Origins*, p. 258.

24 Juan Hernández y Davalos, *Colección de documentos para la historia de la guerra de independencia de México de 1808 a 1821*, 6 vols. (Mexico, 1877), 1:428.

25 CA, 2:26.

26 The information in Tables 1.1 and 1.2 is drawn from the biographies contained in Restrepo Saenz, *Biografías*, pp. 1–18, 295–451, 462–521.

27 This hypothesis comes from my study of the Quito bureaucracy, and is a view that was also shared by both Olivares and the reforming bureaucrats of Charles III's reign.

28 Phelan, "El auge y la caída."

29 Restrepo Saenz, *Biografías*, pp. 460–61. For royal permission granting the children of Fiscal Alvarez the right to marry natives see the consulta, March 4, 1775, AGI/ASF 547. For his retirement see consulta, August 19, 1775, ibid. His biography was discussed in a lecture delivered at Museo Arqueológico del Banco Popular by José de Muir on May 8, 1974 (to be published). His portrait hangs in the Museo Nacional. His seignorial mansion has been tastefully restored by the Banco Popular to house their Museo Arqueológico.

30 Gutiérrez de Piñeres to Gálvez, March 30, 1778, AGI/ASF 659. However critical Gutiérrez de Piñeres was of the Alvarez rosca, he himself was not above practicing some nepotism. He appointed as administrator of the aguardiente monopoly in Mompós his nephew, who became the founder

of a distinguished family in Colombia. Ibid., December 30, 1778. Gálvez himself practiced massive nepotism. Brading, *Miners and Merchants*, p. 37.

31 Gutiérrez de Piñeres to Gálvez, February 28, May 15, 1778, AGI/ASF 659.

32 Flores to Gálvez, November 15, 1777, AGI/ASF 659.

33 Gutiérrez de Piñeres to Gálvez, July 31, 1778, ibid.

34 Brading, *Miners and Merchants*, pp. 40–42.

Chapter 2
From Kingdom to Colony:
The Fiscal and Economic Program of Charles III

1 Bernardo Ward, *Proyecto económico* (Madrid, 1779), p. xiv.

2 Ibid., pp. 225–319. Miguel Artola, "Campillo y las reformas de Carlos III," *Revista de Indias* 12 (1952):685–714.

3 Brading, *Miners and Merchants*, pp. 29–30, 53; Priestley, p. 154; Gutiérrez de Piñeres to Gálvez, December 31, 1779, AGI/ASF 660.

4 Biblioteca Nacional, Bogotá, Libros Raros y Curiosos, ms. 185. Restrepo's figures for 1808 are even somewhat higher: José Manuel Restrepo, *Historia de la revolución de Colombia*, 2 vols. (Medellín, 1969), 1:29.

5 Priestley, *Gálvez*, pp. 131 ff.

6 Flores to cabildo of Socorro, June 20, 1781, AGI/ASF 577-B; Gutiérrez de Piñeres to cabildo of Tunja, May 29, 1780, AGI/ASF 660; Andres V. Castillo, *Spanish Mercantilism: Gerónimo de Uztáriz* (New York, 1930), p. 172.

7 Basilio Vicente de Oviedo, *Cualidades y riquezas del nuevo reino de Granada* (Bogotá, 1930), pp. 174–82. Oviedo, who was pastor of San Gil in the 1750's, reports that tobacco was not cultivated in Socorro but only in San Gil, Barichara, and Zapatoca.

8 José María Ots Capdequí, *Instituciónes* (Barcelona, 1959), p. 485; Gutiérrez de Piñeres to Gálvez, August 31, 1778, AGI/ASF 659; Mesía de la Cerda to Guirior, in *Relaciones de mando de los virreyes de la Nueva Granada*, ed. Gabriel Giraldo Jaramillo (Bogotá, 1954), p. 53.

9 Guirior to Flores, in *Relaciones de mando*, pp. 91–92; AHN, Tabacos, 12:492–512.

10 Guirior to Flores, in *Relaciones de mando*, p. 53.

11 Gutiérrez de Piñeres to Gálvez, January 31, August 31, 1778, AGI/ASF 659; Gutiérrez de Piñeres to Flores, January 27, March 5, 1778, ibid.

12 Climaco Calderón, *Elementos de hacienda pública* (Bogotá, 1911), pp. 539–41; Pablo E. Cárdenas Acosta, *Del vasallaje a la insurrección de los Comuneros: la provincia de Tunja en el virreinato* (Tunja, 1947), pp. 345–47; Gutiérrez de Piñeres to Gálvez, March 30, May 15, August 31, November 18, 1778, AGI/ASF 659; Flores to Gálvez, November 15, 1777, ibid.

13 AHN, Audiencia, Cundinamarca, 9:992—1000; Gutiérrez de Piñeres to Gálvez, February 28, March 30, May 15, 1778, and March 31, 1779, AGI/ASF 659.

14 Cárdenas Acosta, *Del vasallaje*, p. 346; Calderón, *Elementos*, pp. 539—41; Gutiérrez de Piñeres to Gálvez, March 31, 1779, AGI/ASF 659, and January 6, 1780, AGI/ASF 660.

15 Over the course of a year, García Olano had permitted a massive over-production of tobacco and then, miscalculating consumption in the area, had purchased 4,000 *cargas* (a carga weighed about 250 lbs.) when the market could handle only about 2,000 cargas. Tobacco was rotting in the royal warehouses. Calderón, *Elementos*, p. 347; Cárdenas Acosta, *Del vasallaje*, pp. 345—47. For García Olano's defense see AHN, Tabacos, 35:255—87.

16 Berenguer to Mélendez de Arzona, March 22, 1781, AGI/ASF; Salvador Plata to Caballero y Góngora, December 1, 1781, AHN, Los Comuneros, testimony of Plata, 6:97 ff.; cabildo of Socorro to Flores, May 7, 1781, AGI/ASF 663-A; Manuel Briceño, *Los Comuneros* (Bogotá, 1880), pp. 100—103.

17 The most comprehensive study of the tobacco monopoly is John P. Harrison, "The Colombian Tobacco Industry: From Government Monopoly to Free Trade, 1778—1876," unpublished Ph.D. dissertation, University of California, Berkeley, 1951. For a résumé see his "The Evolution of the Colombian Tobacco Trade to 1875," *Hispanic American Historical Review* 32 (1952):163—74. Calderón, *Elementos*, pp. 514—53. The principal primary sources for Gutiérrez de Piñeres's tobacco policy are the following: for a copy of Gálvez's rules for the Mexican monopoly see AHN, Tabacos, 19:860—85. See also Gutiérrez de Piñeres to Gálvez, January 31, February 28, May 15, July 31, August 31, November 20, 1778, AGI/ASF 659; Gutiérrez de Piñeres to Flores, January 28, March 5, 1778, and Flores to Gutiérrez de Piñeres, February 28, ibid.; Gutiérrez de Piñeres to Gálvez, April 30, 1780, AGI/ASF 660; Gutiérrez de Piñeres, August 22, 1781, AGI/ASF 662; Gutiérrez de Piñeres to Pey y Ruíz, May 21, 1781, AGI/ASF 663-A; Flores to cabildo of Socorro, June 20, 1781, and Flores to Gálvez, August 22, 1781, AGI/ASF 577-B; ordinance of viceroy, August 18, 1778, AHN, Los Comuneros, 18:91—98.

18 Harrison, "Colombian Tobacco Industry," ch. 2.

19 Edward C. Kirland, *A History of American Economic Life* (3rd ed., New York, 1952), p. 68.

20 Jacob M. Price, *France and the Chesapeake: A History of the American Tobacco Monopoly, 1674—1691, and Its Relationship to the British and American Tobacco Trades*, 2 vols. (Ann Arbor, 1973), 2:718, 839—42.

21 Ibid.

22 Mesía de la Cerda to Guirior, *Relaciones de mando*, pp. 54—55.

23 For a concise history of the aguardiente monopoly see Calderón, *Elementos*, pp. 497—514. Also see Gutiérrez de Piñeres to Gálvez, May 31, 1779, AGI/ASF 659.

24 The definitive texts of Gutiérrez de Piñeres's fiscal innovations can be found in AHN, Los Comuneros, 1. Gutiérrez de Piñeres to Gálvez, January 31, 1781, AGI/ASF 660.
25 Gutiérrez de Piñeres to Gálvez, April 30, 1780, AGI/ASF 660; junta de tribunales, April 27, 1780, AGI/663-A.
26 The text of the capitulations is published in CA, 2:19, 23–24, 26. At the end of the colonial regime the crown derived the following revenues from those monopolies:

Playing cards	12,000	pesos
Gunpowder	11,500	"
Stamped paper	53,000	"
Salt	65,000	"
Total	141,500	pesos

(Restrepo, *Historia de la revolución de Colombia,* 1:29.)
27 Ibid.
28 Ward, *Proyecto económico,* pp. 235–41.
29 For background on the alcabala see: Salvador de Moxo, *La alcabala, sobre sus orígenes, concepto y naturaleza* (Madrid, 1963); Luis Eduardo Nieto Arteta, *Economía y cultura en la historia de Colombia* (Bogotá, 1962), pp. 15–35; Robert S. Smith, "Sales Taxes in New Spain, 1575–1770," *Hispanic American Historical Review* 28 (1948):2–37; Abel Cruz Santos, *Economía y hacienda pública, Historia extensa de Colombia,* vol. 15 (Bogotá, 1965), 1:121–89; Luis Ospina Vásquez, *Industria y protección en Colombia, 1810–1930* (Medellín, 1955), pp. 1–84; Calderón, *Elementos,* pp. 293 ff.; Cárdenas Acosta, *Del vasallaje,* pp. 271–308.
30 Smith, "Sales Taxes in New Spain," p. 10; *Recopilación de leyes de los reynos de las Indias,* bk. 8, tit. 13.
31 John Lynch, *Spain Under the Habsburgs,* 2 vols. (London, 1969), 2:200.
32 Gutiérrez de Piñeres to Gálvez, October 30, 1780, January 31, 1781, AGI/ASF 660.
33 CA, 1:19.
34 Gutiérrez de Piñeres to Gálvez, April 30, October 30, 1780, AGI/ASF 660.
35 Ibid., September 30, 1780.
36 CA, 1:211–12.
37 For background on this tax see my *Kingdom of Quito,* pp. 109–11, 331.
38 Gutiérrez de Piñeres to Gálvez, March 31, 1781, AGI/ASF 660.
39 Testimony of Salvador Plata, December 1, 1781, AHN, Los Comuneros, 6:97–131, and March 13, 1783, ibid., 18:354–400.
40 CA, 1:99–100.
41 See John Lynch, review of the Steins' *The Colonial Heritage of Latin America, Journal of Latin American Studies* 4 (1972):319–20.
42 For a concise overview of the colonial economy of New Granada see

Jaime Jaramillo Uribe, "La controversia jurídica y filosófica librada en la Nueva Granada en torno a la liberación de los esclavos," *Anuario Colombiano de historia social y de la cultura* 4 (1969):63 ff.

43 Allan J. Kuethe, "Military Reform in the Viceroyalty of New Granada, 1773–1796," unpublished Ph.D. dissertation, University of Florida, 1962, chs. 2 and 3.

44 Gutiérrez de Piñeres to Gálvez, March 31, 1780, AGI/Audiencia de Quito 574.

45 Kuethe, "Military Reform," ch. 4.

46 Caballero y Góngora to Gálvez, October 15, 1782, AGI/ASF 594.

47 Gutiérrez de Piñeres to Gálvez, June 3, 1781, AGI/ASF 662.

48 Ward, *Proyecto económico,* pp. 241–49.

49 The correspondence between the two is in AGI/ASF 659 and 912.

50 Flores to Gálvez, July 15, 1778, AGI/ASF 591; CA, 1:82.

51 Jack P. Greene, *The Quest for Power: The Lower House of Assembly in the Southern Royal Colonies, 1689–1776* (Chapel Hill, 1963); Merrill Jensen, *The Founding of a Nation: A History of the American Revolution, 1763–76* (New York, 1968); Oliver M. Dickerson, *The Navigation Acts and the American Revolution* (Philadelphia, 1951); David Lovejoy, *The Glorious Revolution in America* (New York, 1972). For an interpretation that stresses economic rather than constitutional issues see Marc Egnal and Joseph A. Ernst, "An Economic Interpretation of the American Revolution," *William and Mary Quarterly* 29 (1972):3–32. For a stimulating comparison and contrast see James Lang, *Conquest and Commerce: Spain and England in the Americas* (New York, 1975).

Chapter 3
The Crowd Riots

1 For the history of Socorro see the following: Horacio Rodríguez Plata, "Origen y fundación del Socorro," *BHA* 26 (1939):879–91, and his *La inmigración alemana al estado soberano de Santander en el siglo xix* (Bogotá, 1968), pp. 33–37; Cárdenas Acosta, *Del vasallaje,* pp. 227–92. A much less reliable account is Rito Rueda, *Presencia de un pueblo* (San Gil, 1968).

2 Oviedo, *Cualidades,* pp. 174–76.

3 Biblioteca Nacional, Bogotá, Libros Raros y Curiosos # 185.

4 Finestrad estimated that in the early 1780's there were, on the average, 800 births, 300 deaths, and 200 marriages annually. Joaquín de Finestrad, "El vasallo instruído en el estado del nuevo reino de Granada," in Eduardo Posada, ed., *Los Comuneros* (Bogotá, 1905), pp. 119–20.

5 For overviews of the textile industry see Ospina Vásquez, *Industria,* pp. 61–71; Rodríguez Plata, *La inmigración alemana,* pp. 33–37.

6 Gary W. Graff, "Spanish Parishes in Colonial New Granada: Their Role in Town Building on the Spanish-American Frontier," *The Americas* 33 (1976–77): 336–51.
7 For just a few examples see Oviedo, *Cualidades,* pp. 174–82; Ramiro Gómez Rodríguez, *Chima–vida y hazañas de un pueblo* (Bucaramanga, 1971), pp. 53, 56–62. In AHN, Poblaciones, there are countless lawsuits.
8 Oviedo, *Cualidades,* p. 174; Archivo Histórico Nacional (Madrid), Consejos, leg. 20, 437; AHN, Poblaciones de Santander, 3:753–969. Only the king, and not the audiencia, could bestow the titles of city or town (*Recopilación,* bk. 4, tit. 8, law vi). There was no substantive difference between a city and a town as administrative entities. The former had a larger population than the latter, as evidenced by the fact that cities ordinarily had 12 aldermen and towns 6 (Juan de Solórzano y Pereira, *Política Indiana,* 5 vols. [Madrid, 1647], bk. 5, ch. 1, #1 and 2).
9 Ramiro Gómez Rodríguez, "Socorro, cuna de la libertad Colombiana, 1540–1819," 2 vols. (unpublished ms.), 1, ch. 6.
10 AHN, Cabildos, 10:278–82. The documentation of this dispute can be found, ibid., 1–525, and AHN, Poblaciones de Santander, 3:753–969. See also testimony of Salvador Plata, no date, Lilly Library, Indiana University, ff. 263–64 and 273–74. Plata was an active partisan of Socorro's cause, even though he had once served as alcalde ordinario of San Gil.
11 For this dispute see AHN, Poblaciones de Santander, 3:315–673.
12 For the 1711 figure see ibid., 3:753 ff. For 1753 see ibid., f. 176. For the 1781 figure see Finestrad, "El vasallo," pp. 119–20 and notes 10 and 11. For the 1779 and 1781 census figures see AHN, Censos Nacionales, Varios Departmentos, 6:271.
13 On February 4, 1760, for example, the treasury received 2,625 pesos for the resguardos of Oiba. AHN, Caciques y Indios, 41:325–58; 45: 723–802.
14 AHN, Poblaciones de Santander, 3:176, and Caciques y Indios, 3:392–93.
15 Francisco Silvestre, *Descripción del reyno de Santa Fé de Bogotá* (Bogotá, 1950), pp. 72–75.
16 Will of Salvador Plata, ANS, December 7, 1802, ff. 185–217.
17 ANS, January 26, 1772, f. 9; February 14, 1773, f. 12; November 6, 1784, f. 128; April 16, 1787, f. 132; March 15, 1788, ff. 702–3; January 7, 1789, ff. 702–3.
18 ANS, March 8, 1774, f. 55.
19 For a few examples see ANS, February 12, March 7, May 20, June 10, 1774: ff. 29–30, 49–50, 123, and 141; May 23, November 3, 1778: ff. 72, 164; September 21, November 1, 1780, ff. 177–78.
20 For some examples see ANS, 1774–76, f. 13; September 19, 1774, ff. 186–87; 1781–83, f. 192; July 18, 1785, f. 81.
21 ANS, September 18, 1778, f. 184.

22 Will of Juan Francisco Berbeo, June 29, 1795, in the private archives of Dr. Jorge Cárdenas Acosta.
23 See Jaime Jaramillo Uribe, "Esclavos y señores en la sociedad Colombiana del siglo xviii," *Anuario Colombiano de historia social y de la cultura,* 1.1 (1963): 38.
24 Pedro Fermín de Vargas, *Memoria sobre la población del reino* (Bogotá, 1953), p. 83. For further evidence see note 10, above.
25 For some random samples of minifundia land sales see ANS, 1777, ff. 121, 206; 1778, ff. 3, 85, 87, 163; September 27, 1790, f. 95; May 13, 1784, ff. 64–65. For sales of larger tracts see July 1, 1774, ff. 158–60; October 4, 1790, f. 78; July 14, 1774, ff. 185–86; July 1, 1774, ff. 158–60.
26 Quotations from Oviedo, *Cualidades,* pp. 179–80, 178–79 respectively.
27 Cabildo of Socorro to Flores, May 7, 1781, in Briceño, *Los Comuneros,* pp. 101–3. Flores to Gálvez, December 31, 1781, AGI/ASF 577-B. Procurador of Socorro to Flores, September 15, 1781, ibid. Joaquín de Finestrad, "El vasallo instruído," ms. in the Biblioteca Nacional, Libros Raros y Curiosos, ff. 320–21. See chapter 3, note 5, for the published version, from which several chapters were omitted. Gómez Rodríquez, "La cuna," part 4; AHN, Poblaciones de Santander, 3:462 ff.
28 For a useful chronology of events see CA, 2:313 ff.
29 The sources for the three riots are: Flores to Gálvez, August 22, December 31, 1781, AGI/ASF 577-B; cabildo of Socorro to Gutiérrez de Piñeres, March 16, April 2, 1781, AGI/ASF 663-A; Angulo y Olarte to Gutiérrez de Piñeres, March 27, April 19, 1781, ibid.; Céspedes y Uribe to Gutiérrez de Piñeres, April 3, 1781, ibid.; Gutiérrez de Piñeres to Galvéz, June 3, 1781, AGI/ASF 662. CA, 1:132–35; Angulo y Olarte to Osorio, May 15, 1781, Collection of Horacio Rodríguez Plata, Casa de la Cultura, Socorro. Plata's three testimonies are blatantly self-serving, yet they contain graphic accounts of the riots. One version at the Lilly Library, Indiana University, has no date. The other testimonies, each somewhat different but also repetitious, are dated December 1, 1781, and March 13, 1783, in AHN, Los Comuneros, 6:91–131 and 18:354–405.
30 For her certificate of baptism see Ramiro Gómez Rodríguez, "Datos tomados del archivo parroquial del Socorro," *Archivo* (Academia Colombiana de Historia) 3 (1971):103.
31 CA, 2:65.
32 See the consulta of the fiscal, March 22, 1781, and audiencia to Angulo y Olarte, March 23, 1781, AGI/ASF 663-A.
33 Anonymous account, May 15, 1781, published in *Archivo del General Miranda* (Caracas, 1938), 15:31.
34 Ordinance of the audiencia, April 3, 1781, AGI/ASF 663-A.
35 Gutiérrez de Piñeres to Gálvez, March 31, 1781, AGI/ASF 660; testimonies of Salvador Plata (see n. 29, above).
36 Gutiérrez de Piñeres to Gálvez, June 3, 1781, AGI/ASF 662.

37 Angulo y Olarte to Gutiérrez de Piñeres, April 2, 1781, AGI/ASF 663-A.
38 Céspedes y Uribe to Gutiérrez de Piñeres, April 3, 1781, ibid.
39 Campuzano y Lanz to Gutiérrez de Piñeres, April 8, 1781, ibid.
40 Gutiérrez de Piñeres to Campuzano, April 11, 1781, ibid.
41 Ordinance of corregidor, Chiquinquirá, April 12, 1781, ibid.; Gutiérrez de Piñeres to Campuzano, April 15, 1781, ibid.; Campuzano to Gutiérrez de Piñeres, April 16, 1781, ibid.
42 Fiscales to Gutiérrez de Piñeres, April 8, 1781, AGI/ASF 663-A; ordinance of the audiencia, April, 9, 1781, ibid.; appointment and acceptance of Osorio, April 9 and 10, 1781, ibid.

Chapter 4
Patricians and Plebeians in Socorro

1 Gómez Rodríguez, "Datos," p. 104.
2 For the family history see Gómez Rodríguez, "La cuna," 1, part 5.
3 For chantries see Juan Pablo Restrepo, *La iglesia y el estado en Colombia* (London, 1885), pp. 323–33; Michael P. Costeloe, *Church Wealth in Mexico: A Study of the Juzgado de Capellanías in the Archbishopric of Mexico, 1800–1856* (Cambridge University Press, 1967), pp. 46–62; Germán Colmenares, "Censos y capellanías: formas de crédito en una economía agrícola," *Cuadernos Colombianos* 2 (1974):123–44.
4 Will of Juan Francisco Berbeo, June 29, 1795, personal collection of Dr. Jorge Cárdenas Acosta.
5 ANS, March 13, 1785, ff. 35–36.
6 Will of Juan Manuel Berbeo, March 5, 1788, ANS. His wife Josefa, the sole beneficiary, was a sister of Juan Maldonado de la Zerda, the wealthiest citizen of Socorro in his generation, who died sometime around 1778. For his career see Gómez Rodríguez, "La cuna," ch. 6.
7 Ibid., 1, part 5.
8 Will of Juan Francisco Berbeo, June 29, 1795.
9 CA, 2:295–311.
10 Gómez Rodríguez, "La cuna," 1, part 5.
11 Marriage contract of Juan Francisco Berbeo and Bárbara Rodríguez Terán, January 6, 1771. Collection of Horacio Rodríguez Plata, Casa de la Cultura, Socorro.
12 For Berbeo's purchases of urban and rural real estate see ANS, June 26, 1776, f. 188 and June 8, 1783, ff. 2–3. See also February 17, 1782, ibid. and May 10, 1782, f. 101; July 1, 1774, ibid., ff. 158–60; January 26, 1772, February 14, 1773, ibid., ff. 9, 12.
13 May 1, 1793, ibid., f. 56. In 1796 Rito de Acosta served as alcalde ordinario of Socorro (February 26, 1796, ibid., f. 14).
14 Salvador Plata testimony, March 13, 1783, AHN, Los Comuneros, 18:354–405, #34.

15 Ibid., # 18. Also see testimony of don Fernando Pavón y Gallo, September 23, 1782, in dispatch from Caballero y Góngora to Gálvez, October 15, 1782, AGI/ASF 594 (hereafter cited as testimony of Pavón y Gallo). Pavón y Gallo was a prominent patrician from Tunja who provided the most factual account of Berbeo's activities prior to 1781.

16 Both quotations in this paragraph from ibid.

17 In the late 1780's he became a successful Indian fighter. AHN, Virreyes, 12:362–92 and 13:487–93.

18 For Plata's career see Horacio Rodríguez Plata, "¿Quién fué Salvador Plata?" *BHA* 44 (1957):366–79. Dr. Rodríguez Plata has a manuscript on the history of the Plata clan. For a genealogy of the family see Horacio Rodríguez Plata, *Antonio Santos Plata* (Bogotá, 1969), pp. 11–34. For Plata's role in the Socorro–San Gil dispute see AHN, Poblaciones de Santander, ff. 324 ff., and Gómez Rodríguez, "La cuna," 1, part 5.

19 We have no certificate of baptism for Plata. In 1782 he gave his age as 40. (Plata testimony at García Olano inquest, October 26, 1782, AGI/ASF 736-A.)

20 He bought the farm from the estate of Juan Maldonado de la Zerda, to whose widow he was related. Gómez Rodríguez, "La cuna," 1, part 5.

21 For the text of the will and the litigation in Socorro see ANS, December 7, 1802, ff. 185–87. For the appeal to the audiencia see AHN, Testamentarias de Santander, # 19, ff. 640–871.

22 See Rodríguez Plata as cited in note 19.

23 See Plata testimonies, as cited in ch. 3, note 29, above.

24 The Berbeo-Plata correspondence is attached to the testimony of Juan Francisco Berbeo (September 14, 1782) in the Codice, Los Comuneros, Lilly Library. Briceño published the Berbeo testimony but not the correspondence, in *Los Comuneros*, pp. 205–7.

25 Gómez Rodríguez, "Datos," p. 104.

26 Manuel Berbeo was baptized on February 1, 1741 (Parochial Archive, Socorro, Baptisms, Book 3, f. 241). Clemente José Estévez's baptism was performed on March 20, 1746 (Gómez Rodríguez, "La cuna," 1, ch. 6).

27 AHN, Empleados Públicos de Santander, 1:200–211; 2:633–42; 4: 924–75; 6:651–73; 13:579–735.

28 Gómez Rodríguez has made it clear that the son was the Comunero captain. Rosillo senior married Antonia Fernández de Saavedra, the daughter of an alcalde ordinario of San Gil. Her substantial dowry amounted to 1,405 patacones (a patacón was a peso worth 9 instead of 8 reales). ANS, February 27, 1742, ff. 26–28.

29 Horacio Rodríguez Plata, *Andres María Rosillo y Meruelo* (Bogotá, 1944), pp. 7–13.

30 ANS, August 7, 1780, ff. 144–45.

31 Monsalve and Rosillo to audiencia, November 9, 1781, AHN, Los Comuneros, 5:5–14, 72–84; testimony of Angulo y Olarte, December 9, 1781, ibid., 6:238–42.

32 Gómez Rodríguez, "La cuna," 1, ch. 6; ANS, 1794–95, f. 6; May 8, 1780, April 17, 1787, f. 30; December 12, 1782, f. 124; October 25, 1790, ff. 107–8.

33 AHN, Alcabalas, 3:1–80.

34 Testimony of Angulo y Olarte, December 9, 1781, AHN, Los Comuneros, 6:238–42; Plata testimony, Lilly Library, ch. 201; Gómez Rodríguez, "La cuna," 2, ch. 6.

35 ANS, June 28, 1779, f. 139; August 14, 1786, f. 142.

36 ANS, 1787–89, f. 85; May 13, 1784, ff. 64–65; 1790–93.

37 For an example see cabildo of Socorro to viceroy, May 7, 1781, and captains general to viceroy, May 7, 1781, in Briceño, *Los Comuneros*, pp. 100–104.

38 For examples see cabildo of Socorro to king, September 20, 1781, AHN, Los Comuneros, 6:191–99; Rosillo inquest, November 3, 1781, ibid., 5:4–14; testimony of Rosillo and Monsalve, November 9, 1781, ibid., 72–84; testimony of Angulo y Olarte, December 9, 1781, ibid., 6: 238–42; Plata and Rosillo to Caballero y Góngora, February 10, 1782, AGI/ASF 594.

39 Gómez Rodríguez, "Datos," pp. 103, 105–6.

40 See chapter 3, note 10.

41 For a brief explanation of the Spanish currency see Lynch, *Spain Under the Habsburgs* 1:349; for a more extensive account see Felipe Mateu y Llopes, *La moneda española* (Barcelona, 1946), pp. 231–74.

42 Doris Ladd, "The Mexican Nobility at Independence, 1780–1826" (unpublished Ph.D. dissertation, Stanford University, 1972), p. 48.

43 The marquis of San Jorge purchased the truly seignorial mansion of Fiscal Alvarez in Bogotá in 1774 for 10,000 pesos (Bernardo Sanz de Santamaría, "La casa del marqués de San Jorge," *BHA* 59 [1972]:545–56). Socorro could boast of no such comparable mansions.

44 Camilo Pardo Umaña, *Haciendas de la sabana: su historia, sus leyendas y sus tradiciones* (Bogotá, 1946), pp. 209–33; Frank R. Safford, "Commerce and Enterprise in Central Colombia, 1821–1870" (unpublished Ph.D. dissertation, Columbia University, 1965), p. 12.

45 Safford, "Commerce and Enterprise."

46 For the salaries see Viceroy Francisco Gil y Lemos to king, May 19, 1790, AGI/ASF 562.

47 Oviedo, *Cualidades*, pp. 174–76.

48 Oviedo, *Cualidades*, pp. 177–84.

49 Peter Marzahl, "Creoles and Government: The Cabildo of Popayán," *Hispanic American Historical Review* 54 (1974):647.

50 Pedro Ibañéz, "Los nobles de la colonia," *BHA* 1 (1903):29–40.

51 Lyle N. McAlister, "Social Structure and Social Change in New Spain," *Hispanic American Historical Review* 43 (1963):357.

52 Ibid., and Jaime Jaramillo Uribe, "Mestizaje y diferención social en el nuevo reino de Granada en la segunda mitad del siglo xviii," *Anuario Colombiano de historia social y de la cultura* 2.3 (1965): 21–30. Also see

Juan A. Villamorín, "The Concept of Nobility in the Social Stratification of Colonial Santa Fe de Bogotá," to be published in *Actas XLI Congreso Internacional de Americanistas.*

53 Gutiérrez de Piñeres to Gálvez, March 31, 1781, AGI/ASF 660.

54 Plata testimony, Lilly Library, # 193–204. For the genealogy of the Ardila clan see Gómez Rodríquez, "La cuna," 2, ch. 12.

55 Plata testimony, Lilly Library, # 96.

56 As quoted, ibid., # 206. The square of Chiquinquirá was usually called the *plazuela,* or little square, to distinguish it from the main square.

57 The idea of drawing such a chart first occurred to Peter De Shazo in a paper he submitted to my research seminar in the fall semester of 1973.

58 George Rudé, *The Crowd in the French Revolution* (New York, 1967), ch. 2.

59 For some examples of other plural societies see J. S. Furnivall, *Netherlands India: A Study of Plural Economy* (Cambridge, 1944); M. G. Smith, *The Plural Society in the British West Indies* (Berkeley, 1965); H. Hoetink, *Two Variants in Caribbean Race Relations* (London, 1967).

Chapter 5
A Utopia for the People

1 Testimony of Angulo y Olarte, October 25, 1782, in the García Olano inquest included as an appendix in dispatch from Caballero y Góngora to Floridablanca, January 31, 1783, AGI/ASF 736-A (hereafter cited as the García Olano inquest). Testimony of Salvador Plata, October 26, 1782, ibid.; testimony of Pavón y Gallo; and see my "La trayectoria enigmática de Manuel García Olano durante la revolución Comunera," *BHA* 61 (1974):163–70.

2 Testimony of Pavón y Gallo, in Caballero y Góngora to Gálvez, October 15, 1782, AGI/ASF 594. Guevara y Suescún, one of whose ancestors, Pedro de Lombana, was one of the original conquerors, belonged to the creole bureaucratic establishment. He was appointed oidor of the audiencia of Quito on August 25, 1773, alcalde de crimen in Lima on May 21, 1779, and oidor in Lima on May 29, 1787. This information was supplied to me by Mark Burkholder. Also see the consulta, December 16, 1777, AGI/ASF 547.

3 On the impact of Túpac Amaru see: testimony of Pavón y Gallo; testimony of Angulo y Olarte, and Plata in the García Olano inquest; testimony of Salvador Plata, AHN, Los Comuneros, 6:97–131, # 16, 47, and 18:354–405, # 1, 34.

4 Bernet to Flores, November 22, 1781, AHN, Los Comuneros, 5:104.

5 Testimony of Pavón y Gallo.

6 Testimony of Francisco de Vergara, April 7, 1762, AHN, Cabildos, 10:7–8.

7 Testimony of Plata, AHN, Los Comuneros, 6:97–131, # 18.

8 Testimony of Jorge Miguel Lozano de Peralta, June 15, 1762, AHN, Cabildos, 10:17–18.
9 Raimundo Rivas, "El marqués de San Jorge," *BHA* 6 (1911):721–50; Pedro M. Ibáñez, "Los nobles de la colonia," ibid. 1 (1903):29–40; Eduardo Posada, "El marqués de San Jorge," ibid. 6 (1911):747–50; Francisco de Paula Plazas, "El marqués de San Jorge de Bogotá," ibid. 58 (1971):261–68; Eduardo Zuleta, "El oidor Mon y Velarde," ibid. 16 (1927):273–85; Charles III to Caballero y Góngora, June 26, 1778, AGI/ASF 697. See also Pardo Umaña, *Haciendas de la sabana*, pp. 209–33, and Indalecio Liévano Aguirre, *Los grandes conflictos sociales y económicos de nuestra historia* (3rd ed., Bogotá, 1968), pp. 441–46.
10 Ladd, "The Mexican Nobility," pp. 106–7.
11 Consulta, October 7, 1778, AGI/ASF 696.
12 Marquis of San Jorge to Charles III, October 31, 1783, British Libraries, Egerton 1.807, ff. 604–9.
13 For the pro-Socorro spirit in Bogotá see the anonymous "Relación verdadera de los hechos ocurridos en la sublevación . . . de 1781," *Proceso histórico del 20 de Julio* (Bogotá, 1960), p. 22; see also testimony of Plata, AHN, Los Comuneros, 18:354–405, # 15–17, 34.
14 For a persuasively well-documented analysis of the authorship see Alberto E. Ariza, O.P., *Fray Ciriaco de Archila, primer prócer de la libertad absoluta en Colombia y Fray José Simón de Archila, preceptor y libertador del León de Apure* (Bogotá, 1971), pp. 32–33; see also investigation of the audiencia, April 11, 1781, AGI/ASF 663-A.
15 Rafael Gómez Hoyos, *La revolución granadina de 1810; ideario de una generación y de una época, 1781–1821*, 2 vols. (Bogotá, 1962), 1:170.
16 Testimony of Plata, AHN, Los Comuneros, 18:354–405, # 15–17, 34.
17 Briceño, *Los Comuneros*, pp. 17–25; CA, 1:121–30. There is a complete text of the poem in CR. Until now Gómez Hoyos is the only historian who has made an analysis in depth of the ideological current of the poem. *La revolución granadina*, 1:168–71. For a hostile contemporary critique see my discussion of Finestrad in ch. 17.
18 CA, 1:172.
19 Philip II, for example, never referred to his naval expedition against England as the "invincible armada," but as the "enterprise." So also did some early Jesuits characterize their mission. Garrett Mattingly, *The Armada* (Boston, 1959), p. 40; Enrique Herrera Oria, *La armada invencible* (Valladolid, 1929), p. 151.
20 Finestrad, "El vasallo," p. 156.
21 Gómez Hoyos, *La revolución granadina*, 1:170–72.
22 See below, chapter 6, and ibid., pp. 53–95; R. W. and A. J. Carlyle, *A History of Political Thought in the West*, 6 vols. (Edinburgh and London, 1903–36), 6:344–51; Heinrich Albert Rommen, *La teoría del estado y de la comunidad internacional de Francisco Suárez* (Madrid, 1951), pp. 370–84; Bernice Hamilton, *Political Thought in Sixteenth Century Spain* (New York and Oxford, 1963), pp. 61–63.

23 For the texts see ordinance of the audiencia, April 11, 1781, AGI/ASF 663-A.

Chapter 6
A Utopia for the Nobles

1 CA, 1:137–38.
2 Ibid., p. 131; Angulo y Olarte to Gutiérrez de Piñeres, April 19, 1781, ibid., pp. 132–33.
3 Ibid., pp. 138–39.
4 Ibid., p. 140.
5 For examples see Angel M. Galán, "José Antonio Galán, 1749–1782," in Posada, *Los Comuneros,* pp. 246–47; Germán Arciniegas, *Los Comuneros* (Bogotá, 1960), ch. 12.
6 CA, 1:140. Also see Horacio Rodríguez Plata, *Los Comuneros, curso superior de historia,* 2 vols. (Bogotá, 1950), 1:65–69; Manuel José Forero, *La primera república, Historia extensa de Colombia,* vol. 5 (Bogotá, 1966), pp. 35 ff.
7 For the first tax revolt see Gómez Hoyos, *La revolución granadina,* 1: 155–58; Francisco Elías de Tejada, *El pensamiento político de los fundadores de Nueva Granada* (Seville, 1955), pp. 73 ff.; Cárdenas Acosta, *Del vasallaje,* pp. 271–76; Liévano Aguirre, *Los grandes conflictos,* pp. 201–9. For the 1641 revolt see Gómez Hoyos, *La revolución granadina,* 1: 159–60; Cárdenas Acosta, *Del vasallaje,* pp. 281–87. What little we know about the third tax revolt in Puente Real de Vélez, in which the local patricians protested a forced loan in order to help finance the War of the Spanish Succession, is in Enrique Otero D'Costa, "Levantamiento en Vélez," *BHA* 16 (1925):82–87.
8 For a discussion of the decentralized character of the imperial bureaucracy see my *Kingdom of Quito,* pp. 22, 26–27, 38, 77–78, 123–25, 221–27, and 336–37, and my "Authority and Flexibility in the Spanish Imperial Bureaucracy," *Administrative Science Quarterly* 5 (1960): 47–65.
9 For the debate see: Humphreys and Lynch, *Origins,* p. 9; Charles C. Griffin, "The Enlightenment and Latin American Independence," in Arthur P. Whitaker, ed., *Latin America and the Enlightenment* (2nd ed., Ithaca, 1961), pp. 124–25; Miguel Batllori, S.J., *El abate Viscardo: historia y mito de la intervención de los Jesuitas en la independencia de Hispanoamérica* (Caracas, 1953), pp. 82–93, 145–47; Manuel Giménez Fernández, "Las doctrinas populistas en la independencia de América," *Anuario de estudios americanos* 3 (1946):519–665.
10 In the rare book room of the Biblioteca Nacional in Bogotá there are still many copies of the political works of Suárez, Castillo de Bobadilla, Marquez, Quevedo, and Saavedra y Fajardo. There are now no extant copies of the works of Benavente y Benavides, Lancina, Madariaga, or

Rivadeneira. Over the course of time many books from this collection, which originally belonged to the Jesuits, have disappeared.

11 I encountered only two such references in the unpublished part of the Finestrad manuscript in the rare book room at the Biblioteca Nacional.

12 Humphreys and Lynch, *Origins*, p. 9.

13 Francisco Suárez, *Defensio fidei*, bk. III, ch. 3, no. 2.

14 Ibid., bk. VI, ch. 4, no. 15; *De bello*, disp. XIII, sec. 8. For discussions of the Spanish school see ch. 5, note 22, above. Also see Gómez Hoyos, *La revolución granadina*, 1:53–107; Luis Recasens Sichs, *La filosofía del derecho de Francisco Suárez* (Mexico, 1947); José Antonio Maravall, *La teoría español del estado en el siglo xvii* (Madrid, 1944); Richard Morse, "The Heritage of Latin America," in Louis Hartz, *The Founding of New Societies* (New York, 1964), pp. 153–59.

15 For a persuasive analysis see Gómez Hoyos, *La revolución granadina*, 1: 155–204.

16 For the meaning of the term in Castile in 1520–21 see José Antonio Maravall, *Las comunidades de Castilla: una primera revolución moderna* (Madrid, 1963), pp. 79–124.

17 The seventeenth-century theorists explicitly identified the king's ministers as possible tyrants (Maravall, *La teoría expañola*, pp. 399–411).

Chapter 7
A Utopia for the Indians: The Resguardos

1 Although demographic studies have made considerable progress in Colombia in recent years, they still fall short of the sophisticated quantitative techniques employed by Woodrow Borah and Sherburne Cook for Mexico. The 300,000 figure is in Jaime Jaramillo Uribe, "La población indígena de Colombia en el momento de la conquista y sus transformaciones posteriores," *Anuario colombiana de historia social y de la cultura*, 1:2 (1964): 239–84. The 562,510 figure is Juan Friede, "Algunas consideraciones sobre la evolución demográfica en la provincia de Tunja," ibid. 2.3 (1965): 5–19. Also see his *Los Quimbayas bajo la dominación española* (Bogotá, 1963). For other demographic studies see Germán Colmenares, *Encomienda y población en la provincia de Pamplona, 1549–1650* (Bogotá, 1969); M. Darío Fajardo, *El régimen de la encomienda en la provincia de Vélez* (Bogotá, 1969). For a critique of these studies see Hermes Tovar Pinzón, "Estado actual de los estudios de demografía histórica en Colombia," *Anuario colombiano de historia social y de la cultura* 5 (1970): 65–140. Also see Sherburne F. Cook and Woodrow Borah, *Essays in Population History: Mexico and the Caribbean*, 2 vols. (Berkeley, 1971–74), 1:411–29.

2 Jaramillo Uribe, "La población indígena de Colombia," p. 255. Friede, "Algunas consideraciónes," p. 13.

3 Ibid. In New Granada, as in all other areas of the Americas where Indians and Europeans came into contact, diseases such as smallpox, influenza, and measles in the highlands and malaria in the tropics, took a massive toll in lives among Indian populations with no immunity.

4 The total population of the audiencia kingdom of New Granada was 826,550. Figures compiled from census data in Silvestre, *Santa Fe de Bogotá*, pp. 27–63, by Gary W. Graff, "Cofradías in the New Kingdom of Granada: Lay Fraternities in a Spanish American Frontier Society, 1600–1755," unpublished Ph.D. dissertation, University of Wisconsin–Madison, 1973.

5 Orlando Fals Borda, *El hombre y la tierra en Boyacá* (Bogotá, 1957), pp. 72–105, and his "Indian Congregation in the New Kingdom of Granada: Land Tenure Aspects, 1595–1850," *The Americas* 13 (1957):331–52; Magnus Mörner, *La corona española y los foráneos en los pueblos de Indios de América* (Stockholm, 1970), pp. 285, 287, 354–56, 357, and his "Las comunidades de indígenas y la legislación segregacionista en el nuevo reino de Granada," *Anuario colombiano de historia social y de la cultura* 1.1 (1963): 63–84; Juan Friede, "De la encomienda indiana a la propiedad territorial y su influencia sobre el mestizaje," ibid., 1969, pp. 35–61; Margarita González, *El resguardo en el nuevo reino de Granada* (Bogotá, 1970); Guillermo Hernández Rodríguez, *De los Chichas a la colonia y a la república* (Bogotá, 1949); Liévano Aguirre, *Los grandes conflictos*, pp. 419–23, 517, 519; Ospina Vásquez, *Industria y protección*, pp. 1–20.

6 Ospina Vásquez, *Industria y protección*, p. 15; González, *El resguardo*, pp. 35–42. Also see the other works cited in note 5.

7 Fals Borda, *El hombre y la tierra*, pp. 341–48. For an analysis of the cedula of 1754 see José María Ots Capdequí, *El régimen de la tierra en la América española durante el período colonial* (Cuidad Trujillo, 1946), pp. 110–16. Also see his *Nuevos aspectos del siglo xvii en América* (Bogotá, 1946), pp. 244–50.

8 For some primary sources of the visita of 1635–36 see José Mojica Silva, *Relación de visitas coloniales* (Tunja, 1948), pp. 166–207. For the archival sources see AHN, Visitas of Boyacá and Santander, 4:541–857, 978–88; 8:216–725; 9:637–764; 10:428–646, 969–86; 11:1–345; 12:1–338; 13:247–546. For the 1755–56 visita see ibid., 2:968–79; 3:241–68; 5:417–40, 964–96; 7:1–87; 8:726–58; 10:647–954. For Oidor Verdugo's report of May 7, 1757, see *Anuario colombiano de historia social y de la cultura* 1.1 (1963): 131–96; Germán Colmenares, *La provincia de Tunja en el nuevo reino de Granada, ensayo de historia social* (Bogotá, 1970), pp. 68 ff.; Fals Borda, *El hombre y la tierra*, pp. 82–98.

9 Verdugo report, in *Anuario* 1.1 (1963): 170. For Indian cattle raising in the llanos see José Tapia to Salvador Plata, July 10, 1781, AHN, Los Comuneros, 6:53–56.

10 AHN, Visitas of Boyacá and Santander, 3:903–99; 4:962–77; 7:808–46; 9:892–968, 969–87, 988–1009; 10:197–287; 11:900–91; 14:290–306;

González, *El resguardo*, pp. 71–80; Ulises Rojas, *Corregidores y justicias mayores de Tunja* (Tunja, 1962), pp. 550–68; Colmenares, *Tunja*, pp. 76 ff.

11 Colmenares, *Tunja*, pp. 80–83; González, *El resguardo*, pp. 150–54.

12 For the text of the Gutiérrez de Piñeres opinion see González, *El resguardo*, pp. 154–81.

13 Text in AHN, Reales Cédulas y Ordenes, 12:860–914. Also see Ots Capdequí, *Nuevos aspectos*, pp. 252–60.

14 See, for example, William Paul McGreevey, *An Economic History of Colombia, 1845–1930* (Cambridge, 1971), p. 59. McGreevey followed the argument of Liévano Aguirre, *Los grandes conflictos*, pp. 419–23. Liévano was unaware of Gutiérrez de Piñeres's memorandum of February 3, 1779, first published by González, *El resguardo*, pp. 154–81. He argued that the whole thrust of Bourbon policy was to favor the growth of latifundia—a misleading, if not downright false, claim, as can be seen in Campillo y Cosío's hostility to latifundia and see Ward, *Proyecto económico*, pp. 247–67. The pre-1778 audiencia, sympathetic to creole points of view, favored the landowners but not metropolitan bureaucrats such as Gutiérrez de Piñeres, Caballero y Góngora, and subsequent viceroys. Arciniegas's portrait of Gutiérrez de Piñeres (*Los Comuneros*, pp. 43–53) as a cold-blooded fiscal computer whose principal concern was to extract more revenue from the blood and sweat of the Indians does not square with the documentation.

For an argument in favor of the overwhelming primacy of local conditions over central directives in the seventeenth century see Marzahl, "Creoles and Government."

15 Creole-mestizo pressure against the remaining resguardos did not abate after 1781, but the Indians successfully fought back in the law courts to protect their community lands. For some examples see José María Ots Capdequí, *Las instituciones del nuevo reino de Granada al tiempo de la independencia* (Madrid, 1958), pp. 240–63. See also Liévano Aguirre, *Los grandes conflictos*, pp. 517–19.

16 CA, 2:20.

17 Fals Borda, *El hombre y la tierra*, p. 98. The same request was made by the cabildo of Socorro to New Granada's representatives to the junta in Spain on October 20, 1809 ("Instrucción," *BHA* 28 [1941]:417–23). Although the creole elites put sustained pressure on the authorities before 1778 and periodically continued that agitation until 1810, land hunger was not exclusively confined to creole magnates who wanted to carve out large estates. Small farmers, many of whom were mestizos, were also beneficiaries of the resguardo consolidation of the 1770's. It was the combined pressure of latifundistas and minifundistas that made the coalition so formidable. Liévano Aguirre's analysis ignores the latter and thus exaggerates the importance of "the great magnates of the creole oligarchy," pp. 517–19.

18 Fals Borda, *El hombre y la tierra*, pp. 98–105.

Chapter 8
A Utopia for the Indians: Indians in Revolt

1 My analysis of Túpac Amaru is based on secondary accounts. The two most extensive ones are Boleslao Lewin, *La rebelión de Túpac Amaru y los orígenes de la emancipación americana* (Buenos Aires, 1957), and Carlos Daniel Válcarcel, *La rebelión de Túpac Amaru* (3rd ed., Lima, 1970). Also see Jorge Cornejo Bouroncle, *Túpac Amaru: la revolución precursora de la emancipación continental* (2nd ed., Cuzco, 1963); Lillian Estelle Fisher, *The Last Inca, 1780—83* (Norman, 1966); J. R. Fisher, *Government and Society in Colonial Peru: The Intendant System, 1784—1814* (London, 1970), ch. 1; Vicente Palacio Atard, *Areche y Guirior: observaciones sobre el fracaso de una visita al Perú* (Seville, 1946); Oscar Cornblit, "Levantamientos de masas en Perú y Bolivia durante el siglo dieciocho," *Revista latinoamericana de sociología* 7 (1970):100—43; John H. Rowe, "El movimiento nacional inca del siglo dieciocho," *Revista universitaria* (Cuzco, 1954), no. 107. Also see Rowe's review of Lewin in the *Hispanic American Historical Review* 39 (1959): 278—80 and his "The Incas under Spanish Colonial Institutions," ibid. 37 (1957):155—99. For a comprehensive collection of primary sources see the *Colección documental de la independencia del Perú*, 27 vols. (Lima, 1971—73). The second volume, consisting of four thick tomes edited by Carlos Daniel Válcarcel, concerns Túpac Amaru.

2 Cárdenas Acosta may be quite correct in criticizing Arciniegas for exaggerating the importance of the Indians, but Cárdenas Acosta may also be faulted for calling the Comunero movement "obra exclusiva de los criollos" (*Los Comuneros*, p. 167).

3 García de León y Pizarro to Gálvez, July 18, December 18, 1781, AGI/Audiencia de Quito 241; Caballero y Góngora to Gálvez, February 6, 1783, CR; Actas de cabildo, Archivo Municipal, Quito, 1771—81. García de León y Pizarro reacted to the assassination of a fiscal bureaucrat in Pasto by dispatching 150 veteran soldiers to Ibarra, but no commotions occurred in the Quito district: Archivo Nacional Histórico, Quito, vol. 179, ff. 197—250. For the Pasto uprising see cabildo of Pasto to the junta de tribunales, June 22, 1781, AGI/ASF 663-A. Even Lewin, who saw the rebellion of Túpac Amaru in continental terms, is not able to make out a persuasive case that the Peruvian movement had visible repercussions in Quito (*Túpac Amaru*, pp. 668—72). García de León y Pizarro to Gálvez, AGI/Audiencia de Quito 241. In August 1781 Quito sent a much appreciated subsidy of some 186,000 pesos to the viceroy in Cartagena: García de León y Pizarro to Gálvez, August 18, 1781, AGI/Audiencia de Quito 241.

4 An analysis of these local Indian uprisings in the eighteenth century is the subject of a doctoral thesis being written by Segundo Moreno at the University of Bonn.

5 Pedro Fermín Ceballos, *Resumen de la historia del Ecuador*, 10 vols.

(Quito, 1972), 4:94–103; Federico González Suárez, *Historia general de la republica del Ecuador,* 9 vols. (Quito, 1890–94), 5:206–66; Lewin, *Túpac Amaru,* pp. 126–29.

6 Kuethe, "Military Reform," pp. 94, 116–17.
7 Pisco to fiscal (no date, perhaps late June 1781), AHN, Caciques y Indios, 26:1–10.
8 Inventory of his property, September 4, 1781, AHN, Los Comuneros, 14:16–21. On September 4, 1781, Pisco was arrested and tried by the audiencia for his role in the Comunero movement. A few of the key documents of the trial were published by Posada, *Los Comuneros,* pp. 434–43. Volume 14 of the Comunero collection in the AHN contains the complete documentation of the litigation. Hence my references will be to that collection.
9 Ambrosio Pisco to José Ignacio Ramírez, Cartagena, October 25, 1782, collection of Horacio Rodríguez Plata, in the Casa de la Cultura, Socorro.
10 AHN, Caciques y Indios, 26:1–10.
11 For some references to the Piscos as governors of Chía see ibid., ff. 955–57 (1709) and 49:197–214 (1734).
12 Filippo Salvatore Gilij, *Ensayo de historia americana, o sea la historia natural, civil y sacra de los reinos, y de las provincias de tierra firme en la América meridonal* (Bogotá, 1960), p. 231. Gilij was an Italian Jesuit who was in Bogotá between 1743 and 1749 before serving for many years in the Orinoco missions.
13 In the voluminous section of the AHN entitled Caciques y Indios, there are relatively few cases concerning disputed cacique successions.
14 For his succession see AHN, Caciques y Indios, 26:1–10.
15 He was born in Chía in 1737. Ibid., 26:1–10.
16 See Pisco confession, AHN, Los Comuneros, 14:28–35.
17 Ibid.
18 Testimony of Cabrera, ibid., ff. 10–14; Pisco confession, ibid., ff. 28–35.
19 Pisco's lawyer, December 19, 1781, ibid., ff. 39–42. For a published text of the letter see Posada, *Los Comuneros,* p. 440.
20 Fiscal to audiencia, October 16, 1781, AHN, Los Comuneros, 14:36–39. Pisco's lawyer admitted as much, ibid., ff. 39–42.
21 Ibid., ff. 28–42.
22 Calderón, *Elementos,* pp. 371–409.
23 AHN, Los Comuneros, 14:28–42.
24 Ibid., also AHN, Caciques y Indios, 26:1–10.
25 Such was the considered opinion of the archbishop: Caballero y Góngora to Gálvez, October 15, 1782, AGI/ASF 594. For other interpretations of Ambrosio Pisco that differ from mine in several respects see the following: CA, 1:286–88, 293–98, 2:92–93, 136–37, 223–24; Liévano Aguirre, *Los grandes conflictos,* pp. 470–73; Arciniegas, *Los Comuneros,* pp. 141–48. Only one violent riot occurred, in which several Indians lost their

lives, at Nemocón on September 1, several weeks after Zipaquirá. While that incident precipitated the audiencia's arrest and trial of Pisco three days later, Pisco was then in Bogotá and not in Nemocón. Nor did the audiencia accuse Pisco of any involvement in the riot. For the Nemocón riot see CA, 2:137–38.

26 Pisco's role at Zipaquirá will be chronicled in chapter 11. Chapter 13 contains a detailed analysis of the concessions granted to the Indians in the capitulations.

27 The Indian protest conformed in large measure to Eric J. Hobsbawm's model in *Primitive Rebels* (New York, 1963).

28 José Villalonga to Charles III, June 28, 1784, in Posada, *Los Comuneros,* pp. 425–30.

29 The principal primary sources are in AHN, Los Comuneros, 6:49–62.

30 Silvestre, *Santa Fe de Bogotá,* pp. 44–46.

31 José Manuel Groot, *Historia eclesiástica y civil de Nueva Granada,* 5 vols. (Bogotá, 1956), 2:128–46; Liévano Aguirre, *Los grandes conflictos,* pp. 315–22. The Jesuit historian Juan Manuel Pacheco's carefully documented *Los jesuitas en Colombia* has not yet arrived at the eighteenth century.

32 CA, 1:253.

33 Ibid., p. 252. Also see the full text of this letter in AHN, Los Comuneros, 6:53–56.

34 CA, 1:253.

35 Briceño, *Los Comuneros,* pp. 139–40. Cárdenas Acosta gives the date of the Silos manifesto as June 14, whereas Briceño identifies the date as May 24. Cárdenas Acosta's version of the Silos manifesto is much shorter than Briceño's text, "Que viva el rey de Inga y muera el rey de España y todo su mal gobierno y quien saliese a su defensa!" (CA, 2:92). This text is included in dispatch from Flores to Gálvez, December 31, 1781, AGI/ASF 577-B. The archival source for the Briceño text is in the Lilly Library, Indiana University.

36 Manuel de Mendiburu, *Diccionario histórico-biográfico del Perú,* 8 vols. (1874–90), 8:138; Fisher, *The Last Inca,* pp. 134–35.

37 Lewin, *Túpac Amaru,* pp. 425–29; Válcarcel, *Túpac Amaru,* pp. 176 ff.

38 See the proclamation of the captains of Socorro, June 18, 1781, attached to Flores to Gálvez, December 31, 1781, AGI/ASF 577-B.

39 Válcarcel, *Túpac Amaru,* pp. 176 ff.

40 The principal primary source consists of the trial of the ringleaders: AHN, Los Comuneros, 8:1–15, 292–439.

41 For some other examples in 1798 and in 1804 see Archivo Histórico del Departmento de Antioquia, vol. 332, docs. 6330, 6331. The other side of the coin is that tension and conflict intensified during the second half of the eighteenth century, when fugitive slaves set up several palenques. Jaramillo Uribe, "Esclavos y señores," pp. 38–40, 42–50.

Chapter 9
Confrontation at Puente Real de Vélez

1 Lewin, *Túpac Amaru,* p. 495.

2 CA, 2:327.

3 Osorio received his appointment in Spain on December 7, 1778, but did not take possession in Bogotá until January 25, 1781. Restrepo Saenz, *Biografías,* p. 384. Consulta, December 7, 1778, AGI/ASF 696.

4 Osorio to Gálvez, May 10, 1777 in Archivo del General Herrán 2-A, f. 20, Academia Colombiana de Historia (hereafter cited as Archivo Herrán); CA, 2:353.

5 Gálvez to Osorio, September 15, 1776, May 20, 1778; Osorio to Gálvez, May 10, 1777, November 25, 1778, in Archivo Herrán 2-A, ff. 1–10.

6 CA, 1:150.

7 Kuethe, "Military Reform," p. 107. Also see the discussion in chapter 10 of the battle of Pie de la Cuesta, where the royalists had some cavalry units and the Comuneros none. The former won the battle, but not the victory.

8 Ibid., pp. 106–7; CA, 1:151.

9 Informe of Joaquín de la Barrera, June 8, 1781. For the published text see CA, 1:191. For the archival reference see AGI/ASF 663-A.

10 For these letters of April 26 see the Archivo Herrán.

11 Osorio to villa de Leiva, April 27, 1781, May 2, 1781; Osorio to audiencia, July 17, 1781; the Diary of the expedition, all in Archivo Herrán. Barrera to audiencia, June 8, 1781, in CA, 1:186.

12 For a calendar of the riots see CA, 1:167–71.

13 Kuethe claims that only 500 men besieged Puente Real ("Military Reform," pp. 106–7). Five hundred men did leave Socorro, but they picked up hundreds of recruits along the way. Testimony of Salvador Plata, March 13, 1783, AHN, Los Comuneros, 18:345–405, #22; CA, 1:159; Osorio to Berbeo, June 30, 1781, and Diary (May 3) in the Archivo Herrán; Osorio to captains of Socorro, May 10, 1781, ibid. Filiberto José Estévez estimated that the Comunero army numbered around 4,000 men (see note 15, below).

14 CA, 1:201.

15 Estévez to Osorio, May 1, 1781, ibid., 1:164–65.

16 For Estévez's role as a courier between Berbeo and Caballero before Zipaquirá, see Estévez to Caballero y Góngora, May 20, 1781; Berbeo to Caballero y Góngora, May 31, 1781, and Berbeo to Estévez (no date, about June 1), AGI/ASF 663-A.

17 Barrera to audiencia, June 8, 1781, in CA, 1:186.

18 The correspondence is in the Archivo Herrán and in the AGI/ASF 663-A. For published texts see CA, 1:173, 175.

19 Osorio to audiencia, July 17, 1781, and Diary (May 8), Archivo Herrán.

20 Barrera to audiencia, June 8, 1781, in CA, 1:191; Diary (May 9), Archivo Herrán.

21 CA, 1:181.

22 Ibid., p. 197. The original is in the Archivo Herrán, f. 96.

23 Barrera to audiencia, June 8, 1781, in CA, 1:193–94.

24 Briceño, *Los Comuneros,* p. 31; Lewin, *Túpac Amaru,* pp. 679–81.

25 Although he hailed the Comuneros as precursors of independence, Cárdenas Acosta suggested that the Osorio coronation offer was made to create a rift in the Spanish camp. Yet he also cites the incident as evidence that the creoles aspired to independence, "consecuencialmente de manifesto la poca fidelidad que se profesaba al soberano español." CA, 1:184.

26 For the text of the proclamation see ibid., 1:138–39.

27 The hierarchy of officers consisted of *capitanes territoriales, tenientes, alféreces, sargentos,* and *cabos.* Clause 19 of the capitulations, ibid., 2:25.

28 The following account of the hierarchy and nomenclature of the council comes from ibid., 1:160–63, and Plata testimony, February, 1783?, Lilly Library, Indiana University, #180.

29 There are countless examples in AHN, Los Comuneros, 6. That volume contains a great deal of the correspondence exchanged between Socorro and the other parishes that joined the movement.

30 On the financing of the expedition see the following: testimony of Plata, March 13, 1783, ibid., 18:354–405, #4, and December 1, 1781, ibid., 6:97–131, #44; Ignasio Celi to Plata, May 31, 1781, ibid., f. 181; Molina to Plata, May 12, 1781, ibid., f. 192; Pey to Flores, June 5, 1781, AGI/ASF 577-B; testimony of Berbeo, September 14, 1781, in Briceño, *Los Comuneros,* pp. 215–16.

Chapter 10
A Non-Battle in Bogotá and the Invasion of Girón

1 CA, 1:196.

2 Minutes of the junta de tribunales, May 12, 1781, in AGI/ASF 663-A, hereafter cited as minutes of the junta.

3 Gutiérrez de Piñeres to Gálvez, June 21, 1781, AGI/ASF 662.

4 For a restrained articulation of this nightmare, see Caballero y Góngora to Gálvez, in CA, 2:60–61; AGI/ASF 633.

5 Minutes of the junta, May 12, 1781; CA, 1:207–8.

6 Rojas, *Corregidores,* pp. 569, 571, 595.

7 Minutes of the junta, May 12, 1781.

8 Ibid., May 14, 1781.

9 For the clerical population see Silvestre, *Descripción,* p. 31; minutes of the junta, May 13 and 14, 1781.

10 Minutes of the junta, May 15, 1781.

11 Ibid., CA, 1:211–12.

12 CA, 1:212–14.

13 Minutes of the junta, May 17, 1781.

14 Ibid., May 18, May 23, 1781.

15 An anonymous and contemporary account of events, favorable to the Comuneros, indicates that the reactivation of the militia calmed spirits in the capital and effectively reenforced royal authority. "Levantamiento de Santa Fe de Bogotá" in *Archivo del General Miranda,* 15:37–38.

16 Silvestre, *Descripción,* p. 46; Oviedo, *Cualidades,* pp. 183–84.

17 The key primary sources for the battle of Girón have been published in *BHA* 5 (1907):129–59. For the archival sources see AHN, Los Comuneros, 6:302–11; 7:80–102; 18:78–145, 407–29, 433–67; cabildo of Girón to Flores, May 9, 1781, AGI/ASF 577-B; CA, 1:221–26, 249–51.

18 *Archivo del General Miranda,* 15:31.

19 CA, 1:249.

Chapter 11
"War, War, On to Santa Fe"

1 CA, 1:233.

2 Osorio to captains of Socorro, May 10, 1781, Archivo Herrán 2-A.

3 The document was first published by Briceño, *Los Comuneros,* pp. 104–6.

4 CA, 1:128. Taking Salvador Plata's testimony as his basis, Cárdenas Acosta argued that the grand strategy of marching on the capital originated with Berbeo, but he ignored the internal evidence of the pasquinade. Ibid., 1:233.

5 Ibid., pp. 128, 130.

6 Ibid., p. 292.

7 García Olano inquest.

8 For the text of the letters see Briceño, *Los Comuneros,* pp. 100–104.

9 Flores's reply to Socorro's letter of June 20 is included as an appendix in Flores to Gálvez, August 22, 1781, AGI/ASF 577-B.

10 CA, 1:256–57.

11 According to Berbeo the author of this catchy phrase was Antonio Molina, a plebeian member of the supreme council of war. Berbeo testimony, September 14, 1781, in Briceño, *Los Comuneros,* p. 213.

12 CA, 1:257–58.

13 Ibid., pp. 293–94.

14 Minutes of the junta, June 1, AGI/ASF 663-A; Pisco to Fiscal Silvestre Martínez, June 2, 1781, ibid.; Catani to junta, June 3, ibid.; confession of Pisco, October 8–9, 1781, AHN, Los Comuneros, 14:28–35; Pisco's lawyer, December 19, 1781, ibid., ff. 39–42.

15 Confession of Pisco, AHN, Los Comuneros, 14:28–35, #20.

16 For the other sacerdotal intermediaries see Caballero y Góngora to Gálvez, June 20, 1781, AGI/ASF 663, in CA, 2:65. Also see ch. 9, note 16.

17 Caballero y Góngora to Pey y Ruíz, May 26, and commissioners to Pey, May 26, 27, 1781, AGI/ASF 663-A. On May 27 the junta said no, but after receiving Caballero y Góngora's letter of May 26 it gave a reluctant yes. Pey to Caballero y Góngora, May 27, to commissioners, May 28, ibid.
18 Berbeo to commissioners, May 28, ibid.
19 CA, 1:282–83; testimony of Pavón y Gallo.
20 CA, 1:274–75, 288–92.
21 Bolívar won the battle of Boyacá with an army of 2,850 soldiers. Camilo Riano, *La compaña libertadora de 1819* (Bogotá, 1969), pp. 270–72.
22 Silvestre, *Descripción,* p. 31.
23 Nos los Comunes to Berbeo, May 22, 1781, in Caballero y Góngora to Gálvez, August 19, 1781, AGI/ASF 633-A; Monsalve, Rosillo, Molina to Berbeo, May 23, 1781, ibid.
24 Commissioners to Pey, May 30, 1781, ibid. The archbishop subsequently accepted the explanation of Rosillo and Monsalve that pressure from the plebeians forced them to issue the threat. Caballero y Góngora to Gálvez, August 19, 1781, AGI/ASF 633.
25 For some examples see my *Kingdom of Quito,* pp. 314, 316.
26 CA, 1:299–300.
27 Caballero y Góngora to Pey y Ruíz, May 17, 1781, AGI/ASF 663-A.

Chapter 12
Rendezvous in Zipaquirá

1 Pey y Ruíz to Flores, June 5, 1781, AGI/ASF 663-A.
2 Minutes of the junta, June 1, 1781, ibid.
3 Caballero y Góngora to Gálvez, June 20, 1781, AGI/ASF 663; CA, 2:60–61.
4 CA, 1:61.
5 Ibid., p. 11.
6 Ibid., pp. 61–62.
7 Barrera to audiencia, June 8, 1781, ibid., 1:195; 2:12; AGI/ASF 663-A; commissioners to Pey, May 31, 1781, ibid.
8 Caballero y Góngora to Gálvez, June 20, 1781, in CA, 1:62; Caballero y Góngora to junta, June 6, 1781, AGI/ASF 663-A. That the archbishop was distributing presents in Zipaquirá was well known in Bogotá—see the anonymous "Relación verdadera de los hechos ocurridos en la sublevación de los pueblos, ciudades y villas," August 31, 1781, in *Proceso histórico del 20 de Julio* (Bogotá, 1960), p. 24. Caballero y Góngora candidly admitted that he continued to distribute his largesse to selected individuals in order to win their support throughout his term as viceroy: Caballero y Góngora to Floridablanca, March 26, 1789, AGI/ Estado 54.
9 Testimony of Pavón y Gallo.
10 Flores to Gálvez, August 22, 1781, AGI/ASF 577-B; Flores to Gutiérrez de Piñeres, May 18, ibid.

11 Gutiérrez de Piñeres to Flores, May 9, 1781, AGI/ASF 663-A.

12 Flores to Gálvez, August 22, 1781, AGI/ASF 577-B.

13 See the exchange of letters between Flores and Gutiérrez de Piñeres attached as appendices to ibid.

14 Ibid.; CA, 2:110–14.

15 Berbeo to Caballero y Góngora, May 31, 1781, AGI/ASF 663-A.

16 For the text of the letter see CA, 2:16–17.

17 Minutes of the junta, June 1, AGI/ASF 663-A.

18 Caballero y Góngora to Pey y Ruíz, June 4, 1781, ibid.

19 Berbeo's testimony, September 14, 1782, in Briceño, *Los Comuneros,* pp. 208–9; Testimony of Pavón y Gallo.

20 Ibid.; CA, 2:17–18.

21 Commissioners to Pey y Ruíz, June 5, 1781, AGI/ASF 663-A; Caballero y Góngora to Pey, June 6, ibid.; Caballero y Góngora to Gálvez, June 20, 1781, in CA, 2:62.

22 Minutes of the junta, June 6, 1781, AGI/ASF 663-A.

23 Caballero y Góngora's résumé is the only information available about the contents of the letter: Caballero y Góngora to the junta, June 6, 1781, ibid.; CA, 2:36.

24 Ibid. Berbeo to Caballero y Góngora, May 8, 1782, Lilly Library, Indiana University; Pey to Flores, June 5, 1781, AGI/ASF 663-A.

25 Caballero y Góngora to Gálvez, June 20, 1781, in CA, 1:62–63.

26 CA, 1:62–63; Caballero y Góngora to the junta, June 6, 1781, AGI/ASF 663-A.

27 Minutes of the junta, June 7, AGI/ASF 663-A. One of the commissioners at Zipaquirá, Eustaquio Galavis, allegedly issued some kind of secret protest against the capitulations on June 6 before the junta gave its official approval. In fact, Galavis's protest was not made until September 13, when Bogotá was conducting a full-scale counterrevolution against the Comuneros. Silvia M. Broadbent, "La 'protesta secreta' de Eustaquio Galavis revisada," *BHA* 56 (1969):657–66.

28 CA, 2:47–48.

29 Berbeo to Estévez, May 31, 1781, in minutes of the junta.

30 Caballero y Góngora to Pey, June 2, ibid.

31 Pey to Caballero y Góngora, June 4, ibid.

32 In addition to Briceño and Cárdenas Acosta, the following historians have interpreted the Comuneros as precursors or advocates of independence. Lewin, *Túpac Amaru;* Rodríguez Plata, *Los Comuneros;* Eugenio Ortega, "Informe," *BHA* 6 (1911):423–34; Manuel Carreño, ibid., pp. 361–86; Posada, *Los Comuneros.* Among those historians who have rejected the independence interpretation are the following: Liévano Aguirre, *Los grandes conflictos;* Galán, "Galán"; Raimundo Rivas, "Duda histórica," *BHA* 6 (1910):125–61; Groot, *Historia eclesiástica y civil;* Forero, *La primera república;* José Antonio de Plaza, *Memorias para la historia de Nueva Granada desde su descubrimiento* (Bogotá, 1850); Armando Gómez Latorre, *Enfoque social de la revolución comunera* (Bogotá, 1973); Jaime

Jaramillo Uribe, *El pensamiento colombiano en el siglo xix* (Bogotá, 1964); Orlando Fals Borda, *Subversión y cambio social* (2nd ed., Bogotá, 1968); Angel Camacho Baños, *Sublevación de los comuneros en el virreinato de Nueva Granada* (Seville, 1925); Jesús María Henao and Girardo Arrubla, *History of Colombia,* translated by J. Fred Rippy (Chapel Hill, 1958); *Obras completas de doctor Carlos Martínez Silva,* Gustavo Otero Muñoz and Luís Martínez Delgado, eds. (Bogotá, 1937), 8:203–14; Restrepo, *Historia de la revolución de Colombia.*

33 Liévano Aguirre has formulated the most reasoned articulation of this hypothesis. For somewhat more rhetorical and emotional expressions see the following: Arciniegas, *Los Comuneros;* Galán, "Galán"; Latorre, *Enfoque social;* José Fulgencio Gutiérrez, *Galán y los Comuneros* (Bucaramanga, 1939); Luís Torres Almeyda, *La rebelión de Galán, el Comunero* (Bucaramanga, 1961).

34 CA, 2:295–311.

35 Ibid., 2:225–60; Briceño, *Los Comuneros,* pp. 92–94, 218–43.

36 See my "La misión de Luis Vidalle a Londres: realidad y mito," *BHA,* in press.

37 One of the first to formulate the thesis of the "frustrated and betrayed social revolution" was Luís López de Mesa, *Escrutinio sociólogo de la historia Colombiana* (Bogotá, 1956). For an application of this hypothesis to the republican period see Fals Borda, *Subversión.*

38 Caballero y Góngora commented on the attitude of the Comuneros toward their Indian allies "de los indios a quienes miraban con desprecio." Caballero y Góngora to Gálvez, June 20, 1781, in CA, 2:61.

39 Caballero y Góngora to Pey y Ruíz, May 17, 1781, AGI/ASF 663-A.

40 Forero, *La primera república,* pp. 51–65.

41 Silvio Zavala, *Las instituciones jurídicas en la conquista de América* (Mexico, 1971), p. 105; José María Ots Capdequí, "El derecho de propiedad en nuestra legislación de Indias," *Anuario de historia del derecho español* 2 (1925):49–169.

Chapter 13
The Capitulations of Zipaquirá: Fiscal Aspects

1 Jaramillo Uribe, *El pensamiento colombiano,* pp. 114–19.

2 See my *Kingdom of Quito,* pp. 119–21.

3 Gómez Hoyos, *La revolución granadina,* 1:181–82.

4 Daniel Mornet, *Les origines intellectuelles de la révolution française* (Paris, 1967), pp. 452–65; George V. Taylor, "Revolutionary and Non-revolutionary Content in the Cahiers of 1789: An Interim Report," *French Historical Studies* 7 (1972):479–502.

5 For a convincing analysis of the indirect influence of the thought of Suárez on the tone and the spirit of the capitulations, see Gómez Hoyos, *La revolución granadina,* 1:183–85. Also see ch. 6, notes 9–17.

6 Cárdenas Acosta published the definitive text of the capitulations (CA, 2:18-19). For the whole text see ibid., pp. 18-29. The only note references for specific clauses henceforth will be for direct quotations, given in square brackets in the text. The text of the capitulations in Briceño, *Los Comuneros,* pp. 121-37, is a next-to-final draft, which has no substantive difference from the final text. There are, however, differences in language: the next-to-final draft employs harsher rhetoric on some occasions. Those differences will be noted when significant.

7 Confession of Ambrosio Pisco, October 8, 1781, AHN, Los Comuneros 14:28-35. For Indians' complaints about their resguardo lands addressed to Berbeo at Zipaquirá, see Quaderno de varias representaciones ante ... Berbeo, AGI/ASF 663.

8 For background on the salt mines see Calderón, *Elementos,* pp. 371-409.

9 Moreno to Flores, November 18, 1778, in González, *El resguardo,* pp. 144-45. By 1810 the Indian tribute tax earned for the royal treasury only 47,000 pesos out of total annual income of 2,453,096 pesos (Restrepo, *Historia de la revolución de Colombia,* 1:29).

10 For some examples of Indian complaints see AHN, Caciques y Indios, 58:891-996.

11 Colmenares is the only historian who mentions, if only briefly, this key sentence, in *Tunja,* pp. 209-10.

12 This aspect of the seventh clause apparently escaped the attention of the Peruvian ex-Jesuit Viscardo, when he praised the magnanimity and liberality of the creoles toward the Indians. Cárdenas Acosta somewhat uncritically cites Viscardo's words (CA, 2:54).

13 For the resguardos after 1781, see ch. 7, notes 12-19.

14 Jaramillo Uribe, *El pensamiento colombiano,* pp. 114-19.

15 Gutiérrez de Piñeres to Gálvez, June 3, 1781, AGI/ASF 662. For a similar statement also see Gómez Hoyos, *La revolución granadina,* 1:184.

16 For the armada de Barlovento and the alcabala sales taxes see ch. 2, notes 27-34. For background on the tobacco and aguardiente monopolies see ch. 2, notes 7-25.

17 The treasury annually derived from this tax a mere 12,000 pesos out of a total income of some 2,453,096 pesos (Restrepo, *Historia de la revolución de Colombia,* 1:29).

18 Briceño, *Los Comuneros,* p. 122.

19 See ch. 2, notes 37-40.

20 Stamped paper annually yielded 53,000 pesos, some 5,000 pesos more than the Indian tribute tax (Restrepo, *Historia de la revolución de Colombia,* 1:29).

21 Gómez Hoyos, *La revolución granadina,* 1:186-88; Victor Frankl, "La filosofía social Thomista del arzobispo virrey Caballero y Góngora y la de los Comuneros," *Bolívar* 14 (1952):597-626.

22 Gómez Hoyos, *La revolución granadina,* 1:186-87.

23 Briceño, *Los Comuneros,* p. 134.

24 Germán Colmenares, *Las haciendas de los jesuítas en el nuevo reino de Granada* (Bogotá, 1969), p. 29.
25 Gómez Hoyos, *La revolución granadina,* 1:194–196, stresses the Catholicism of the Comuneros, which is undeniable, but he ignores the resentment they felt toward what they regarded as excessive fees charged by the clergy. Complaints against the clergy continued after 1781. See Juan Manuel Pacheco, *La ilustración en el nuevo reino de Granada* (Caracas, 1975), p. 159.
26 Nancy M. Farriss, *Crown and Clergy in Colonial Mexico, 1759–1822: The Crisis of Ecclesiastical Privilege* (London, 1968).
27 For Gutiérrez de Piñeres's attempts to limit the privileges of the clergy see ch. 2, note 34.
28 This content analysis does not coincide precisely with the number of clauses of the capitulations—34. The majority of the clauses dealt with only one issue, but some did not: the seventh clause, for instance, contained four quite different concessions to the Indians and one to the freed blacks. In dealing with those two ethnic groups all those concessions which directly affected them in the category of the plebeians were counted—5 for the Indians and 6 for the freed blacks.
29 Liévano Aguirre, *Los grandes conflictos,* p. 480, stresses that Berbeo had to secure massive concessions for the plebeians in order to persuade them not to occupy the capital. It should be added that Caballero y Góngora followed the same policy of granting significant concessions to the plebeians.

Chapter 14
The First Written Constitution of New Granada

1 Biblioteca Nacional, Bogotá, Libros Raros y Curiosos, ms. 185. For data on Tunja see the following sources: Rojas, *Corregidores;* Cárdenas Acosta, *Del vasallaje;* Oviedo, *Cualidades,* pp. 119 ff.; Silvestre, *Santa Fe de Bogotá,* pp. 60–63.
2 Briceño, *Los Comuneros,* p. 135.
3 Viceroy Francisco Gil y Lemos to king, May 19, 1790, AGI/ASF 561.
4 For the ordinance of the audiencia see Briceño, *Los Comuneros,* pp. 183–87. One historian attempted to defend Berbeo against the charge of being avaricious on the grounds that he was wealthy (Rodríguez Plata, *Los Comuneros,* pp. 130–53). In fact, Berbeo was not rich (see ch. 4, notes 2–17). Another historian regards Berbeo's acceptance of the office as evidence of self-aggrandizement (Liévano Aguirre, *Los grandes conflictos,* pp. 490–91). I share neither view. Berbeo was a precursor of regional autonomy; in his attitudes one sees the genesis of subsequent federalism.
5 Rojas, *Corregidores,* pp. 606–7.

6 For the pertinent stanzas see CA, 1:121–22.

7 Fernando Guillén Martínez, *Raíz y futuro de la revolución* (Bogotá, 1963), and *El poder, los modelos estructurales del poder político en Colombia,* Centro de Investigaciones para el Desarrallo-CID, Universidad Nacional de Colombia, 1973, Xerox, pp. 92–112.

8 Solórzano y Pereira, *Política indiana,* bk. V, ch. i, #30, 37, 38, and 40.

9 This was an office that in many localities was purchased, but the custom in Socorro was for the alcaldes ordinarios to appoint the alcalde de la santa hermandad. See ibid., #18.

10 For a description of the functioning of the residencia and visita general see my *Kingdom of Quito,* pp. 215–18.

11 Rafael Gómez Hoyos published the 1771 Mexican manifesto in *BHA* 47 (1960):426–76. For the copy in the archives see AHN, Virreyes, 14:420–26. Also see Peggy K. Korn, "The Problem of the Roots of Revolution: Society and Intellectual Ferment in Mexico on the Eve of Independence," in Frederick B. Pike, *Latin American History: Select Problems* (New York, 1969), pp. 101–14.

12 Gómez Hoyos, *La revolución granadina,* 1:190.

13 Ibid., 2:7–44; Liévano Aguirre, *Los grandes conflictos,* pp. 583–87.

14 My discussion of the issue in *Kingdom of Quito,* p. 122, places its emphases incorrectly, I now believe.

15 Lázaro de Aspurz, O.F.M., *La aportación extranjera a las misiones españolas del patronato regio* (Madrid, 1946); Juan Manuel Pacheco, S.J., *Los jesuitas en Colombia,* 2 vols. (Bogotá, 1962), 2:199–205.

16 CA, 2:53; Gutiérrez de Piñeres to Flores, July 2, 1781, and appendix of Flores to Gálvez, August 22, 1781, AGI/ASF 577-B.

17 See chapter 18 for an extended discussion of the question of higher education—the lay university so heatedly discussed at the time. This is the only major issue confronting New Granada that did not appear in the capitulations.

Chapter 15
José Antonio Galán: Myth and Fact

1 Briceño, *Los Comuneros,* pp. 36–40 and 76–84, was one of the first historians to view Galán as a hero. In Santander itself, until the late nineteenth century the patriotic heroes extolled in the regional newspapers were not Bolívar and Santander as much as the Comuneros, in particular, Galán (David Johnson, pers. comm.).

2 In his confession of October 9, 1781, Galán gave his age as 32 (Briceño, *Los Comuneros,* p. 168). Gómez Rodríguez, "La cuna," 1, ch. 7, has located his certificate of baptism.

3 For his wedding certificate see Gómez Rodríguez, "Datos," pp. 105–6.

4 Germán Arciniegas's portrait of him (*Los Comuneros,* p. 130) is the

product of that great writer's imagination. Pablo E. Cárdenas Acosta, *Los Comuneros* (Bogotá, 1945), pp. 169–70.
5 Torres Almeyda, *La rebelión de Galán,* pp. 17–32.
6 Gutiérrez, *Galán,* p. 230.
7 Galán confession in Briceño, *Los Comuneros,* p. 168. For an example of his signature see AHN, Los Comuneros, 18:212.
8 Gómez Rodríguez, "La cuna," ch. 7. See also note 16 below.
9 Constancio Franco Vargas, *Galán, el Comunero* (Bogotá, 1891). The voluminous criminal files of the audiencia reveal no trace of any litigation involving Galán. Not all the Galanista historians accepted the Franco fable. Gutiérrez, *Galán,* has a sensible critique, pp. 235–37. Arciniegas, *Los Comuneros* (1938 ed., pp. 187–88), originally accepted the story but in the 1968 edition he sensibly eliminated all reference to it. Cárdenas Acosta, *Los Comuneros,* pp. 170–71, assailed the Franco account as a myth, but he provided no analysis. Angel Galán, "Galán," does not mention the incident. Among those who have repeated the Franco myth are Torres Almeyda, *La rebelión de Galán,* pp. 61–63, and Gómez Latorre, *Enfoque social,* pp. 242–43.
10 CA, 2:176.
11 Such was the somewhat harsh observation of Oviedo, circa 1761, *Cualidades,* pp. 174–82.
12 For this incident, see ch. 9, note 20. The charge comes from government sources, but the claim seems credible. Commissioners to Pey, May 20, 24, 1781, AGI/ASF 633-A. This news was confirmed by the usually well-informed pastor of Oiba, Filiberto José Estévez, writing to Caballero y Góngora, May 24, 1781, ibid., and CA, 1:265. Estévez claimed that Galviño confiscated a good deal of money which was in Galán's possession.
13 CA, 2:176.
14 For the text of his formal appointment see Briceño, *Los Comuneros,* pp. 38–39, and CA, 1:266–68.
15 CA, 1:283–85; commissioners to Pey, May 29, 1781; Pey to commissioners, May 29; commissioners to Pey, May 30; minutes of the junta, June 1; junta to Caballero y Góngora, June 1; commissioners to Pey, June 1; Pey to Flores, June 5; all in AGI/ASF 663-A.
16 Galán to García Olano, May 30, 1781, ibid. Also see García Olano inquest. This letter clearly implies that Galán's stay in Socorro extended into 1777, when García Olano was administrator of the tobacco monopoly.
17 García Olano inquest.
18 Ibid.; Minutes of the junta, May 29, May 30, and June 1, AGI/ASF 663-A.
19 For the text of the letter see CA, 2:80–81.
20 Ibid., p. 82–83. A manuscript copy is in the minutes of the junta.
21 CA, 2:80–89.

22 Gómez Latorre, *Enfoque social,* p. 247. Since the Galán letters were not published by Cárdenas Acosta until 1960, the accounts prior to that date obviously do not discuss the incident. They are Galán, Gutiérrez, and Arciniegas. For another superficial explanation see Zárate Francisco Posada, *El movimiento revolucionario de los Comuneros* (Bogotá, 1971), p. 98. Liévano Aguirre, *Los grandes conflictos,* pp. 491–92, who portrays Galán as a precursor of social revolution, ignores the incident. There are no surviving written instructions from Berbeo to Galán. The supreme commander probably had the good sense not to put anything in writing, but Galán's words reveal Berbeo's intent.

23 Torres Almeyda, *La rebelión de Galán,* pp. 183–86.

24 Gutiérrez de Piñeres to Gálvez, July 6, August 27, October 20, 1781, AGI/ASF 662. Gutiérrez de Piñeres sent copies of the Galán letters to the authorities, but he did not mention them in his correspondence.

25 CA, 2:88–89.

26 Arciniegas, *Los Comuneros,* pp. 132–33; Torres Almeyda, *La rebelión de Galán,* pp. 64–69.

27 For the population of Mariquita see Silvestre, *Santa Fe de Bogotá,* pp. 59–60; for Antioquia, ibid., p. 57.

28 CA, 2:98.

29 Ibid., pp. 87–88; Tello de Meneses to Flores, July 7, 1781, AHN, Los Comuneros, 6:128–29.

30 CA, 2:95–96.

31 For the text of Nieto's letter to Angulo y Olarte, October 21, 1781, see ibid., p. 106.

32 Ibid., p. 105.

33 Ibid., pp. 93–101; Tello de Meneses to audiencia, June 19, 1781, AHN, Los Comuneros, 3:39–40; Juan Blas de Aranzazu to audiencia, June 21, 1781, ibid., 3:134–38.

34 Ibid.

35 For the route of the Bernet expedition and the force sent by Flores see CA, 2:112, 113–14.

36 Ibid., p. 114.

37 For the edict of the audiencia, July 14, 1781, see ibid., p. 115.

38 For this and the succeeding incidents of Galán's return see ibid., pp. 107, 114.

39 As quoted in Peter H. Smith, "Political Legitimacy in Spanish America," Richard Graham and Peter H. Smith, eds., *New Approaches to Latin American History* (Austin, 1974), p. 234; Max Weber, *The Theory of Social and Economic Organization,* Talcott Parsons, ed. (New York, 1964), pp. 324–423. For the charismatic aspects in the Spanish American colonial system see my *Kingdom of Quito,* pp. 320–23.

40 Constancio Franco Vargas, *Galán, el Comunero,* p. 59, was perhaps the first person to coin the phrase, *unión de los oprimidos contra los opresores.* He attributes it to Galán, but he provides no proof. Torres

Almeyda, *La rebelión de Galán,* pp. 330–37, does not claim that Galán was the author, but he argues that the phrase aptly summarizes his goals.
41 CA, 2:175–76.

Chapter 16
The Second Enterprise against Santa Fe

1 Caballero y Góngora to Gálvez in CA, 2:61.
2 Ibid., 2:145.
3 Ibid., 2:136–38; Bernet to Flores, September 8, 1781, Lilly Library, Indiana University.
4 CA, 2:136–38.
5 Caballero y Góngora to Flores, September 14, 1781, AGI/ASF 577-B. Flores committed this tactical blunder, which Caballero y Góngora rectified, under pressure from Gutiérrez de Piñeres. See Gutiérrez de Piñeres to Flores, July 6, 1781, AGI/ASF 662.
6 Salvador Plata to Flores, December 31, 1781, AGI/ASF 577-B.
7 Caballero y Góngora to Flores, September 14, 1781, ibid.
8 Confession of Gálan, October 18, 1781, in Briceño, *Los Comuneros,* pp. 168–69.
9 Cárdenas Acosta, *Los Comuneros,* pp. 293–94.
10 Briceño, *Los Comuneros,* pp. 156–57.
11 Parochial archive, Socorro, IX-A, 163–64. Copy lent to me by Ramiro Gómez Rodríguez.
12 CA, 2:151.
13 Torres Almeyda, *La rebelión de Galán,* pp. 334–35. A militant defender of Galán, he argues that the man from Charalá wanted the support of both the elites and the others, ibid., pp. 103–4.
14 Molina to Galán, September 14, 1781, in Briceño, *Los Comuneros,* p. 154; confession of Isidro Molina, October 20, 1781, AHN, Los Comuneros, 5:271–79; confession of Manuel Ortíz, November 14, 1781, ibid., pp. 280–86; CA, 2:150.
15 Salvador Plata, who hated the Ardila clan, tried to implicate them with Galán. Plata testimony, no date, Lilly Library, Indiana University, #193–207. Several members of the Ardila clan signed the anti-Galán statement (see note 11).
16 Galán confession, Briceño, *Los Comuneros,* p. 169.
17 Ibid., p. 170.
18 CA, 2:153.
19 Ibid.
20 Ibid.; Plata testimony, December 1, 1781, AHN, Los Comuneros, 6:97–131, and March 13, 1783, ibid., 18:354–405; Plata testimony, Lilly Library. All three contain lengthy accounts of the expedition.
21 As translated from Arciniegas, *Los Comuneros,* p. 235. Arciniegas chides

Caballero y Góngora for "practicando a su manera la fórmula cristiana de que ignore su izquierda lo que haga su derecha." For a somewhat naive defense of Caballero y Góngora see Gutiérrez, *Galán,* pp. 280–81. Also See Caballero y Góngora to Gálvez, February 9, 1782, AGI/ASF 594.

22 CA, 2:155–60.

23 See AHN, Los Comuneros, 4:269–70, 287–88; 5:295–99; 10:77–82, 154–61, for some examples. For Zapata y Porras's brilliant defense of José Antonio's brother Juan Nepomuceno, see ibid., 4:388–406. The key documents that we lack in José Antonio's trial are: (1) the charges and evidence submitted by the prosecution; (2) José Antonio's rebuttal; and (3) his counsel's defense. For his confession, taken in Socorro on October 18, 1781, see Briceño, *Los Comuneros,* pp. 167–75.

24 For the text of the sentence see CA, 2:175–80. Subsequent quotations all from this source.

25 AHN, Los Comuneros, 18:322–38.

26 José Toribio Medina, *La imprenta en Bogotá* (Santiago de Chile, 1904), p. 29.

27 Vincente Diago admitted that Galán had returned the bulk but not all the jewels. He sued for the recovery of the remaining ones. AHN, Los Comuneros, 18:217–25.

28 For the text of the letter see the García Olano inquest.

29 The late Francisco Posada in his brief but sophisticated Marxist interpretation claims that Galán stood for drastic changes in labor and production. But he makes his case rather unconvincing by confessing that Galán never defined in his own mind what social changes he advocated (*Los Comuneros,* pp. 77–78, 149–53).

30 See his confession in Briceño, *Los Comuneros,* p. 169.

31 Some of the pro-Galanista historians are vitriolic critics of Juan Francisco Berbeo. The most notable example is Arciniegas. Both Liévano Aguirre and Francisco Posada, less rhetorical and more reasoned defenders, extol Galán without denying Berbeo's qualities of leadership. Posada, *Los Comuneros,* pp. 133–41; Liévano Aguirre, *Los grandes conflictos,* pp. 467–88.

Chapter 17
The Reconquest of Socorro from Its "Infidelity"

1 For background on the Capuchins, see Antonio de Alcacer, *La Capuchina, iglesia y convento de capuchinos en Santa Fe de Bogotá* (Puente del Común, 1959) and *Las misiones capuchinas en el nuevo reino de Granada* (Puente del Común, 1959).

2 Richard Herr, *The Eighteenth Century Revolution in Spain* (Princeton, 1958), pp. 11–36.

3 Alcacer, *Las misiones,* p. 252.

4 Caballero y Góngora to Gálvez, July 31, 1783, AGI/ASF 600.

5 Finestrad to Valensuela, June 8, 1786, AHN, Los Comuneros, 17: 112–27; Alcacer, *La Capuchina,* pp. 86–87.

6 Finestrad, *El vasallo instruído,* p. 6. In the published edition Posada did not include the last four chapters "por carecer de importancia histórica," p. 204. These chapters, however, are the most revealing about ideology. The unpublished version will hereafter be cited as Finestrad ms. The manuscript is vol. 198 of the manuscript collection in the rare book room of the Biblioteca Nacional in Bogotá.

7 Finestrad ms., pp. 297, 401.

8 Ibid., p. 365. Victor Frankl has correctly pointed out that the paternal image to justify obedience, which was congenial to Finestrad as well as Caballero y Góngora, was characteristic of Spanish political theory in the seventeenth century: "La estructura barroca del pensamiento político, histórico y económico del arzobispo-virrey Antonio Caballero y Góngora," *Bolívar* 5 (1951):822–33. True enough, but it should also be pointed out that a principal goal of the Caroline state, in contrast to that of the Habsburgs, was to promote economic change energetically in order to increase royal revenues.

9 Finestrad, *El vasallo instruído,* pp. 153–54.

10 Bossuet's works had been well known at the University of Valencia, where Finestrad was educated, since the middle of the eighteenth century. Herr, *Eighteenth Century Revolution,* pp. 26–27.

11 Many of these were Jesuits, whom by royal decree it was forbidden to cite. Finestrad ms., pp. 464, 484–85; Gómez Hoyos, *La revolución granadina,* 1:197–202.

12 Finestrad, *El vasallo instruído,* pp. 156–57.

13 Finestrad ms., p. 289.

14 Ibid., pp. 297, 410–11.

15 Ibid., p. 285.

16 Ibid., pp. 229–30, 414 ff.

17 Ibid., p. 417.

18 Ibid., pp. 413, 415, 421–43.

19 Ibid., p. 463.

20 Ibid., pp. 476–77.

21 The title of ch. 11, ibid.

22 Ibid., p. 326.

23 Elagabulus (218–22 A.D.) was a Roman emperor celebrated for his cupidity and lust. Ibid., p. 320.

24 Finestrad, *El vasallo instruído,* pp. 113 ff.

25 For the text of the poem see CA, 2:173–75. After Caballero y Góngora was named proprietary viceroy, Finestrad organized in Socorro an elaborate series of secular and religious ceremonies that lasted for 15 days. For a description of the fiestas see *Colección,* 1:12–21.

26 Alcalde of Vélez to audiencia, November 15, 1781, AHN, Los Comuneros, 5:115–17.

27 Pastor of Chiquinquirá to audiencia, December 7, 1781, ibid., ff. 265–69, and March 28, 1782, ibid., 11:282.

28 CA, 2:163–65.

29 For some examples see declaration of Francisco Rosillo, November 3, 1781, AHN, Los Comuneros, 5:5–14.

30 Caballero y Góngora to Gálvez, February 6, 1783, CR and AGI/ASF 663; Charles III to Caballero y Góngora, January 2, 1782, ibid.

31 Berbeo to Flores, November 26, 1781, AGI/ASF 577-B; CA, 2:193.

32 Finestrad to Caballero y Góngora, September 16, 1782, attached to Caballero y Góngora to Gálvez, October 15, 1782, AGI/ASF 594.

33 Angulo y Olarte to Caballero y Góngora, February 21, 1782, and Filiberto José Estévez to Caballero y Góngora, March 4, 1782, in CA, 2:191–92.

34 Cabildo of Socorro to Charles III, September 20, 1781, AHN, Los Comuneros, 4:191–99.

35 For a host of such resignations see ibid., ff. 136–40, 262–63.

36 Ordinance of the audiencia, December 24, 1781, AGI/ASF 594.

37 Cabildo of Socorro to Flores, November 19, 1781, AHN, Los Comuneros, 5:135–37.

38 For the text of this pastoral letter (September 25, 1782) see Caballero y Góngora to Gálvez, October 15, 1782, AGI/ASF 594.

39 Caballero y Góngora to Finestrad, AHN, Los Comuneros, 12:283–85.

40 Ibid., 13:116–29.

41 Cabildo of Socorro to Caballero y Góngora, December 6, 12, 1782, ibid., 13:83, 85–86, 106; 15:139–40.

42 For the request of 1776 see Archivo Provincial Franciscano de Bogotá, 5:407–24.

43 "Our royal decree" had predicted that the Capuchin friars and not the Franciscans would be sent to "pacify" Socorro. See stanza 38 in CA, 2:129.

44 For the founding and a brief history of the Capuchin monastery see Ramiro Gómez Rodríguez, "La cuna," ch. 8, and Rodríguez Plata, *La antigua provincia del Socorro y la independencia* (Bogotá, 1963), pp. 245–47.

Chapter 18
The Carrot and the Stick

1 AHN, Los Comuneros, 4:162. Flores acted in response to the prodding of Gutiérrez de Piñeres. Gutiérrez de Piñeres to Gálvez, July 28, 1781, AGI/ASF 662.

2 Gutiérrez de Piñeres to Gálvez, February 28, 1782, AGI/ASF 661.

3 Gálvez to Caballero y Góngora, January 21, 1782, AGI/ASF 633.

4 CA, 2:194–97.

5 Ibid., pp. 194–202.

6 Caballero y Góngora to Gálvez, June 19, 1782, AGI/ASF 594, and January 31, 1783, AGI/ASF 736-A. Gutiérrez de Piñeres sided with Caballero y Góngora: Gutiérrez de Piñeres to Gálvez, June 20, 1782, AGI/ASF 658.

7 Michael Flamingo, "Viceregal Recruitment Patterns in the Spanish-American Colonies," seminar paper for Professor Peter H. Smith, fall of 1971, University of Wisconsin–Madison.

8 Gálvez to Caballero y Góngora, AHN, Los Comuneros, 12:172; Charles III to Caballero y Góngora, April 7, 1783, AGI/ASF 633.

9 Caballero y Góngora to Gálvez, January 31, 1783, AGI/ASF 736-A.

10 See marginal comment of king, June 12, 1783, ibid. The cedulas were issued four days later on June 16 (ibid.).

11 Caballero y Góngora to Gálvez, October 15, 1782, AGI/ASF 594. This letter makes it clear that the archbishop and not the king was the author of this policy. Cárdenas Acosta quite correctly criticizes Arciniegas for arguing that the policy originated in Spain (*Los Comuneros*, pp. 195–200). The pardon was printed on the new printing press. For a copy see AHN, Los Comuneros, 12:46–56. For a more accessible copy see CA, 2: 205–17.

12 García Olano inquest. For samples of García Olano's sympathy for the Comuneros see CA, 2:219–20. Also see my "García Olano."

13 Caballero y Góngora to Gálvez, February 6, 1783, AGI/ASF 736-A.

14 CA, 2:219; Caballero y Góngora to Gálvez, January 31, 1783, AGI/ASF 736-A. Cárdenas Acosta apparently did not see another letter of Caballero y Góngora to Gálvez, October 31, 1783, AGI/ASF 663.

15 Caballero y Góngora to Gálvez, June 20, 1782, in CA, 2:221.

16 Caballero y Góngora to Gálvez, October 15, 1782, AGI/ASF 594.

17 Ariza, *Fray Ciriaco de Archila*, p. 43.

18 For don Jorge's feuds with the audiencia see his letter to the king, October 31, 1785, British Libraries 1, Egerton 807, ff. 604–8. See also Ariza, *Fray Ciriaco de Archila*, p. 32, and CA, 1:135. My analysis disagrees with that of Raimundo Rivas, who argues that don Jorge's punishment had nothing whatsoever to do with his role in 1781: "El marqués de San Jorge," *BHA* 6 (1911):721–50.

19 Caballero y Góngora to Gálvez, May 31, 1783, AGI/ASF 600; to Floridablanca, January 31, 1783, AGI/ASF 736-A. García Olano was originally sentenced to exile in Spain, but the sentence was subsequently reduced to exile in Cartagena: AHN, Juicios Criminales, 183:154–58.

20 Caballero y Góngora to Floridablanca, January 31, 1783, AGI/ASF 736-A. Indicative of the crown's desire to conciliate the creole elites was the decision of the council of the Indies to allow the former marquis's son to resume the title in 1787. See Rivas, "El marqués de San Jorge," pp. 749–50. Caballero y Góngora refused the marquis's request for a high military post in the reorganized militia, but he granted a commission to

his son, whom he did not distrust: Caballero y Góngora to Gálvez, April 30, 1785, AGI/ASF 603. For another expression of Caballero's awareness of the need to conciliate the creole bureaucratic establishment see Caballero y Góngora to Gálvez, October 31, 1783, AGI/663. For the return of the creoles to office in the reign of Charles IV see ch. 1, note 26. Another indication of the revival of the creoles was the audiencia's interim appointment on December 19, 1781, of Eustaquio Galavis y Hurtado as corregidor of Tunja. His proprietary appointment was enthusiastically recommended by Caballero y Góngora: Rojas, *Corregidores,* pp. 571, 573.

21 Restrepo Saenz, *Biográfias,* pp. 388–93.

22 CA, 2:208.

23 Ibid., p. 209.

24 Pérez Ayala, *Caballero y Góngora,* p. 7.

25 CA, 2:213.

26 The crisis of 1781 was Caballero y Góngora's explanation for not introducing the intendant system to New Granada. See his Relación de Mando (February 20, 1789) in Pérez Ayala, *Caballero y Góngora,* p. 371 (hereafter cited as Relación de Mando). Also see my *Kingdom of Quito,* pp. 174–75, and Lillian Estelle Fisher, *The Intendant System in Spanish America* (Berkeley, 1929). The most thoughtful and best-documented study of the intendant system is that of Lynch, *Spanish Colonial Administration.* Also see Navarro García, *Intendencias de Indias;* J. R. Fisher, *Colonial Peru.* For a recent and stimulating study see Horst Pietschmann, *Die Einführung des Intendantensystems in Neu-Spanien im Rahmen der allgemeinen Verwaltungsreform der spanischen Monarchie im 18 Jahrhundert* (Cologne, 1972). When Flores was viceroy in Mexico from 1787 until 1789, he was hostile to the intendant system: Brading, *Miners and Merchants,* p. 33.

27 For the treasury statistics see Restrepo, *Historia de la revolución de Colombia,* 1:29. Francisco Antonio Moreno y Escandón, "El estado del virreinato de Santa Fe, 1772," *BHA* 23 (1936):605.

28 Caballero y Góngora to Gálvez, October 15, 1782, AGI/ASF 594; Victor Frankl, "Estructura barroco," has persuasively argued that Caballero y Góngora was a disciple of the baroque concept of "reason of state" which held that governments can break any law—positive, natural, or even divine—if the safety and welfare of the state is in danger. Although I respect his erudition, I cannot agree with his principal thesis; Caballero's style may have been that of the seventeenth-century Habsburgs but the content of his policies was Caroline in spirit.

29 Gutiérrez de Piñeres to Gálvez, July 31, 1782; August 31, 1782, AGI/ASF 658. In his Relación de Mando, pp. 298–307, Caballero y Góngora goes out of his way to praise the accomplishments and diplomatic manner of Viceroy Flores. He tactfully implied that the crisis of 1781 was precipitated to some extent by the intransigent and undiplomatic tactics of Gutiérrez de Piñeres.

30 Gutiérrez de Piñeres to Gálvez, January 31, 1781, AGI/ASF 736-A. Those same magistrates had been the principal critics of Gutiérrez de Piñeres. For that controversy see the following: Minutes of the junta, July 9, 1781, AGI/ASF 663-A, and junta to Charles III, July 31, 1781, AGI/ASF 662. For the regent's reply see Gutiérrez de Piñeres to Gálvez, August 27, 1781, ibid. This voluminous memorandum consisted of some 48 folios divided into 26 chapters which he entitled *Reflexiones.* See also Charles III to Gutiérrez de Piñeres, March 18, 1782, ibid.

31 Gutiérrez de Piñeres to Gálvez, January 15, 1783, AGI/ASF 658.

32 Archivo General de Simancas, Sección XXIII (Dirección General de Tesoro), Inventario 13, legajo 9, doc. 122. Samuel Chandler kindly supplied this citation.

33 CA, 2:209.

34 For the Campillo-Ward program see Ward, *Proyecto económico,* pp. 225–319. Caballero y Góngora's program of economic development is most articulately spelled out in his Relación de Mando, pp. 315–22, 327–62.

35 Cruz Santos, *Económia,* 1:124–25.

36 Toribio Medina, *La imprenta,* pp. 30–31.

37 Robert Jones Smith, *The Economic Societies in the Spanish World, 1763–1821* (Syracuse, 1958), pp. 154–56, 235–36.

38 Kathleen Romoli, *Colombia, Gateway to South America* (Garden City, 1944), p. 72. Also see Diego Mendoza, *Expedición botánica de José Celestino Mutis al nuevo reino de Granada* (Madrid, 1909). Pérez Ayala, *Caballero y Góngora,* pp. 145–50, 341–42. For some basic primary sources see Guillermo Hernández de Alba, *Archivo epistolar del sabio naturalista José Celestino Mutis,* 2 vols. (Bogotá, 1947–49). For a succinct bibliography see Pacheco, *La ilustración,* p. 15, note 41.

39 Relación de Mando, pp. 345–53. For an explanation of this failure see Arthur P. Whitaker, "The Elhuyar Mining Missions and the Enlightenment," *Hispanic American Historical Review* 31 (1931):557–85.

40 Relación de Mando, p. 341.

41 Perhaps the most comprehensive synthesis of the educational controversy is provided by the classic publications of Guillermo Hernández de Alba, among them *Aspectos de la cultura en Colombia* (Bogotá, 1947), pp. 117–27, 132–74, and *Crónica del muy ilustre colegio mayor de Nuestra Señora del Rosario,* 2 vols. (Bogotá, 1950), 2:87–96, 127–37, 141–53, 157–65, and 187–91. For a succinct and recent summary see Pacheco, *La ilustración,* pp. 104–22. Also containing useful information but somewhat biased in favor of the Dominicans are José Abel Salazar, *Los estudios eclesiásticos superiores en el nuevo reino de Granada, 1563–1810* (Madrid, 1946), pp. 401–56, 532–625; Agueda María Rodríguez Cruz, O.P., *Historia de las universidades hispano-americanas,* 2 vols. (Bogotá, 1973), 1:383–88; Gómez Hoyos, *La revolución granadina,* 1:319–22, 325–30. Also see Frank Safford, *The Ideal of the Practical: Colombia's*

Struggle to Form a Technical Elite (Austin, 1976), pp. 86–97. For some key primary sources see Carlos Restrepo Canal, "Documentos del archivo nacional," *BHA* 24 (1937): 332–71; AHN, Colegios, 2:264–337, 710–96; 4:893–901; AHN, Instrucción Pública, 2:38 ff.

42 Relación de Mando, pp. 339–41.

43 Ibid., pp. 165–66.

44 Hernández de Alba, *Crónica,* 2:224.

45 Relación de Mando, p. 339.

46 Ibid., pp. 339–40.

47 Salazar, *Estudios,* p. 453.

48 For the text of plan see Pérez Ayala, *Caballero y Góngora,* pp. 267–83.

49 Ibid., p. 340.

50 Ibid., p. 166. The relationship between this intellectual revolution and independence will be explored in the next chapter.

51 Gutiérrez de Piñeres to Gálvez, March 31, 1780, AGI/Audiencia de Quito 574.

52 Pérez Ayala, *Caballero y Góngora,* p. 380. Also see Caballero y Góngora to Gálvez, May 29, 1782, AGI/Audiencia de Quito 574.

53 For the military statistics see Kuethe, "Military Reform," chs. 4 and 7.

54 Ibid., ch. 7.

55 Pérez Ayala, *Caballero y Góngora,* pp. 187–94, 197–201, 285–96.

56 For a partial list of his alms see ibid., pp. 160–62. Both ecclesiastical establishments and many laymen received offerings from the archbishop in order to repair their homes. Several among them belonged to elite creole families such as the Ricaurtes, Caicedos, Alvarezes, Casals, and Vélezes. Caballero y Góngora to Gil y Lemos, May 15, 1789, AGI, Estado 54.

57 Caballero y Góngora to Floridablanca, March 26, 1789, ibid. All the material concerning his debts is in this legajo.

Chapter 19
Caballero y Góngora and the Independence of Colombia

1 For some examples see my *Kingdom of Quito,* pp. 66–85, and my *Hispanization of the Philippines: Spanish Aims and Filipino Responses, 1565–1700* (Madison, 1959), pp. 93–120.

2 See his Relación de Mando, pp. 298–307.

3 Harrison, "The Evolution of the Colombia Tobacco Trade," 163–74.

4 McGreevey, *Colombia,* pp. 19–48.

5 For his career as bishop of Córdova see Pérez Ayala, *Caballero y Góngora,* pp. 203–38.

6 Smith, "Political Legitimacy," in *New Approaches to Latin American History,* p. 238.

7 For a stimulating analysis of the goals of Núñez see Indalecio Liévano Aguirre, *Rafael Núñez* (Bogotá, 1944), pp. 168–81.

8 Smith, "Political Legitimacy," pp. 229–55.
9 For a more extended analysis of the rather complex character of traditional legitimacy in the Spanish Empire see my *Kingdom of Quito*, pp. 320–37.
10 Such an argument was forcefully presented to me by Frank Safford in a personal conversation.
11 Pérez Ayala, *Caballero y Góngora*, pp. 243–47.

Index

293

aspect of, 4; resistance to changes of, 6; and viceroys, 6, 7; and Habsburgs, 6, 237; technocrats, 7; and creoles, 10; and bureaucracy, 16; goals of, 17, 18, 230; and Colbert, 23; and hereditary privilege, 98; and the "unwritten constitution," 134, 135; and capitulations of Zipaquirá, 155, 159; colonies and the metropolis, 157; and taxes, 163; and clergy, 170, 236; in Mexico, 171; defensive modernization, 186; patriotism, 215; fiscal program, 230; and royal revenues, 230; and higher education, 235; and military, 236; and centralized monarchy, 237; and economic development, 243, 285*n8*; enlightened despotism, 244

Cartagena: 22, 24, 26, 31, 34, 52, 70, 101, 114, 123, 126, 127, 128, 132, 135, 142–46, 172, 185, 190, 194, 195, 197, 201, 208, 213, 218, 223, 226, 227, 237

Casal, María Josefa del, 14

Casal y Montenegro, Benito, 11, 181

Casanare, 22

Castile: crown of, 3, 157, 183; Comuneros of, 87; mentioned, 84, 88, 103, 156, 181

Castillo de Bobadilla, Jerónimo de, 85

Castro, Alfonso de, 85

Casuistry, 158

Catani, Pedro: and junta de tribunales, 122; and internal subversion, 126; and military, 126–27; success of, 127; and García Olano, 192; transfer of, 225, 231; and Gutiérrez de Piñeres, 231; and Caballero y Góngora, 231

Cauca Valley, 22

Cédulas. *See* Royal legislation

Cepita, 44

Chanchón, 42, 54

Chandler, D. S., 10

Charalá, 21, 22, 41–45 passim, 116, 189, 190, 196–98 passim, 203, 209, 219, 228

Charcas, 10

Charles II, 13, 24

Charles III: demanded obedience to authority, xviii; goals of, xviii, 18, 84, 237; and subjects, xviii, 243–44; lesson from Comuneros, xix; as King of the Two Sicilies, 4; and riots of 1766, 4; advantage over predecessors, 4; innovations of, 4, 84, 229; and sale of judicial offices, 9–10; and creoles, 10, 11, 71, 227, 287*n20*; unitary state, 10–11, 185, 239; and the "unwritten constitution," 17; political revolution of, 17, 84, 123, 185; and tobacco monopoly, 19, 20, 83; and taxation, 20, 29, 81, 163, 230, 237; and Flores reorganization, 22; and intendancy units, 23, 229; forced loans, 28–29; and representative assemblies, 35; and nuestra cédula, 77; and the cabildo, 82; ministers of, and common good, 87, 88; Indian policy, 89, 93; and the Silos manifesto, 106; on colonies and metropolis, 183; and Italian-born ministers, 184; and citizens' militia, 185; and Viceroy Flores, 223; and Caballero y Góngora, 224; modernization of Spanish empire, 232; neomercantilist program, 237; political concessions, 240; suspensive veto, 240; enlightened despotism, 243

Charles V: Comunero revolt against, in 1521, 87; mentioned, 10, 35

Chía, 101

Chibchas: preconquest, 89; and forced labor, 90; and Ambrosio Pisco, 99, 103; mentioned, 43, 101, 138

Chile, 10, 109

Chima, 41, 45, 116, 204

Chiquinquirá: bridge at, and capitulations of Zipaquirá, 167; loyalty to king, 203; mentioned, 48, 63, 73, 139, 143, 197, 208, 217

Chire, 105

Chochos, 54

Church, 170–71. *See also* Clergy

Ciriaco de Archila: and nuestra cédula, 72, 75; imprisoned, 72, 227; background of, 73; and anonymous letter, 148

Clergy: and aguardiente production, 24; tax exemptions, 27, 29; education of, 61; and nuestra cédula, 75; and defense of Bogotá, 126; and capital funds, 168; and riot control, 170

Cochabama, 95

Cocuy, 106, 108, 109

Cocuy manifesto, 106, 109, 137

Colbert, Jean Baptiste, 23

Philip II, 10, 81
Philip V, 9, 10, 24, 41, 83
Philippines, 90
Physiocrat school, 44
Pie de la Cuesta, 117, 129
Pilcorvaco, Juana, 95
Pimental, 102
Pinchote: riots, 45; mentioned, 54, 204
Pisco, Abmrosio: and business, 100; and
  royal monopolies, 100; and Indians,
  100, 102, 103–4, 139, 226; fortune of,
  100–101; career of, 100–104; and
  Comuneros, 101–2; loyalty to king, 102;
  as lord of Chía, 102; as prince of Bogotá,
  102; political role of, 102–4, 226; and
  Spanish authorities, 103; and Manuel
  Silvestre Martínez, 103; as cacique of
  Bogotá, 103; cooptation of, 104, 138,
  153; at Puente Real de Vélez, 116; and
  Berbeo commission, 137; and drafting
  of capituations, 159; and audiencia, 201;
  exile of, 226
Pisco, Ignacio, 101
Pisco, Luis, 101
Pista, 105
Pizarro, José Alfonso, 157, 167
Plata, Basilio, 204
Plata, Hipólito José, 53
Plata, Juan Dionisio, 57, 203–4
Plata de Acevedo, José Vicente, 56
Plata de Acevedo, Juan Bernardo, 56, 72,
  205
Plata Domínguez, Francisco Felix de la, 53
Plata y González, Salvador: leadership
  qualifications of, 53; and Bogotá creole
  elite, 53; bureaucratic posts of, 53; and
  Comuneros, 53, 54, 55; background of,
  53–54; career of, 53–54; and Socorro
  riots, 54; and tobacco monopoly, 54;
  and local military force, 54; and Berbeo,
  54, 55; wealth of, 54, 58; and government cause, 201, 204–5; and Juan
  Dionisio Plata, 203–4; and plebeians,
  204; and Galán, 205, 219; and Capuchin
  monastery, 222
Plebeians: and peninsulares, 30; and taxes,
  30, 110, 162–63, 228; as colonizers, 44;
  craftsmen, 60; occupations of, 60, 64;
  butchers, 63; leaders of, 64; and Túpac
  Amaru, 67–68; and royal authority, 78;

and creole elites, 81, 84, 153, 165;
  golden age of, 84, 154; and innovations
  of Charles III, 84; and occupation of
  Bogotá, 132, 147, 153; at Mortiño,
  149; aspirations of, 153; discipline of,
  153–54; and social revolution, 154; and
  capitulations of Zipaquirá, 162–66; and
  aguardiente, 164; fines, 165; and forced
  loan, 165; and imprisonment, 165; role
  in Comunero movement, 165; unrest,
  201; and Capuchin friars, 203; and
  Galán, 210, 217; and Caballero y Gón-
  gora, 217–18
Police, 22, 25, 133
Political legitimacy, xviii, 153, 242–44
  passim
Polonia, 79
Ponce, Francisco, 123
Popayán, 23, 31, 100, 124, 142, 227
Population: increases in, 93, 230
Pore, 22, 105
Portobelo, 52, 145
Portuguese empire, 9
Positivists, 242, 243
Postal service, 167, 242
Prada, Pedro Alejandro de la, 56–59
  passim, 117–18, 205
Prieto family, 15, 16, 225
Printing press, 85, 207, 232
Puente Real de Vélez, 81, 102, 104,
  112–21 passim, 123 131, 139, 145, 150

Quechua, 97
Quesada, Jiménez de, 173
Quevedo y Villegas, Francisco de, 85
Quito: and audiencia, 10, 226; 1765
  aguardiente riot, 31, 99, 100; unrest in,
  99; tranquility of, 99; and aguardiente
  monopoly, 99; and capitulations of
  Zipaquirá, 99; and Túpac Amaru rebellion, 99; Indians, 99, 100; military, 100;
  mentioned, 94, 109, 124, 142

Radical Liberals, 241, 243
Ramírez, José Antonio, 129
Ramírez, Ramón, 56–58 passim, 128–29,
  222
Ramírez de Arellano, Juan Félix, 197–98
Ráquira, 133
Raynal, Abbé, 214

Terán, Bárbara Rodríguez, 51, 54, 55
Textile production, 40, 172, 173
Tobacco: and royal revenues, 19; reign of,
20; overproduction of, 21, 255n15;
North American, 22; Spanish American,
22; world market for, 22; export of, 22,
241; destruction of, during Comunero
Revolution, 25, 154; prices, 29, 45, 126,
153, 220, 228; as cash crop, 164; restricted cultivation of, 164; use of, 164;
in Socorro and San Gil, 220
Tobacco monopoly: establishment of, in
Spain, 19; profits from 19, 229, 230;
and tax farming, 20; centralization of,
20; local interests, 20; administration of,
20; reorganization of, 20, 22; establishment of, in New Granada, 20, 83, 157;
restrictions on, 21, 22; abolition of, 22,
229, share of French market, 22–23;
structure of, 23; state capitalism, 23; reform of, 84; target of wrath, 164; and
damage during disturbances, 221; and
Caballero y Góngora, 229
Tocaima, 197
Tornaguías, 28, 126, 133, 167, 220,
228–29
Torreazar Díaz Pimienta, Juan de, 223
Torres, Blas Antonio, 116, 135, 202, 206
Torres, Camilo, 181
Torres, Manuel, 245
Torres Almeyda, Luis, 193–94
Trujillo Molina, Rafael, 243
Tungasuca, 96
Tunja: property destruction in, 25; and
royal monopolies, 26, 29; and ecclesiastical tithes, 39; and taxes, 45, 81, 173;
corregidor of, 60, 174, 175; resguardos,
90; unrest in, 95; alliance with
Comuneros, 113, 118, 119, 139;
strategic importance of, 118; and battle
of Puente Real de Vélez, 118; fall of,
121; and negotiating commissioners,
143; military force of, 143; defection
from Comunero camp, 143, 144, 195;
Cajica war camp, 146; captains general,
150; founding of, 172; textile industry,
172; and encomienda, 172; territorial
extent of, 172–73; sources of wealth,
172–73; rivalry with Socorro, 172–75;
aristocratic class, 173; population, 173;

religious houses of, 173; Indian population, 173; and tension between Socorro
and San Gil, 175
Túpac Amaru, Jose Gabriel Concordanqui
Noguera: rumors about, in Socorro, 67;
revolutionary example of, 67–68;
execution of, 68, 97, 106, 113; and
visitor general, 96; and Indians, 96;
background of, 96; as victim of tension
between heritages, 96; as king of the
Indies, 106; and the Silos manifesto,
107; and political independence, 108;
and the Catholic church, 110
Túpac Amaru rebellion: and peninsulares,
96; failure of, 96; and Indians, 96, 98;
and mestizos, 96, 98; and creoles, 96,
98; example of, in New Granada, 98;
and Comunero Revolution, 98; as race
war, 98; and other Indian chiefs, 98
Turbaco, 237

Ubaté, 102, 103, 113, 197
United States. *See* North America
"Unwritten constitution": essence of,
xviii, 17; and Caballero y Góngora,
xix, 186, 244; evolution of, 81; and
Spanish political theory, 85, 134–35;
and Gutiérrez de Piñeres, 157; corrosion
of, 157; and creoles, 181, 239–40;
triumph of, 237; and Berbeo, 240;
mentioned, 34, 183, 186
Upper class. *See* Creole elites; Patricians
Uribe, Miguel de, 63

Valcárcel, Daniel, 108
Valencia, 212
Vargas, 79
Vargas, Francisco de, 67, 68, 79
Vargas, José Groot de, 71
Vargas, Pedro Fermín de, 44
Vasco y Vargas, Joaquín: and junta de
tribunales, 122, 124; as commissioner,
124; and audiencia, 124, 225; transfer
of, 225, 231; and Caballero y Góngora,
231; and Gutiérrez de Piñeres, 231
Vélez, Francisco Antonio, 68, 146–47,
226
Vélez: resguardos, 90; unrest at, 95;
mentioned, 39, 40, 44, 89, 92, 100,
103, 104, 167

DESIGNED BY IRA NEWMAN
COMPOSED BY THE COMPOSING ROOM, GRAND RAPIDS, MICHIGAN
MANUFACTURED BY THOMSON-SHORE, INC., DEXTER, MICHIGAN
TEXT IS SET IN PRESS ROMAN, DISPLAY LINES IN BASKERVILLE

ⓌⓊ

Library of Congress Cataloging in Publication Data
Phelan, John Leddy, 1924–1976.
The people and the king.
Includes bibliographical references and index.
1. Colombia—History—Insurrection of the Comuneros,
1781.   2. Colombia—Politics and government—To 1810.
3. Spain—Colonies—America—Administration.
I. Title.
F2272.P45   1977   986.1'02   76-53654
ISBN 0-299-07290-8